An Introduction to
Crime and
Crime Causation

An Introduction to

Crime and Crime Causation

Robert C. Winters
Professor, Kaplan University

Julie L. Globokar
Kent State University

Cliff Roberson
Professor emeritus
Washington University
Topeka, Kansas

CRC Press
Taylor & Francis Group
Boca Raton London New York

CRC Press is an imprint of the
Taylor & Francis Group, an **informa** business

CRC Press
Taylor & Francis Group
6000 Broken Sound Parkway NW, Suite 300
Boca Raton, FL 33487-2742

© 2014 by Taylor & Francis Group, LLC
CRC Press is an imprint of Taylor & Francis Group, an Informa business

Printed on acid-free paper
Version Date: 20140502

International Standard Book Number-13: 978-1-4665-9710-5 (Hardback)

Library of Congress Cataloging-in-Publication Data

Winters, Robert C.
  An introduction to crime and crime causation / Robert C. Winters, Julie L. Globokar, Cliff Roberson.
       pages cm
  Includes bibliographical references and index.
  ISBN 978-1-4665-9710-5 (hardback)
  1. Forensic sciences. 2. Criminal behavior. 3. Crime prevention. I. Globokar, Julie L. II. Roberson, Cliff, 1937- III. Title.

HV8073.W528 2014
364--dc23

2014009430

Visit the Taylor & Francis Web site at
http://www.taylorandfrancis.com

and the CRC Press Web site at
http://www.crcpress.com

To my wife Sue,
for her endless inspiration, motivation, and support and to my son
Michael for his reminders of just what a thirsty young mind can
dream, think, and achieve.

Robert

To Michael,
for his love and support, and to my family. With love always.

Julie

To my partner,
Dr. Elena Azaola, Senior Investigator, Centro de Investigaciones
y Estudios Superiores en Antropología Social, Mexico City,
Mexico—she is a tireless advocate for human rights.

Cliff

To Carolyn Spence,
Thanks Carolyn

Robert, Julie, and Cliff

Contents

Preface

An Introduction to Crime and Crime Causation is designed to provide an understanding of issues involving the phenomena of crime. This book examines crime, the extent of it, and other facts in an attempt to educate the reader regarding the steps that need to be taken before a significant reduction in crime can occur. We also cover the major crime causation theories and some of the lesser-known ones that impact our society.

The three authors have different and distinct backgrounds, and therefore there are differences in their views on crime. These differences allow them opportunities to discuss and debate their differences. Their differences ensure that the various issues covered are examined from different viewpoints. Robert C. Winters (the lead author) is a former attorney and present professor of criminal justice. Julie L. Globokar is a sociologist and college professor. Cliff Roberson, a human behaviorist, is a professor emeritus of criminology and criminal justice.

The text matter is presented in a manner that is designed to enhance student learning. For example, the materials in Chapters 1 and 2 overlap to some extent. The two chapters could have been structured as one long chapter, but we decided that rather than start the book with a massive first chapter, it would be easier for readers to have the material divided into two smaller chapters. After the introductory material in Chapters 1 and 2, the text focuses on criminal causation theories. We have covered many of the current and popular theories, but no one book could cover the vast number of theories that exist today. The final chapters of the book discuss and examine the criminal justice system, the types of crime, specialized crimes involving governments and big business, and drugs.

Any corrections, suggestions for improvement, or comments should be forwarded to Cliff Roberson at cliff.roberson@washburn.edu.

Robert C. Winters
Kaplan University

Julie L. Globokar
Kent State University

Cliff Roberson
Washburn University

Acknowledgments

While the three of us are listed as coauthors, numerous professionals have contributed to the development of this text. First, our understanding and flexible editor, Carolyn Spence, gave us the opportunity to write this book as well as encouragement throughout the process. Copyeditors P. S. Smitha and Shirley Vigin and project manager Dhayanidhi Karunanidhi did a professional, quality job and were there when we needed them.

chapter one

An introduction to concepts involving crime and crime causation

Chapter objectives

After studying this chapter, the reader should be able to

- Discuss what constitutes criminal behavior
- Discuss who should be labeled as a criminal
- Define and explain the concepts of crime, criminal law, and criminology
- Provide descriptions and explanations of sources of crime data
- Describe the importance of crime data

Introduction

This book is designed as a textbook on criminology. Criminology is the study of criminals, crime prevention, crime causation, and the social processes that shape the label of "criminal." Criminologists work to identify the etiological variables related to criminal behavior.

The study of criminal behavior is exciting for numerous reasons, including the fact that it is an analysis of human nature, people, drama, and how human beings both create and solve problems.[1] Many of our current entertainment venues are centered on crime. Take a look at the list of the top 10 movies that played in your city last week. How many were based on crimes? In addition, crime-related industries are a significant economic force. How many individuals in today's society have a job because of crime, including law enforcement personnel, correctional personnel, private security, and prison and jail construction companies? If all crime disappeared tomorrow and we no longer needed those occupations, how much of an impact would it have on unemployment?

To understand crime and criminology, we must first have a foundation regarding the criminal justice system. We refer to the criminal justice system as a "system," but the term inaccurately implies that its various components are heavily interrelated, closely knit, and highly coordinated. In reality, it would be more accurate to refer to it as a nonsystem: Although each component plays an important role in society's responses to crime, they each play a relatively independent role in the process. The criminal justice system is actually composed of three separate elements:

1. Law enforcement
2. Courts
3. Corrections

Not only does each of these components operate relatively independently, but in many cases, the orientation of the various elements within a local jurisdiction is in conflict with each other as to the main goals of the criminal justice system. Thus, the system can best be described as "fragmented" or "divided." Accordingly, the criminal justice system is a group of agencies organized around various functions that each is assigned. In addition, there is no single criminal justice system in this country, and there is a great deal of variation among the systems that operate within different jurisdictions. In reality, we have many criminal justice systems, each of which has their main components in common but are otherwise highly unique in regard to specific laws, cultures, and practices. The laws in any given system determine who comes to be deemed "criminal," and the operation of the system determines how those individuals will be handled. For convenience and out of habit, we will use the phrase "criminal justice system" to refer generally to the three structures that are tasked with the enforcement of criminal laws and processing of criminal law violators.

Criminals are apprehended, tried, and punished by means of this loose confederation of agencies at all levels of the government. The present system of justice evolved from English common law into a complex series of procedures and decisions. Unlike the situation in many other nations, private citizens are actively involved in the U.S. criminal justice system, through aspects such as service on juries and the public nature of proceedings.

Under the federal form of government, each state and the federal government has its own criminal justice system. Although state constitutions and state statutes define many aspects of each state's criminal justice system, all the systems must work within the outer bounds set by the U.S. Constitution as interpreted by our courts. Regardless of other forms of variation among the states, all must respect the Constitutional rights of individuals.

Criminal behavior

> A crime is anything that a group in power chooses to prohibit.
>
> **Freda Adler, 1974**[2]

What constitutes criminal behavior? This may seem like an easy question, but what is considered criminal by one group may not be considered criminal by others. Take for example the societal debate on the right to have an abortion. To a large number of people, the right to have an abortion is in effect the woman's right to choose. To others, an abortion is murder. Because of this conflict in our beliefs and values, this conflict over the right to an abortion may never be solved in a manner that can be supported by the vast majority of the population. The states with the most restrictive laws on abortion include Arkansas and North Dakota, whereas California is included in those states that have the least restrictions on abortion. There are valid arguments for both sides of this conflict, but what is certain is that if we polled the population about whether having an abortion (or preventing a woman from having an abortion) should be deemed "criminal," we would receive a broad variety of responses.

Prostitution is a crime in 49 states and the U.S. territories. It is not a crime under Nevada state law. Selling your body for sex is a crime in New York and under certain conditions is fully legal in Nevada. If we define criminal behavior as a violation of a criminal law, then location becomes relevant to whether or not someone is a "criminal." If we instead consider criminal behavior in a broader context (using a social, not legal, definition), then serious violations of our social/moral code might be considered criminal behavior, and the individual committing an act of prostitution in any location would be considered as engaged in criminal behavior.

Legal definitions of crime also vary over time. Consider the following scenario: In 1932, Julie, Robert, and Cliff are walking down a street in New York City. Both Robert and Cliff have a pint of whiskey in their coat pockets. Julie has a gold coin in hers. Which individuals are committing criminal acts? Robert and Cliff would be violating a criminal law because of the prohibition laws. Julie would not be.

Change the date to 1935: Then Julie would be violating a criminal law because the possession of gold coins without special permission was in that year a violation of the currency laws. Robert and Cliff, however, could legally enjoy their whiskey because the prohibition laws had been repealed.

Who is a criminal?

> Terming an act a crime involves a series of judgments. First, the judgment is made that the act is harmful. Next, the decision is made that the act should be regulated by law. Finally, the decision is made that the law regulating the act should be a criminal statute rather than a civil one.
>
> **Cliff Roberson, 1994[3]**

Simply defining a criminal as a person who has violated a criminal law means that we all are criminals. Everyone at one time or another has violated one of the many criminal laws that presently exist in the United States or in your home state. Most people have, at the very least, broken the speed limit. Does this make everyone the potential focus of criminological inquiry? In December 1955, Rosa Parks, a black seamstress in Montgomery, Alabama, refused to take a seat in the rear section of a public transit bus as then required by state law. Was she a criminal? If so, was she no longer a criminal when the state law was declared unconstitutional by a federal court?

Can you answer all of the below questions with a "never" answer? Have you ever

- Exceeded the speed limit in a school zone?
- Taken a pencil that belongs to your employer?
- Failed to report all of your income on an income tax return?
- Taken part in an office or school basketball or football betting pool?
- Taken an alcoholic drink in a public park or at a public beach?
- Lied to a customs agent to avoid paying customs fees?
- Served an alcoholic drink to a person under the lawful age?
- Consumed alcohol under the lawful age?
- Made the unauthorized sale of a ticket to a sporting event?
- Lied on a job application?
- Parked illegally?
- Shoplifted?
- Committed adultery?
- Possessed small amounts of a controlled substance?
- Illegally copied music, computer software, or movies?

As you can observe by the preceding list of questions, few people, if any, could entirely escape the label of "criminal" if we use the standard legal definition.

Does the person have to be convicted of a crime before he or she is labeled as a criminal? When using this requirement, you are focusing not on the conduct of the individual but on the ability of the police to detect and investigate a crime and then the court system to obtain a conviction. This would in large part mean that who should be labeled criminal is dependent on factors such as the efficiency of the criminal justice system, not just the conduct of the individual. Ultimately, it may be best to think of crime as a broad category of human behaviors that have been (legally or socially) deemed problematic in a given social and historical context. The causes for crime are as diverse as its many forms, as will be seen throughout this chapter.

**THE CHALLENGE OF CRIME IN A FREE SOCIETY: EXCERPTS
FROM THE PRESIDENT'S CRIME COMMISSION (1967)**

Many Americans think of crime as a very narrow range of behavior. It is not. An enormous variety of acts make up the "crime problem." Crime is not just a tough teenager snatching a lady's purse. It is a professional thief stealing cars "on order." It is a well-heeled loan shark taking over a previously legitimate business for organized crime. It is a polite young man who suddenly and inexplicably murders his family. It is a corporation executive conspiring with competitors to keep prices high. No single theory, no single generalization can explain the vast range of behavior called crime....

The most understandable mood into which many Americans have been plunged by crime is one of frustration and bewilderment. For "crime" is not a single, simple phenomenon that can be examined, analyzed and described in one piece. It occurs in every part of the country and in every stratum of society. Its practitioners and its victims are people of all ages, incomes and backgrounds. Its trends are difficult to ascertain. Its causes are legion. Its cures are speculative and controversial. An examination of any single kind of crime, let alone of "crime in America," raises a myriad of issues of the utmost complexity.

Source: President's Commission on Law Enforcement and Administration of Justice, Washington, DC, 1967, pp. 3–5.

Classification of crimes

As will be discussed later in this chapter, crimes are classified in numerous ways. Probably the most familiar classification is based on the severity of the misconduct, which allows us to prioritize our study of different problematic behaviors. This generally entails four categories: treason, felonies, misdemeanors, and infractions. Treason, since it threatens the very existence of our nation, is considered the most serious. Because of its rarity, treason will not be further discussed in this chapter. The majority of crimes are classified as either felonies or misdemeanors. Because infractions are relatively minor offenses, such as fishing without a license, they will not be a substantial focus of this chapter. Still, infractions can be useful in thinking about the factors that contribute to a willingness to break the law in everyday contexts.

Felony or misdemeanor

In common law, a felony was considered any crime for which the offender would be compelled to forfeit property to the king. Most common law felonies were punishable by the death penalty. The common law felonies included murder, rape, assault and battery, larceny, robbery, arson, and burglary. Presently, the death penalty is much more rarely used—only in cases of aggravated murder—and felonies are generally defined as those crimes punishable by a year or more in prison. By contrast, misdemeanors are punishable by a maximum of a fine and up to a year in jail. The guide in distinguishing between a felony and a misdemeanor is not the punishment actually given in court, but the punishment that could have been imposed. For example, Joe commits the crime of burglary of an inhabited building and could receive 10 years in prison. The judge sentences him to only 6 months in the local jail, the sentence typically given for a misdemeanor. As the maximum possible punishment that Joe could have received entailed prison time, his crime is still considered a felony, despite the lesser sentence actually applied in his case.

Although most states distinguish between felonies and misdemeanors based on whether the crime is eligible for a prison sentence, a few states use a combination of place of incarceration and character of offense to make the distinction between the two categories. The Model Penal Code (MPC) provides that a crime is a felony if it is so designated, without regard to the possible penalty. In addition, any crime for which the permissible punishment includes imprisonment in excess of 1 year is also considered a felony under the MPC. All other crimes are misdemeanors. A few states, such as California, have crimes that are referred to as "wobblers," based on the fact that the court can treat the violation as either a felony or a misdemeanor.

Felonies and misdemeanors are frequently subdivided into classes. For example, in Texas, misdemeanors are subdivided into classes A, B, and C, and felonies are subdivided into classes of first, second, and third degree. In Texas, under this classification, promotion of prostitution is a felony of the third degree, and forcing someone to commit prostitution is a felony of the second degree. The burglary of an inhabited building is a felony of the first degree, whereas the burglary of an uninhabited building is a felony of the second degree. The MPC also creates degrees of felonies. A first- or second-degree felony under the MPC carries a $10,000 fine plus imprisonment and a third-degree felony carries a $5,000 fine plus imprisonment.

The classification of a crime as a felony or misdemeanor is important. A felony conviction on a person's record can prevent the individual from entering many professions and obtaining certain jobs. A felony conviction has been used to deny a person the right to enter the armed forces or obtain employment with a law enforcement agency, and it may even affect one's ability to obtain credit or adopt a child. In the state of New York, a felon (a person who has been convicted of a felony) may not obtain a license to sell chickens wholesale. In addition, conviction of a felony can be grounds to impeach a public official. At one time, many states did not allow a convicted felon to vote, hold office, or serve on a jury. Today, in all but eight states, most of the disabilities commonly associated with a criminal conviction are removed after the criminal has served his or her time.

Infractions

In many states, infractions are the lowest level of criminal activity. An infraction is an act that is usually not punishable by confinement, such as a traffic ticket. In several states, the term petty misdemeanor is used in lieu of infraction. Similar to infractions are violations of municipal ordinances. In some states, ordinance violations are not considered crimes, based on the theory that a crime is a public wrong created by the state and thus prosecuted in the name of the state. An ordinance is a rule created by a public corporation (the municipality) and prosecuted in the name of the municipality.

Mala in se or mala prohibita

Crimes may also be classified as either mala in se or mala prohibita. Mala in se crimes are those acts that are not only crimes but are also almost universally considered morally wrong—for example, rape, murder, and theft. Generally, all common law crimes are considered mala in se crimes. Mala prohibita crimes are those crimes that are not the focus of broad moral consensus even though they are technically against the law—for example, insider trading or failure to have a business license. Mala prohibita crimes are wrong simply because they are prohibited by statutes.

Victimless crimes

Victimless crimes are those crimes where there are no direct victims, such as gambling, prostitution, and abuse of control substances. Unlike murder, rape, or robbery, a victimless crime is usually committed by two or more people, all of whom readily participate in the crime. In some cases, these crimes are also called "public order" crimes. Although many of these offenses are called "victimless crimes," many individuals contend that these crimes do have victims, whether conceived as society as a whole, or those individuals who are otherwise affected by the behaviors. For example, many would hold that the relatives of drug addicts are "victims" in light of the stressors and consequences of the individual's substance abuse.

Public and private laws

Not all laws deal with criminal behavior. Laws may be classified as either public or private. Private laws generally are concerned with relationships between people, in which the government has only an indirect interest. Family law (marriage, divorce, etc.), property law, and probate law (wills and trusts) primarily regulate the relationships between individuals and/or companies. The government has only an indirect interest.

By contrast, public laws are those in which the government has a more direct interest. They include constitutional law, criminal codes, vehicle codes, and public health laws. Criminal codes, which are most relevant to this chapter, are a subset of this category. At one time in early England, rules prohibiting crimes against the individual, such as rape, robbery, and theft, were considered private laws, on the theory that these crimes did not affect the state. Eventually, English law recognized that crime was not a personal affair but a wrong against society, a violation of the peace and dignity of the people, resulting in their transformation to criminal law.

In the present day, some actions fall under both public and private law, and the statutes that establish certain crimes provide the state or federal government with the option to proceed civilly rather than criminally. The matters in which the government has this option include insider trading, civil rights, antitrust, obscenity, and consumer fraud. In civil court, the offender may be found civilly liable and ordered to pay compensatory and punitive damages.

MODEL PENAL CODE

The American Law Institute, a nonprofit organization sponsored by the American Bar Association, has drafted the MPC. This code was developed by a group of judges, lawyers, and scholars and is designed to reflect in general the criminal law of the

United States. The project was started in 1952, its rationale being that states enacted criminal laws in a piecemeal fashion, often based on public perceptions of need without a thorough examination of the situation. The project was basically completed in 1962 after 13 tentative drafts. Since 1962, approximately two-thirds of the states have adopted new criminal codes greatly influenced by the MPC. Although some states have adopted this code with slight changes, other states refer to it when redrafting criminal laws.[4]

Crime or tort

> The first requirement of a sound body of law is, that it should correspond with the actual feelings and demands of the community, whether right or wrong.

> **Justice Oliver Wendell Holmes, *The Common Law*, 1881**

Private wrongs are usually considered either a tort or a breach of contract. A tort is a wrong that violates a private interest and thus gives rise to civil liability. A crime is a public wrong, as it involves the violation of the peace and dignity of the state. In theory, it is committed against the interest of all of the people of the state. Crimes are prosecuted in the name of the "State," the "People," or the "Commonwealth." If in the earlier example, Joe was prosecuted for robbery, the title of the case would be the People of the State of ___ v. Joe ___. In the five states that are considered commonwealths, the title would be, for example, the People of the Commonwealth of Virginia, Plaintiff v. ___, Defendant.

When conduct violates both public and private laws, it may be both a crime and a tort. For example, if a woman is forcibly raped by a neighbor, the conduct is viewed as a crime because it is a violation of the peace and dignity of the state. In the criminal courts, the action is handled as a crime against all the people in the state. At the same time, it is also a violation of the private interest of the victim, and she may file a civil suit and obtain civil damages against the offender.

Hall of Fame football player O.J. Simpson was tried by the State of California for the murder of his wife and her friend. In that case entitled the *People of the State of California, Plaintiff v. Orenthal James Simpson, Defendant*, note that for the criminal case, the plaintiff was the state. O.J. Simpson was found not guilty. The estate of Nicole Simpson then sued O.J. Simpson in civil court under a tort action. That case, a civil case, was entitled *Louis H. Brown, as Executor and personal representative of the Estate of Nicole Brown Simpson, deceased, Plaintiff, v. Orenthal James Simpson, Defendant*. As the burden of proof is higher for a criminal trial, where the case must be proven beyond a reasonable doubt, than for civil cases, where the burden of proof is the preponderance of evidence, it is possible to be found not guilty in a criminal trial but civilly liable for the private wrong. In the O.J. case, that is exactly what happened. The estate recovered money damages in the civil suit against O.J. Simpson even though he had been acquitted at the criminal trial.

Criminology

What exactly is the phenomenon called criminology? Society has been studying crime for centuries. Individual scientists have attempted to discover the cause of crime and how we can stop it. There are a few detractors who claim that criminology is not a true academic discipline, that we can never determine the true causes of crime, and that people who study criminology are typically doing so only to obtain a job in the criminal justice system. In reality, though, there are professionals who study crime, criminals, and criminal behavior. There are several national societies dedicated to the study of criminology. National, regional, and state conferences are conducted where criminologists and other academic professionals present their research to peers. Finally, there are a number of referred academic journals that review, accept, and publish research in the area of criminology. By any standard, criminology can be referred to as a valid academic discipline.

Just as there are a number of different definitions of crime so are there a variety of sources to draw upon when defining criminology. One of the best known and accepted definitions comes from Edwin Sutherland, a well-known researcher and criminologist who stated that criminology consists of three principal divisions:

1. The sociology of law
2. Scientific analysis of the causes of crime
3. Crime control[5]

However, for our purposes, we will use a more comprehensive definition of criminology. Criminology from our perspective is the scientific study of crime and criminal behavior. This definition includes all of Sutherland's elements of criminology. In addition, this definition allows for an examination of other parties that interact with criminals, such as prosecutors, judges, correctional officials, and victims. As will be illustrated, criminology is continuously growing, evolving, and maturing.

EXCERPTS FROM CHIEF JUSTICE EARL WARREN'S OPINION IN *MIRANDA V. ARIZONA*

The quality of a nation's civilization can be largely measured by the methods it uses in the enforcement of the criminal law.... All of these policies point to one overriding thought: the constitutional foundation underlying the privilege is the respect a government—state or federal—must accord the dignity and integrity of its citizens. To maintain a fair state–individual balance, the government must shoulder the entire load.

Associated with the *Individual Rights v. Law and Order* issue is the concept of due process. This concept restricts the power of the state and more particularly the police, courts, and corrections. The Bill of Rights, the first nine amendments to the U.S. Constitution, contains 23 separate individual rights, 12 of them concern procedural rights for persons accused of criminal conduct. In 1798, the U.S. Supreme Court ruled that the prohibitions against government action contained in those amendments were restrictions only on the federal government and not on state governments. The case, *Calder v. Bull*, involved a statute passed by the legislature of Connecticut, which set aside a probate court judgment and directed the probate judge to refuse the recording of a will (an ex posto law).[6]

Measuring crime

> Hence, no reliable measure exists of the number of crimes that might be falsely reported or of the number of crimes that might be under-reported in the NCVS data.
>
> **Frank Schmalleger, 2009[7]**

Measuring crime is not an exact science. There is no way to directly count every crime that takes place, and so there is no such thing as a "perfect" measure of crime. Consider the number of times you have broken the speed limit versus the number of tickets you have received, or the number of people you know who have consumed alcohol before the age of 21 or used other illegal substances, compared to those who have been arrested or received tickets for their violations. Not every crime comes to police attention, not every victim will speak up about their experiences, and certainly not every offender will confess to their crimes. Therefore, most researchers believe that the actual crime rate is significantly higher than is indicated by any of the available measures of crime. The number of crimes that forever remain unknown or unreported is sometimes termed the "dark figure of crime." Because there is no way to count every single crime that takes place, researchers are left to figure out the best strategy for assessing crime trends and patterns. To do this, they seek approximate measures from the three sources that can be expected to know the most about crime: police, victims, and offenders.

The Uniform Crime Report

The best national source of crime data from the police is the Uniform Crime Report (UCR), an annual report composed by the Federal Bureau of Investigation (FBI) based on information gathered from law enforcement agencies nationwide. The UCR was designed in 1929 and implemented in 1930,[8] meaning that it allows for a good comparison of national crime trends over the last 80 years. The UCR also celebrates widespread participation: More than 18,000 law enforcement agencies submit information for the report, representing those responsible for 98.1% of the U.S. population.[9] The UCR includes information on two categories of crime. "Part I offenses" are generally considered more serious and include murder, rape, robbery, aggravated assault, burglary, larceny-theft, motor vehicle theft, and arson.[10] Rates of each crime are calculated for every 100,000 of the population, allowing for comparison of crime prevalence across areas of different population sizes, and "clearance rates" are calculated to indicate how many of those crimes are considered closed by arrest or exceptional means.[11] The UCR also keeps track of arrests for "Part II offenses," which include gambling, forgery, vandalism, and other minor offenses. The FBI provides an online UCR data tool that allows users to compare crime rates over time and across states and agencies.[12] So, for example, users can pull up tables to compare violent crime in Alaska and Illinois to discover that in 2012, Illinois had a far higher rate of robbery and a slightly higher rate of murder, whereas Alaska had far higher rates of forcible rapes and aggravated assaults. Any number of states or agencies can be compared in this way.

The UCR remains an especially valuable tool for assessing trends in murder and other serious crimes. For obvious reasons, murder statistics cannot be derived from victimization surveys, and few offenders, if surveyed about their criminal activity, would volunteer that they committed murder (if not yet caught for it). At the same time, serious crimes are those most likely to come to police attention: Few individuals would catch wind of a murder without notifying law enforcement. This makes the UCR the nation's best source of data for most types of serious crimes. News reports indicating that murder rates have increased or decreased nationwide or in a given state have usually based their information on the UCR.

By contrast, the UCR contains no information on crimes such as prostitution, drug use, or drunk driving. It also makes a poor source of information on forcible rape, because that particular crime is heavily underreported to the police. There are also weaknesses to relying on law enforcement agencies to report crimes in their own jurisdictions. The reports may be subject to human error and vulnerable to manipulation, as with agencies that might be tempted to inflate their crime statistics to try to get more funding, or under-report their crime statistics to cast a more positive light on their communities. Although such manipulation is not likely widespread, it was recently discovered that the NYPD—the largest police department in the nation—engaged in "numbers games" to minimize the appearance of serious crimes in the city's statistics.[13] The UCR data are limited by the "hierarchy rule," which dictates that only the most serious offense of any criminal incident be counted. For example, if an offender breaks into a home, rapes one resident, and kills another, the incident would be counted as one murder according to the UCR reporting guidelines. Finally, the UCR provides only limited information on any given criminal incident, including little (if any) information on the victim or the criminal.

In recent years, the FBI responded to criticism about the limitations of UCR data by designing the more detailed National Incident-Based Reporting System (NIBRS). This new system, first implemented in 1991, was first envisioned as a replacement for the UCR. Slow adoption by law enforcement agencies has kept this transition from becoming a reality: As of 2011, only 5880 law enforcement agencies were participating in the NIBRS,[14] representing only 28% of the population.[15] The advantage of the NIBRS is the extent of the information gathered on any criminal incident, including the age, race, and sex of victims and known offenders.[16] Unfortunately, the level of detail expected of reports may be the very reason that reporting is not yet more widespread.

**ACCORDING TO THE FBI, INFORMATION COLLECTED
FOR NIBRS INCLUDES THE FOLLOWING[17]**

- Data for 22 offense categories
- Victim data for all offenses
- Offender data for all offenses
- Relationship of victims to offenders for select offenses
- Location data for all offenses
- Time of day for all incidents
- Weapon data for select offenses
- Drug and alcohol involvement in offenses
- Gang involvement in offenses
- Attempted versus completed offenses
- Clearances by incidents

National Crime Victimization Survey

The Bureau of Justice Statistics (BJS) directs the collection of data for the National Crime Victimization Survey (NCVS). The NCVS, which started in 1973, provides a detailed picture of crime incidents, victims, and trends. In 1993, the survey completed an intensive methodological redesign. The redesign was undertaken to improve the questions used to uncover crime, update the survey methods, and broaden the scope of crimes measured. The redesigned survey collects detailed information on the frequency and nature of the crimes of rape, sexual assault, personal robbery, aggravated and simple assault, household burglary, theft, and motor vehicle theft. It does not measure homicide or commercial crimes such as burglaries of stores.

Once a year, U.S. Census Bureau personnel interview household members in a nationally representative sample of approximately 90,000 households. Approximately 160,000 interviews of persons age 12 or older are conducted annually. Households stay in the sample for 3 years. New households are rotated into the sample on an ongoing basis. Questions are asked regarding crimes suffered by individuals and households, and whether or not those crimes were reported to law enforcement. This allows for an estimate of the proportion of each crime type reported to law enforcement and a summary of the reasons that victims give for reporting or not reporting.

The survey provides information about victims (age, sex, race, ethnicity, marital status, income, and educational level), offenders (sex, race, approximate age, and victim–offender relationship), and the crimes (time and place of occurrence, use of weapons, nature of injury, and economic consequences). The survey questions also cover the experiences of victims with the criminal justice system, self-protective measures used by victims, and possible substance abuse by offenders. Supplements are added periodically to the survey to obtain detailed information on topics such as school crime.

The first data from the redesigned NCVS were published in a BJS bulletin in June 1995. BJS publication of NCVS data includes *Criminal Victimization in the United States*, an annual report that covers the broad range of detailed information collected by the NCVS. BJS publishes detailed reports on topics such as crime against women, urban crime, and gun use in crime. The NCVS and UCR data files are maintained in the National Archive of Criminal Justice Data at the University of Michigan to enable researchers to perform independent analysis.

BUREAU OF JUSTICE STATISTICS STATISTICAL PRINCIPLES AND PRACTICES

The BJS is a unit of the U.S. Department of Justice whose principal function is the compilation and analysis of data and the dissemination of information for statistical purposes. It adheres to the following principles and practices:[18]

- Clearly defined and well-accepted mission
- Strong position of independence
- Continual development of more useful data
- Openness about the sources and limitations of the data provided
- Wide dissemination of data
- Cooperation with data users
- Fair treatment of data providers
- Commitment to quality and professional standards of practice
- Active research program
- Professional advancement of staff
- Coordination and cooperation with other statistical agencies

Comparing the Uniform Crime Report and National Crime Victimization Survey

Because the NCVS was designed to complement the UCR program, the two programs share many similarities. As much as their different collection methods permit, the two measure the same subset of serious crimes, including rape, robbery, aggravated assault, burglary, theft, and motor vehicle theft. The two measures hold the definitions of most crimes in common, as with virtually identical definitions of rape, robbery, theft, and motor vehicle theft. One key difference, though, is that while rape is defined analogously aside from this detail, the UCR Crime Index measures the crime against women only, whereas the NCVS measures it as a crime against either sex.

There are also significant differences between the two programs. First, the two programs were created to serve different purposes. The UCR program's primary objective is to provide a reliable set of criminal justice statistics for law enforcement administration, operation, and management. The NCVS was established to provide previously unavailable information about crime (including crime not reported to police), victims, and offenders.

Second, the two programs measure an overlapping but nonidentical set of crimes. The NCVS includes crimes both reported and not reported to law enforcement. The NCVS excludes, but the UCR includes, homicide, arson, commercial crimes, and crimes against children under age 12. The UCR captures crimes reported to law enforcement, but it excludes sexual assaults and simple assaults from the Crime Index.

Third, because of methodology, the NCVS and UCR definitions of some crimes differ. For example, the UCR defines burglary as the unlawful entry or attempted entry of a structure to commit a felony or theft. The NCVS, not wanting to ask victims to ascertain offender motives, defines burglary as the entry or attempted entry of a residence by a person who had no right to be there.

Fourth, for property crimes (burglary, theft, and motor vehicle theft), the two programs calculate crime rates using different bases. The UCR rates for these crimes are per capita (number of crimes per 100,000 persons), whereas the NCVS rates for these crimes are per household (number of crimes per 1,000 households). Because the number of households may not grow at the same rate each year as the total population, trend data for rates of property crimes measured by the two programs may not be comparable.

In addition, some differences in the data from the two programs may result from sampling variation in the NCVS and from estimating for nonresponse in the UCR. The NCVS estimates are derived from interviewing a sample and are therefore subject to a margin of error. Rigorous statistical methods are used to calculate confidence intervals around all survey estimates. Trend data in NCVS reports are described as genuine only if there is at least a 90% certainty that the measured changes are not the result of sampling variation. The UCR data are based on the actual counts of offenses reported by law enforcement jurisdictions. In some circumstances, the UCR data are estimated for nonparticipating jurisdictions or those reporting partial data.

Each program has unique strengths. The UCR provides a measure of the number of crimes reported to law enforcement agencies throughout the country. The UCR's *Supplemental Homicide Reports* provide the most reliable, timely data on the extent and nature of homicides in the nation. The NCVS is the primary source of information on the characteristics of criminal victimization and on the number and types of crimes not reported to law enforcement authorities.

By understanding the strengths and limitations of each program, it is possible to use the UCR and NCVS to achieve a greater understanding of crime trends and the nature of crime in the United States. For example, changes in police procedures, shifting attitudes toward crime and police, and other societal changes can affect the extent to which people report and law enforcement agencies record crime. The NCVS and UCR data can be used in concert to explore why trends in reported and police-recorded crime may differ. Apparent discrepancies between statistics from the two programs can usually be accounted for by their definitional and procedural differences or resolved by comparing NCVS sampling variations (confidence intervals) of those crimes said to have been reported to police with UCR statistics.

For most types of crimes measured by both the UCR and NCVS, analysts familiar with the programs can exclude from analysis those aspects of crime not common to both. Resulting long-term trend lines can be brought into close concordance. The impact of such adjustments is most striking for robbery, burglary, and motor vehicle theft, whose definitions most closely coincide. For example, with robbery, researchers can use the NCVS data and exclude victimizations that were not reported to the police, resulting in a calculation of annual victimization rates based only on NCVS robberies that were reported to the police. With the UCR data, while the definition of robbery is more expansive than the NCVS because it includes crimes against both households and commercial establishments such as gas stations, convenience stores, and banks, it is possible for researchers to exclude commercial robberies from analysis. When the resulting NCVS police-reported robbery rates are compared to UCR noncommercial robbery rates, the results reveal closely corresponding long-term trends, increasing the level of confidence we can have in the accuracy of both measures.

Some Major Differences between the Uniform Crime Report and the National Crime Victimization Survey

	Uniform Crime Report (UCR)	National Crime Victimization Survey (NCVS)
Geographic coverage	National and state estimates, local agency reports	National estimates
Collection method	Reports by law enforcement to the FBI on a monthly basis	Survey of as many as 90,000 households and 160,000 individuals age 12 or older
Measures	Index crimes reported by law enforcement	Reported and unreported crime; details about the crimes, victims, and offenders

Other Crime Data Collections by the Bureau of Justice Statistics

Violent Crime against Youth, 1994–2010: Presents patterns and trends in violent crime against youth ages 12–17 from 1994 to 2010.

Crime against Persons with Disabilities, 2009–2011—Statistical Tables: Presents estimates of nonfatal violent victimization (rape, sexual assault, robbery, aggravated assault, and simple assault) against persons age 12 or older with disabilities from 2009 to 2011.

Violent Victimization Committed by Strangers, 1993–2010: Presents findings on the rates and levels of violent victimization committed by offenders who were strangers to the victims, including homicide, rape, sexual assault, robbery, aggravated assault, and simple assault.

Firearms Stolen during Household Burglaries and Other Property Crimes, 2005–2010: Presents findings on the theft of firearms during household burglaries and other property crimes from 2005 to 2010.

Criminal Victimization, 2011: Presents 2011 estimates of rates and levels of criminal victimization in the United States. This bulletin includes violent victimization (rape or sexual assault, robbery, aggravated assault, and simple assault) and property victimization (burglary, motor vehicle theft, and property theft).

Prevalence of Violent Crime among Households with Children, 1993–2010: Presents data from the National Crime Victimization Survey (NCVS) on nonfatal violent crime involving members of a household as victims and reports on the annual prevalence of that violent crime among U.S. households with children from 1993 to 2010.

(Continued)

Other Crime Data Collections by the Bureau of Justice Statistics (*Continued*)

Victimizations Not Reported to the Police, 2006–2010: Presents findings, for a 5-year period from 2006 to 2010, on the characteristics of crime victimizations that went unreported to police, according to data from the NCVS.

Violent Crime against the Elderly Reported by Law Enforcement in Michigan, 2005–2009: Presents statistics about violent victimization of persons age 65 or older reported by law enforcement agencies into the FBI's National Incident-Based Reporting System (NIBRS) from 2005 to 2009.

Methods for Counting High-Frequency Repeat Victimizations in the NCVS: Examines the nature and extent of series victimization in the NCVS.

Indicators of School Crime and Safety, 2011: Presents data on crime and safety at school from the perspectives of students, teachers, and principals.

National Incident-Based Reporting System

Over the years, a broad utility for UCR data evolved, and law enforcement expanded its capabilities to supply crime information. In the late 1970s, the law enforcement community called for a thorough evaluation of the UCR program to recommend an expanded and enhanced data collection system to meet the needs of law enforcement in the twenty-first century. The result of this assessment was the design of a more comprehensive database that would include more details about each criminal incident. The South Carolina Law Enforcement Division was the first entity to use the proposed system to determine its workability. At a national UCR conference in March 1988, participants approved the new system.

The National Incident-Based Reporting System (NIBRS)[19] is an incident-based reporting system in which law enforcement agencies collect data on each single crime occurrence. Data are collected on each incident and arrest within 22 offense categories made up of 46 specific crimes called Group A offenses. For each of the offenses coming to the attention of law enforcement, specified types of facts about each crime are reported. In addition to the Group A offenses, there are 11 Group B offense categories for which only arrest data are reported. NIBRS data come from local, state, and federal automated record systems. It permits a law enforcement agency to build a system to suit its own needs, including any collection/storage of information required for administration and operations, as well as to report data required by the NIBRS to the FBI for the compilation of national statistics.

The benefits of participating in the NIBRS are the following:

- The NIBRS can furnish information on nearly every major criminal justice issue facing law enforcement today, including terrorism, white-collar crime, weapons offenses, missing children where criminality is involved, drug/narcotics offenses, drug involvement in all offenses, hate crimes, spousal abuse, abuse of the elderly, child abuse, domestic violence, juvenile crime/gangs, parental abduction, organized crime, pornography/child pornography, driving under the influence, and alcohol-related offenses.
- Using the NIBRS, legislators, municipal planners/administrators, academicians, sociologists, and the public will have access to more comprehensive crime information than the summary reporting can provide.
- The NIBRS produces more detailed, accurate, and meaningful data than the traditional summary reporting. Armed with such information, law enforcement can better make a case to acquire the resources needed to fight crime.
- The NIBRS enables agencies to find similarities in crime-fighting problems so that agencies can work together to develop solutions or discover strategies for addressing the issues.

- Full participation in the NIBRS provides statistics to enable a law enforcement agency to provide a full accounting of the status of public safety within the jurisdiction to the police commissioner, police chief, sheriff, or director.

One of the key weaknesses of the NIBRS is that it has been adopted slowly. As of 2012, only 23 states had agencies participating in the program, with the data reflecting the experiences of only 29% of the nation's population.[20]

What crimes are reported in the National Incident-Based Reporting System?

The following offense categories, known as Group A offenses, are those for which extensive crime data are collected in the NIBRS:

1. Arson
2. Assault offenses: Aggravated assault, simple assault, intimidation
3. Bribery
4. Burglary/breaking and entering
5. Counterfeiting/forgery
6. Destruction/damage/vandalism of property
7. Drug/narcotic offenses: Drug/narcotic violations, drug equipment violations
8. Embezzlement
9. Extortion/blackmail
10. Fraud offenses: False pretenses/swindle/confidence game, credit card/automatic teller machine fraud, impersonation, welfare fraud, wire fraud
11. Gambling offenses: Betting/wagering, operating/promoting/assisting gambling, gambling equipment violations, sports tampering
12. Homicide offenses: Murder and nonnegligent manslaughter, negligent manslaughter, justifiable homicide
13. Kidnapping/abduction
14. Larceny/theft offenses: Pocket picking, purse snatching, shoplifting, theft from building, theft from coin-operated machine or device, theft from motor vehicle, theft of motor vehicle parts or accessories, all other larceny
15. Motor vehicle theft
16. Pornography/obscene material
17. Prostitution offenses: Prostitution, assisting or promoting prostitution
18. Robbery
19. Sex offenses, forcible: Forcible rape, forcible sodomy, sexual assault with an object, forcible fondling
20. Sex offenses, nonforcible: Incest, statutory rape
21. Stolen property offenses (receiving, etc.)
22. Weapon law violations

There are 11 additional offenses, known as Group B offenses, for which only arrest data are reported:

1. Bad checks
2. Curfew/loitering/vagrancy violations
3. Disorderly conduct
4. Driving under the influence
5. Drunkenness
6. Family offenses, nonviolent

7. Liquor law violations
8. Peeping tom
9. Runaway
10. Trespass of real property
11. All other offenses

Terms Commonly Used in Describing Crime Measures[21]

Age category	The appropriate age category is determined by the respondent's age on the last day of the month preceding the interview.
Aggravated assault	An attack or attempted attack with a weapon, regardless of whether an injury occurred, and an attack without a weapon when serious injury results. With injury: An attack without a weapon when serious injury results or an attack with a weapon involving any injury. Serious injury includes broken bones, lost teeth, internal injuries, loss of consciousness, and any unspecified injury requiring two or more days of hospitalization. Threatened with a weapon: Threat or attempted attack by an offender armed with a gun, knife, or other object used as a weapon that does not result in victim injury.
Assault	An unlawful physical attack or threat of attack. Assaults may be classified as aggravated or simple. Rape, attempted rape, and sexual assaults are excluded from this category, as well as robbery and attempted robbery. The severity of assaults ranges from minor threats to nearly fatal incidents.
Burglary	Unlawful or forcible entry or attempted entry of a residence. This crime usually, but not always, involves theft. The illegal entry may be by force, such as breaking a window or slashing a screen, or may be without force by entering through an unlocked door or an open window. As long as the person entering has no legal right to be present in the structure, a burglary has occurred. Furthermore, the structure need not be the house itself for a burglary to take place; illegal entry of a garage, shed, or any other structure on the premises also constitutes household burglary. If breaking and entering occurs in a hotel or vacation residence, it is still classified as a burglary for the household whose member or members were staying there at the time the entry occurred. Attempted forcible entry: A form of burglary in which force is used in an attempt to gain entry. Completed burglary: A form of burglary in which a person who has no legal right to be present in the structure successfully gains entry to a residence, by use of force, or without force. Forcible entry: A form of completed burglary in which force is used to gain entry to a residence. Some examples include breaking a window or slashing a screen. Unlawful entry without force: A form of completed burglary committed by someone having no legal right to be on the premises, even though no force is used.
Collection year	The set of victimizations reported to the NCVS in interviews conducted during the same calendar year. This set may include victimizations that occurred in the previous calendar year, due to the retrospective nature of the NCVS interview. Collection year data are used in tables beginning in 1996.
Crimes of violence	Rape, sexual assault, personal robbery, or assault. This category includes both attempted and completed crimes. It does not include purse snatching and pocket picking. Murder is not measured by the NCVS because of an inability to question the victim. Completed violence: The sum of all completed rapes, sexual assaults, robberies, and assaults. See individual crime types for definition of completed crimes. Attempted/threatened violence: The unsuccessful attempt of rape, sexual assault, personal robbery, or assault. Includes attempted attacks or sexual assaults by means of verbal threats. See individual crime types for definition of attempted crimes.

Criminal history records

The FBI administers national systems that permit interstate access to criminal records maintained in all 50 states. These systems include the following:

- National Instant Criminal Background Check System Index
- National Crime Information Center
- Interstate Identification Index
- National Protection Order File
- National Sex Offender Registry
- Automated Fingerprint Identification System

AUTOMATED FINGERPRINT IDENTIFICATION SYSTEM

Automated Fingerprint Identification System (AFIS) is an automated system for searching fingerprint files and transmitting fingerprint images. AFIS computer equipment can scan fingerprint impressions (or use electronically transmitted fingerprint images) and automatically extract and digitize ridge details and other identifying characteristics in sufficient detail to enable the computer's searching and matching components to distinguish a single fingerprint from thousands or even millions of fingerprints previously scanned and stored in digital form in the computer's memory.

The process eliminates the manual searching of fingerprint files and increases the speed and accuracy of 10-print processing (arrest fingerprint cards and noncriminal justice applicant fingerprint cards). AFIS equipment also can be used to identify individuals from "latent" (crime scene) fingerprints, with even fragmentary prints of single fingers in some cases. Digital fingerprint images generated by AFIS equipment can be transmitted electronically to remote sites, eliminating the necessity of mailing fingerprint cards and providing remote access to AFIS fingerprint files.

Criminal Justice Data Improvement Program

The Criminal Justice Data Improvement Program works to fulfill BJS's mission of improving the criminal record keeping of states and local governments while improving the ability of states and localities to produce statistics on crime and the administration of justice.

Criminal history records describe offenses and offenders and include offender fingerprint identification and notations of arrest and subsequent dispositions. All states have established a criminal record repository that maintains criminal records and identification data and responds to law enforcement inquiries and inquiries for other purposes such as background checks and national security. Criminal records include data provided by all components of the criminal justice system: law enforcement, prosecution, courts, and corrections. Automated interfaces with courts and prosecutors are critical to ensuring that all criminal records include dispositions at each stage of the criminal process. Criminal records include records of protection orders, sex offender registries, and other records of contacts with the justice system.

The program allows accurate, timely, and complete criminal history records that

- Enable states to immediately identify persons who are prohibited from firearm purchase or are ineligible to hold positions of responsibility involving children, the elderly, or the disabled

- Enable criminal justice agencies to make decisions on pretrial release, career criminal charging, determinate sentencing, and correctional assignments
- Are critical to assist law enforcement in criminal investigations and decision making
- Are required for background checks for national security, employment, licensing, and related economic purposes, as required under recent legislation

References

1. Masters, R., & Roberson, C. (1990). *Inside criminology.* Englewood Cliffs, NJ: Prentice-Hall.
2. Adler, F. (1974). *Sisters in crime: The rise of the new female criminal* (p. 32). New York: McGraw-Hill.
3. Roberson, C. (1994). *Introduction to criminal justice* (p. 20). Incline Village, NV: Copperhouse.
4. Wallace, H., & Roberson, C. (2012). *Principles of criminal law* (5th ed., pp. 13, 14). Columbus, OH: Prentice-Hall.
5. Sutherland, E. (1974) *Principles of criminology* (4th ed., p. 1). New York: Lippincott.
6. Miranda v. Arizona, 384 U.S. 436 (1966).
7. Schmalleger, F. (2009). *Criminology today: An integrative introduction* (p. 48). Columbus, OH: Pearson.
8. Federal Bureau of Investigation. (n.d.). *Uniform Crime Reports.* Retrieved March 5, 2013, from http://www.fbi.gov/about-us/cjis/ucr/ucr
9. Federal Bureau of Investigation. (n.d.). *Crime in the United States, 2012.* Retrieved March 3, 2013, from http://www.fbi.gov/about-us/cjis/ucr/crime-in-the-u.s/2012/crime-in-the-u.s.-2012/resource-pages/about-ucr/aboutucrmain
10. Federal Bureau of Investigation. (n.d.). *Crime in the United States, 2012.* Retrieved March 4, 2013, from http://www.fbi.gov/about-us/cjis/ucr/crime-in-the-u.s/2012/crime-in-the-u.s.-2012/resource-pages/about-ucr/aboutucrmain
11. Federal Bureau of Investigation. (n.d.). *Crime in the United States, 2012.* Retrieved from http://www.fbi.gov/about-us/cjis/ucr/crime-in-the-u.s/2012/crime-in-the-u.s.-2012/resource-pages/about-ucr/aboutucrmain
12. Uniform Crime Reporting Statistics, Department of Justice, Retrieved August 20, 2013, from http://www.ucrdatatool.gov/
13. Ruderman, W. (2012, June 28). Crime report finds manipulation is common among New York Police, study finds. *New York Times.* Retrieved March 4, 2013, from http://www.nytimes.com/2012/06/29/nyregion/new-york-police-department-manipulates-crime-reports-study-finds.html?_r=0
14. Federal Bureau of Investigation. (n.d.). A word about NIBRS. Retrieved March 4, 2013, from http://www.fbi.gov/about-us/cjis/ucr/nibrs/2011
15. Federal Bureau of Investigation. (2011). NIBRS participation by state. Retrieved March 4, 2013, from http://www.fbi.gov/about-us/cjis/ucr/nibrs/2011/resources/nibrs-participation-by-state
16. Federal Bureau of Investigation. (n.d.) Summary of NIBRS 2011. Retrieved March 4, 2013, from http://www.fbi.gov/about-us/cjis/ucr/nibrs/2011/resources/summary-of-nibrs-2011
17. Federal Bureau of Investigation. (n.d.) Summary of NIBRS 2011. Retrieved March 4, 2013, from http://www.fbi.gov/about-us/cjis/ucr/nibrs/2011/resources/summary-of-nibrs-2011. List drawn from p. 1.
18. National Research Council. (2005). *Principles and practices for a federal statistical agency* (3rd ed.). Washington, DC: National Academy Press.
19. The information on the NIBRS was adapted from The FBI website. Retrieved March 1, 2013, from http://www2.fbi.gov/ucr/faqs.htm
20. Justice Research and Statistics Association. (2012). *Status of NIBRS in the United States.* Retrieved March 4, 2013, from http://www.jrsa.org/ibrrc/background-status/nibrs_states.shtml
21. The definitions set forth in this section were taken from the DOJ website as noted in Reference 8.

chapter two

The concept of crime

Chapter objectives

After studying this chapter, the reader should be able to

- Identify the characteristics of law and the role of criminal law in shaping behavior
- Describe the relationship between actions that are deemed "criminal," and those that result in social harm
- Explain the complex nature of crime causation
- Define the five goals of punishment
- Compare and contrast the approaches to crime most typical of Native American tribes to those of other primitive societies
- Describe the nature of punishment in colonial America
- Identify key developments in criminal law and punishment in the United States from the 1800s to the present day

Introduction

> Crime is common. Logic is rare. Therefore it is upon the logic rather than upon the crime that you should dwell.
>
> **Sir Arthur Conan Doyle, *The Adventures of Sherlock Holmes*, "The Adventure of the Copper Beeches"**[1]

> Crime is a sociopolitical artifact, not a natural phenomenon. We can have as much or as little crime as we please, depending on what we choose to count as criminal.
>
> **Herbert Leslie Packer, 1968**[2]

Not all societies have had "crime" in the manner that we think of it today, and the landscape of crime in contemporary times continues to change with alterations to the underlying causes of crime, definitions of crime, and mechanisms of crime control. This chapter first sets the context with a brief introduction to the inextricable link between criminal law and "crime," and then goes on to explore some of the historic evolution of criminal behavior and changes to how society has defined and responded to criminal behavior.

Thinking about criminal law

> The essential characteristic of crime is that it is behavior which is prohibited by the State as an injury to the State and against which the State may react, at least at the last resort, by punishment.
>
> **Edwin Sutherland, 1949**[3]

Crime is typically defined as a violation of criminal law. Laws are rules that are codified into the status of law by our government to secure the orderly functioning of the society. They attempt to reduce, control, or eliminate behaviors that are believed to threaten the social order. This is why criminal cases are viewed as the state versus the defendant rather than the individual victim(s) versus the defendant—the offense in question is legally viewed as an action against the greater social order (as represented by the government), rather than the individual. Laws have the following three characteristics:

1. They are enforced by government entities.
2. The enforcement is carried out through standardized techniques.
3. The laws include clearly established sanctions.

Laws can take the form of constitutions, statutes, codes, and judicial decisions.

Criminal law is not the only way to maintain order or combat socially harmful behaviors. If you have ever been grounded (or grounded someone else), or reined in your behavior at a school dance or company party so that you would not draw the judgment of others, you are familiar with the idea that people's behavior can be controlled without the threat of legal sanctions. Law is not even the most effective form of social control—the most effective control is the internalization of social norms, as it is not until we have internalized a social expectation that we abide by it regardless of whether we think anyone is watching. So, for example, if a person only drives under the speed limit because they do not want a ticket, they will continue to speed when they do not see police officers or speed detection cameras. On the other hand, if the same individual has internalized the understanding that high speeds can jeopardize public safety, they are more likely to obey the speed limit regardless of whether they think they would be caught for doing otherwise.

Although laws are not the only way to affect human behavior, it is widely accepted that as society increases in complexity, there is an increasing need for criminal law. When people from several cultures or with conflicting sets of values and priorities converge in a given society, conflicts may arise regarding the norms that should be enforced, and how stringently so. Debates surrounding abortion, illicit drug use, and the "stand your ground" law are just a few examples of ongoing controversies surrounding the appropriateness of what should or should not be deemed "criminal."

The contours of criminal law are constantly changing, which serves as a good reminder that while some behaviors are clearly more socially harmful than others, the dividing line between "criminal" and "noncriminal" is sometimes quite arbitrary. Consider the following scenario: You are standing on the bank of a river. There is a rescue rope beside you. You see a young child drowning. In most states, if you have no statutory duty or relationship to the child you would have no legal obligation to save him or her. Of course, it would be a violation of most moral codes to standby and not do anything. This example also points out that there is a difference between moral standards and legal requirements. That is why individuals often remark that the law only covers the minimum requirements of living in a society and does not cover what makes us good and useful citizens. All states have statutes that require parents to take care of and protect their children, so if you were the parent (or caretaker) of that child, you would have a duty to act. If you were only a friend or a stranger, you might not have any legal duty to do so. In this scenario, is a parent who allows their child to drown inherently more "criminal" than a person who allows someone else's child to drown? Both might be seen as actions resulting in an equal amount of social harm, and yet they are handled differently by criminal law. The following diagram represents this imperfect overlap between the full scope of socially harmful behaviors, not all of which are criminalized, and the full scope of criminal behaviors as legally defined, not all of which everyone will agree are socially harmful.

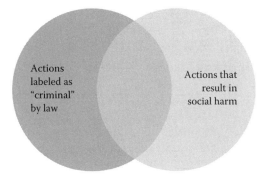

So, for example, failure to provide adequate mental health care to those with serious illness is clearly socially harmful, but it is not illegal. Similarly, charging exorbitant interest rates to someone in dire economic circumstances is potentially socially harmful but not, up to a point, illegal. On the other hand, conduct that is labeled as "criminal" by law may result in minimal social harm. Although excessive speeding can place people at risk, it is unlikely that driving 26 mph in a 25 mph zone will result in tangible social harm, but it is technically illegal. Drinking responsibly and in moderation under the age of 21 is unlikely to cause harm, and yet it is still a violation of the legal code.

Thinking about crime

Frequently, we hear the question "What can we do to solve crime?" This question seems to imply that there is a holy grail of crime prevention. In fact, the question is the equivalent of asking a doctor "What can we do to cure sickness?" Just as a treatment plan would vary widely depending on whether a person is battling cancer, a bacterial infection, or the common cold, the nature and causes of crime are widely varied, and, by consequence, so are the solutions. As will be discussed in the Chapters 3 through 9, the "causes" of crime range from the influence of family and friends, to individual traits, to the circumstances of the criminal event—many offenses are committed impulsively rather than carefully and thoughtfully planned.

The wide array of factors that influence crime should not be surprising given the diversity of human experience. Whenever we are talking about human behavior, the answers will not be straightforward. Consider, for example, the question of why people go to college. Is it due to the influence of parents who are college graduates, or due to a determination to be the first college graduate in their family? Are students interested in knowledge for the sake of learning, or earning a degree to make more money? Likely, each of these explanations is true in at least some cases, but clearly no single explanation can adequately account for the broad range of human motivations. The same goes for criminal behavior.

Furthermore, any given crime is likely to result from the convergence of several risk factors. Just as the risk for a common cold varies based on a person's level of exposure to the virus, the strength of their immune system, and the preventive steps they take, the risk of committing crime will be amplified among those individuals who are at risk based on their social circumstances, personal characteristics, and their exposure to criminal opportunities. No single risk factor automatically compels an individual into criminal activity, but cumulatively the risk factors identified in this book sometimes converge to significantly increase the likelihood that any given person will engage in crime.

The various causes of crime mean that serious effort to reduce crime cannot be monolithic. Just as antibiotics are powerless against viral infections and even the most promising cancer treatment will not cure the common cold, efforts to prevent crime need to be tailored to its different causes. A community that relies on only one strategy for crime reduction is akin to a hospital that carries only one type of medication. Traditional "crime-fighting" tactics such as aggressive policing or long prison sentences will work in some cases, as with those circumstances in which crime is committed due to a rational calculation of potential benefits relative to potential costs. On the other hand, people who turn to crime due to addiction, mental illness, or a lack of viable alternatives or coping skills are unlikely to be swayed by heavy-handed criminal justice policies. By consequence, the burden for crime prevention permeates all of the major institutions of life, including the economy, educational system, and family unit.

Goals of punishment

There are generally five widely held goals to any criminal punishment, the first three of which relate directly to the reduction of crime:

1. Incapacitation: Prevents the offender from continuing to engage in crime through physical controls, such as incarceration
2. Deterrence: Reduces crime through the threat of criminal punishment
3. Rehabilitation: Reduces crime by changing the offender in some fundamental way, as with the application of treatment or educational programs
4. Retribution: Exacts vengeance against the wrongdoer
5. Restoration: Attempts to "make right" the wrongs caused by the crime

Some types of punishment can fulfill multiple goals at once. For example, incarceration can incapacitate, deter, and fulfill retributive purposes simultaneously.

The historic evolution of responses to criminal behavior addressed in this chapter can be viewed within the framework of these goals. Many of the earliest responses to crime were focused on retribution or restoration, meaning that early criminal law was not perceived as a mechanism for reducing overall crime rates. It has only been in relatively recent times—perhaps in the last 300 years of the more than 4000-year history of written criminal laws—that formal punishments have started to shift toward goals of crime reduction.

Goal of Punishment	Example
Incapacitation	Johnny receives a prison sentence of 25 to life with the reasoning that so long as he is behind bars, he will not be able to victimize anyone else.
Deterrence	The state legislature passes a law requiring a mandatory minimum sentence of 10 years in prison for aggravated robbery, with the belief that people will be less likely to commit robbery out of fear of the long sentence.
Rehabilitation	Jane is convicted of possession of crystal methamphetamine in a drug court. She is ordered to attend drug treatment and report back to the judge periodically on her progress.
Retribution	Larry is sentenced to the death penalty after being convicted of two counts of aggravated murder. The intention is to help provide some closure to the victims' families with the sense that justice was served.
Restoration	Karen is found guilty on counts of vandalism and destruction of property. She is ordered to return, replace, or repair all items for the victim.

Early historic responses to socially harmful behavior

Primitive societies

Historically, some societies have maintained order entirely without written law. For example, the Lakota tribe in the mid-1800s was regulated through unwritten but commonly accepted rules.[4] As just one example, consider the following:

> [It] was allowed … for a woman to walk away from a man who had been unfaithful. It was even allowed for a woman to beat the man who had been caught having an affair. If she chose to humiliate him, he would not be allowed to defend himself. He could only run away. If he defended himself, he would be the object of ridicule by all. On the other hand, if there was no reason for a woman to walk away, she would not be allowed to return, in our culture, if she abandoned her home. If she walked away, she would lose all rights to her home and everything in it.[5]

These rules were widely accepted and implemented without being codified into a body of law, and without a government bureaucracy in place to enforce them. Although individuals within the Lakota tribe, as with any society, sometimes engaged in socially harmful behavior, there were no "criminals" per say, as there were no criminal laws to violate. Similarly, there was no formal correctional system of the kind that we take for granted in the present day, leaving tribes to rely on informal mechanisms such as humiliation or social exclusion to enforce social rules.

In many Native American societies, the primary focus was on restoration for the harms resulting from the offense. Even murders were often forgiven through various mechanisms, although sometimes retribution was sought. For example, among the Iroquois,

> a killer's family met with him to convince him to admit his guilt, then sent a strip of white wampum to the victim's clan to signal their willingness to make reparations … if the victim's family accepted the strip, the death was pardoned; their refusal, on the other hand, meant that they chose to retaliate by claiming a life from the killer's clan.[6]

Similarly, the Karok of California had "an elaborate compensation system for deaths and other crimes."[7] Another approach comes from the Ojibway:

> Instead of deciding who is at fault, the Ojibway focus on cleansing the spirits of the victim and the offender to repair the injury done to both and to improve their futures as whole community members; compensation, if chosen, is dealt with privately between the victim and offender.[8]

Primitive societies in Europe and elsewhere also used some restorative elements, but generally speaking the punishments tended to emphasize retribution above all other goals. Working on the premise that "only blood may wash away blood,"[9] those who were harmed by violence were expected to seek vengeance against their attackers without the intervention of a legal authority. A "vendetta," or "blood feud," was carried out when the victim or his or her family or tribe exacted revenge on the offender, offender's family, or tribe. In these societies, it was viewed as the responsibility of the victim's kin to make things right through revenge.[10] This practice was problematic and an alternative custom of "wergild" developed in which the offender or offender's kin could make restitutive payments of money or property in lieu of the vendetta. This practice is still used in some Middle Eastern countries.

Early criminal laws

Definitions of crime in early Europe and elsewhere were strongly wedded to religious concepts of sin. Where crime was viewed as a sin against church and/or state as well as the individual victim, a supplemental practice of "friedensgeld" developed, in which the offender would pay to the church or later to the crown in addition to their wergeld. Over time, centralized governance—whether in the form of tribal leadership, religious leadership, or, eventually, government—began to play a more active role in settling disputes and assume greater responsibility for carrying out punishments and issuing fines in the place of vendettas and wergeld. Dykes described the transition to formal law:

> To the most primitive types of law crime is unknown. Theft, robbery, and even homicide, are regarded as private injuries for which, at most, an appropriate indemnification or revenge may be exacted, but not as crimes which it is to the interest of the community to discourage by penalties. In the earliest phase of Roman law, for theft and robbery the injured party avenged himself at his own hand without judicial or public warrant.... But at Rome an exception was very early established by instituting a public prosecution for treason and murder. The former was obviously an injury to the State in its corporate capacity; and the relegation of murder to the sphere of private revenge doubtless produced blood feuds which were found to be disturbing to the peace. Hence criminal law arose.[11]

Slowly, offensive behaviors such as violence and theft came to be viewed as public rather than private harms, and thus in need of state action. It was at this stage that criminal law was conceived as an avenue for protecting the public from wrongdoing. Those who failed to fulfill their punishment were sometimes banished or exiled, and thus considered "outlaws."

The earliest known written laws have been traced to about 2000 BC. The "Code of Hammurabi," from the ancient city of Babylon, is often identified as the earliest known example of written laws, but Sumerian codes have been located that predate the Code of Hammurabi by about 200 years.[12] These codes outlined regulations for slavery, taxation, property ownership, civil liability, family relations and criminal culpability, and the penalties for violation. Serving as evidence of the close relationship between religion and state power at the time, both of the codes contained explicit reference to the "power and authority of the gods."[13] Demonstrating the evolution of society's primary concerns over time, the Sumerian codes included several pieces of regulation pertaining to the rental of oxen:

- If a man rented an ox and injured the flesh at the nose ring, he shall pay one-third of (its) price.
- If a man rented an ox and damaged its eye, he shall pay one-half of (its) price.
- If a man rented an ox and broke its horn, he shall pay one-fourth of (its) price.[14]

The criminal penalties outlined in these codes could be quite severe. Under the Code of Hammurabi, the death penalty could be imposed for any of the following crimes:

- Witchcraft
- Threatening witnesses in death penalty cases
- Perjury
- Theft of property belonging to "the king or the temple"
- Kidnapping
- Harboring a fugitive slave
- Breaking into a home
- Robbery[15]

Other punishments were quite harsh, including mutilation, whipping, or forced labor, and in many cases, the victim or nearest relative were allowed personally to inflict punishment. Originally, punishments were reserved almost exclusively for slaves and bondservants; later, punishments were extended to all offenders.

When the Roman legions under Emperor Claudius conquered England, Roman law, customs, and language were forced upon the English people. Roman law at that time was based on the Twelve Tables, which had been developed around 450 BC. The tables listed basic rules that governed family, religious, and economic life. The tables were later replaced by the Justinian Code. The Justinian Code was developed under the rule of Emperor Justinian I between 527 and 565 BC. The Code was actually three lengthy documents: (1) the Institutes, (2) the Digest, and (3) the Code.

Before the Norman Conquest (1066), there was no uniform criminal law in England. The village courts were governed by sheriffs who often enforced the rules as they saw fit. After the conquest, when William the Conqueror was King of England, he decreed that all prosecution was to be conducted in the name of the king to reduce the arbitrariness of the prior system. New laws were created, and the king, the judges, and the church authorities determined the elements and the scope of criminal offenses. Judicial decisions were based on general customs, usages, and moral concepts. By the 1600s, criminal law in England was based on mandatory rules of conduct that the judges had laid down. The rules became the "common law" of England. Prior court decisions were accepted as authoritative precepts and were applied to future cases in a system of case law that came to be central to the common law tradition. In medieval times, punishments continued to be quite brutal, including death sentences for minor crimes such as theft. Punishments overlapped with religious beliefs, as with the burning of witches.

Historic definitions and responses to crime in the United States

Colonial law

When the English settlers came to America in the 1600s, they brought with them the English common law[16] with modifications. Many components of common law persist to the present day: Just as laws were prosecuted in the name of the king under William, present-day laws are prosecuted as "State v. defendant," or, for federal laws, "United States v. defendant," and case law continues to be recognized at the stature of legal codes. All states except Louisiana can trace their legal systems to the English common law system. (Louisiana, whose system was originally based on the French and Spanish code law concept, officially adopted the common law of England as the basis for their system in 1805.)

LEGAL TRADITIONS

Although the United States continues to operate in the common law tradition, this is not the most typical legal tradition internationally. Many countries in Europe and elsewhere instead operate under "civil law," in which there is a heavy emphasis on writing comprehensive criminal codes that provide judges with adequate guidance in a variety of circumstances. By contrast, laws in the United States are less comprehensive when originally written, but continue to be refined through case law, or the decisions of the courts pertaining to their interpretation of the laws. Other nations operate within an Islamic legal tradition, which is heavily based on the religious tenets of Islam just as early common law was often clearly grounded in the principles of Christianity.

Early colonial approaches to criminal law and punishment were also heavily influenced by the religious beliefs of the colonists, with criminal laws often formed around the idea of moral sins. In colonial America, those who committed crimes were also considered to be "offenders against the divine." Punishments integrated components of humiliation, physical pain, penance, fines, and, sometimes, death, often taking the form of corporal punishment carried out in public, or, if the offender could afford it, fines. "Corporal punishment" refers to physical, sometimes quite brutal, punishments meant to inflict pain on the offender. The term is sometimes used in the present day to refer to spanking in the context of child rearing, but the punishments of colonial times extended well beyond this current use of the term. Offenders were whipped, branded, or put to death, often in full view of the public. One researcher, Joseph J. Thompson, commented on the cruelty of these punishments as follows:

> As one studies the making and execution of laws for the punishment of offenses of days long past it [is] apparent that the law maker never had himself in mind, but always fixed the penalties for others; but it will strike one as strange that it never seems to have occurred to the law makers that they might sometime have the machinery of punishment turned upon them.[17]

Other punishments were intended to shame the offender. For example, the offender would be placed in "stocks," or a wooden framework with two holes for their ankles, in a public location such as the town square, sometimes for days at a time, where they would be subject to the ridicule of passersby.[18] These shaming punishments sometimes also integrated physical cruelty: In the "pillory," offenders would place their head and hands into the holes of a wooden framework in full view of the public as a shaming measure, but in some instances, their ears were nailed to the wood, only to be torn off when the offender was released. Individualized sentences often reflected the dominance of religion in public life, as with orders that offenders pull weeds on church property or perform repairs for the church (p. 331).

Punishments were often stratified by class/social status. Those who were wealthy enough to pay fines could often do so in lieu of corporal punishment, and punishments were shaped in part by the relative status of the victim and offender. One author offered the following description:

> Whippings of up to 40 lashes were most frequently administered for immorality, being the form of payment which could be made

by servants, who accounted for most of these cases. More severe application of the lash appears to have been reserved for insubordinate behavior: the scattered instances of mutiny of slaves against an overseer, a wrongful accusation of bastardy, a servant woman's false accusation of her mistress of acts of unchastity were punished by 100 lashes on the bare back. Servants who could not pay fines could have additional time added to their term of service.... Where master and servant were charged with the same offense the master was sentenced to pay a fine in tobacco, the servant was whipped.[19]

Developments in the 1800s

The practice of separate punishments based on one's social status continued to pervade criminal law in many states well into the 1800s, and became increasingly based explicitly on race, particularly in the south as a way of enforcing systems of slavery and, later, racial segregation. "Black codes" were laws that explicitly criminalized actions among black populations that did not apply to others. For example, Missouri in 1847 passed a law that explicitly outlawed the education of blacks and those of mixed race (at the time, referred to as "negroes" and "mulattoes," respectively):

> No person shall keep or teach any school for the instruction of negroes or mulattoes, in reading or writing, in this State.... All meeting of negroes for the purposes mentioned ... shall be considered unlawful assemblages, and shall be suppressed by sheriffs, constables, and other public officers ... if any person shall violate the provisions of this act, he shall, for every such offence, be indicted and punished by fine not exceeding five hundred dollars, or by imprisonment not exceeding six months, or by both such fine and imprisonment.[20]

At the same time, in some parts of the country and for some populations, punishment began to take other forms. It was in the late 1700s that the most significant experiments with incarceration as punishment first took place, as with the Walnut Street Jail in Philadelphia. Influenced heavily by Pennsylvania Quakers, the jail was a move away from corporal punishment, with the hope that offenders could be reformed by a period of isolated penance. Jails quickly earned a reputation as criminogenic, though, with the thought that they simply expose offenders to like-minded individuals and, in some cases, subject them to cruelty at the hands of guards that approximated the physical punishments the penitentiary movement was intended to curb.

A few decades later, in 1841, probation was first used in a Boston courtroom when a local shoemaker volunteered to take the responsibility for a drunkard in order to keep him out of jail. The shoemaker agreed to look after a drunkard to keep him out of jail. Probation allows offenders to be conditionally released to the community under supervision. Around the same time, also in the 1840s, parole was developed as an incentive for good behavior within a prison colony in Australia. The practice was brought to the United States just a few decades later. From the penitentiary movement to probation and parole, the emphasis of reformers during this time, particularly with the changes that were taking place in the Northeast, was distinctly on shifting the primary goal of punishment from retribution to rehabilitation. Another important development was the creation of the nation's first juvenile court in Chicago in 1899, opened in recognition that juveniles had different needs and levels of culpability for their actions relative to adults.

THE LAST PUBLIC EXECUTION

The last execution to be carried out in public in the United States did not occur until 1936. In many ways, it was an event typical of public executions in the south, although the size and rowdiness of the crowd has been implicated in speeding up the end of public executions in Kentucky. A woman had been raped and murdered, and her apartment burglarized.[21] Ex-convict Rainey Bethea confessed to the crime and directed the police to the woman's missing items. He was convicted by a jury and sentenced to death. George Wright described the event:

> As noted by the city's historian, in the days leading up to the execution, thousands of people came to Owensboro [Kentucky] by horseback, automobiles, excursion trains, buses, and even airplanes. The usual vendors arrived … to profit from the [execution]. Many citizens held "hanging parties," inviting out-of-town friends to Owensboro. Others had spontaneous barbecues and sporting activities. Some twenty thousand people attended the hanging, even though it took place at 5:30 in the morning. National newspaper accounts … told of people rushing to the gallows to rip off the hangman's hood and the clothes worn by Bethea for souvenirs.[22]

David Garland's research affirms that this crowded atmosphere was not unusual. In the south, in the late 1800s and early 1900s, in addition to the public state execution of offenders and the lynching of thousands of people for other reasons, there were also hundreds of executions that were carried out in response to criminal accusations but without proper procedure, which were also "highly publicized, took place before a large crowd, were staged with a degree of ritual, and involved elements of torture, mutilation, or unusual cruelty,"[23] similar to the Bethea execution event. It was not unusual for professional photographers to sell souvenir pictures of these events for attendees to mail to their friends and family. The crowd would participate in the mutilation of the accused, sometimes engaging in great brutality while the accused was still alive. The body would not only be hanged but also shot and sometimes burned. Members of the crowd would take souvenirs that sometimes included "pieces of the rope, links of the chain, or pieces of the tree where [the accused] had been tied. Some took scraps of his clothes or bones and body parts that had survived the fire."[24]

Developments from the 1900s to the present

Punishment in the early part of the 1900s was a mix of remnants of the public, physical punishments of colonial days, particularly in the executions of the south, and the rehabilitative reforms that increasingly taken hold in the latter part of the 1800s. The rehabilitative movement continued through the mid-1900s, with correctional practices focused on treatment of the offender. The early 1900s saw distinct growth in the number of people being labeled "criminal," though, with an expansion of criminal laws that included a constitutional prohibition on alcohol that remained in effect from 1920 to 1933. The 18th Amendment to the U.S. Constitution prohibited "the manufacture, sale, or transportation of intoxicating liquors within, the importation thereof into, or the exportation thereof from the United States," including all U.S. territories.

The Prohibition era serves as an interesting study in the effects of criminal laws and punishment on criminals and crime. First, any time that a new action becomes criminalized, it will expand the scope of those labeled criminal, even when any given individual's behavior remains unchanged. By the period 1929–1934, 43.4% of sentences to federal prison were for liquor law violations[25]—behaviors that would not have even been considered criminal several years prior. At the same time, the prohibition of alcohol also opened up a new black market for alcohol manufacture and sales that strengthened organized crime in the United States. The outlawing of one set of behaviors—the manufacture and sale of alcohol—had effects on other forms of crime, ranging from political corruption to violence to other forms of vice.

The midpoint of the century witnessed a series of civil rights efforts that led to the dismantling of the explicitly race- and class-based laws and punishments that had become so common through the 1800s and into the 1900s. At the same time, growing social unrest resulting from the antiwar, civil rights, counterculture, and gay rights movements in the 1960s led to a growing sense of insecurity as police and protesters clashed, prominent figures were assassinated, and riots burned entire neighborhoods. This set into motion a renewed effort for "law and order" politics, this time not rooted in the moral or religious underpinnings that characterized Prohibition so much as fear over the radical social changes that were taking place. The previously dominant goal of rehabilitation was overtaken with an emphasis on incapacitation as states and the federal government adopted longer sentences for a broad range of crimes, including relatively minor drug offenses.

In their well-known work on this "new penology," Malcolm Feeley and Jonathan Simon observed the following changes:[26]

- A shift from a moral or rehabilitative language within corrections to actuarial discourse about the risks posed by offenders
- An emphasis on risk management rather than rehabilitation or social work
- A general pessimism regarding the potential to change offenders in any fundamental way

The United States now incarcerates a greater portion of its population than any other nation in the world.

Summary

- Crime is typically defined as a violation of criminal law.
- Laws have three characteristics that collectively set them apart from other forms of social control: They are enforced by government entities, through standardized techniques, with clearly established sanctions in place.
- Laws are most effective when the norms they represent have been internalized.
- Criminal law is constantly changing, and so is the population deemed "criminal."
- Acts that are labeled as "criminal" by law overlap, but not perfectly, with acts that result in social harm.
- There is no single answer to the question of what causes crime.
- Crime is most likely to result when multiple risk factors converge.
- The potential solutions to crime are as varied as crime itself.
- Society's responses to crime aim to fulfill one or more of five commonly held goals: incapacitation, deterrence, rehabilitation, retribution, and restoration.

- The goals of incapacitation, deterrence, and rehabilitation are all targeted at reducing crime.
- Not all societies throughout history have had formal written laws.
- The responses to socially harmful behaviors in Native American societies were most strongly characterized by an emphasis on restoration.
- Primitive societies in Europe and elsewhere responded to social harm with retributive justice, as with the practice of blood feuds.
- Justice in primitive societies was exacted between private parties.
- Friedensgeld was one of the earliest examples of the church or state taking an active role in carrying out justice for socially harmful behaviors.
- Over time, socially harmful behaviors increasingly came to be viewed as public, rather than just private, harms, and thus in need of state action.
- The earliest known written laws were the Code of Hammurabi and the Sumerian codes, which date to around 2000 BC.
- The Code of Hammurabi and the Sumerian codes were relatively well developed, including criminal law as well as laws for taxation, property ownership, family relationships, and civil liability.
- Early state-applied punishments tended to be physical in nature, with the death penalty applied for a wide range of offenses.
- After the Norman Conquest in 1066, William the Conqueror applied a system of common law across England, which provided the model for the American legal system.
- Approaches to crime and punishment in early colonial times were heavily influenced by religion and by English law.
- Punishments in colonial America were often physical and carried out in public, although fines and other alternatives were sometimes used.
- The severity of criminal punishment in colonial America was contingent, in part, upon the social standing of the offender and the victim.
- The American system of slavery contributed to the development of black codes, which explicitly outlawed behaviors among blacks—sometimes both free and slave—that were not considered illegal if committed by other segments of the population.
- Incarceration was first used as a punishment in the late 1790s, prompted by Quakers' efforts to reform punishment toward a focus on the penance of the offender.
- Probation and parole both date to the mid-1800s.
- The first juvenile court was created in Chicago in 1899.
- Punishment into the 1900s was increasingly targeted at rehabilitation.
- The 1900s witnessed the dismantling of race-based criminal legislation.
- From 1920 to 1933, the criminalization of alcohol helped shape the nature of crime and punishment in the United States.
- The unrest of the 1960s led to increasingly conservative criminal justice practices, including a shift away from rehabilitation toward incapacitation.
- The United States now incarcerates a greater portion of its population than any other nation in the world.

Questions in review

1. What is the relationship between criminal law and socially harmful behaviors?
2. In early Native American societies, what tended to be the primary goal of the tribe's response to socially harmful behavior?

3. What were blood feuds?
4. What is the significance of the Code of Hammurabi and the Sumerian codes?
5. What significant developments in criminal justice took place in the mid- to late-1800s?

Practicum

As described in this chapter, criminal law has a complex relationship with criminal behavior. The law defines what is criminal. The legal system stands to address socially harmful behaviors through deterrence, incapacitation, or rehabilitation, but in other cases, as evidenced by Prohibition, expansions to criminal law can actually aggravate socially harmful behaviors. Thinking about the nation's current use of incarceration, respond to the following questions:

1. In what ways would you expect a high rate of incarceration to reduce crime? Do you feel these benefits are likely to be realized, and why or why not?
2. In what ways could a high incarceration rate actually cause crime? Do you think this is a realistic concern, and why or why not?

Common terms used in criminal law

"Crime": An act or omission that violates the law and is punishable by a criminal sentence.

"Common-law crime": An offense that was a crime under the common law. Nearly all crimes, including offenses that were common-law crimes, are now defined by statute and are, thus, statutory crimes.

"Computer crime": A crime, such as committing fraud over the Internet, that requires the knowledge or use of computer technology. Also known as cybercrime.

"Crime of passion": A crime committed in a moment of sudden or extreme anger or other emotional disturbance sufficient enough for a reasonable person to lose control and not reflect on what he or she is doing.

"Hate crime": A crime motivated mostly by bias, ill will, or hatred toward the victim's actual or perceived race, color, ethnicity, country of national origin, religion, or sexual orientation. Many states impose extra penalties if a crime is committed due to such motivation.

"Inchoate crime": One of the three crimes (attempt, conspiracy, solicitation) that are steps toward the commission of another crime. Inchoate crime is also known as anticipatory crime, anticipatory offense, and inchoate offense.

"Infamous crime": At common law, any one of the crimes that were considered particularly dishonorable and the punishment for which included ineligibility to hold public office, to serve on a jury, or to testify at a civil or criminal trial. These crimes included treason, any felony, forgery, and perjury. In addition, any crime punishable by death or by imprisonment of more than 1 year was considered an infamous crime.

"Malum in se crime": An act is said to be malum in se when it is inherently and essentially evil, that is, immoral in its nature and injurious in its consequences, without regard to the fact that it violates the law.

"Mala prohibitum crime": A wrong prohibited; a thing which is wrong because it is prohibited; an act which is not inherently immoral, but becomes so because its commission is expressly forbidden by positive law.

"Status crime": A crime that is defined by a person's condition or character rather than by any wrongful act that they have done. For example, a minor drinking beer in a state that prohibits minors from consuming alcoholic beverages is a status crime because of his or her minority status.

"Statutory crime": An offense that was not a crime under the common law, but has been made a crime by a statute or any crime that is defined by a statute.

"Violent crime": Any crime that has as an element the use, attempted use, or threatened use of physical force against the person or property of another or any felony that entails a substantial risk that physical force will be used against the person or property of another.

"White-collar crime": Any business or financial nonviolent crime, such as bribery, consumer fraud, corruption, embezzlement, and stock manipulation, committed by business executives, professionals, public officials, and others in their profession.

References

1. Arthur Conan Doyle. (June 1892). *The Adventures of Sherlock Holmes*. Strand Magazine.
2. Packer, H. L. (1968). *The limits of criminal sanction* (p. 364). Stanford, CA: Stanford University Press.
3. Sutherland, E. (1949). *White collar crime*. New York: Holt, Rinehart and Winston.
4. Red Shirt, D. (2002). *Turtle lung woman's granddaughter*. Lincoln, NE: University of Nebraska Press.
5. Red Shirt, D. (2002). *Turtle lung woman's granddaughter* (p. 58). Lincoln, NE: University of Nebraska Press.
6. Meyer, J. F. (1998). History repeats itself: Restorative justice in Native American communities. *Journal of Contemporary Criminal Justice, 14*, 42–57.
7. Meyer, J. F. (1998). History repeats itself: Restorative justice in Native American communities. *Journal of Contemporary Criminal Justice, 14*, 44.
8. Meyer, J. F. (1998). History repeats itself: Restorative justice in Native American communities. *Journal of Contemporary Criminal Justice, 14*, 44, 45.
9. Grutzpalk, J. (2002). Blood feud and modernity: Max Weber's and Emile Durkheim's theories. *Journal of Classical Sociology, 2*, 115–134.
10. Grutzpalk, J. (2002). Blood feud and modernity: Max Weber's and Emile Durkheim's theories. *Journal of Classical Sociology, 2*, 118.
11. Dykes, D. O. (1904). Code of Hammurabi. *Juridical Review, 16*, 72–85.
12. Steele, F. R. (1948). The Code of Lipit-Ishtar. *American Journal of Archaeology, 52*(3), 425–450.
13. Steele, F. R. (1948). The Code of Lipit-Ishtar. *American Journal of Archaeology, 52*(3), 446.
14. Bulleted list drawn verbatim from Steele, F. R. (1948). The Code of Lipit-Ishtar. *American Journal of Archaeology, 52*(3), 444.
15. Dykes, D. O. (1904). Code of Hammurabi. *Juridical Review, 16*, 83.
16. Gardner, T. J., & Anderson, T. M. (2009). *Criminal law* (10th ed., p. 23). Belmont, CA: Thomson/Wadsworth.
17. Thompson, J. J. (1923). Early corporal punishments. *Illinois Law Quarterly, 6*, 37–49.
18. See, for example, Thompson, J. J. (1923). Early corporal punishments. *Illinois Law Quarterly, 6*, 44.
19. Preyer, K. (1982). Penal measures in the American colonies: An overview. *The American Journal of Legal History, 26*(4), 326–353.
20. Missouri State Law. (1847). *Negroes and mulattoes: An act respecting slaves, free Negroes and Mulattoes*. Retrieved April 11, 2013, from http://www.sos.mo.gov/archives/education/aahi/earlyslavelaws/An%20Act%20Respecting%20Slaves,%201847.pdf
21. Description of the Bethea execution based on Wright, G. C. (1991). Executions of Afro-Americans in Kentucky, 1870–1940. *Georgia Journal of Southern Legal History, 1*, 321–355.
22. Wright, G. C. (1991). Executions of Afro-Americans in Kentucky, 1870–1940. *Georgia Journal of Southern Legal History, 1*, 337–338.

23. Garland, D. (2005). Penal excess and surplus meaning: Public torture lynchings in twentieth-century America. *Law & Society Review, 39*(4), 793–833.
24. Garland, D. (2005). Penal excess and surplus meaning: Public torture lynchings in twentieth-century America. *Law & Society Review, 39*(4), 805.
25. Cahalan, M. W., with Parsons, L. (1986). *Historical corrections statistics in the United States, 1850–1984* (p.153). (NCJ 102529). Washington, DC: Bureau of Justice Statistics.
26. Feeley, M. M., & Simon, J. (1992). The new penology: Notes on the emerging strategy of corrections and its implications. *Criminology, 30*(4), 449–474.

chapter three

Early development of crime causation theories

Chapter objectives

After studying this chapter, the reader should be able to

- Explain the difference between a paradigm and a theory
- Identify the significant paradigms in the history of criminological thought
- Describe the core assumptions of the prescientific, classical, positivist, and postmodern paradigms
- Define and provide examples of trials by ordeal
- Outline the contributions of Cesare Beccaria and Jeremy Bentham
- Differentiate between general and specific deterrence
- Define and identify examples of situational crime prevention
- Differentiate between the Franco-Belgian and Italian schools of criminology
- Describe early American criminology, including the anthropological and hereditary traditions
- Discuss the relevance of social Darwinism to early positivist theories
- Define eugenics and explain its relationship to early American criminology
- Describe how positivist theories have evolved with time
- Discuss the policy implications of classicalism and positivism
- Identify critiques of classicalism and positivism
- Compare and contrast positivism and postmodernism

Introduction

This chapter addresses the historical development of criminological theory. Just as criminal behaviors have evolved with time (see Chapter 2), so too has society's understanding of its causes. A few key points set the context for this chapter:

- Predominant explanations of crime have varied over time.
- The history of criminological thought can be roughly divided into four eras: prescientific, classical, positivist, and postmodern.
- While these eras represent key changes in the *prevailing* explanations of criminal behavior across time, the eras are not clearly demarcated—to a greater or lesser extent, the core beliefs developed in each era continue to shape discussions of crime and crime causation.

Examining these different eras can support an understanding of society's changing responses to crime, since punishments are often designed to address what are believed to be the underlying causes of crime.

Paradigms: Setting the context

Different eras of criminological thought can be attributed to shifting paradigms. A "paradigm" is a worldview—a way of knowing and making sense of the world. Paradigms create the lens through which we view and interpret all that we see. When there is a shift in the predominant paradigm, it affects where attention is focused, how phenomena are explained, and what is done in response. Shifting paradigms drive changes in our awareness, how we define problems, and the social institutions that result. Thus, the dominant paradigm at any given point in time often has the power to shape criminological theories, punishments, and general views of crime and criminals.

A paradigm is more expansive than a theory. A "theory" is a set of propositions about the specific relationships that exist among phenomena. For example, a theory might attempt to explain the relationship between family structure and crime. As will be seen in this chapter, the predominant paradigm, on the other hand, will affect whether the specific theories in any given era will tend to be grounded in supernatural, rational, scientific, or critical understandings of the world. The identification of significant paradigm shifts in criminology allows us to understand the broader context within which theories are formed.

This chapter will cover the paradigms that have shaped thoughts about criminal behavior in four eras of criminological thought.

- Prescientific. Until about the 1300s, many nations relied on religious or supernatural explanations to make sense of errant behavior.
- Classical. During the Age of Enlightenment in the 1600s and 1700s, the tendency shifted toward explaining criminal behavior through logic and rationality.
- Positivist. Beginning in the late 1700s, those looking to explain crime increasingly turned to the scientific method.
- Postmodern. In the mid-1900s, a critical strain of thought turned attention to the subjective and power-laden processes by which laws are formed and criminals are defined.

Although each paradigm shift represents a key development in how crime has tended to be viewed within different eras, the contributions of each era continue to have an influence on the present day. When a crime is so heinous that it seems to defy prevailing explanations of human behavior, some will still refer to offenders as evil or monstrous, harkening back to supernatural explanations of crime. Classical explanations experienced a resurgence of popularity in the 1970s with the introduction of neoclassical theories, and positivism remains the dominant thread in criminological research, even as postmodern theories have gained traction. The rest of this chapter explores the origins of each paradigm in greater detail.

Prescientific explanations of crime

Before the era of scientific thought, religion provided the core paradigm for making sense of the world's mysteries. Human behavior and other natural phenomena were believed to have godly or mythical roots, and extreme forms of deviance were often explained in spiritual terms. Although contemporary offenders might be viewed as psychopathic, sociopathic, or mentally ill, in early times they were more likely to be understood as sinners fallen to temptation, or, in more extreme circumstances, as evil or befallen to demonic possession.

Supernatural beliefs about crime have, at times, been reflected in the trial process. In a "trial by ordeal" (as opposed to a judge or jury trial), the accused was subject to some kind of physical test, the outcome of which was believed to be in the hands of god. Trials by ordeal were viewed as a mechanism for appealing to a "divine witness"[1] to discover the ultimate truth about the defendant's guilt or innocence, particularly in serious civil or criminal cases that lacked sufficient evidence to determine the guilt of the accused. These ordeals were most commonly used by ancient cultures, and again in several European countries from the years 800 to 1200,[2] including heavy use in England for a brief period of time in twelfth century.[3]

TYPES OF TRIALS BY ORDEAL

Trials by ordeal took several forms, with the common thread being the expectation that a divine power would intervene to protect the innocent. Some examples of trials by ordeal included the following:

- Trial by cold water. The accused was to jump into a lake. Sinking (rather than floating) was seen as a sign of innocence, at which point the accused would be retrieved from the water before drowning.[4]
- Trial by boiling water. The accused had to retrieve an item from boiling water. If no physical burns resulted, the accused would be deemed innocent.[4]
- Trial by hot iron. The accused had to lift a hot iron and carry it a certain distance. The hand would then be bandaged for three days. If, at the end of the three days, the hand was without sign of a burn, the party would be found innocent.[5]
- Trial by hot ploughshares. The accused had to walk, blindfolded and barefoot, across a series of red-hot ploughshares (plow blades). The accused was determined to be innocent if they successfully completed the task without injury.[5]

A similar strategy to assess guilt in cases with insufficient evidence was "trial by battle," in which the accuser and accused (or representatives for them) engaged in a duel on the basis that God would intervene on behalf of the rightful party.[5]

A belief in the supernatural also affected the punishments applied to offenders. From this paradigm appropriate outcomes might include efforts to save the sinner, appease the gods, or exorcise the demons. If a person was viewed as beyond salvation, exile or execution might be acceptable options for casting the "evil" individual from society. Other punitive responses were guided by religious principles, as with the concept of "an eye for an eye."

The classical school

The Enlightenment brought new ways of making sense of human behavior. Religion and spirituality did not go away, but they were increasingly supplanted with reasoning and logic as the primary mechanism for understanding deviance. It was in this era that classical theorists set forth the idea that behavior is shaped by a rational assessment of anticipated consequences. This perspective is rooted in a presumption that individuals have free will—that they have the agency to determine their own actions—but it also moves beyond it. To stop at the idea of free will suggests that people choose what to do and when to do it, but says nothing of why they choose any given behavior over another. Classical theory emphasizes that individuals predictably choose to engage in behaviors that maximize their pleasure and minimize pain. If this is true, the prevalence of crime can be reduced through a manipulation of its costs and benefits.

Cesare Beccaria

Cesare Beccaria laid the groundwork for the classical school in his work *An Essay on Crimes and Punishments*, first published in 1764. Beccaria believed that punishments, if thoughtfully designed, could deter offenders from repeating their crimes and deter the general public from contemplating crime.[6] Beccaria set forth several principles to guide the development of just and effective punishments:

- Proportionality. The strength of the sanction should be proportionate to the seriousness of the crime. To do any less would not only be unjust, but would invite offenders to commit more serious crimes to gain the most advantage for their risk.
- Severity. The strength of the punishment should be enough to counteract the seduction of crime. Beccaria held that individuals are drawn to act in their own best interest as though it held gravitational pull, with the implication that "the legislator acts … like a skillful architect, who endeavors to counteract the force of gravity."[7] Those who are compelled to crime must be met with a threat of punishment substantial enough to repel them from the temptation.
- Swiftness. The more quickly the punishment takes place after the crime, the stronger the two will be associated in the minds of potential offenders. This also spares offenders from the "torment of uncertainty."
- Certainty. To cement the association between crime and punishment, potential offenders should perceive punishment as "the unavoidable and necessary effect" of crime.[8]

On the whole, punishments that are severe, swift, and certain will be more effective than those with none of those qualities. Beccaria prioritized certainty over severity, for moral reasons as well as practical. He held that, for a rational actor,

> The certainty of a small punishment will make a stronger impression than the fear of one more severe, if attended with the hopes of escaping; for it is the nature of mankind to be terrified at the approach of the smallest inevitable evil, whilst hope … hath the power of dispelling the apprehension of a greater [punishment] if supported by examples of impunity.[9]

EXPLORING BECCARIA'S VIEWS ON SENTENCE SEVERITY

During the eighteenth century, when Beccaria wrote his groundbreaking work, punishments were typically carried out in public and involved corporal (physical) punishment, including brutal, torturous executions. For example, Voltaire described the execution of a man in England who had been convicted of treason for voicing dissent with the government: "they ripped up [his] belly … tore out his heart, dashed it in his face, then threw it upon the fire."[10] A similarly grisly scene was described from an execution in France in 1757, in which a convicted murderer had flesh torn away with "red-hot pincers," the wounds of which were then aggravated with a boiling mixture of oil, lead, wax, and other ingredients before he was "drawn and quartered by four horses and his limbs and body consumed by fire."[11] In the colonial United States, the death penalty was used for crimes ranging from murder to theft and counterfeiting.[12]

It was this context that set the backdrop for Beccaria's work, which helps explain the coexistence of what might otherwise be interpreted as two contradictory arguments—that punishment should deter, but also that it should be limited in severity. In this way, Beccaria's recommendations had both rational and moral underpinnings. His work is riddled with reference to the dangers of tyranny and the need to place limits on the state's right to punish. He argued that punishment severity should be constrained for three reasons

- "It may brutalize the population": Frivolously harsh punishments appear to provoke the same spirit in the public. Beccaria observed

    The countries and times most notorious for severity of punishments were always those in which the most bloody and inhuman actions and the most atrocious crimes were committed; for the hand of the legislator and the assassin were directed by the same spirit of ferocity.[13]

- "Sentence severity operates on a scale of diminishing returns": Beccaria observed that governments had exercised great creativity in formulating new forms of torture, but "the human frame can suffer only to a certain degree."[14] Thus, continual efforts to expand the cruelty of punishment were unlikely to alter the effectiveness of deterrence.
- "Governments that engage in harsh punishments are not sustainable": Beccaria believed that governments derive the right to govern from the will of the people. If a government engages in brutality against its own, society will fight until they secure reform or revolution. This sets an outer boundary on the brutality with which governments can rule.

Jeremy Bentham

Just a couple of decades after Cesare Beccaria's work, Jeremy Bentham published a corresponding treatise: *An Introduction to the Principles of Morals and Legislation*.[15] Bentham proposed that most human behavior is shaped by the "principle of utility," which holds that people seek to maximize pleasure and minimize their pain. He elaborated on Beccaria's idea of proportionality by suggesting that both pleasure and pain can be measured along four dimensions:[16]

1. Intensity
2. Duration
3. Certainty or Uncertainty
4. Propinquity or Remoteness (i.e., how quickly the pleasure or pain is realized)

Generally speaking, the likelihood that a person will engage in a particular activity will increase as the intensity, duration, certainty, and propinquity of the anticipated pleasure rise, whereas it will decrease as the anticipated pain rises on these same four dimensions.

Bentham's propositions provide a more nuanced understanding of human decision making. Individuals commonly engage in behaviors that carry potentially dire consequences to acquire minimal gains, as with risking a car accident to run to the store for a bag of chips (or, to use a criminal example, committing an armed robbery for a small financial yield). Bentham's work helps to make sense of these seemingly irrational choices. So long as the potential risk appears remote and unlikely, regardless of its potential severity, individuals remain susceptible to the enticement of more certain and immediate gains, no matter how small.

THINKING LIKE A CLASSICAL CRIMINOLOGIST

Recent years have witnessed a rebound in the popularity of heroin within the United States. Rates of use have increased steadily from 2007, when 373,000 people aged 12 and older reported using heroin within the last year, to 2012, when 669,000 reported doing the same.[17] Heroin is a highly addictive drug that slows users' mental, cardiac, and pulmonary functions, sometimes to the point of death.[18] States across the nation are experiencing spikes in heroin overdose deaths.

Can this surge in heroin use be addressed by applying the principles of classical criminology? Design a punishment for heroin possession that meets the criteria set forth by Beccaria and Bentham. How would you determine proportionality for the possession of heroin for personal use? What about possession with intent to distribute?

Neoclassical theories

Classical thought experienced a resurgence of popularity in criminology in the 1970s and 1980s. Skepticism grew around the effectiveness of the rehabilitative interventions that had come to dominate correctional work, culminating in a well-known 1974 publication (commonly called the "Martinson report") that questioned whether any treatment-based intervention could successfully reduce crime rates.[19] Criminologists began to refocus on ways that crime might instead be prevented through deterrent strategies.

"Deterrence" refers to the reduction of crime through the threat of punishment. Deterrence can take two different forms. With "general deterrence," the general public is compelled to abstain from crime due to fear of threatened punishments. For example, a storeowner may prominently post a sign with the penalties for shoplifting to deter would-be thieves, or a state might post signs along the highway to communicate the penalties for speeding in a construction zone. A general deterrent strategy was recently used by the National Highway Traffic Safety Administration with its highly publicized "Drive Sober or Get Pulled Over" campaign, which included the prominent dissemination of information about the dangers and criminal penalties of driving under the influence.[20] By contrast, "specific deterrence" holds that offenders who experience adequate punishment will refrain from future criminality due to their fear of repeating penalties they had personally incurred. For example, steep fines or long prison sentences may be enough to compel offenders to abstain from further crimes.

The only difference between specific and general deterrence is the intended audience: Whereas general deterrence aims to prevent crime through the threat of possible punishment, specific deterrence is intended to prevent repeated criminal involvement among those who have been subject to punishment. This means that some punishments can simultaneously serve as both general and specific deterrents. A long prison sentence may not only help the former inmate decide to abstain from future criminality, but also send a message to others about the likely penalties if they were to follow in the offender's footsteps. Similarly, "shaming" strategies such as making an offender stand in front of the courthouse with a sign stating their offense can have a deterrent effect on both the offender and the general public alike.

Rational choice theory

In 1986, Ronald Clarke and Derek Cornish[21] edited a book that helped bring the "rational offender" back to the fore in criminology. The work drew upon early classical beliefs about crime, but also represented some key departures from the works of Beccaria and Bentham. First, Clarke and Cornish acknowledge that individual pathology may play a role in some crime, although they stress that even the actions of a pathological offender may be shaped in part by rationality. Second, they clarify that acts do not need to be carefully premeditated to be considered rational. Rather, even the most impulsive of offenders will likely conduct a quick, if imperfect, assessment of the likely costs and benefits of their actions before committing a crime. Carroll and Weaver[22] differentiate between two forms of rationality:

> "Normative rationality" occurs when potential offenders carefully weigh the most likely outcomes of both criminal and noncriminal behaviors to determine which path is most beneficial.
> "Limited (bounded) rationality" occurs when individuals pursue the best possible outcome for their self-interest, but they rely solely on easily available information in their decision making.

Carroll and Weaver argue that those who engage in limited rationality are still technically "rational" in that they try to act in their own best interest, but their willingness to act on minimal or potentially inaccurate information can result in poor decision making.

The works of the original classical theorists were consistent with the idea of normative rationality, whereas Clarke and Cornish give more attention to limited rationality. From this perspective, even many "stupid criminal" cases might be viewed as rational if the offender was unaware of the factors that made their crime "stupid" at the time of the offense. For example, one man stole a credit card from a car, only to walk into a bar and unwittingly attempt to use the card to buy beer from the very man to whom the card belonged.[23]

Situational crime control

Another contribution of neoclassical theorists has been an increased awareness of strategies for "situational crime prevention," which includes strategies that increase the perceived effort needed to carry out a crime and minimize the anticipation of potential gains. To the extent that potential offenders are often poorly informed about criminal penalties, this approach provides a broader array of strategies for altering their cost–benefit analysis.

Target hardening and defensible space are two specific types of situational crime prevention. "Target hardening" increases the effort necessary to victimize the target, as with installing bars on windows, locks, or security systems. Many jewelry stores now use replicas rather than real gems in their display cases to decrease thieves' access to valuable items, and clothing stores may use ink tags or other security devices to increase the effort necessary to carry out a successful theft.

"Defensible space" specifically refers to the use of architectural design to facilitate prosocial surveillance.[24] For example, a building might be designed to have all apartments cluster around a common area with open stairwells to minimize the isolated areas in which crime could flourish. Other architectural details might include improved lighting or the use of fences to block alleyways and channel foot traffic. Such efforts have also been called "crime prevention through environmental design."[25]

Routine activities theory

Lawrence Cohen and Marcus Felson's routine activities theory,[26] presented in 1979, provides a framework for identifying situations that present a high risk for criminal behavior. They suggested that crime is likely to result when three factors converge in time and space:

1. "Motivated offenders." Those inclined to commit criminal offenses, whether due to need, desire, or some other factor.
2. "Suitable targets." The suitability of a target is determined by its value, visibility, accessibility, and inertia (mobility).
3. "The absence of capable guardianship." Crime is most likely to take place when there is nobody present with the capability of intervening.

Cohen and Felson devised the theory in their attempt to explain post–World War II crime patterns. They observed, for example, that the increase of females in the workforce left more homes unattended during the day, increasing their vulnerability to burglary. Similarly, the increased "portability" of consumer electronics facilitated an increase in theft.

URBAN REVITALIZATION AND CRIME PREVENTION

Many cities are revitalizing their downtown business districts as a means for encouraging commerce, attracting tourism, and improving residents' quality of life. Such revitalization efforts often incorporate design elements intended to minimize crime. If you were on a planning commission for such a project, what types of design features would you encourage developers to use to deter crime? What situational crime prevention strategies might you use? Would you expect these efforts to be effective? Why or why not?

Criticisms of the classical school

Although the classical school has made many significant contributions to criminology and penology, criticisms include the following:

- "It fails to explain why some individuals are more easily deterred than others": Biological, psychological, and social factors all play a role in human behavior. Although individuals do have free will, factors such as depression, alcohol consumption, and peer pressure have the power to influence decision making. Examining these factors opens up new avenues for addressing crime. For example, a person who has lost the will to live is unlikely to be deterred by the threat of harsh punishments. In this situation, the policy implications of the classical perspective lose their relevance unless they are adopted in conjunction with other interventions, such as mental health treatment.

- "It overestimates the rationality of offenders": The practical implications of this perspective are predicated on the ability of potential offenders to be deterred through an alteration of the consequences of crime. This loses applicability where offenders commit crimes in the heat of the moment, without considering the implications of their actions.
- "A deterrence approach might simply displace rather than prevent crime": Motivated offenders may recognize the risks of crime as too great in certain contexts, but this may simply lead them to pursue easier targets. For example, drug dealers may position themselves in neighborhoods with limited police surveillance, or burglars may bypass houses with security systems but continue to target more vulnerable homes.

Early positivist theories

After the initial decline of classical thought in the mid-1800s and before the rise of neoclassical theories, "positivism," a paradigm that values the scientific method over deductive reasoning, took hold. Rooted in the hard sciences, positivists believe that knowledge is best obtained through careful observation and measurement. Observations allow scientists to identify truths about natural phenomena that shape the world and, once these natural laws are understood, allow for prediction of future events. Applied to the social sciences, positivism holds that human behavior is shaped by natural laws similar to other biological phenomena. Just as scientists can identify the factors that contribute to cell degeneration, criminologists should be able to identify the factors that contribute to crime.

Specific assumptions of positivist criminologists include the following:

- Human behavior is shaped in predictable ways by factors that can be observed and identified.
- Human behavior is thus best understood through an application of the scientific method (observation and hypothesis testing).
- Once the factors that shape human behavior are identified, steps can be taken to alter those factors to modify human behavior.

This is a more deterministic approach to crime than was true of the classical school—rather than stressing free will, positivists believe that human behavior is largely determined by a wide range of factors that may be outside of a person's control.

The Franco-Belgian school

As positivism took hold in Europe, two distinct traditions of criminology emerged. The Franco-Belgian school of criminology emphasized the role of social factors in shaping human behavior. Andre-Michel Guerry was a lawyer and statistician who worked with the earliest known national database of crime statistics, composed by French authorities beginning around 1825.[27] He is credited with creating the earliest known crime maps, which showed the geographic distribution of different types of crime across France.[27]

Guerry is thus credited with founding the "cartographic method" of crime analysis,[28] which provided a foundation for later socioecological examinations of crime (see Chapter 5). Guerry argued that any theory of criminality must be grounded in "numerical observation," a component that was lacking in classical theorists' logic-based arguments.[27]

Consistent with Guerry's work, Belgian Adolphe Quetelet focused on the social correlates of criminality. Quetelet was quintessentially positivistic: He contended that human behavior was subject to the same "law-like, mechanical regularity that had been determined to exist in the ... world of nature."[29] He observed that crime varied in predictable ways according to social factors such as employment, occupation, and social status. Although it was not possible to fully predict any individual offense, he found it possible to predict overall crime rates based on social factors. Quetelet ultimately concluded that

> The crimes which are annually committed seem to be a necessary result of our social organization.... Society prepares crime, and the guilty are only the instruments by which it is executed.[30]

This deterministic assertion was a far cry from the classicalists' emphasis on free will and human agency.

The Italian school

The second emerging thread of European positivism was the Italian school of criminology, which focused on natural rather than social phenomena. This school of thought focused heavily on the physical examination of offenders. Among criminologists in this tradition, "the weighing and measuring of criminals was [viewed as] the only scientific method of studying criminals."[31] This school was heavily influenced by "phrenology," first posited by German physician Franz Joseph Gall in 1798 with the suggestion that the bumps in a person's skull might correlate to their psychological characteristics,[32] and "physiognomy," which held that a person's facial features could indicate differing propensities toward criminal behavior.

Cesare Lombroso was the best-known criminologist of the Italian school, with the lasting influence of his work sometimes resulting in his identification as the "father of criminology." He engaged in an ambitious undertaking to determine the relationship of crime to skull shape, facial features, and other natural phenomena including factors such as climate, disease, and heredity.

Of his specific contributions, Lombroso is most remembered for one that no longer holds weight in the scientific community: the proposition that some criminals are atavistic, or throwbacks to earlier periods in human evolution. Not all criminals fit this classification according to Lombroso. Rather, he proposed four broad categories of offenders:

1. "Atavistic offenders" are born criminals. Products of the "hereditary nature of moral insanity,"[33] they were described as prone to "primitive instincts, like passion for orgies and vendettas."[34] Lombroso held that these individuals were "born with evil inclinations"[35] and could be identified through physical characteristics and abnormalities. Setting out to identify these features through an examination of inmates, Lombroso at one point proposed that "Nearly all criminals have jug ears, thick hair, thin beards, pronounced sinuses, protruding chins, and broad cheekbones."[36]
2. "Insane criminals" are those suffering from madness or simply lacking a moral compass (deemed "moral insanity"). They tend to be more susceptible to provocation,

less sensitive to pain, and lacking in emotional connectedness to others. Their condition may be aggravated by alcoholism or trauma. Some insane criminals may share the physiological markings of born criminals.[37]

3. "Criminals of passion," often young and intensely emotional, surrender to impulses "that explode unforeseen, like rage, love, or offended honor."[38] Relative to other types of offenders, these individuals are less likely to make excuses or attempt to cover up their offenses, and more amenable to treatment.

4. "Occasional criminals" are "normal individuals who are pushed by social forces or bad companions to break the law."[39] This category includes "criminaloids" who hold some characteristics of born criminals but not enough to be considered atavistic, and who served as evidence to Lombroso that the lines between criminals and honest individuals was not always clear.

Although Lombroso's focus on physical characteristics had a formative impact on some of the earliest American theories of criminality, his designation as the "father of criminology" has been disputed. Critics of his work have pointed out that Lombroso's work was plagued by

- "Faulty methods": Lombroso's work was based on insufficient sample sizes gathered without random selection or adequate control groups.[40]
- "Racial bias": Blatantly racist statements are scattered throughout Lombroso's work, and he failed to acknowledge or examine the sociological foundations of racial inequity.
- "Insufficient attention to sociological factors": Although this issue was addressed somewhat in Lombroso's later works, he generally prioritized physical attributes over the sociological variables that had already been identified as relevant among Franco-Belgian criminologists.[41]

THE HUMAN AS ANIMAL

Cesare Lombroso's ideas were strongly grounded in the idea of crime as a natural phenomenon, to the extent that he argued that carnivorous plants—those that trap, kill, and digest insects—were representative of "the dawn of criminality."[42] Pointing to examples of murder, theft, child abandonment, and sexual aggression among monkeys, cuckoos, and other animals, Lombroso argued that human nature should be no less attributed to the deterministic forces of nature:

Are these actions crimes or simply the necessary effects of heredity—an organic structure imposed by competition for survival, by sexual selection, by the social necessity to quell discord, or by the need for food among voracious animals? These examples underline the absurdity of a concept of justice based on free will and explain why we find criminal tendencies among all creatures, even within the most civilized races.[43]

Consider the following questions:

1. Is there value in Lombroso's comparison of human crime to examples of aggressive and predatory behavior in the animal (and plant) kingdom? Explain your answer.
2. On the other hand, is there justification for the argument that humans have more control over their innate tendencies than other species? Explain your answer.

Criticisms of the Italian school

Several criticisms of the early Italian school criminologists can be highlighted:

- "The perspective placed too much faith in the ability of science to reveal 'ultimate truths' about human behavior": Scientific inquiry (and its subsequent discoveries) can be highly politicized and subject to the biases of those doing the research.
- "The conclusions were based on now-antiquated scientific techniques": Scientific explanations are inherently susceptible to the limits of scientific vision. For example, while phrenology turned out to be correct in its assumption that different regions of the brain are responsible for different aspects of human behavior, technology at the time did not allow for brain imaging. Phrenologists wrongly assumed that the only measurement capability available to them—the external features of the human skull—could be used to assess the functioning of the brain underneath. As the saying goes, "you don't know what you don't know," and it was not until the development of brain imaging technology that more robust theories of brain functioning could be developed.
- "The idea of innate criminality overlooks the fluidity of human behavior": Criminal involvement tends to peak in adolescence and early adulthood, and then decline throughout the rest of the life course, a pattern difficult to explain if working from the assumption that some people are simply "born criminal." Within a given life stage, even the individuals most heavily involved in criminal behavior do not commit crime all the time. The Italian school would encounter difficulty explaining this phenomenon of "drift."
- The application of scientific methods to social phenomena without an acknowledgement of social dynamics risks confusing cause and effect. Many societies have engaged in overtly racist practices that criminalize and persecute certain aspects of the population. When early positivists based their conclusions about "inborn criminality" on the evaluation of prison populations, their results were just as (or more) likely to reflect biased laws and enforcement practices as differences in actual criminal tendencies. In societies that criminalize racial, religious, or other minority populations, any examination of offender populations will reveal hereditary commonalities not because those parties are inherently more criminal, but rather because they are more likely to be criminalized in that society. Africans and southern Italians in Mussolini's Italian regime, Jews and gypsies in Hitler's Germany, and blacks and immigrant populations in the United States have all received disproportionate attention by law enforcement. By the 1930s, this key weakness of Italian school criminology helped support the development of social structural explanations of crime.

Early American criminology

Many of the earliest American criminologists followed in the tradition of the Italian school, believing that crime was rooted in the physicality of the offender. Criminal anthropologists and hereditary criminologists took note of the tendency for social problems such as poverty, mental illness, and criminality to cluster within the same individuals, and thus argued that crime must be rooted in the characteristics of the offender (rather than their environment). These criminologists were similar in their beliefs, but differed in their methods. "Criminal anthropologists" focused on examining parts of the body that may serve as markers of crime, whereas "hereditary criminologists" relied on genealogical mapping.

Criminal anthropology

Criminal anthropologists were the most closely aligned with Lombroso's legacy, as their focus was on identifying the physical markers of criminality. Earnest Hooton and W.H. Sheldon, both Harvard researchers, kept this thread of criminology alive through the 1940s and 1950s. For example, Earnest Hooton composed a profile of the physical features that he believed could differentiate criminals from noncriminals, which included

- Tattoos
- Thinner beards and body hair, but thicker hair on the head
- Low and sloping foreheads
- Large necks and sloping shoulders

These physical manifestations were seen as variant among types of offenders, with rapists and forgers characterized as heavy, but forgers proclaimed to be taller, and robbers being more likely to be undersized. Hooton concluded that criminals were biologically inferior, suggesting that the only proper response to crime was to separate offenders from the general population and sterilize them to prevent their proliferation.

W.H. Sheldon's work on the relationship between somatotype (body type) and temperament culminated in the publication of *The Atlas of Men* in 1954. According to Sheldon's "somatotype theory," people can be categorized as follows:

- Endomorphs: Those with a round body, which is linked to a relaxed temperament
- Mesomorphs: Those with a muscular body, who are aggressive
- Ectomorphs: Those with a lean body, who are sensitive

Although there were some supporters of Hooton and Sheldon's work, most mainstream criminologists did not take their contributions seriously. Hooton's work, for example, was critiqued by one reviewer as "the funniest academic performance that has appeared since the invention of movable type." The reviewer openly questioned how "one derives social conclusions from biological and physical measurements" and accused Hooton of unsound methodology and invalid conclusions.[44] Hooton was critiqued for failing to take a representative sample and reporting only details that supported his hypothesis of an anthropological distinction between criminals and noncriminals, while selectively excluding any details that challenged his proposition.

CONTROVERSIAL METHODS OF W.H. SHELDON[45]

Some criminologists' emphasis on physical anthropology led to research methods that would be shocking to contemporary sensibilities. To test the assertion that physical characteristics were linked to behavioral outcomes, these researchers needed access to large pools of data based on measurements and photographs of subjects. For example, W.H. Sheldon based his work on temperament and body type on an analysis of the nude photographs of thousands of college students and "some 46,000 individuals photographed at military and medical institutions."[45]

(Continued)

CONTROVERSIAL METHODS OF W.H. SHELDON (*CONTINUED*)

Some controversy exists over whether these subjects were willing participants. Most of the college students in Sheldon's studies were photographed under the pretext of "posture photographs" that were taken for college administrators to identify students with posture issues in need of remediation, while at least in some cases at Harvard students were told that their photos were being taken to assist with the design of new railroad seats.[46] Posture photos were routinely taken of all incoming freshmen at universities that included Yale, Harvard, and other Ivy League institutions. In some cases, these photographs were part of an established practice that predated Sheldon's research, but as Sheldon advanced his work he approached new schools to take such photos to expand his trove of data. Sheldon sometimes took the photographs himself; in other instances, schools provided the photos to Sheldon unbeknownst to students.

Although some schools continued to take posture photographs into the 1960s and 1970s, the practice sometimes drew substantial controversy. Sheldon faced one such outcry after he began to take nude photos of female freshmen at the University of Washington in 1950. A *New York Times* article described the incident and posed some relevant questions:

> One of [the female students] told her parents about the practice. The next morning, a battalion of lawyers and university officials stormed Sheldon's lab, seized every photo of a nude woman, [and proceeded to burn them]. A short-lived controversy broke out: Was this a book burning? A witch hunt? Was Professor Sheldon's nude photography a legitimate scientific investigation into the relationship between physique and temperament, the raw material of serious scholarship? Or [was it] just raw material—pornography masquerading as science?[45]

Many of these photographs were eventually burned as universities became increasingly concerned about the privacy of their students. At least until recently, though, other photos were still held in the Smithsonian archives, and some were included as illustrations in Sheldon's *Atlas of Men*.[47]

Heredity and crime

"Hereditary criminologists" attempted to explain what they believed to be the intergenerational transmission of crime, but they were working without the benefit of modern-day genetics. They held that crime could be passed through the generations along with the related ills of pauperism, promiscuity, disease, alcoholism, and a lack of industriousness. The core argument was that sustained immoral behavior could damage one's "germ plasm" (genes), thus rendering future generations susceptible to the transmission of criminal tendencies.[48] Rather than the physical examinations favored by criminal anthropologists, this school of researchers turned to family trees to understand the hereditary transmission of crime.

Robert Dugdale's *The Jukes*,[49] published in 1877, was one of the most influential works in hereditary criminology, although ironically his conclusions openly refuted its arguments. Dugdale approached the study of crime as a genealogical exercise that might lend insight into the transmission of criminality across generations. He examined the lineage of one family (for which "Jukes" was a pseudonym) for signs of promiscuity, alcoholism, disease, industriousness (or the lack thereof), and crime. His data spanned seven generations and included 709 individuals related through blood or marriage.

Dugdale concluded that the family's influence on criminality was twofold. Although heredity can play a role—in Dugdale's words, "capacity, physical and mental, is limited and determined mainly by heredity"[50]—he stressed the shaping of the moral environment as the primary mechanism by which parents transmitted their behavior to children. By extension, he suggested that efforts to curb crime should focus on altering the social environment. He describes crime as akin to other public health issues: Like a disease, it can be spread from person to person, so "sanitary precautions" should be taken to separate youth from sources of contaminated morality. Despite Dugdale's emphasis on processes of socialization, many of his readers focused on his terminology and methodology and went on to misapply his conclusions as supportive of a purely genetic explanation of crime. They used his book to bolster more literal arguments of hereditary criminality, stressing that immorality could damage one's "germ plasm" and render future generations susceptible to physically (rather than socially) transmitted criminal tendencies.[48]

Social Darwinism

Many of those who held that crime could be inherited were heavily influenced by Charles Darwin's work on evolution. In his landmark book *On the Origin of the Species*,[51] Darwin argued that in any given species, the most vigorous specimens would survive the longest and enjoy the greatest success in attracting mates, thereby passing their competitive advantage on to their offspring. This process of selection results in "evolution," the propagation of well-suited traits and the diminishment of weak traits over the course of generations. Although Darwin was attempting to explain biological rather than social phenomena, "social Darwinists" held that criminals might in fact be individuals who are less advanced on the scale of humans' evolutionary development, akin to Lombroso's atavists.

Some social Darwinists went so far as to support "eugenics," or efforts to improve the human race through controlled breeding. Eugenicists believed that the advancement of the human race could be sped by discouraging "defective" individuals from having children while simultaneously encouraging reproduction among those with desirable traits. By the early 1900s, broader public attention to the concepts of heredity, genetics, and evolution increased support for eugenicists' agenda. Policy initiatives built around the dual strategies of sterilization and institutionalization—both of which were intended to prevent the reproduction of "defective" populations and, as a result, prevent them from passing on their "defects" to the next generation[52]—were openly discussed and pursued. For example, a report published by the Eugenics Record Office from the Committee to Study and to Report on the Best Practical Means of Cutting Off the Defective Germ-Plasm in the American Population advocated for both sterilization and institutionalization:

> The ultimate extinction of the anti-social strains must consist in the segregation of the members of these strains before their reproductive periods, and in the sterilization of such of them as are returned to society at large while still potential parents.… The relation between segregation and sterilization is, under the model law, automatically complementary. If segregation ceases and the individual of potential parenthood of defectives is about to be returned to society, he is first to be sterilized.[53]

In some cases, eugenics laws and practices were implemented. Josephine Shaw Lowell, an influential reformer who supported the opening of an "Asylum for Feeble-minded Women" in Newark in 1878, argued that the asylum was needed to prevent the spread of criminality and other moral ills.[54] She stated the following:

> What right have we today to allow men and women who are diseased and vicious to reproduce their kind, and bring into the world beings whose existence must be one long misery to themselves and others?[55]
>
> … Shall the State of New York suffer a moral leprosy to spread and taint her future generations, because she lacks the courage to set apart those who have inherited the deadly poison and who will hand it down to their children, even to the third and fourth generations?[55]

Indiana became the first state to pass a law that allowed forced sterilization in 1907, and several states followed. Kansas, Utah, Idaho, Oklahoma, and other states specifically allowed for the sterilization of those with criminal tendencies. The Nebraska law went so far as to require forced sterilization as a prerequisite for release among inmates whom a Board of Examiners deemed to be habitual criminals "likely to produce offspring which would have a tendency to criminality."[56] Involuntary sterilization was carried out by court order, by conducting vasectomies on men or tubal ligations or hysterectomies on women.

The eugenics movement in the United States gained enough of a foothold to be an influence to Adolph Hitler, who looked to its laws for guidance. He stated in *Mein Kampf* that he "studied with great interest the laws of several American states concerning prevention of reproduction by people whose progeny would, in all probability, be of no value or be injurious to the racial stock."[57] Germany adopted a Habitual Offender Law in 1933 that allowed for the indefinite confinement of "incorrigibles."[58] Hitler's eugenics efforts developed into an extermination program that called for the execution of those deemed criminally insane, juveniles from "homes for wayward youth,"[58] and other antisocial individuals, using arguments about hereditary criminality as partial justification for the program. The Nazi regime began to characterize Jews, Gypsies, alcoholics, political opponents, delinquents, and others as "hereditary degenerates" best eliminated from the gene pool.[58]

SKINNER V. OKLAHOMA (1942)

The topic of forced sterilization of convicted offenders in the United States made it to the U.S. Supreme Court in *Skinner v. Oklahoma* (1942). An Oklahoma law passed in 1935 allowed anyone convicted of two or more "felonies involving moral turpitude" to be sterilized. Skinner had been convicted of stealing chickens in 1926, and subsequently convicted of armed robberies in 1929 and 1935. Proceedings began for his sterilization, and he appealed based on his right to equal protection and on the basis that sterilization constituted cruel and unusual punishment.

The Supreme Court ultimately ruled that Oklahoma's specific law for the forced sterilization of repeat felons was unconstitutional, striking down the law not because they disagreed with forced sterilization in principle, but rather because the law specifically excluded felonies related to "prohibitory laws, revenue acts, embezzlement, or political offenses"—in other words, the law systematically excluded the types of crimes most likely to be committed by white collar offenders. A person could be sterilized for stealing $20, but not if they embezzled the same amount of money. The court held this practice was just as discriminatory "as if [the state] had selected a particular race or nationality for oppressive treatment." The court reasoned that such a law "in evil or reckless hands ... can cause races or types which are inimical to the dominant group to wither and disappear." The *Skinner* ruling was not the end of the eugenics movement—it only struck down the specific law in Oklahoma. Involuntary sterilization continued through the 1960s and remained on the books in some states into the 1970s.

Lasting influence of the positivist school

Positivism continues to play a central role in criminological inquiry, albeit in a different form than those of criminal anthropology, hereditary criminology, or the related eugenics movement. These early perspectives began to lose steam by the 1930s and 1940s, as public sensibilities turned against eugenics due to its growing association with the atrocities being carried out by Hitler in Europe. Many of the specific contributions of the Italian school have been debunked as pseudoscience. For example, with developments in the fields of psychology, psychiatry, and the neurosciences, there is no longer a belief that bumps on an individual's skull correlate to their psychological traits, nor do we any longer measure individuals' ears, noses, or cranial circumference in an effort to measure criminal propensity. In the present day, the contributions of criminologists such as Lombroso, Hooton, and Sheldon are most often viewed as antiquated theories that serve as evidence of criminology's naive and in some cases racist past.

Although many specific assertions of early Italian school theorists have since been debunked, their contributions provided the starting point for modern-day positivist theories of crime. The same holds true for the works of Guerry and Quetelet, who heavily influenced works that focus on social factors such as employment, education, and social class. Over time, these two schools of early positivism developed into the following modern-day theories:

- "Trait theories," which continue to focus on personal traits but now emphasize psychology, psychiatry, and subtle biological or genetic influences (see Chapter 4) rather than criminal anthropology or inborn criminality.
- "Social structure theories," which follow in the footsteps of the Franco-Belgian school by emphasizing the social roots of crime (see Chapter 5).

Many of the theorists in the social process (Chapter 6) and integrated (Chapter 7) traditions also ground their work in the scientific method, representing new schools of positivist thinking. The positivist paradigm remains the most widely accepted and used within criminology.

Critiques of positivism

Positivist criminology has come a long way since the early days of examining offenders' skull shapes and mustache thickness to better understand crime. Even though contemporary studies appear to have a stronger foundation in both the hard sciences and sociology, there are still some who question the very premise that crime can be understood through objective examination. The positivist approach has been questioned on the basis that

- "It neglects the existence of free will." Although choices are certainly influenced by factors such as biology and social environment, it is impossible to predict with certainty the behavior of any given individual at any given time. Thus, positivist theories take an overly deterministic stance on human behavior, failing to account for human agency.
- "It is based on the wrongful assertion that it is possible to conduct truly objective studies." Although positivists claim to be guided by objectivity, all research is shaped to some extent by the interests and perspectives of the researchers involved. The biases of criminologists affect the nature of their research, the questions asked, the variables considered, and how the results are interpreted and presented.
- "It takes for granted who should be deemed 'criminal.'" Most positivists uncritically assume that those who have broken the law compose a unique population worthy of study. This fails to acknowledge that most offenders drift in and out of crime, thus blurring the line between criminal and law-abiding. Positivists' acceptance of a legalistic definition of "criminal" prevents them from exploring deeper questions about how certain acts come to be deemed criminal and often results in the failure to study individuals who engage in socially harmful, but not necessarily criminal, behavior, thus arbitrarily limiting the scope of their studies.

Key Differences between Classicalism and Positivism

	Classicalism	Positivism
Core assumption	Human behavior is shaped by the rational exercise of free will	Human behavior is shaped by deterministic influences such as biological, psychological, and social forces
Approach	Deductive reasoning	Inductive reasoning and the application of the scientific method
Early contributors	Jeremy Bentham, Cesare Beccaria	Cesare Lombroso, Adolphe Quetelet
Modern theories	Rational choice theory; neoclassicalism	Social structural, psychological, and biological theories
Policy implications	Punishment should be swift and certain; its severity should be proportionate to the offense	Punishment should address the underlying causes of crime: mental health treatment for psychological causes, biological interventions for biological causes, and so on. It should be tailored to the individual offender

Emergence of postmodernism

Although positivist criminology still very much dominates the field, an alternative approach to criminology has emerged in the form of postmodernism. Postmodernism differs from positivism in that it

- "Questions the existence of an objective reality." According to postmodernists, all truths are mediated through the filter of an observer's perceptions, rendering truly objective studies impossible.

- "Stresses the social construction of meaning and reality." Since there is no objective truth, postmodernists broaden their gaze to examine the process by which concepts and processes are "constructed" by the people involved. For example, rather than limiting their research to the causes of crime, postmodernists are just as likely to examine the processes by which certain individuals come to be defined as "criminal."
- "Acknowledges the role of power in the definition of crime." Postmodernism pays particular attention to the distribution of power in society. The laws are believed to systematically work to the advantage of those in power while criminalizing the behavior of others.

Since who is identified as criminal will depend on the laws in effect at any given point and how they are enforced, criminality cannot be an inborn trait. Postmodernists go one step further in questioning the meaningfulness of examining "criminals" without considering those who engage in other social harms. For example, companies that knowingly sell dangerous products or maintain unsafe work conditions are most often held accountable through civil lawsuits against the corporation; rarely are the responsible individuals brought to criminal court, so they often fall outside the scope of traditional positivist studies despite the immense harm of their actions. Postmodernism provides the paradigmatic framework for critical theories of crime (Chapter 8).

Summary

- Predominant explanations of crime have varied across space and time.
- The prevailing explanations of crime in any given society often help shape its punitive responses.
- Four dominant paradigms can be identified through the history of criminological thought: prescientific, classical, positivist, and postmodern.
- Prescientific explanations described crime as the outcome of supernatural or religious forces.
- In the prescientific era, trials by ordeal were sometimes used to assess the guilt of the accused.
- The classical school of thought explained crime as the exercise of free will by rational actors who were seeking to maximize pleasure and minimize pain.
- Classical theorists argued that punishment should be designed around the goal of deterrence.
- According to the classical school, to deter crime, punishments should be swift, severe, and certain, with certainty being the most important.
- Cesare Beccaria and Jeremy Bentham were the primary contributors to the classical school.
- Classical criminology stresses the swiftness, certainty, severity, and proportionality of punishment.
- Neoclassical theories stress general and specific deterrence as well as situational crime prevention as methods for reducing crime.
- Positivism uses the scientific method to examine crime as a natural phenomenon that results from deterministic forces.
- Early positivist theories can be divided into two schools of thought: the Franco-Belgian and Italian schools.
- The Franco-Belgian school of criminology, led by the work of Andre-Michel Guerry and Adolphe Quetelet, emphasized the role of social forces.

- Guerry is credited with founding the cartographic method that later inspired socio-ecological theories of crime.
- The Italian school, often associated with Cesare Lombroso, focused on the personal traits of offenders.
- Early American theories, which were heavily influenced by the Italian school and social Darwinism, focused on criminal anthropology and heredity.
- Early American criminology played a role in the eugenics movement, which advocated the sterilization or institutionalization of offenders to prevent them from having children.
- Over time, the emphasis of positivist criminology shifted to psychological and social factors.
- Postmodernism questions positivists' assumption of an objective, knowable reality, emphasizing instead the importance of subjectivity and social constructivism.
- In contemporary criminology, positivism continues to guide most research, although classical and postmodern thought also have an influence.

Questions in review

1. What is the difference between a paradigm and a theory?
2. Compare and contrast classicalism and positivism.
3. What were the primary contributions of Cesare Beccaria?
4. How might a punitive system modeled after classical thought differ from one based on positivism?
5. Explain the relationship of early positivist theories to social Darwinism and eugenics.
6. What criticisms of positivism are set forth by postmodernists?

Practicum

The famous case of Phineas P. Gage

In psychology courses, the case of Phineas P. Gage is often used as an illustration of the influence of the brain's physical structure on personality. In 1848, Mr. Gage was working on a railroad when an accidental explosion drove a long iron rod through his cheek and straight through his skull.[59] Mr. Gage not only survived, but he retained his memory and was able to function after a period of recovery. Still, the incident resulted in marked changes to his personality. The once hard worker was now crass, rude, and unrestrained. From the notes of his doctor, he became

> fitful, irreverent, indulging at times in the grossest profanity (which was not previously his custom), manifesting but little deference for his fellows, impatient of restraint or advice when it conflicts with his desires…. A child in his intellectual capacity and manifestations, he has the animal passions of a strong man.[60]

In other words, the man had survived, but his personality had not.

At the time of Mr. Gage's injury, the field of neuroscience had not yet developed, so phrenology was used to explain the personality changes. Phrenology was founded on the belief that the "psychological characteristics of an individual are determined by the size and proportion of controlling organs in the brain" and that an examination of the skull could reveal information about these organs because "the cranium corresponds closely to the shape of the brain beneath."[61] The *American Phrenological Journal* published an analysis in 1851 that suggested Mr. Gage's changes could be attributable to damage to his "organs of veneration and benevolence."[62] It was not until several years later, in 1878, that neurologist David Ferrier drew the connection between Mr. Gage's transformation and similar observed effects in animal studies of brain function, leading him to conclude that damage to the prefrontal cortex could have resulted in the behavioral changes.[59] This explanation is more consistent with contemporary understandings of brain structure and functioning.

The various analyses of Mr. Gage's case are illustrative of the transition from early scientific explanations of human behavior to the more nuanced understandings brought by modern science. On one hand, phrenologists were on the right track with the idea that different parts of the brain correlate to different types of functioning. On the other, they were misguided in thinking that the functioning of different brain regions is indicative of different "brain organs" that can be examined based on externally observable characteristics, such as skull irregularities or forehead size. It is thus accurate to think of phrenology both as an outdated form of pseudoscience with little relevance to modern-day understandings of human behavior, but also to consider it an early precursor to the modern fields of psychology, neuroscience, and criminology.

Questions regarding the Gage case

1. What connections do you see between the case of Phineas P. Gage and the material from this chapter?
2. Can classical theory account for the change in Mr. Gage's behavior? If so, how?
3. If Mr. Gage had committed a crime after his accident and you were the judge in the case, would his history affect your decision about an appropriate punishment? If so, how? Describe your reasoning.

References

1. Bartlett, R. (1986). *Trial by fire and water: The medieval judicial ordeal* (p. 13). New York: Oxford University Press.
2. Bartlett, R. (1986). *Trial by fire and water: The medieval judicial ordeal* (pp. 29–33). New York: Oxford University Press.
3. Kerr, M. H., Forsyth, R. D., & Plyley, M. J. (1992). Cold water and hot iron: Trial by ordeal in England. *Journal of Interdisciplinary History*, 22(4), 573–595.
4. Lombroso, C. (2006). *Criminal man* (M. Gibson, & N. H. Rafter, Trans., p. 186). Durham, NC: Duke University Press.
5. Bartlett, R. (1986). *Trial by fire and water: The medieval judicial ordeal*. New York: Oxford University Press.
6. Beccaria-Bonesana, C. (1953). *An essay on crimes and punishments, with commentary by M.D. Voltaire*. Stanford, CA: Academic Reprints. (Reprinted from *An essay on crimes and punishments*, translated from the Italian of Caesar Bonesana, Marquis Beccaria, to which is added, a commentary, by M. D. Voltaire & E. D. Ingraham, Trans., 2nd American ed., Philadelphia, PA: Philip H. Nicklin.)
7. Beccaria-Bonesana, C. (1953). *An essay on crimes and punishments, with commentary by M.D. Voltaire* (p. 29). Stanford, CA: Academic Reprints. (Reprinted from *An essay on crimes and punishments*, translated from the Italian of Caesar Bonesana, Marquis Beccaria, to which is added, a commentary, by M. D. Voltaire & E. D. Ingraham, Trans., 2nd American ed., Philadelphia, PA: Philip H. Nicklin.)

8. Beccaria-Bonesana, C. (1953). *An essay on crimes and punishments, with commentary by M.D. Voltaire* (p. 75). Stanford, CA: Academic Reprints. (Reprinted from *An essay on crimes and punishments*, translated from the Italian of Caesar Bonesana, Marquis Beccaria, to which is added, a commentary, by M. D. Voltaire & E. D. Ingraham, Trans., 2nd American ed., Philadelphia, PA: Philip H. Nicklin.)

9. Beccaria-Bonesana, C. (1953). *An essay on crimes and punishments, with commentary by M.D. Voltaire* (p. 93). Stanford, CA: Academic Reprints. (Reprinted from *An essay on crimes and punishments*, translated from the Italian of Caesar Bonesana, Marquis Beccaria, to which is added, a commentary, by M. D. Voltaire & E. D. Ingraham, Trans., 2nd American ed., Philadelphia, PA: Philip H. Nicklin.)

10. In Beccaria-Bonesana, C. (1953). *An essay on crimes and punishments, with commentary by M.D. Voltaire* (p. 165). Stanford, CA: Academic Reprints. (Reprinted from *An essay on crimes and punishments*, translated from the Italian of Caesar Bonesana, Marquis Beccaria, to which is added, a commentary, by M. D. Voltaire & E. D. Ingraham, Trans., 2nd American ed., Philadelphia, PA: Philip H. Nicklin.)

11. The original rules and procedures book of Robert-Francois Damiens [*Pièces originales et procedur és du proc ès fait à Robert-François Damiens*], III, 1757 (pp. 372–374). Cited in Foucault, M. (1995). *Discipline and punish: The birth of the prison* (Sheridan, A. Trans., 2nd ed., p. 3). New York: Vintage Book.

12. Banner, S. (2002). *The death penalty: An American history*. United States: Harvard University Press.

13. Beccaria-Bonesana, C. (1953). *An essay on crimes and punishments, with commentary by M.D. Voltaire* (p. 94). Stanford, CA: Academic Reprints. (Reprinted from *An essay on crimes and punishments*, translated from the Italian of Caesar Bonesana, Marquis Beccaria, to which is added, a commentary, by M. D. Voltaire & E. D. Ingraham, Trans., 2nd American ed., Philadelphia, PA: Philip H. Nicklin.)

14. Beccaria-Bonesana, C. (1953). *An essay on crimes and punishments, with commentary by M.D. Voltaire* (p. 95). Stanford, CA: Academic Reprints. (Reprinted from *An essay on crimes and punishments*, translated from the Italian of Caesar Bonesana, Marquis Beccaria, to which is added, a commentary, by M. D. Voltaire & E. D. Ingraham, Trans., 2nd American ed., Philadelphia, PA: Philip H. Nicklin.)

15. Bentham, J. (1823). *An introduction to the principles of morals and legislation*. London: Oxford University Press. (First edition published in 1789.)

16. Bentham, J. (1823). *An introduction to the principles of morals and legislation* (p. 29). London: Oxford University Press. (First edition published in 1789.)

17. U.S. Department of Health and Human Services. (2013). Results from the 2012 National Survey on Drug Use and Health: Summary of National Findings. Retrieved, from http://www.samhsa.gov/data/NSDUH/2012SummNatFindDetTables/NationalFindings/NSDUHresults2012.htm#ch2

18. National Institute on Drug Abuse. (2005). What are the immediate (short-term) effects of heroin use? Retrieved, from http://www.drugabuse.gov/publications/research-reports/heroin-abuse-addiction/what-are-immediate-short-term-effects-heroin-use

19. Martinson, R. (1974). What works? Questions and answers about prison reform. *Public Interest*, 5(Spring), 22–35.

20. National Highway Traffic Safety Administration. (2013). *Drive sober or get pulled over*. Retrieved, from http://www.nhtsa.gov/drivesober/

21. Cornish, D. B., & Clarke, R. V. (Eds.). (1986). *The reasoning criminal: Rational choice perspectives on offending*. New York: Springer-Verlag.

22. Carroll, J., & Weaver, F. (1986). Shoplifters' perceptions of crime opportunities: A process-tracing study. In D. B. Cornish, & R. V. Clarke (Eds.), *The reasoning criminal: Rational choice perspectives on offending* (pp. 20–38). New York: Springer-Verlag.

23. Huffington Post. (2012, September 12). *David Weber, Miami Beach man, tried to buy beer with bartender's own stolen credit card*. Retrieved, from http://www.huffingtonpost.com/2012/09/12/man-stole-bartenders-credit-card_n_1877059.html?utm_hp_ref=stupid-criminals

24. See Newman, O. (1972). *Defensible space: Crime prevention through urban design*. New York: Macmillan.

25. Jeffery, C. R. (1971). *Crime prevention through environmental design*. Thousand Oaks, CA: Sage.

26. Cohen, L. E., & Felson, M. (1979). Social change and crime rate trends: A routine activity approach. *American Sociological Review, 44*(August), 588–608.

27. See Rafter, N. (Ed.). (2009). *The origins of criminology: A reader* (pp. 270–272). New York: Routledge.

28. Lindesmith, A., & Levin, Y. (1937). The Lombrosian myth in criminology. *American Journal of Sociology, 42*(5), 653–671.

29. Beirne, P. (1987). Adolphe Quetelet and the origins of positivist criminology. *American Journal of Sociology, 92*(5), 1140–1169.

30. Quetelet cited in Beirne, P. (1987). Adolphe Quetelet and the origins of positivist criminology. *American Journal of Sociology, 92*(5), 1158.

31. Lindesmith, A., & Levin, Y. (1937). The Lombrosian myth in criminology. *American Journal of Sociology, 42*(5), p. 664.

32. See discussion of Gall's work in Simpson, D. (2005). Phrenology and the neurosciences: Contributions of F.J. Gall and J.G. Spurzheim. *ANZ Journal of Surgery, 75*(6), 475–482.

33. Lombroso, C. (2006). *Criminal man*. (M. Gibson, & N. H. Rafter, Trans., p. 218). Durham, NC: Duke University Press.

34. Lombroso, C. (2006). *Criminal man*. (M. Gibson, & N. H. Rafter, Trans., p. 213). Durham, NC: Duke University Press.

35. Lombroso, C. (2006). *Criminal man*. (M. Gibson, & N. H. Rafter, Trans., p. 48). Durham, NC: Duke University Press.

36. Lombroso, C. (2006). *Criminal man*. (M. Gibson, & N. H. Rafter, Trans., p. 53). Durham, NC: Duke University Press.

37. See Rafter, N. (Ed.). (2009). *The origins of criminology: A reader* (pp. 74–79). New York: Routledge.

38. Lombroso, C. (2006). *Criminal man*. (M. Gibson, & N. H. Rafter, Trans., p. 106). Durham, NC: Duke University Press.

39. Lombroso, C. (2006). *Criminal man*. (M. Gibson, & N. H. Rafter, Trans., p. 228). Durham, NC: Duke University Press.

40. See, for example, Hooton, E. A. (1939). *The American criminal: An anthropological study. Vol. 1: The native white criminal of native parentage*. Cambridge, MA: Harvard University Press.

41. See discussion in Lindesmith, A., & Levin, Y. (1937). The Lombrosian myth in criminology. *American Journal of Sociology, 42*(5), 653–671.

42. Lombroso, C. (2006). *Criminal man*. (M. Gibson, & N. H. Rafter, Trans., p. 168). Durham, NC: Duke University Press.

43. Lombroso, C. (2006). *Criminal man*. (M. Gibson, & N. H. Rafter, Trans., p. 171). Durham, NC: Duke University Press.

44. Reuter, E. B. (1939). Crime and the man by Earnest Albert Hooton. *American Journal of Sociology, 45*(1), 123–126.

45. Based on Rosenbaum, R. (1995, January 15). The great Ivy League nude posture photo scandal: How scientists coaxed America's best and brightest out of their clothes. *New York Times*. Retrieved, from http://www.nytimes.com/1995/01/15/magazine/the-great-ivy-league-nude-posture-photo-scandal.html?pagewanted=all&src=pm

46. Chong, C. R. (1995, March 18). Posing for posture. *The Harvard Crimson*. Retrieved, from http://www.thecrimson.com/article/1995/3/18/posing-for-posture-pbabs-an-american/

47. Sheldon, W. H. (1954). *Atlas of men: A guide for somatotyping the adult male at all ages*. New York: Harper.

48. See Rafter, N. H. (1997). *Creating born criminals* (esp. pp. 36–39). Urbana, IL: University of Illinois Press.

49. Dugdale, R. L. (1877/1910). *The Jukes: A study in crime, pauperism, disease, and heredity* (4th ed.). New York: G.P. Putnam's Sons.

50. Dugdale, R. L. (1877/1910). *The Jukes: A study in crime, pauperism, disease, and heredity* (4th ed., p. 65). New York: G.P. Putnam's Sons.

51. Darwin, C. (1859). *On the origin of the species: Or the preservation of favoured races in the struggle for life*. London: John Murray.

52. Laughlin, H. H. (1914). *Eugenics Record Office, Bulletin No. 10 B*. Retrieved, from http://dnapatents.georgetown.edu/resources/Bulletin10B.pdf

53. Laughlin, H. H. (1914). *Eugenics Record Office, Bulletin No. 10 B* (p. 9). Retrieved, from http://dnapatents.georgetown.edu/resources/Bulletin10B.pdf

54. Rafter, N. H. (1997). *Creating born criminals* (esp. pp. 35–43). Urbana, IL: University of Illinois Press.

55. Cited in Rafter, N. H. (1997). *Creating born criminals* (esp. p. 41). Urbana, IL: University of Illinois Press.

56. H.R.C. (1942). The sterilization laws and their relation to criminal law administration. *Virginia Law Review, 29*(1), 93–102.

57. In Kuhl, S. (1994). *The Nazi Connection: Eugenics, American racism, and German national socialism* (p. 37). New York: Oxford University Press.

58. Rafter, N. (2008). Criminology's darkest hour: Biocriminology in Nazi Germany. *The Australian and New Zealand Journal of Criminology, 41*(2), 287–306.

59. Based on O'Driscoll, K., & Leach, J. P. (1998). "No longer Gage": An iron bar through the head: Early observations of personality change after injury to the prefrontal cortex. *British Medical Journal, 317*(7174), 1673–1674.

60. Cited in O'Driscoll, K., & Leach, J. P. (1998). "No longer Gage": An iron bar through the head: Early observations of personality change after injury to the prefrontal cortex. *British Medical Journal, 317*(7174), 1673.

61. Parssinen, T. M. (1974). Popular science and society: The phrenology movement in Early Victorian Britain. *Journal of Social History, 8*(1), 1–20.

62. Macmillan, M. (2001). John Martyn Harlow: "Obscure country physician"? *Journal of the History of the Neurosciences, 10*(2), 149–162.

chapter four

Biological and psychological approaches to crime causation

Chapter objectives

After studying this chapter, the reader will be able to

- Differentiate between early and contemporary trait theories
- Describe the nature of the relationship between genes and crime
- Identify the ways that alcohol consumption and drug abuse can contribute to crime
- Define the key concepts of the evolutionary perspective
- Outline the policy implications of the biological approach to crime
- Explain the construct of psychopathy
- Describe the role of cognition in criminal behavior
- Discuss the relationship of mental illness to crime

Introduction

This chapter introduces "trait theories," which explore the influence of biology and psychology on criminal behavior. They attempt to answer the following question: Why do people respond differently to identical environmental influences? For example, why do some people succumb to peer pressure while others do not? How is it that siblings who share their upbringing can sometimes vary widely in their level of criminal activity? The theories in this chapter provide some possible answers to these questions by looking to "individual differences" as a possible source of criminal behavior.

Modern trait theories can be categorized as either biologically focused, which explore the physiological components that underlie behavior, or psychologically focused, which explore thought processes and personality traits. Collectively, the theories in this chapter hold the following assumptions:

- Individuals vary in their propensity to commit crime.
- Biological factors such as genes, diet, and hormones, and psychological factors such as personality and mental health can explain this variation.
- The criminogenic effects of biological and psychological factors are mediated through environmental experiences.

The contemporary trait perspective

The theories in this chapter may sound reminiscent of the Italian school theories of the 1800s and mid-1900s (Chapter 3), in that both perspectives examine the role of individual characteristics in criminality. Still, they differ in important ways. First, modern trait theorists place much more emphasis on the interaction of personal traits and environmental factors, whereas early trait theorists subscribed to biological determinism. To stress this acknowledgment of the trait–environment interplay, some have referred to modern trait theories as psychosocial or biosocial. This is in sharp contrast to early trait theorists' view of crime as biologically determined and relatively unyielding to environmental influences.

Second, modern trait theorists have more advanced tools at their disposal. Genetic testing, brain imaging techniques, and other measurement strategies have greatly developed in recent decades. None of these tools can by themselves fully account for human behavior, but they do offer more nuanced insights into cause-and-effect relationships than early trait theorists' seemingly absurd focus on factors such as ear size and forehead slope.

	Key Differences between Early and Modern Trait Theories	
	Early Trait Theories (1800s to Early 1900s)	Modern Trait Theories (1970s to Present)
Main assumption	People's behavior is biologically determined; in some cases, criminality is an inherited trait	Biological and psychological traits interact with environmental influences in ways that make crime more or less likely
Common research methods	Inheritability charts, measurement of facial features, examination of skull shape and body type	Brain imaging, hormone measurement, genetic tests, psychological inventories, twin/adoption studies

Although modern trait theories offer important insights into the question of why people vary in their propensity toward crime, this perspective has been slow to gain popularity within mainstream criminology. Contemporary criminologists may be reluctant to examine the biological and psychological underpinnings of crime because of

- The stigma that lingers from the work of early trait theorists such as Lombroso
- The tendency for criminologists to be trained in the social sciences
- A lack of access to the specialized equipment and training necessary to use neuroimaging, genetic tests, and other specialized methods in their research
- Concern that trait theories could be misused to support unethical crime control efforts, as with the eugenics movement
- The belief that crime is best controlled through social programs, thus limiting the policy implications of biological and psychological research

By consequence, there is a dearth of fully developed biological and psychological theories of crime. Instead, criminologists interested in the trait perspective often draw heavily on research from fields such as psychology and behavior genetics. Proponents of the trait perspective, on the other hand, hold that it represents an intellectually exciting and methodologically rich aspect of the field, and that their contributions are an indispensable component to any comprehensive understanding of crime.

Biology and crime

> Few serious scientists in psychology and psychiatry would deny that biological factors are relevant to understanding crime, and public interest in and understanding of this perspective are increasing. The discipline of criminology, on the other hand, has been reluctant to embrace this new body of knowledgew.... For whatever reason, these data have been largely ignored by criminologists and sociologists.
>
> **Adrian Raine, 2002[1]**

Biological theorists posit that physiological and environmental factors interact in a manner that can render crime more or less likely. This perspective most often supports an indirect relationship between biology and crime: genes, hormones, diet, and environmental factors such as stress can alter biochemistry, which in turn can shape perception, mood, disposition, and, by consequence, behavior. This relationship is complex, with physiology and the environment both acting on one another and both proving integral to an understanding of human behavior. Consider the following examples of the interplay between biological and sociological influences:

- Jane is studying for final exams. The stress is aggravating her anxiety, and the lack of sleep is making it difficult to concentrate. Her friend offers her some Adderall to help her focus. Jane accepts the offer, thus being in illegal possession of a controlled substance.
- After a long week at work, Jimmy sits down at a bar to unwind. Several beers later, a patron starts harassing him. Irritable from the stress at work and experiencing the reduced inhibitions of alcohol, he shoves the patron away, and a fight ensues. The police are called, and Jimmy is arrested for assault.
- John was recently diagnosed with clinical depression, a condition rooted in an imbalance of neurotransmitters. His lack of energy and inability to concentrate compromises his productivity at work, and ultimately he is fired. He turns to alcohol to self-medicate, but his mood, the stress of unemployment, and the effects of the alcohol lead to escalating tensions between John and his family. One day, in a particularly heated argument, John hits his wife and throws a lamp at her. She calls the police, and John is arrested for domestic violence.

Social context played an important role in each of the above scenarios, as Jane would have been unlikely to try Adderall if not for her finals and her friend offering the drug; Jimmy might have enjoyed a peaceful evening at the bar had he not been provoked; and John might not have been as prone to violence without the effects of unemployment. At the same time, the physiological effects of sleep deprivation, stress, alcohol, and depression are also apparent: Absent these factors, each party might well have successfully abstained from crime, even when faced with the same social situations.

Biological explanations of crime can be broken down into the following broad categories:

- "Genetic" theories explore the relationship between inherited predispositions and crime.
- "Neurophysiological" theories investigate the role of brain functioning and nervous system activity in criminal behavior.

- "Biochemical" theories posit that diet, hormones, and environmental contaminants can affect internal chemistry in ways that can influence behavior.
- "Evolutionary" theories consider the possibility that evolved human characteristics play a role in some forms of crime.

Each of these areas presents unique insight into the underlying sources of individual variance in criminal propensity.

Genetic influences

> It is imperative to understand that ... there is no neat cryptography by which certain kinds of gene build certain kinds of brain, which in turn produce certain kinds of behavior. [Genes] do not *cause* us to behave or feel one way or another, they *facilitate* our behaviors and our feelings .... It might be better yet to think of genes as modulators of how we respond to the environment, since the gene products that facilitate behavior and emotions are produced in response to environmental stimuli.

> **Anthony Walsh and Kevin M. Beaver, 2009[2]**

Genes are the basis for heredity—they provide the vehicle by which inherited traits transfer from one generation to the next. Most of the estimated 25,000 human genes are the same among all people and serve to differentiate humans from other species. Differences among humans can be traced to the 1% of genes that have some variance across the population.[3] Variations of genes are referred to as "alleles." Every individual inherits two copies of each gene—one allele from each parent. Collectively, the pair of alleles forms an individual's specific "genotype," or variant, for a particular gene.

Although we cannot readily "see" genetic coding with the naked eye, we can see the outward expression of underlying genes in a person's characteristics, such as eye color, skin tone, hair texture, and, most relevant to criminology, disposition and behavior. "Phenotype" refers to these observable manifestations of genotype. Phenotypes are mediated by environmental factors. Just as there is a genetic basis for hair texture but the resultant phenotype can be altered somewhat by environmental factors such as humidity, nutrition, and the use of hair products, there may be a genetic basis for behavior, but it is one that is mediated by social contexts and experiences.

Research has supported an underlying genetic foundation for behavioral phenotypes such as violence, addictions[4] including alcoholism,[5] and mental illnesses such as bipolar disorder.[6] Genes provide the "building blocks" that interact with environmental factors to shape the other biological and psychological factors discussed in this chapter, including neurological functioning, biochemical sensitivities, personality traits, and propensity for mental illness.

The link between genes and crime is indirect. Most often, genes affect crime through their role in regulating neurotransmitters that can, in turn, affect criminological risk factors such as behavior disorders and addictive tendencies.[7] In many instances, it is not a single gene, but variations of multiple genes that collectively shape an individual's propensity toward crime. "Polygenic traits" are phenotypes that are attributable to multiple genes. This is particularly relevant to discussions of crime as there is no single gene solely responsible for complex behavioral tendencies, such as propensities toward

Genes Associated with Specific Criminogenic Risk Factors[8]

Criminogenic Risk Factor	Dopamine Transporter Gene (DAT1)	Dopamine D2 Receptor Gene (DRD2)	Dopamine D4 Receptor Gene (DRD4)	Serotonin Transporter Gene (5-HTTLPR)	Catechol-O-Methyltransferase Gene (COMT)	Monoamine Oxidase A Gene (MAOA)
Attention-deficit hyperactivity disorder	X		x	x		
Gambling	X	X	x			
Violence/aggression	X	X		x	x	X
Conduct disorder				x		X

violence or addictive behaviors. Consider the identified relationships between genes and risk factors mentioned in the table.

Genes can also influence crime by affecting the environment to which a person is exposed. The different relationships that exist between genes and environment have been identified as follows:[9]

- "Passive correlation" occurs when parents pass their genes along to children and are also responsible for shaping their environment.
- "Reactive correlation" occurs when the manifestation of a person's genes affects how others respond to them.
- "Active correlation" occurs when individuals actively seek out environments compatible with their genetic predispositions.

With each of these correlations, genetics can have a compounded effect by acting directly on criminogenic propensities, and indirectly through shaping the environmental influences with which a person comes into contact.

Behavior genetics

Some researchers have suggested that crime is highly concentrated in a small number of families, with one study finding that 5% of families accounted for 53% of the arrests in the sample.[10] Given that children often share both genes and environment with one or both parents, though, how can we determine how much of the familial concentration of crime is attributable to genes versus environment? The complicated task of disaggregating the social and genetic influences of one's family has long been recognized. "Behavior geneticists" are researchers dedicated to disentangling the effects of genes from environment.

There are two primary methodologies used by behavior geneticists. In "twin studies," identical twins provide a natural control for genetic variation. Researchers can compare the relative behavioral similarity of identical (monozygotic) twins, who share all of their genes, with fraternal (dizygotic) twins, who do not. Any variation in the behavioral similarity of twin sets between the twin types is presumed to be attributable to genetics. In "adoption studies," adopted children are evaluated for their relative similarity to their biological parents, with whom they share genes, and their adopted parents, with whom they share an environment.

Efforts to disentangle the relative effects of genes and environment have led some researchers to conclude that the direct and indirect effects of genes may account for as much as "40% to 50% of the population variation in antisocial behavior."[11]

Neurophysiology and crime

Neurophysiology refers to the study of the brain and nervous system. Changes in brain structure or functioning can have an observable impact on behavior, as with the case of Phineas P. Gage, the railroad foreman who survived an explosion that sent a yard-long iron rod through his skull but was left with a forever altered personality (see Chapter 3). Other recent examples include the following:

- A Wisconsin boy, once talkative and loving, who became withdrawn and impulsive after sustaining permanent brain damage from an accident at the age of 10. Three years later, in 2012, he and a friend broke into his great-grandmother's house, robbed her, and killed her with a hatchet and knife.[13]

GENETIC ENGINEERING

Advancements in genetic sequencing have given experts the ability to assess an embryo's susceptibility to different diseases and read its genetic code for physical traits. Prenatal genetic testing is used in the first trimester of pregnancy to provide expectant mothers with information about their child's risk of some types of abnormalities. Preimplantation genetic diagnosis (PGD) is used to screen embryos for genetic diseases or abnormalities before in vitro fertilization.

For a short period in 2009, a Los Angeles fertility clinic advertised offering parents the opportunity to choose the eye and hair color of their children with PGD, until public pressure pushed them to retract the offer.[12] Such efforts arouse concerns about a trend toward "designer babies." Aggravating this concern are advancements in "genetic engineering," or the direct manipulation of DNA to "program" for desirable traits. Genetic engineering is already widely used in agriculture but, at the time of this writing, has only been used in experiments with human embryos to correct faulty DNA. In the near future, we could theoretically develop the necessary technology to identify and replace sections of DNA that increase the risk of undesirable traits such as alcoholism, attention deficit hyperactivity disorder (ADHD), or aggression.

Some critics view genetic engineering as little more than a new-age eugenics movement. Take some time to consider the implications of genetic engineering. Do you see connections to the eugenics movement of the past, or is the potential move toward "designer babies" an entirely different phenomenon? What are the potential benefits and risks of genetic engineering? Should it play a role in the future of crime prevention?

- A doting, affectionate husband in the United Kingdom, who fell down the stairs in 2006, incurring severe injury to the frontal lobe of his brain. Both his 42-year-old wife and their daughter noticed "a definite huge personality change" after the incident, which left him paranoid and aggressive. In 2010, experiencing delusions that his wife was trying to leave him, he stabbed her to death.[14]
- World famous wrestler Chris Benoit, who killed his wife and 7-year-old son and then hanged himself in 2007. This was a shocking move for a "devoted dad and husband who cherished time with his family." Research revealed evidence of substantial brain damage from the blows to the head Benoit had had during his career, which may have played a role in the double-murder suicide.[15]

Different regions of the brain are responsible for different functions, with damage to the "prefrontal cortex," the part of the brain responsible for complex reasoning and goal-directed behavior,[16] most commonly associated with criminal outcomes.

Behavior can also be impacted by the neurotransmitters that transport information from one region to another. Neurons have mechanisms for both sending (axons) and receiving (dendrites) messages among themselves. "Neurotransmitters" are the chemical messengers that carry information from the axon of one neuron to the dendrite of another. The two neurotransmitters most associated with crime are the following:

1. "Dopamine," a neurotransmitter associated with pleasurable feelings. For example, dopamine is released from sexual activity or eating.[17] Dopamine levels that fall outside

the normal range have been associated with mental illness. Genes that affect dopamine processing and receptors have been linked to violence, aggression, mental illness, ADHD, and novelty seeking, all of which are correlates to antisocial behavior.[18]

2. "Serotonin," a neurotransmitter that inhibits activity within the brain, "including aggressive tendencies and primitive impulses."[19] Deficits in serotonin are believed to increase the risk of violence, particularly when combined with a criminogenic environment.[20] A variation in a serotonin-relevant gene has been linked to ADHD, alcoholism, nicotine addiction, and conduct disorder.[21]

Hormones and crime

There is evidence that male hormones (collectively called "androgens"), and testosterone in particular, account for at least some of the sex variance in violent criminality. Testosterone is associated with aggression, competitive behavior, and violence.[22] Ellis[23] has suggested that androgens affect crime by

- Maintaining a lower baseline level of arousal within the nervous system, which encourages sensation seeking and decreases sensitivity to negative consequences
- Rendering males more prone to minor seizures such as "limbic psychotic trigger reaction," a rare event in which a trigger alters the electrical or chemical functioning of the brain and causes a brief and out-of-character episode that may include hallucinations, delusions, and a regression to basic drives, which may include extreme violence[24]
- Favoring right-brain dominance, which is more spatially and temporally inclined and less associated with "empathy-based moral reasoning"[25]

Environmental toxins

The "neurotoxicity hypothesis" holds that exposure to environmental toxins such as lead and manganese can contribute to negative outcomes in behavior. This argument has some logical appeal to the extent that the uptake of certain metals can affect the absorption of nutrients, which in turn can impact behavior.[26] There is also some evidence that lead exposure is correlated to crime at the county level.[27] Still, the evidence in support of this hypothesis is limited. Exposure to pollutants is often concentrated in the most disadvantaged areas, making it difficult to disentangle the effects of toxin exposure and social structural factors in drawing a causal explanation of crime.

Alcohol and crime

The link between alcohol and crime is undisputed. Consider the following statistics from a Bureau of Justice study of correctional populations in the 1990s:

- Nearly 40% of probationers and jail inmates and more than 32% of prison inmates self-reported being under the influence of alcohol at the time of their offense.[28]
- Of those who reported alcohol consumption in the 8 hours leading up to their offense, "probationers were estimated to have consumed … the equivalent of about 9 beers.… Jail inmates self-reported ethanol consumption equaling about 11 beers, and prisoners drank the equivalent of 15 beers."[29]
- Among state prison inmates, alcohol was commonly a factor in cases of domestic violence and manslaughter.[30]

This is consistent with the National Crime Victimization Survey, which found that offenders were under the influences of alcohol or drugs in 44% of all violent crimes,[31] and that substance abuse was more commonly a factor in cases of intimate partner violence (75%), particularly in cases involving spouses (81%).[32]

Although the existence of an alcohol–crime link is clear, the exact nature of this relationship is less certain.[33] Does alcohol cause crime, or do other risk factors, such as having an alcoholic parent or being raised in poverty, contribute to both crime and alcohol consumption? Ultimately, as with the examples presented earlier in this chapter, it is most likely that alcohol and other risk factors have an interactive effect on crime, with each magnifying the effect of the other when both are present.[34] There are some recognized mechanisms through which alcohol contributes to violence. Alcohol

- Alters receptors in the brain to be less anxious about risky behavior[35]
- Reduces impulse control through its effect on serotonin and dopamine[36]
- Reduces sensitivity to pain
- Impairs cognition

These effects suggest that alcohol is likely to lower inhibitions, impair judgment, and encourage risk-taking behavior. The social acceptance of alcohol-induced behaviors in contexts such as bars and parties may magnify alcohol's disinhibiting effects.

Drugs and crime

Similar to alcohol, drugs can play a multifaceted role in criminal behavior. Illegal drug use is, of course, a crime in and of itself (see the discussion of drug laws in Chapter 11). Goldstein set forth a three-part model of the relationship between drugs and other forms of crime:[37]

- "Psychopharmacological violence" represents the most direct link between crime and the physiological effects of drugs. To the extent that drugs increase an individual's excitability and irrationality, they can by consequence increase the risk of violence.
- "Economic compulsive" crimes represent an indirect link between crime and biology. Cash-strapped drug addicts may turn to burglary, robbery, shoplifting, prostitution, or other crimes to fund their next high.
- "Systemic violence" is that which stems directly from the "business" of the drug trade, as with disputes over turf.

Even systemic violence can be seen as the indirect result of biological factors, since the drug trade would arguably be substantially weaker if not for drug addiction.

Dietary effects on crime

It is widely believed that diet affects behavior. People may feel that certain foods make them sluggish, or anticipate that a high dose of sugar will make their children "hyper." This belief has even worked its way into the courtroom, when the defense in a high-profile double-murder case in the 1970s invoked what was later termed the "Twinkie defense": It was argued that the defendant had impaired judgment due to the combined effects of depression and a diet high in sugared sodas, candy, and other junk foods.[38]

Is there truth to the belief that diet affects behavior, and could it play a role in crime? Perhaps surprisingly, research has not supported that sugar intake, by itself, affects behavior—although one study found that parents who were falsely told their child had consumed sugar reported more hyperactivity, indicating a "placebo effect."[39] Instead, dietary effects appear to be more closely related to individual food sensitivities or a dearth of proper nutrients. A meta-analysis of the behavioral impact of diet found the following to increase the risk of violence or other antisocial behavior:[40]

- Exposure to foods to which people have an individual intolerance
- Deficits in omega-3 and omega-6 fatty acids, which are associated with greater behavioral problems in those with ADHD[41]
- Low levels of blood glucose, as with hypoglycemia[42]

Nutritional supplements appear to reduce antisocial behavior, possibly through their positive effect on neurotransmitters that assist with brain functioning.[43]

Efforts to assess the relationship between diet and behavior face several methodological hurdles. The highly individual nature of food sensitivity makes it difficult to draw broad conclusions about problematic foods. It may not be practical to hide dietary interventions from participants in experimental settings, making it difficult to differentiate between actual and placebo effects. With survey methods it is difficult to disentangle the effects of diet from other variables that may cause both a poor diet and involvement in crime, such as poverty.

Evolution and crime

Evolutionary theorists hold that evolution naturally results in the propagation of traits that most successfully support survival and reproductive success. Accordingly, they evaluate all human behavior, including crime, in relation to mating and parenting effort. "Mating effort" refers to the energy invested in securing sexual partners and engaging in sexual activity to conceive children. "Parenting effort" refers to the time and energy invested in maximizing the survival of one's offspring.

Evolutionary theorists assume that the persistence of criminal behavior indicates that it provides (or at some point has provided) strategic advantages in reproduction. In this conception of crime (no pun intended), it is believed that male jealousy and aggressiveness are evolutionary traits rooted in men's competition for reproductive partners. In contrast, since females have a more substantial obligatory investment in childbearing due to the nature of pregnancy, they have evolved to place more emphasis on parenting effort, resulting in more conservative and nurturing behavior. This view is consistent with gendered patterns of criminality, particularly in explaining crimes attributable to male jealousy and competitiveness. It may also explain crimes committed to gain status in the eyes of potential mates, as with some cases of theft, drug dealing, or even white-collar crime.

Researchers have found support for the proposition that mating effort and criminality are linked. Criminal activity is positively correlated with number of sexual partners and with an earlier age of first sexual encounter.[44] Cross-cultural comparisons have found that cultures that emphasize mating effort also have higher rates of antisocial behavior.[45] At the same time, the perspective oversimplifies the differences between men and women, whose behavior is far more diverse than this perspective suggests. It also fails to explain crimes that are discordant with reproductive and parenting success, as with child neglect.

Evolutionary neuroandrogenic theory

In 2005, Lee Ellis[46] published one of the few comprehensive modern theories of biology and crime. In his "evolutionary neuroandrogenic" (ENA) theory, he begins with the assumption that evolution has favored competitiveness and "aggressive and acquisitive" behavior among males who must compete for status to attract mates. He then presents several interrelated propositions regarding the biological basis of male behavior, which may be summarized as follows:

- Since males and females share most of their genes, differences in competitive and victimizing behavior must be attributable to the Y-chromosome and the resulting androgens, including testosterone.
- Although androgens support competitive behavior among all males, those with high levels of intelligence and cognitive functioning are able to find noncriminal outlets for attaining the status they desire.
- Alternatively, biological factors that impair cognitive functioning, such as fetal exposure to maternal smoking or other neurotoxins, increase the likelihood that male competitiveness will manifest in crude and potentially criminal forms of victimization.

The strength of Ellis's theory is that it addresses both sex differences and age patterns in criminality. The increase of crime in adolescence and early adulthood is consistent with a pubescent spike in testosterone, whereas aging out is consistent with Ellis's description of the adaptation of some men to socially acceptable outlets for status attainment. At the same time, Ellis's theory is controversial in its heavy emphasis on intelligence and cognitive functioning. His arguments fail to take into account differences in social opportunities and social learning, and cannot easily account for female crime, intelligent or otherwise successful males who commit crude forms of crime, or males with impaired cognitive functioning who abstain from criminality.

Policy implications for biology and crime

A biological approach to criminology offers several policy implications, such as

- The treatment of chemical imbalances with prescription drugs
- The alteration of diets to improve nutrition and address individual food sensitivities
- Providing drug and alcohol treatment for those with addictions, and regulating the availability and use of addictive substances
- Limiting exposure to environmental contaminants such as lead

Other possible implications are more controversial. For example, what should be done with an offender who possesses several genetic risk factors for antisocial or violent behavior? There is some fear that this perspective may be misapplied to support eugenics, genetic engineering, or unduly harsh punishments for affected individuals.

Robinson[47] acknowledges that a biological approach to crime could be interpreted to support unethical policies, but doubts that such policies would gain widespread support. Instead, he argues that the value of genetic research lies in its ability to guide the alteration of environmental triggers and insulators for criminal behavior, and to inform the development of medical interventions that can regulate brain chemistry in a manner that reduces crime.

Criticisms of a biological approach to crime

Contemporary biological theorists remain largely marginalized from mainstream criminology, despite strong evidence that biological factors do affect human behavior. Criticisms of a biological approach include the following:

- It underemphasizes the role of human choice and agency in criminal behavior.
- It fails to account for individual variation in how genes or other biosocial factors manifest in behavior.
- Since genes have only an indirect effect on behavior, it may be more effective to address crime via intervening environmental factors, raising questions about the value of investing in genetic research.
- It fails to adequately account for social and geographic patterns of criminal activity.
- Crime is a socially and legally defined phenomenon, raising questions about the validity of looking for a biological basis.
- The research in this area may convolute biological and environmental effects. Often those who are subject to criminogenic social conditions are also at the greatest risk for poor nutrition and exposure to environmental toxins, so without carefully controlled experimental studies, it is difficult to determine whether biology–crime relationships are causal.
- Research findings may lead to the inappropriate labeling of offenders as possessing some inherently criminal quality, when in fact many of their behaviors are heavily mediated by social conditions.
- This perspective overstates its ability to identify mechanical processes that guide social phenomena. Many biological criminologists claim to be able to draw definitive connections between observable physical phenomena and criminal behavior. Although biosocial theories offer more "hard data" in regard to independent variables, theorists in this tradition often overlook alternative causal explanations, oversimplify the nature of human behavior, and fail to critically analyze how "crime" is defined in their studies.

Psychology and crime

"Psychology" examines the role of "the mind" (including emotions, cognitive functions, and personality traits) in shaping behavior. The field has a long history in the study, assessment, and treatment of criminal offenders. In the 1920s and 1930s psychology became the dominant perspective in the treatment of offenders.[48] Beginning in the late 1970s, when the focus began to shift from rehabilitation back to punishment,[49] the field of psychology remained relevant for its contributions to risk assessment and management.[50] "Forensic psychology" is the umbrella term used to refer to the application of psychological expertise to the functioning of the legal system.[51]

Personality and crime

Psychologists use the term "personality" to describe the aspects of character and temperament that render individuals unique from one another. These aspects are relatively "enduring" in that they maintain some consistency across time and social contexts. As applied to crime, personality theories provide a mechanism for understanding why some people are more inclined than others to exploit criminal opportunities or give in to criminal temptations.

FORENSIC PSYCHOLOGY: THE REAL STORY

Television shows such as *Criminal Minds* have increased public awareness of the role that psychology can play in criminal justice, but not always accurately.[52] In these shows, psychologists act as detectives who identify and hunt down criminals in time-sensitive situations and demonstrate an uncanny ability to anticipate offenders' moves based on criminal profiling. In reality, forensic psychology plays a different but no less important role than is usually portrayed in the media.

The field of forensic psychology has grown substantially over the past 50 years[53] as licensed psychologists have been called upon to

- Assess defendants' mental competency to stand trial
- Serve as expert witness in criminal and civil trials
- Engage in crisis intervention, including hostage negotiations
- Mediate or negotiate disputes
- Screen potential police officers for fitness for duty and provide counseling after critical incidents
- Provide mental health treatment in a prison setting
- Treat probationers and parolees for specific issues such as sexual deviance and anger management

Criminal profiling does exist, but it is not central to the work of most forensic psychologists.

Psychologists' efforts to conceptualize personality, interestingly, began with a thorough review of the dictionary. Researchers carefully catalogued and then tried to make conceptual sense of all terms that could possibly be used to distinguish among different individuals' behaviors.[54] Since then, several different models of personality have gained prominence. This section explores some of the most widely used personality models as they relate to criminology.

Eysenck's three-dimensional personality model

Well-known psychologist Hans Eysenck posited that personality can be measured on three dimensions: introversion/extraversion, stability/neuroticism, and normality/psychoticism.[55] Each dimension exists on a continuum, meaning that gradations of any given characteristic are possible. For example, some people may be slightly neurotic, whereas others may rate extremely high on the neurotic scale.

According to Eysenck's model,

- Extroverts tend to be sociable, impulsive, and excitement seeking.
- Neurotics lack emotional stability.
- Psychopaths tend to disregard the rights of others and fail to take responsibility for their own behavior.

He identifies high ratings in extraversion, neuroticism, and psychoticism as risk factors for most types of crime.

NEUROPHYSIOLOGICAL UNDERPINNINGS OF PERSONALITY

In his book *Crime and Personality*, Hans Eysenck suggested that individual variations in introversion/extraversion might be attributable to the autonomic nervous system (ANS). The ANS is composed of two parts: The "sympathetic system" aids survival by providing the body's fight/flight mechanism, whereas the "parasympathetic system" regulates the fight/flight system by dampening the body's response to external stimuli.[56] Eysenck argues that introverts have a higher base rate of arousal, rendering them more sensitive to external stimuli. This heightened state of arousal can serve to limit criminal behavior by rendering them more sensitive to risks. He cites research indicating that introverts are faster to develop conditioned responses to stimuli—for example, in tests of subjects exposed to a tone followed by an air puff to the eye, introverts develop a conditioned blinking reflex in response to the tone at about twice the rate of extroverts.[57] Applied to crime, this suggests that introverts will more readily respond to the deterrent effects of punishment, whereas extroverts, who are less sensitive to outside stimuli, will be slower to respond.

More recently, the "five-factor model" or "big five" has taken hold as the dominant model of personality. Although the model has varied slightly over the years, Costra and McCrae as described in Digman[58] first introduced its most broadly accepted form in 1985. The Revised NEO-Personality Inventory identifies the big five as follows:[59]

1. Extraversion: Warmth, gregariousness, assertiveness, activity, excitement seeking, and positive emotions
2. Agreeableness: Trust, straightforwardness, altruism, compliance, modesty, and tender-mindedness
3. Conscientiousness: Competence, order, dutifulness, achievement striving, self-discipline, and deliberation
4. Emotional stability versus neuroticism: Anxiety, anger/hostility, depression, self-consciousness, impulsiveness, and vulnerability
5. Intellect or openness: Fantasy, aesthetics, feelings, actions, ideas, and values

Other theories argue that the human personality is composed of a greater number of constructs, as with Cloninger and colleagues' proposition that it includes seven factors, among which are novelty seeking, harm avoidance, reward dependence, and persistence.[60]

There is some evidence that personality traits do vary between offending and nonoffending populations. One meta-analysis concluded that antisocial behaviors were most strongly associated with Eysenck's construct of psychoticism, followed by (lack of) agreeableness and a propensity toward novelty seeking.[61] Another study using different constructs found arrests to be correlated with angry hostility, impulsiveness, and excitement seeking.[62]

Freud's psychodynamic theory

According to famed psychologist Sigmund Freud, personality results from the dynamics of three underlying components:[63]

1. The "id" represents the subconscious, primitive impulse to pursue pleasure.
2. The "superego" counterbalances the id with morals and inhibitions that are largely internalized during childhood.
3. The "ego," or conscious mind, is responsible for reconciling the opposing demands of the id and superego according to the "reality principle."

There are several ways in which this theory can help us understand crime. Most directly, it would predict that children raised without strong moral guidance may fail to develop an adequate superego to balance the impulses of the id, leading to a bias toward impulsive, pleasure-driven behavior. Perhaps counterintuitively, others have argued that children raised in overly repressive environments may develop such a strong superego that it leads to a buildup of pressure in the id, ultimately backfiring. This is consistent with crimes in which a person seems to "snap."

Psychopathy

> Psychopaths can be described as intraspecies predators who use charm, manipulation, intimidation, and violence to control others and satisfy their own selfish needs. Lacking in conscience and in feelings for others, they cold-bloodedly take what they want and do as they please, violating social norms and expectations without the slightest sense of guilt.
>
> **Robert D. Hare, 1996[64]**

Among the general public, it is not unusual to hear the offender of a particularly heinous crime labeled a "psychopath," but exactly what does the label mean? In the early 1900s, when persistent antisocial behavior could not otherwise be explained, psychiatrists sometimes applied the term "psychopathic personality" with the presumption that the behavior was rooted in an underlying psychiatric disorder.[65] Today, psychopathy is often associated with "antisocial personality disorder,"[66] a diagnosable psychiatric condition characterized by pervasive offending against others. Still, there is some debate over the precise meaning of the word.

Walsh and Wu[67] describe psychopathy as an inborn trait that exists in the population at a stable rate. Although psychopaths experience personal emotions such as anger or joy, they are distinguished by their "greatly reduced ability to experience the social emotions of shame, embarrassment, guilt, empathy, and love,"[68] which in turn renders them more likely to engage in behaviors that are exploitive of others. The authors summarize the research that documents physiological indicators of psychopathy, reporting that psychopaths

- Do not show increased brain wave pattern activity on electroencephalograms when exposed to emotionally laden words, such as "cancer," relative to emotionally neutral words, such as "apple"[69]
- Fail to show physical signs of nervousness when engaging in deceitful activities[70]
- Do not experience the same increase in fear or anxiety, as measured by electrodermal activity, as nonpsychopaths in anticipation of negative stimuli[71]

Research has linked psychopathy to various personality dimensions, including low scores on agreeableness and conscientiousness.[72] A survey of experts on psychopathy revealed the belief that psychopaths are likely to rate high in impulsiveness, excitement seeking, anger/hostility, and gregariousness.[73] Psychopaths often have low levels of fear and empathy and reduced sensitivity to social cues and classical conditioning[74] and engage in violent, varied, and frequent offenses.[75]

The Psychopathy Checklist—Revised (PCL-R) is the most widely used measurement tool for psychopathy. The PCL-R rates individuals on each of 20 characteristics such as shallow affect, impulsivity, irresponsibility, and lack of empathy[76] on a scale of 0–2, resulting in a total maximum score of 40.[77] Those scoring 30 or above are typically classified as psychopathic.[78]

Psychopathy is sometimes confused with sociopathy, but the two are not one and the same. Walsh and Wu[79] explain that while both are characterized by predatory behavior, sociopaths are made, not born—sociopathy is often tied to socially and economically disadvantaged circumstances, meaning that its prevalence will vary in different social contexts. Research has found that sociopaths tend to score between psychopaths and the rest of the population on physiological measures of emotional response, possibly as a result of desensitization due to exposure to abuse or neglect in childhood.[80]

ANTISOCIAL PERSONALITY DISORDER

The *Diagnostic and Statistical Manual of Mental Disorders* (*DSM-V*) defines antisocial personality disorder (APD) as follows:

A pervasive pattern of disregard for and violation of the rights of others, occurring since age 15 years, as indicated by three (or more) of the following:

1. Failure to conform to social norms with respect to lawful behaviors, as indicated by repeatedly performing acts that are grounds for arrest
2. Deceitfulness, as indicated by repeated lying, use of aliases, or conning others for personal profit or pleasure
3. Impulsivity or failure to plan ahead
4. Irritability and aggressiveness, as indicated by repeated physical fights or assaults
5. Reckless disregard for safety of self or others
6. Consistent irresponsibility, as indicated by repeated failure to sustain consistent work behavior or honor financial obligations
7. Lack of remorse, as indicated by being indifferent to or rationalizing having hurt, mistreated, or stolen from another[81]

To be diagnosed with APD, the individual must be at least 18 years old, but have symptoms predating the age of 15.[82] It is most common among males, particularly among those in forensic settings (such as prison) who experience alcohol and other substance abuse issues.[83] Although the term "psychopath" is sometimes viewed as synonymous with an APD diagnosis, the connection has been strongly disputed. Robert Hare, the creator of the PCL-R, has suggested that only a small subset of those diagnosed with APD fit the criteria for psychopathy, although most psychopaths will fit the criteria for APD.[84]

	Psychopathy, Sociopathy, and Antisocial Personality Disorder
Psychopathy	An inborn quality characterized by a lack of social emotions, most often measured by the PCL-R
Sociopathy	A pattern of antisocial behavior attributed to a disadvantaged upbringing
APD	A diagnosable psychiatric disorder characterized by a chronic pattern of antisocial behavior

Crime and cognition

> Behavior follows in the wake of thought. To eliminate criminal behavior, it is essential first to change the way a man ... thinks.

> **Stanton E. Samenow, 2004/1984**[85]

In 1976, Samuel Yochelson and Stanton Samenow published *The Criminal Personality*, a landmark book on the topic of cognition and criminal behavior. On the basis of their experience working with criminal offenders in a psychiatric hospital, the authors concluded that criminal behavior stemmed from the deeply ingrained thinking patterns of offenders. They identified 52 "thinking errors" that characterized criminal thought processes. For example, they found that offenders were often closed to criticism, refused to accept responsibility for their own behaviors, and were present- (rather than future-) oriented. The authors held that in order for these thinking patterns to change, offenders must undergo "habilitation," the process of learning new ways of thinking that enable a responsible path in life.

Lifestyle theory

Yochelson and Samenow's contributions inspired others to explore the importance of thought patterns in criminal behavior, most notably Glenn Walters.[86] In his lifestyle theory, he proposed that crime was the result of three elements:

1. Conditions: Criminal opportunities are shaped by a convergence of a person's individual traits, their social environment, and the interaction of the two.
2. Choice: Acknowledging the role of free will, he argued that individuals would then select from the options available to them.
3. Cognition: The offender's thinking would then adapt in a manner that would alleviate their feelings of guilt for their offenses.

Walters did not view any one of these factors as primary—rather, he viewed all of them as exerting influence over one another in complex ways. He explained that:

> Conditions, choices, and cognitions merge over time to form a complex, dynamic, and multidirectional system of interacting influences .... Cognitions not only arise in support of choice but also modify the decision-making process and the individual's perception of assorted life conditions. Similarly, choices are both influenced by, and exert an influence over, conditions and cognition.[87]

Walters elaborated on eight thinking patterns commonly present in the cognition of offending populations:[88]

1. Mollification: The use of rationalizations and self-justifications to reject responsibility for one's own actions
2. Cutoff: A strategy consciously invoked to overcome their fear of committing an offense, which sometimes includes the use of drugs or alcohol
3. Entitlement: The sense that society's rules do not apply, and that the offense is a necessary action to fulfill a personal need
4. Power orientation: A preoccupation with gaining control over the environment, including the people within it
5. Sentimentality: Self-serving efforts to prove that they are "good" people
6. Superoptimism: An overestimation of ability to commit risky actions without negative consequence
7. Cognitive indolence: A tendency to prefer the path of least resistance in thought, planning, and action
8. Discontinuity: Disjointed thoughts, including the ability to "compartmentalize," and a lack of follow-through in action

Walters posits that discontinuity is the most supportive of a criminal lifestyle, as it can interfere with the success of offenders even when they begin with genuinely positive intentions.[89]

COGNITIVE INTERVENTION PROGRAMS

The work on crime and cognition has contributed to the development of cognitive intervention programs, now commonly used with offender populations. These programs help offenders recognize the role of their thought process in shaping their problematic behavior and then work to develop methods for altering those thought patterns to improve future behavior. Research has supported the potential effectiveness of these programs, with one meta-analysis concluding approximately a 25% reduction in recidivism.[90]

One of the authors of this book had the opportunity to observe a cognitive intervention group for probationers. An offender convicted of domestic violence was quite proud to share a story of how he had benefited from the class: He returned home after a stressful day at work only to find that his wife had finished his favorite ice cream. Historically, he said that he would have been angered by her apparent lack of consideration (consistent with Yochelson and Samenow's "victim stance") and it would have resulted in an abusive incident. Instead of lashing out, he decided to take a walk to reflect on how to better respond—was this really his wife's fault, or was he overlooking an "error" in his interpretation of events? He finally realized that instead of pointing fingers and getting angry at his wife, a little bit of problem solving could solve what upset him: If he simply purchased an ample supply of ice cream, then he and his wife could both enjoy it without issue. He went on to fully stock the freezer. In other words, he now possessed the tools to identify and interrupt the "thinking errors" that previously supported his violence.

Mental illness and crime

The question of a potential link between mental illness and crime has been widespread in the wake of high-profile, mass casualty shootings such as those at Columbine High School, Virginia Tech, and Sandy Hook Elementary School. Although mental illness likely played a role in some of these cases, it is also the case that mental illness is fairly common, and the onset of a mental illness does not send individuals spiraling toward inevitable criminality. The National Institute of Mental Health reports that in any given year, more than one in four adults will experience a diagnosable mental illness.[91] Many forms of mental illness have little if any connection to criminality, as with those who experience panic disorder.

So what is the relationship between crime and mental illness? Although mental illness does not always manifest in crime, under the right circumstances some symptoms of mental illness can increase the likelihood of criminal behavior. To the extent that mental illness alters an individual's perceptions and cognitive functioning, in certain situations it may

- Reduce perceptions of risk
- Increase perceptions of reward

For example, those who have bipolar disorder (also known as manic depression) fluctuate between periods of depression and mania. Manic episodes entail feelings of high energy, invincibility, and lessened concern for long-term consequences.[92] The sense of invincibility in the manic stage can manifest itself in legal but self-destructive ways, as with promiscuity, binge eating, or spending sprees, but it can also lead people to take criminal risks that they might not otherwise take, as with getting into fights, stealing, driving recklessly, or taking drugs.

In other cases, mental illness may increase the perceived rewards of criminal behavior. For example, paranoid schizophrenia is characterized by delusions that the sufferer is the target of a plot. The illness is also sometimes accompanied by auditory hallucinations that support these delusions.[93] If an individual hears voices that threaten harm if (s)he fails to harm another, or if the voices convincingly suggest that another person poses a threat, the schizophrenic may engage in violence with the belief that the action was necessary for self-defense.

One common misconception is that mental illness is frequently used as an excuse to evade responsibility for criminal behavior. In fact, this is rarely the case. Because mental illness is fairly common in society, and most mental illnesses are not serious enough to disconnect a person from reality to the extent that would be necessary for a successful plea of "not guilty by reason of insanity," or even "guilty but mentally ill," most offenders with mental illness are processed through the criminal justice system without any particular leniency. In fact, two trends converged in recent decades to lead to a relatively strong prevalence of mental illness in the nation's prisons and jails.

First, the United States underwent a dramatic "deinstitutionalization" of the mentally ill (a reduction in the number of inpatient beds at mental health facilities) in favor of outpatient treatment and the use of prescription medications. Among those who have serious mental illness and lack strong social and community supports, this has in some cases led to a failure to manage symptoms properly, which in turn contributes to unemployment, homelessness, and self-medication with alcohol or other drugs.

Second, from the 1970s and into recent years, the United States more heavily criminalized public order offenses such as drug possession, public intoxication, trespassing in parks after hours, and loitering. These policing efforts have disproportionately impacted the mentally ill and channeled those who once would have been hospitalized into the nation's jails and prisons. As of 2005,

> More than half of all prison and jail inmates had a mental health problem, including 705,600 inmates in State prisons, 78,800 in Federal prisons, and 479,900 in local jails. These estimates represented 56% of State prisoners, 45% of Federal prisoners, and 64% of jail inmates.[94]

The concentration of the mentally ill within the criminal justice system has become notable to the point that several media sources have referred to prisons and jails as the "new asylums."

The prevalence of mental illness in prisons and jails is a concern for several reasons. The stress and, in some cases, isolation behind bars can exacerbate the symptoms of mental illness. In practice, sufficient treatment may not be available in a prison or jail setting.[95] Rule violations are also more common among the mentally ill, which could post security challenges within facilities.[96]

Policy implications for psychology and crime

Possible policy suggestions from the psychological perspective include the following:

- Improvement in the diagnosis and treatment of mental illnesses that are strongly associated with crime, such as APD
- Increased availability of screening and treatment resources for all forms of mental illness
- The availability of cognitive intervention programs to help offenders recognize and overcome their "thinking errors"

The practical implications of trait theories are more questionable. Most psychological theorists would argue that personality is strongly rooted in physiological and genetic underpinnings, and therefore cannot easily be altered. For example, it is unclear whether those who rate low in agreeableness or high in novelty seeking can be changed, and if so, how such changes might be initiated.

Criticisms of a psychological approach to crime

The psychological perspective is faced with the following criticisms:

- It underemphasizes the role of social factors in shaping behavior.
- The concept of a stable personality fails to account for changes in offending over the life course.
- The practical implications of trait theories are unclear.
- Efforts to search for a criminal personality are akin to early trait theorists' efforts to identify inborn criminality.

Summary

- Trait theories explore the influence of biology and psychology on criminal behavior.
- Unlike early trait theorists, modern trait theorists acknowledge that the effects of biology and psychology are mediated by environmental factors.
- Modern trait theorists benefit from tools such as genetic testing and brain imaging to gather data.
- Contemporary criminologists have been slow to embrace the trait perspective, tending to favor sociological explanations of crime.
- Because of the dearth of fully developed biological and psychological theories of crime, modern trait theorists draw heavily on other fields such as psychology and behavior genetics.
- Biological theories of crime can be broken down into four categories: genetic, neurophysiological, biochemical, and evolutionary.
- There is some evidence of a genetic basis for criminal behavior, although the effects are heavily mediated by the environment.
- Crime can best be understood as a polygenic trait—no single gene can explain criminal behavior.
- There are three types of genes–environment correlations: passive, reactive, and evocative.
- Changes in brain structure and functioning can affect behavior.
- There is evidence that androgens, or male hormones, are linked to aggressiveness, competitive behavior, and violence.
- The neurotoxicity hypothesis holds that exposure to environmental toxins can increase the risk of criminal behavior.
- Alcohol consumption is strongly correlated to crime.
- Alcohol can affect crime through several mechanisms: It reduces impulse control, sensitivity to pain, and perceptions of risk, and impairs cognition.
- Drugs are linked to crime through several mechanisms: The effects of some drugs are conducive to violent crime, addiction can foster economic compulsive crimes, and the illegal drug trade is characterized by systemic violence.
- Individual food sensitivities and nutritional deficits can foster antisocial behavior.
- Evolutionary theorists examine the relationship of mating effort and parenting effort to crime.
- The evolutionary perspective holds that males' developed emphasis on mating effort contributes to competitive and potentially criminal behaviors.
- Lee Ellis developed the ENA theory, which posits that crime is related to androgens, low intelligence and cognitive functioning, and exposure to neurotoxins.
- Psychological studies of crime explore the role of emotions, cognitive functions, and personality traits.
- Forensic psychology is an umbrella term that refers to the application of psychological expertise to the functioning of the legal system.
- Personality theorists attempt to identify the types of character and temperament that are the most conducive to crime.
- Hans Eysenck suggested that those who rank high in extraversion, neuroticism, and psychoticism would be most susceptible to crime.
- Research has found a link between crime and high ratings in psychoticism and novelty seeking and low ratings in agreeableness.

- Sigmund Freud's psychodynamic theory suggests that crime may result when the id and superego are out of balance.
- Psychopathy is an inborn trait characterized by a reduced ability to feel social emotions.
- The PCL-R is the most common measure of psychopathy.
- Sociopathy is similar to psychopathy, but is not believed to be inborn.
- APD is a diagnosable disorder listed in the *DSM-V* that reflects the presence of factors such as failure to conform, deceitfulness, impulsivity, irritability, and a reckless disregard for the well-being of others.
- Yochelson and Samenow suggest that crime is the result of thinking errors, which can best be addressed by habilitation.
- In his lifestyle theory, Glenn Walters argued that crime is the result of conditions, cognition, and choice. He identified several thinking patterns that represent cognitive risk factors for crime.
- Cognitive intervention programs are now commonly used in correctional settings.
- Some symptoms of mental illness can alter the individual's subjective perceptions of risk and reward in ways that make crime more likely.
- The deinstitutionalization of the mentally ill and the criminalization of minor offenses have contributed to a large population of the mentally ill within prisons and jails.

Questions in review

1. How do modern trait theories differ from early trait theories?
2. Explain the nature of the relationship between genes and crime.
3. How does alcohol and drug abuse contribute to crime?
4. What are some of the weaknesses of the biological perspective?
5. Compare and contrast psychopathy and sociopathy.
6. What is the relationship between mental illness and crime?

Practicum

The Sandy Hook Elementary School shooting

On December 14, 2012, 20-year-old Adam Lanza killed his mother and then drove to Sandy Hook Elementary School in Newtown, Connecticut, and opened fire, killing 20 children and 6 adults before taking his own life. In the days after the shooting, the nation struggled to understand why it happened. What could motivate someone to take innocent lives, many of whom were only six or seven years old? This was not the first time the nation has been faced with trying to make sense of apparently senseless mass casualty shootings: Similar incidents have taken place at Columbine High School, Virginia Tech, and at Aurora, Colorado, movie theater, among others.

In the days and weeks following the Sandy Hook shooting, new details became available about the shooter's past. Lanza had autism,[97] a neurodevelopmental disorder that results from a combination of genes and environment[98] and can affect a person's social interactions and communication abilities.[99] According to the National Institutes of Health,

> Studies of people with ASD [autism spectrum disorder] have found irregularities in several regions of the brain. Other studies suggest that people with ASD have abnormal levels of serotonin or other

neurotransmitters in the brain. These abnormalities suggest that ASD could result from the disruption of normal brain development early in fetal development caused by defects in genes that control brain growth and that regulate how brain cells communicate with each other, possibly due to the influence of environmental factors on gene function.[100]

Although the news media made much of Lanza's diagnosis, there is no evidence that autism has a direct effect on crime. Some have suggested that his autism had an indirect effect based on Lanza being bullied and ridiculed throughout his schooling, to the point that his mother ultimately decided to home-school him,[101] an argument consistent with a reactive genes–environment correlation.

Lanza also had a form of sensory integration disorder (also known as sensory processing disorder) that increased his sensitivity to noise and touch.[102] As with autism, there is no evidence that this disorder increases the risk of crime. It did, on the other hand, cause Lanza to get upset when others touched him growing up. A hypothesis might be that this condition increased his sensitivity to bullying in a manner that ultimately led to the shooting. Other observations about Lanza's past focused instead on the fact that he had been raised around firearms, with his mother's home containing "a cache of weapons— including an assault-style rifle and two handguns"[103]—at the time of the incident.

Questions regarding the Lanza case

1. What connections do you see between this case and the material from this chapter?
2. Do you think Lanza's actions could have been prevented, and if so, how? Explain your answer.
3. Can the biological and psychological arguments in this chapter inform schools' practices in the prevention of school shootings?

References

1. Raine, A. (2002). The biological basis of crime. In J. Q. Wilson & J. Petersilia (Eds.), *Crime: Public policies for crime control* (pp. 43–74). Oakland, CA: ICS Press.
2. Walsh, A., & Beaver, K. M. (2009). Introduction to biosocial criminology. In A. Walsh & K. M. Beaver (Eds.), *Biosocial criminology: New directions in theory and research* (pp. 7–28). New York: Routledge: Taylor & Francis Group.
3. National Library of Medicine. (2013, October 21). *What is a gene?* Retrieved from http://ghr.nlm.nih.gov/handbook/basics/gene
4. For example, Saxon, A. J., Oreskovich, M. R., & Brkanac, Z. (2005). Genetic determinants of addiction to opioids and cocaine. *Harvard Review of Psychiatry, 13*(4), 218–232. See also Le Foll, B., Gallo, A., Le Strat, Y., Lu, L., & Gorwood, P. (2009). Genetics of dopamine receptors and drug addiction: A comprehensive review. *Behavioural Pharmacology, 20*(1), 1–17.
5. Agrawal, A., & Lynskey, M. T. (2008). Are there genetic influences on addiction: Evidence from family, adoption, and twin studies. *Addiction, 103*(7), 1069–1081.
6. Alsabban, S., Rivera, M., & McGuffin, P. (2011). Genome-wide searches for bipolar disorder genes. *Current Psychiatry Reports, 13*(6), 522–527.
7. Beaver, K. M. (2009). Molecular genetics and crime. In K. M. Beaver & A. Walsh (Eds.), *Biosocial criminology: New directions in theory and research* (pp. 50–72). New York: Routledge.
8. Adapted from Beaver, K. M. (2009). Molecular genetics and crime. In K. M. Beaver & A. Walsh (Eds.), *Biosocial criminology: New directions in theory and research* (table 3.1, p. 64). New York: Routledge.

9. Plomin, R., DeFries, J. C., & Loehlin. J. C. (1977). Genotype–environment interaction and correlation in the analysis of human behavior. *Psychological bulletin, 34*(2), 309–322.

10. Beaver, K. M. (2013). The familial concentration and transmission of crime. *Criminal Justice and Behavior, 40*(2), 139–155.

11. Miles & Carey (1997) and Rhee & Waldman. (2002). Cited in Moffitt, T. E. (2005). The new look of behavioral genetics in developmental psychopathology: Gene-environment interplay in antisocial behaviors. *Psychological Bulletin, 131*(4): 533–554.

12. Keim, B. (2009, March 9). Designer babies: A right to choose? *Wired*. Retrieved from http://www.wired.com/wiredscience/2009/03/designerdebate/

13. Lintereur, J. (2013, July 21). A dramatic change: Barbeau family says teen's brain injury was a factor in murder. *Green Bay Press Gazette*. Retrieved from http://www.greenbaypressgazette.com/article/20130721/GPG0101/307210326/A-dramatic-change-Barbeau-family-says-teen-s-brain-injury-factor-murder.

14. Daily Mail Reporter. (2010, October 25). *Doting husband stabbed wife to death after brain injury made him 'a different man.'* Retrieved from http://www.dailymail.co.uk/news/article-1323642/Doting-husband-stabbed-wife-death-brain-injury-different-man.html

15. Nelson, E., & Sherwood, R. (2010, August 26). Chris Benoit's murder, suicide: Was brain damage to blame? *ABC News*. Retrieved from http://abcnews.go.com/Nightline/chris-benoits-dad-son-suffered-severe-brain-damage/story?id=11471875

16. Miller, E. K., & Cohen. J. D. (2001). An integrative theory of prefrontal cortex function. *Annual Review of Neuroscience, 24*(1): 167–202.

17. Beaver, K. M. (2009). Molecular genetics and crime. In K. M. Beaver & A. Walsh (Eds.), *Biosocial criminology: New directions in theory and research* (p. 62). New York: Routledge.

18. See review in Beaver, K. M. (2009). Molecular genetics and crime. In K. M. Beaver & A. Walsh (Eds.), *Biosocial criminology: New directions in theory and research* (pp. 62–65). New York: Routledge.

19. Beaver, K. M. (2009). Molecular genetics and crime. In K. M. Beaver & A. Walsh (Eds.), *Biosocial criminology: New directions in theory and research* (p. 66). New York: Routledge.

20. Beaver, K. M. (2009). Molecular genetics and crime. In K. M. Beaver & A. Walsh (Eds.), *Biosocial criminology: New directions in theory and research* (p. 67). New York: Routledge.

21. Beaver, K. M. (2009). Molecular genetics and crime. In K. M. Beaver & A. Walsh (Eds.), *Biosocial criminology: New directions in theory and research* (p. 67). New York: Routledge.

22. See review in Book, A. S., Starzyk, K. B., & Quinsey. V. L. (2001). The relationship between testosterone and aggression: A meta-analysis. *Aggression and Violent Behavior, 6*(6), 579–599.

23. Ellis, L. (2005). A theory explaining biological correlates of criminality. *European Journal of Criminology, 2*(3), 287–315.

24. Explanation of LPTR based on Pontius, A. A. (1996). Forensic significance of the limbic psychotic trigger reaction. *Bulletin of the American Academy of Psychiatry and the Law 24*(1), 125–134.

25. Ellis, L. (2005). A theory explaining biological correlates of criminality. *European Journal of Criminology, 2*(3), 287–315.

26. Masters, R. D., Hone, B., & Doshi, A. (1998). Environmental pollution, neurotoxicity, and criminal violence. In J. Rose (Ed.), *Environmental toxicity: Current developments* (pp. 11–46). London: Taylor and Francis.

27. Stretesky, P. B., & Lynch, M. J. (2004). The relationship between lead and crime. *Journal of Health and Social Behavior, 45*(2), 214–229.

28. Greenfeld, L. A. (1998). *Alcohol and crime: An analysis of national data on the prevalence of alcohol involvement in crime* (NCJ 168632). Washington, DC: Office of Justice Programs, U.S. Department of Justice.

29. Greenfeld, L. A. (1998). *Alcohol and crime: An analysis of national data on the prevalence of alcohol involvement in crime* (NCJ 168632, p. 22). Washington, DC: Office of Justice Programs, U.S. Department of Justice.

30. Greenfeld, L. A. (1998). *Alcohol and crime: An analysis of national data on the prevalence of alcohol involvement in crime* (NCJ 168632, p. 28). Washington, DC: Office of Justice Programs, U.S. Department of Justice.

31. Statistics reflect those who were able to describe the offender's alcohol or drug use at the time of the offense. From Greenfeld, L. A. (1998). *Alcohol and crime: An analysis of national data on the prevalence of alcohol involvement in crime* (NCJ 168632). Washington, DC: Office of Justice Programs, U.S. Department of Justice.

32. Statistics reflect those who were able to describe the offender's alcohol or drug use at the time of the offense (pp. 3–4).

33. See Martin, S. E. (2001). The links between alcohol, crime and the criminal justice system: Explanations, evidence and interventions. *American Journal of Addictions, 10*(2), 136–158.

34. Martin, S. E. (2001). The links between alcohol, crime and the criminal justice system: Explanations, evidence and interventions. *American Journal of Addictions, 10*(2), 144.

35. Martin, S. E. (2001). The links between alcohol, crime and the criminal justice system: Explanations, evidence and interventions. *American Journal of Addictions, 10*(2), 141.

36. Martin, S. E. (2001). The links between alcohol, crime and the criminal justice system: Explanations, evidence and interventions. *American Journal of Addictions, 10*(2), 142.

37. Goldstein, P. J. (1985). The drugs/violence nexus: A tripartite conceptual framework. *Journal of Drug Issues, 39*, 143–174.

38. See Pogash, C. (2003, November 23). Myth of the 'Twinkie defense': The verdict in the Dan White case wasn't based on his ingestion of junk food. *San Francisco Chronicle*. Retrieved from http://www.sfgate.com/health/article/Myth-of-the-Twinkie-defense-The-verdict-in-2511152.php

39. Pogash, C. (2003, November 23). Myth of the 'Twinkie defense': The verdict in the Dan White case wasn't based on his ingestion of junk food. *San Francisco Chronicle*, pp. 758–759. Retrieved from http://www.sfgate.com/health/article/Myth-of-the-Twinkie-defense-The-verdict-in-2511152.php

40. Benton, D. (2007). The impact of diet on anti-social, violent and criminal behavior. *Neuroscience and Biobehavioral Reviews, 31*(5), 752–774.

41. Benton, D. (2007). The impact of diet on anti-social, violent and criminal behavior. *Neuroscience and Biobehavioral Reviews, 31*(5), p. 759.

42. Benton, D. (2007). The impact of diet on anti-social, violent and criminal behavior. *Neuroscience and Biobehavioral Reviews, 31*(5), pp. 762–764.

43. See argument in Benton, D. (2007). The impact of diet on anti-social, violent and criminal behavior. *Neuroscience and Biobehavioral Reviews, 31*(5), pp. 764–766.

44. Ellis, L., &. Walsh, A. (2000). *Criminology: A global perspective*. Boston: Allyn & Bacon.

45. For example, Barber, N. (2004). Single parenthood as a predictor of cross-national variation in violent crime. *Cross-cultural Research, 38*(4), 343–358.

46. Ellis, L. (2005). A theory explaining biological correlates of criminality. *European Journal of Criminology, 2*(3), 287–315.

47. Robinson, M. (2009). No longer taboo: Crime prevention implications of biosocial criminology. In A. Walsh & K. M. Beaver (Eds.), *Biosocial criminology: New directions in theory and research* (pp. 243–263). New York: Routledge.

48. Rothman, D. J. (1980/2002). *Conscience and convenience: The asylum and its alternatives in progressive America* (p. 54). New York: Aldine de Gruyter.

49. Garland, D. (2001). *The culture of control: Crime and social order in contemporary society* (p. 8). Chicago: University of Chicago Press.

50. Feeley, M. M., & Simon, J. (1992). The new penology: Notes on the emerging strategy of corrections and its implications. *Criminology, 30*(4), 449–474.

51. For example, American Psychological Association. (2013). Specialty guidelines for forensic psychology. *American Psychologist, 68*(1), 7–19.

52. Ramsland, K. (2009). The facts about fiction: What Grissom could learn about forensic psychology. *Journal of Psychiatry & Law, 37*(1), 37–50.

53. American Psychological Association. (2013). Specialty guidelines for forensic psychology. *American psychologist, 68*(1), 7–19.

54. See review in John, O. P., & Srivastava, S. (1999). The big five trait taxonomy: History, measurement, and theoretical perspectives. In L. A. Pervin & O. P. John (Eds.), *Handbook of personality: Theory and research* (2nd ed., pp. 102–138). New York: Guilford.

55. Eysenck, H. J. (1964/1977). *Crime and personality*. London: Routledge and Kegan Paul.

56. Eysenck, H. J. (1964/1977). *Crime and personality* (pp. 81–82). London: Routledge and Kegan Paul.

57. Eysenck, H. J. (1964/1977). *Crime and personality* (pp. 90–91). London: Routledge and Kegan Paul.

58. Digman, J. M. (1996). The curious history of the five-factor model. In J. S. Wiggins (Ed.), *The five-factor model of personality: Theoretical perspectives* (pp. 1–20). New York: Guilford Press.

59. Costa, P. T., Jr., & McCrae., R. R. (1992). *Revised NEO Personality Inventory (NEO-PI-R) and NEO Five-Factor Inventory (NEO-FFI) professional manual*. Odessa, FL: Psychological Assessment Resources. See application in Miller, J. D., Lynam, D. R., Widiger, T. A., & Leukefeld., C. (2001). Personality disorders as extreme variants of common personality dimensions: Can the five-factor personality model adequately represent psychopathy? *Journal of Personality*, *69*(2), 253–276.

60. Cloninger, C. R., Svrakic, D. M., & Przybeck, T. R. (1993). A psychobiological model of temperament and character. *Archives of General Psychiatry, 50*(12), 975–990.

61. Miller, J. D., & Lynam, D. (2001). Structural models of personality and their relation to antisocial behavior: A meta-analytic review. *Criminology, 39*(4), 765–798.

62. Samuels, J. S., Bienvenu, O. J., Cullen, B., Costra, P. T., Jr., Eaton, W. W., & Nestadt, G. (2004). Personality dimensions and arrest. *Comprehensive Psychiatry, 45*(4), 275–280.

63. Freud, S. (1933). *New introductory lectures on psychoanalysis*. Sprott, W. J. H. (Transl.). New York: W.W. Norton.

64. Hare, R. D. (1996). Psychopathy: A construct whose time has come. *Criminal Justice and Behavior, 23*(1), 25–54.

65. Gilbert, G. M. (1970). *Personality dynamics: A biosocial approach* (p. 302). New York: Harper & Row. See also Wiebe, R. P. (2009). Psychopathy. In A. Walsh & K. M. Beaver (Eds.), *Biosocial criminology: New directions in theory and research* (pp. 225–242). New York: Routledge: Taylor & Francis Group.

66. Miller, J. D., Lynam, D. R., Widiger, T. A., & Leukefeld, C. (2001). Personality disorders as extreme variants of common personality dimensions: Can the five-factor personality model adequately represent psychopathy? *Journal of Personality*, *69*(2), 253–276.

67. Walsh, A., & Wu, H.-H. (2008). Differentiating antisocial personality disorder, psychopathy, and sociopathy: Evolutionary, genetic, neurological, and sociological conditions. *Criminal Justice Studies, 21*(2), 135–152.

68. Walsh, A., & Wu, H.-H. (2008). Differentiating antisocial personality disorder, psychopathy, and sociopathy: Evolutionary, genetic, neurological, and sociological conditions. *Criminal Justice Studies, 21*(2), 140.

69. Walsh, A., & Wu, H.-H. (2008). Differentiating antisocial personality disorder, psychopathy, and sociopathy: Evolutionary, genetic, neurological, and sociological conditions. *Criminal Justice Studies, 21*(2), 141.

70. Walsh, A., & Wu, H.-H. (2008). Differentiating antisocial personality disorder, psychopathy, and sociopathy: Evolutionary, genetic, neurological, and sociological conditions. *Criminal Justice Studies, 21*(2), 142.

71. Walsh, A., & Wu, H.-H. (2008). Differentiating antisocial personality disorder, psychopathy, and sociopathy: Evolutionary, genetic, neurological, and sociological conditions. *Criminal Justice Studies, 21*(2), 142

72. Miller, J. D., Lynam, D. R., Widiger, T. A., & Leukefeld., C. (2001). Personality disorders as extreme variants of common personality dimensions: Can the five-factor personality model adequately represent psychopathy? *Journal of Personality*, *69*(2), 257–258.

73. Miller, J. D., Lynam, D. R., Widiger, T. A., & Leukefeld., C. (2001). Personality disorders as extreme variants of common personality dimensions: Can the five-factor personality model adequately represent psychopathy? *Journal of Personality*, *69*(2), 263.

74. See review in Wiebe, R. P. (2009). Psychopathy. In A. Walsh & K. M. Beaver (Eds.), *Biosocial criminology: New directions in theory and research* (pp. 230–233). New York: Routledge: Taylor & Francis Group.

75. Miller, J. D., Lynam, D. R., Widiger, T. A., & Leukefeld., C. (2001). Personality disorders as extreme variants of common personality dimensions: Can the five-factor personality model adequately represent psychopathy? *Journal of Personality*, *69*(2), 254.

76. Hare, R. D., & Neumann, C. S. (2007). The PCL-R assessment of psychopathy: Development, structural properties, and new directions. In C. J. Patrick (Ed.), *Handbook of psychopathy* (pp. 58–88). New York: Guilford Press.
77. Hare, R. D., & Neumann, C. S. (2007). The PCL-R assessment of psychopathy: Development, structural properties, and new directions. In C. J. Patrick (Ed.), *Handbook of psychopathy* (p. 58). New York: Guilford Press.
78. Hare, R. D., & Neumann, C. S. (2007). The PCL-R assessment of psychopathy: Development, structural properties, and new directions. In C. J. Patrick (Ed.), *Handbook of psychopathy* (p. 58). New York: Guilford Press.
79. Walsh, A., & Wu, H. -H. (2008). Differentiating antisocial personality disorder, psychopathy, and sociopathy: Evolutionary, genetic, neurological, and sociological conditions. *Criminal Justice Studies, 21*(2): 135–152.
80. Walsh & Wu, pp. 146–147.
81. American Psychiatric Association. (2013). *Diagnostic and statistical manual of mental disorders* (5th ed.). Arlington, VA: Author.
82. American Psychiatric Association. (2013). *Diagnostic and statistical manual of mental disorders* (5th ed.). Arlington, VA: Author.
83. American Psychiatric Association. (2013). *Diagnostic and statistical manual of mental disorders* (5th ed.). Arlington, VA: Author.
84. Hare, R. D., & Neumann, C. S. (2007). The PCL-R assessment of psychopathy: Development, structural properties, and new directions. In C. J. Patrick (Ed.), *Handbook of psychopathy* (p. 61). New York: Guilford Press.
85. Samenow, S. E. (2004/1984). *Inside the criminal mind*. New York: Crown Publishers.
86. Walters, G. D. (1990). *The criminal lifestyle: Patterns of serious criminal conduct*. Newbury Park, CA: Sage.
87. Walters, G. D. (1995). The psychological inventory of criminal thinking styles: Part I: Reliability and preliminary validity. *Criminal Justice and Behavior, 22*(3), 307–325.
88. Walters, G. D. (1990). *The criminal lifestyle: Patterns of serious criminal conduct* (pp. 128–155). Newbury Park, CA: Sage.
89. Walters, G. D. (1990). *The criminal lifestyle: Patterns of serious criminal conduct* (p. 151). Newbury Park, CA: Sage.
90. Lipsey, M. W., Landenberger, N. A., & Wilson, S. J. (2007). Effects of cognitive-behavioral programs for criminal offenders. *Campbell Systematic Reviews,* 6. doi: 10.4073/csr.2007.6.
91. National Institute of Mental Health. *The numbers count: Mental disorders in America*. Retrieved from http://www.nimh.nih.gov/health/publications/the-numbers-count-mental-disorders-in-america/index.shtml
92. National Institute of Mental Health. (n.d.). *Bipolar disorder*. Retrieved from http://www.ncbi.nlm.nih.gov/pubmedhealth/PMH0001924/
93. National Institute of Mental Health. (n.d.). *Schizophrenia—Paranoid type*. Retrieved from http://www.ncbi.nlm.nih.gov/pubmedhealth/PMH0001932/
94. James, D. J., & Glaze, L. E. (2006). *Mental health problems of prison and jail inmates*. (NCJ 213600, p. 1). Washington, DC: U.S. Department of Justice, Bureau of Justice Statistics.
95. James, D. J., & Glaze, L. E. (2006). *Mental health problems of prison and jail inmates* (NCJ 213600, p. 5). Washington, DC: U.S. Department of Justice, Bureau of Justice Statistics.
96. James, D. J., & Glaze, L. E. (2006). *Mental health problems of prison and jail inmates*. (NCJ 213600, p. 10). Washington, DC: U.S. Department of Justice, Bureau of Justice Statistics.
97. Adam Lanza's mom was alarmed by his gruesome images. (2013, April 8). *USA Today*. Retrieved from http://www.usatoday.com/story/news/nation/2013/04/08/adam-lanza-nancy-daily-news-shooter-gruesome-images/2063381/
98. What Causes Autism? Autism fact sheet (2013, May 7). National Institute of Neurological Disorders and Stroke: National Institutes of Health. Retrieved from http://www.ninds.nih.gov/disorders/autism/detail_autism.htm
99. What are some common signs of autism? Autism fact sheet (2013, May 7). National Institute of Neurological Disorders and Stroke: National Institutes of Health. Retrieved from http://www.ninds.nih.gov/disorders/autism/detail_autism.htm

100. What are some common signs of autism? Autism fact sheet (2013, May 7). National Institute of Neurological Disorders and Stroke: National Institutes of Health. Retrieved from http://www.ninds.nih.gov/disorders/autism/detail_autism.htm
101. Kleinfield, N. R., Rivera, R., & Kovaleski, S. F. (2013, March 28). Newtown killer's obsessions, in chilling detail. *New York Times.* Retrieved from http://www.nytimes.com/2013/03/29/nyregion/search-warrants-reveal-items-seized-at-adam-lanzas-home .html?pagewanted=all&_r=0
102. Breslow, J. M. (2013, February 19). For Adam Lanza, a debated diagnosis that meant "more to be worried about." *PBS.* Retrieved from http://www.pbs.org/wgbh/pages/frontline/social-issues/raising-adam-lanza/for-adam-lanza-a-debated-diagnosis-that-meant-more-to-be-worried-about/
103. Martinez, M., &. Ariosto, D. (2012). Adam Lanza's family: Mom liked parlor games, guns; dad, a tax exec, remarried. *CNN.* Retrieved from http://www.cnn.com/2012/12/15/us/connecticut-lanza-family-profile

chapter five

Social structures as a cause of crime

Chapter objectives

After studying this chapter, the reader should be able to

- Explain how the social structural approach differs from other criminological perspectives
- Identify the main contributions of the social structural perspective
- Discuss the relationship of urban growth to criminality
- Explain the concept of social disorganization
- Describe broken windows theory
- Compare and contrast the social disorganization, strain, and subcultural traditions
- Describe how American cities have changed since the early 1900s, and its relevance for understanding crime
- Identify weaknesses of the social structural perspective

Introduction

This chapter presents social structural explanations of crime. It has long been recognized that crime is not evenly distributed across space, with studies dating back to the early 1800s observing higher rates of crime in cities compared to rural areas.[1] The theories in this chapter attempt to explain that spatial pattern by looking to the dynamics of social status, relationships, and social institutions such as the economy and family.

The assumptions of social structural theorists include the following:

- Crime is a normal response to certain social conditions.
- Social problems tend to cluster among structurally disadvantaged populations, and particularly within areas of concentrated disadvantage.
- Crime is most likely to occur in neighborhoods with deteriorated housing, low rates of home ownership, high rates of residential mobility, and low collective efficacy.
- Race- and class-based social exclusion perpetuates disadvantage and, by extension, encourages crime.
- Crime can be reduced through neighborhood-level interventions and changes in the overall social structure.

Structural disadvantage can lead to crime via three mechanisms, which form the subcategories of this perspective. Although all three focus on crime in impoverished neighborhoods, they can be distinguished as follows:

1. "Social disorganization theories" focus on the neighborhood's physical conditions, including the populations present, economic resources, and the state of physical structures (e.g., deterioration or overcrowding).

2. "Strain theories" examine the location of these communities within opportunity structures, and the resulting effects on the population.
3. "Subcultural theories" identify the alternative value systems that arise from disadvantaged circumstances.

Central to the social structural perspective is the idea that human behavior is more than a matter of choice or personal characteristics. Two people with similar dispositions can have different propensities toward crime depending on their position within the social structure. All other things being equal, the perspective holds that someone in a disadvantaged neighborhood who faces discrimination and limited employment opportunities will be at greater risk for criminality than an individual raised in an affluent area with high status and ample employment opportunities.

Anomie

> The urbanization of the world, which is one of the most impressive facts of modern times, has wrought profound changes in virtually every phase of social life. The recency and rapidity of urbanization in the United States accounts for the acuteness of our urban problems and our lack of awareness of them.
>
> **Louis Wirth, 1938[2]**

> Urbanism represents a revolutionary change in the whole pattern of social life.
>
> **Kingsley Davis, 1955[3]**

The social structural perspective has its roots in sociological studies of urbanization and industrialization from the late 1800s and early 1900s. Rapid developments in factory technology encouraged population movement into cities, where different racial groups and new immigrants competed for employment. Racial groups settled into different areas as the result of a combination of housing policies, discriminatory banking and real-estate practices, and racially motivated violence. Relations not just among groups, but also among individuals, underwent a dramatic transformation: People were now coming into greater contact with one another, but any given interaction was likely to be more superficial and utilitarian in nature than would have been the case within smaller communities.[4]

The nature of these rapid changes drew the attention of sociologists. Emile Durkheim, one of the "fathers of sociology," observed that these new social arrangements brought new sources of tension and conflict.[5] He suggested that small agricultural communities of the past were characterized by shared traditions and values, and thus benefited from "mechanical solidarity," in which people of like mind would collectively enforce social norms. In the new urban environment, society could no longer rely on shared traditions and values to bond the community together, resulting in a state of "anomie" or normlessness. This represented a fundamental change in social organization that called for new ways to maintain social cohesion.

According to Durkheim, stability in this new social environment would come from individuals' growing dependence on one another for services. He coined this form of cohesion "organic solidarity." Similar to organs in a body, each individual fulfills a different purpose through their specialized tasks, but all are rendered reliant on one another to keep society functioning smoothly. In this new economic structure, a person who specializes in medicine, for example, becomes dependent on others for services such as manufacturing, construction and food production, whereas workers in each of those areas are in turn reliant on doctors and other professionals to meet their needs.

Durkheim's concept of anomie has served as the basis for future theorists' work on the effects of urbanization on social relations. Although over time criminologists have begun to focus less on the initial process of urbanization and more on the effects of inequality within urban communities, social disorganization, strain, and subcultural theorists all explore various norm conflicts and cultural divergences and thus might be seen as extensions of Durkheim's early work.

Social ecology

Durkheim's work laid the foundation for criminologists to explore social dynamics in urban areas, including those relevant to crime and control. A group of researchers associated with the sociology program at the University of Chicago, collectively known as the "Chicago School," shared Durkheim's curiosity about the effects of urbanization. Working from the premise that social life was subject to natural patterns similar to those observed in the field of biology, they used Chicago as their "natural laboratory" to identify and understand these patterns.

The Chicago School viewed the urban environment as a particularly rich landscape for studying human nature. Specifically, they held that urban life magnifies natural human tendencies by

- Allowing people to seek out like-minded individuals, whose association results in the cultivation of shared interests
- Reducing informal social controls through the anonymity of urban life
- Introducing greater temptation

In the words of Robert Park,

> The small community often tolerates eccentricity. The city, on the contrary, rewards it. Neither the criminal, the defective, nor the genius has the same opportunity to develop his innate disposition in a small town than he invariably finds in a great city.[6]

By simultaneously presenting new temptations and the weakening of inhibiting social forces, the city becomes a perfect laboratory for the examination of a range of human behaviors, particularly crime and vice.[7]

Burgess[8] observed that urban areas tended to develop in certain patterned ways just as we might observe patterns in how ants structure colonies or beavers construct dams. According to his concentric zones model, the natural pattern of urban development starts with the formation of central business districts and develops outward in a process of succession. As the area immediately surrounding the city center becomes aged, heavily populated, and industrialized, it experiences urban decay. Those with adequate financial resources move to newer developments farther from the city center to escape the deteriorating conditions. Burgess[9] explained the resulting urban pattern in his "concentric zones model":

Zone 1: Central Business District. The downtown area that serves as the center of "economic, cultural, and political life," typified by the presence of government offices, a substantial retail presence, office buildings, transportation hubs, museums, and other businesses.[10]

Zone 2: Area of Transition. The least desirable space in the city. As the housing stock deteriorates, it becomes inhabited by those who cannot afford to live elsewhere, including recently settled immigrant populations. The proximity to factories further decreases its desirability as a residential area.

Zone 3: Workingmen's Homes. Occupied by those who want to reside close to their employment, but have attained sufficient economic success to move from Zone 2.

Zone 4: Residential Zone. Dominated by expensive apartments or gated communities.

Zone 5: Commuters' Zone. Composed of suburban areas that allow an escape from urban life while remaining within commutable distance to the city center.

According to Burgess, recent immigrants and other city newcomers tend to live in the affordable zone of transition. As they adjust to city life, they undergo a "reorganization of attitudes and conduct" as they shed old habits and beliefs and adopt new goals and ways of life.[11] Although at the individual level anomie, or the breakdown of norms, is a temporary experience associated with the adjustment to urban life, the constant influx of new residents through the zone of transition leads to anomie becoming a stable presence within the zone.

Social disorganization

> The urban world, with its anonymity, its greater freedom, the more impersonal character of its relationships, and the varied assortment of economic, social, and cultural backgrounds in its communities, provides a general setting particularly conducive to [deviance]. In the low-income areas, where there is the greatest deprivation and frustration, where, in the history of the city, immigrant and migrant groups have brought together the widest variety of divergent cultural traditions and institutions, and where there exists the greatest disparity between the social values to which the people aspire and the availability of facilities for acquiring these values in conventional ways, the development of crime as an organized way of life is most marked.
>
> **Clifford Shaw and Henry McKay, 1942**[12]

In the early twentieth century social ecologists began to explore spatial patterns of urban crime in greater depth. Chicago School researchers Clifford Shaw and Henry McKay produced the landmark study in this area, in which they analyzed patterns of juvenile delinquency in Chicago using Park and Burgess's model of urban zones. They found that delinquency was highest in the transitional zone, and that this pattern held remarkably stable throughout the decades under study and despite high rates of residential turnover in that zone. Similar patterns were found in other cities throughout the United States.[12] This supported Burgess's observation that the transitional zone is characterized by a concentration of social ills.

Shaw and McKay posited that these areas were vulnerable to crime because of the presence of "social disorganization"—conflicting value systems that stem from weak social institutions and limited opportunities for conventional success. They believed that within such neighborhoods criminogenic values are passed from one generation to the next through a process of "cultural transmission," which serves to sustain the high rates of delinquency over time. The weakness of prosocial institutions in these areas facilitated the cultural transmission of crime through their inability to effectively impart conventional beliefs to youth in the face of competing value systems.

A key finding within their work was that race and ethnicity do not independently affect crime rates. Shaw and McKay found that delinquency rates in certain areas remained elevated regardless of changes in racial/ethnic composition. They also noted that as members of all racial and ethnic groups moved outside those areas, they no longer engaged in high rates of delinquency. This supported that crime was attributable to qualities of the place, not the demography of its population, providing a powerful counterdiscourse to some of the racist perspectives dominant at the time (see Chapter 3). Their work also countered the notion that criminality was inborn, since crime patterns were more strongly wedded to specific spaces than specific people.

Shaw and McKay's work was significant for confirming that crime is not evenly distributed, and that it tends to concentrate in areas plagued by other social ills, such as disadvantage and dilapidated housing. In turn, crime reduction efforts that stem from this perspective focus on working with neighborhood residents "to modify those aspects of the community life which provide the appropriate setting for delinquency careers."[12]

THE CHICAGO SCHOOL OF CRIMINOLOGY: REALITY OR MYTH?

The phrase "Chicago School" is often used to identify a tradition of research stemming from the Department of Sociology at the University of Chicago in the early 1900s. In criminology, the Chicago School is often held as the gold standard for research on urban crime. William Julius Wilson, who had a career at the University of Chicago spanning from the 1970s to the 1990s, described the legacy of the Chicago School as follows:

> The most distinctive phase of this research ... was completed before 1950.... These studies often combined statistical and observational analyses in making distinctive empirical and theoretical contributions to our understanding of urban processes, social problems and urban growth, and, commencing in the late 1930s, the nature of race and class subjugation in urban areas. The Chicago social scientists recognized and legitimized the neighborhood—including the ghetto neighborhood—as a subject for scientific analysis. Chicago, a community of neighborhoods, was considered a laboratory from which generalizations about broader urban conditions could be made.[13]

(Continued)

THE CHICAGO SCHOOL OF CRIMINOLOGY: REALITY OR MYTH? (*CONTINUED*)

Howard Becker,[14] who studied at the University of Chicago in the 1940s and 1950s, challenged the notion that the Department's professors ever formed a cohesive school of thought as he held that they never shared a uniform approach to research or theory. Louis Wirth, an urban sociologist who studied under Robert Park, "often said that he could never understand what people were taking about when they spoke of the Chicago School, since he could find nothing, no idea or style of work, that he and his colleagues shared."[15]

What is not in doubt is the significance of the Chicago School for criminology. Collectively, researchers in this tradition

- Drew attention to the conditions in disadvantaged urban areas
- Provided insight into the social dynamics of urban environments
- Modeled the application of both statistical and qualitative methods to understand crime in urban settings

Significant contributions from the Chicago School include the works of Park and Burgess and Shaw and McKay, along with famous ethnographies on topics such as poverty,[16] gangs,[17] and homelessness.[18] More recently, Sudhir Venkatesh, a 1997 graduate of the University of Chicago's doctoral program, has extended the tradition of qualitative sociology with his ethnographic work on gangs.

Broken windows theory

> Untended property becomes fair game for people out for fun or plunder and even for people who ordinarily would not dream of doing such things and who probably consider themselves law-abiding.
>
> **James Wilson and George Kelling, 1982**[19]

Social disorganization theory was influential in laying the groundwork for more recent theoretical developments. James Wilson and George Kelling's "broken windows theory"[19] honed in on the physical aspects of disorganization in the assertion that visual signs of neighborhood deterioration can directly contribute to more serious forms of criminality. They based their argument on an experiment by Stanford psychologist Phillip Zimbardo. In the experiment, cars were staged to appear abandoned and left in two different areas to observe each community's response. A car left in a working-class neighborhood in New York was quickly targeted for stripping and vandalizing, whereas another left in a more affluent community in Palo Alto, California, remained untouched for more than a week. When Zimbardo stepped in and took a sledgehammer to the car, though, passersby quickly joined in. The conclusion was that people are more willing to engage in destructive behavior if they believe nobody cares about the target. Once the proverbial window is broken, it sends a cue to other potentially motivated offenders.

Evidence of broken windows theory can be observed in everyday life. When a visitor enters a spotless home, they are more likely to make an extra effort to respect the space by removing their shoes and taking other steps to maintain its cleanliness. If a property is not well tended, others will be less conscientious about taking steps to care for it. Extrapolated to the neighborhood level, Wilson and Kelling argued that visual signs of disorder such as unkempt properties and public drunkenness pave the way for more serious crime. They identified two mechanisms for this effect:

1. It signals to motivated offenders that nobody cares, thus increasing their willingness to engage in crime.
2. It creates fear among law-abiding citizens, rendering them less likely to intervene when they see misbehavior.

As signs of disorder feed crime, the presence of crime perpetuates further disorder, sending the neighborhood into a spiral of decline. Because law-abiding residents will be hesitant to disrupt this cycle as they become more fearful, Wilson and Kelling argued that police must step in to aggressively police signs of disorder and save the community from the "broken windows" phenomenon. Many large urban police departments did move toward order maintenance strategies, and cities increasingly passed laws that criminalized actions such as loitering, drinking and urinating in public, and aggressive panhandling[20] as part of a strategy to reduce crime.

Broken windows theory carries logical appeal. Reductions in visible disorder can increase community pride, contribute to residents' quality of life, and reduce fear of crime, in addition to its potential effect on crime rates. At the same time, there are also some scathing criticisms of the order maintenance approach:

- It may encourage aggressive policing practices, leading area residents to feel harassed.
- The crackdown on physical signs of disorder can have the practical effect of criminalizing the homelessness via trespassing, loitering, and panhandling laws.
- To the extent that criminal justice involvement can limit one's future employment opportunities and economic success,[21] expanding the net of criminal justice involvement in a community may actually contribute to further disadvantage.

ORDER MAINTENANCE POLICING IN NEW YORK[22]

New York City (NYC) gained international attention for a dramatic crime drop that began in the 1990s. The reduction in crime was astonishing: Between 1990 and 2009, homicides dropped nearly 80%. Internationally, police leaders were so impressed by NYC that they began to look at it as a model for their own agencies. William Bratton, the police chief at the time, attributed the dramatic crime drop in part to the adoption of an order maintenance approach:

> The NYPD targeted low level social disorder and crime … focusing its efforts on "graffiti, aggressive panhandling, fare beating, public drunkenness, unlicensed vending, public drinking, public urination and other misdemeanor offenses."[23]

The department cracked down heavily on these offenses, and began to implement an aggressive policy of "stop, question, and frisk" to seize guns and detect low-level drug offenders.

(Continued)

ORDER MAINTENANCE POLICING IN NEW YORK (*CONTINUED*)

Although on its surface NYC appears to be the poster city for a broken windows approach, order maintenance policing is only part of the story. Although nowhere else quite as dramatically as NYC, the entire nation has experienced a significant crime drop since the early 1990s; whatever factors contributed to the nationwide trend likely also played a role in NYC. The NYPD also adopted new crime analysis software that enabled a data-driven policing strategy, which likely also contributed to police effectiveness. Finally, while there is no doubt that NYC's crime rate has experienced a substantial decline, its precise magnitude has been called into question by the discovery that the NYPD manipulated some of its crime statistics.[24]

There is also a less popular side to order maintenance policing. The NYPD has faced intense criticism for the impact of their policing efforts on citizens' quality of life. Residents complained about the disproportionate targeting of poor minority youth; an inefficient stop and frisk policy that rarely results in the detection of contraband but frequently affects law-abiding citizens; and more frequent abuses of police power, which have resulted in an increase in complaints against the police. For example, almost 90% of those stopped were minorities, and by 2008 only 0.15% of frisks (or 1 in 650) resulted in the recovery of a gun.[25] At the time of this writing, a federal district judge had ruled the NYPD's stop and frisk policy in violation of residents' 4th and 14th Amendment rights, although the ruling was still being challenged in court.[26] This complex set of circumstances has led New York to serve as both a model and a cautionary tale regarding order maintenance policing.

Collective efficacy

Sampson et al.[27] sought to identify protective factors that could shield neighborhoods from processes of decline. They focused their effort on "collective efficacy," which they defined as "the linkage of mutual trust and the willingness to intervene for the common good."[28] By extension, Sampson et al. predicted that a community in which residents are willing to actively engage in opposition to antisocial behavior might be able to successfully protect against the development of criminal subcultures.

To test their theory, they surveyed residents from different parts of Chicago, asking them to rate the accuracy of statements such as "people around here are willing to help their neighbors" and "this is a close-knit neighborhood." Respondents were also asked to rate the likelihood that they would intervene if they witnessed children skip school, disrespect adults, vandalize a building in the neighborhood, or engage in other deviant behaviors.[29] On the basis of an analysis of their findings, Sampson and Laub concluded that collective efficacy could in fact effectively buffer the impact of social disorganization on violent crime rates.

The social disorganization tradition provides an important starting point for thinking about spatial patterns of crime, and recognizing that social structural factors have the power to influence criminal behavior. That said, the approach also has weaknesses:

- Its explanatory power is limited to crime in disadvantaged urban areas.
- It does not account for the many people in disorganized areas who abstain from crime.
- It minimizes the role of human agency in criminal behavior.

- The term "disorganization" overlooks the ordered social patterns that exist in even the highest crime communities.
- This approach ignores the tendency of people to "drift" in and out of criminality, and to desist from crime as they age.
- It gives insufficient attention to the macro-level social forces that shape socially disorganized areas, such as racism and class inequality.

Strain theories

> Certain aspects of the social structure may generate countermores and antisocial behavior precisely because of differential emphases on goals and regulations. In the extreme case, the latter may be so vitiated by the goal-emphasis that the range of behavior is limited only by considerations of technical expediency.... As this process continues, the integration of the society becomes tenuous and anomie ensues.
>
> **Robert Merton, 1938**[30]

Shaw and McKay suggested that crime may be more likely where residents experience barriers to conventional success, but they did not elaborate on the mechanisms by which this might happen. Strain theories build on Durkheim's concept of anomie to explore these mechanisms in greater depth. The first "strain theory" was presented by Robert Merton,[31] who proposed that crime is rooted in a disjunction between a person's goals and their ability to achieve them through legitimate means. Merton observed that success in the United States is almost universally measured by individual economic achievement, but the conventional pathways for economic success are not universally accessible. The discord of these combined circumstances causes strain among the disadvantaged.

Merton recognized that not everyone who experiences strain turns to crime. In a stable society, most people will continue to follow the rules and work toward their goals. Others might continue to go through the socially accepted motions, even after they have given up on achieving their goals. In other cases, though, strain can contribute to criminal behavior, as when those cut off from the socially approved pathways for financial success pursue alternative, sometimes criminal paths to attain it.

Merton identified five possible adaptations to strain, the first two of which are noncriminal:

1. Conformity: Acceptance of both conventional goals and the institutionalized means for attaining them. Conformists help maintain stability in society by respecting its rules.
2. Ritualism: Rejection of commonly held cultural goals, but continued engagement in the institutionalized mechanisms for attainment. A ritualist may give up on dreams of material wealth, but nonetheless continue to "go through the motions."
3. Innovation: Acceptance of the conventional goals of society, but not the institutionalized means for attaining them. An innovator may continue to strive for financial success, but decide to pursue it through illegal means.
4. Retreatism: Rejection of broadly held cultural goals and the accepted means for achieving them. A retreatist withdraws their efforts to be successful in life.
5. Rebellion: Replacement of broadly held cultural goals and the institutionalized means of achieving them with new goals and standards for achievement substituted in their place.

Merton's Five Means of Adaptation

Adaptation	Conventional Goals	Conventional Means	Example
Conformity	Accepts	Accepts	Rachel goes to school and works hard with the goal of becoming a successful lawyer.
Ritualism	Rejects	Accepts	Jimmy continues to go to school every day, even though he has given up on his goals of going to college and obtaining a high-paying job.
Innovation	Accepts	Rejects	Michael wants to make a good living but refuses to "play by the rules." He decides to sell drugs to make some fast money.
Retreatism	Rejects	Rejects	Angela has given up on her prospects for education and financial success. She drops out of school and passes her days hanging out with friends. Sometimes she turns to drugs to pass the time and ease her depression.
Rebellion	Rejects and replaces	Rejects and replaces	Frustrated with society's emphasis on financial success, David drops out of school and joins a revolutionary group. Their goal is to overthrow what is seen as an unfair and unjust capitalist system.

Merton called attention to the role of society's opportunity structure vis-à-vis its cultural standards measures of success. Those who have goals that are rendered unattainable by conventional means due to their structurally disadvantaged position may be tempted to break the rules. Still, Merton left several questions unanswered:

- What accounts for the selection of one mode of adaptation over others?
- Why do some people with ample access to legitimate pathways for success still engage in crime?
- What accounts for nonutilitarian crimes, such as domestic violence or sexual assault?

Differential opportunity theory

Although blocked access to conventional goals may explain why economically disadvantaged individuals are more prone to criminality, it does not explain why criminality is not more widespread within the middle and upper classes. If those of the higher classes freely choose between legitimate and illegitimate means for obtaining success, would not more individuals choose crime to gain a competitive advantage over those who play by the rules? Richard Cloward[32] took on this question in his "differential opportunity theory," and concluded that just as access to conventional means is differentially distributed, so too are opportunities to engage in illicit behavior. Even those individuals of economic advantage who are motivated to engage in crime may not know where to start. They may face limitations including the following:

- Few opportunities to learn illegitimate skills, such as theft or burglary
- Lack of access to criminal networks, as with accessing a distributor for drug dealing
- Greater disapproval and intolerance from the surrounding community

Cloward thus argued that both legitimate and illicit opportunities are unequally distributed according to one's ethnicity, gender, and, most importantly, class.[33]

Institutional anomie theory

Messner and Rosenfeld[34] saw insight in Merton's strain theory, but also suggested that it fell short by failing to account for people who do have access to legitimate means of success but nonetheless engage in economically driven crime, as with white-collar criminals. In response to this weakness, Messner and Rosenfeld suggest that the emphasis on financial success causes crime not directly as a result of offenders striving for goal attainment, but rather indirectly via its effect on culture. They hold that the emphasis on material success within the United States is so strong that it

- Encourages people to strive for wealth by any means necessary
- Plays the dominant role in shaping other major social institutions, such as family, politics, and education
- Weakens the power of other normative institutions

This proposition can still explain the concentration of crime in poor urban areas, where it can be expected that residents are that much more driven to commit crime to achieve material success, but it also provides a mechanism for understanding why those with access to conventional means may still engage in crime to further their position.

This theory challenges the notion that simply increasing access to conventional opportunities can reduce crime. "Greater equality of opportunity and a redistribution of economic resources would not by themselves diminish the importance of winning and losing, nor would they eliminate the strong temptations to try to win by any means necessary."[35] Rather, there would need to be a fundamental redefinition of success in our culture to reinforce the importance of institutions such as family and education over financial gain.

General strain theory

Robert Agnew expanded Merton's concept of strain in a different direction. The core argument in "general strain theory" is that strain may result from either an inability to obtain a desired state—including but not limited to financial wealth—or an inability to escape an undesired state. Thus, Agnew reconceptualizes strain to refer to any life stressor. Those who find themselves facing stressful situations without appropriate coping mechanisms may be compelled to crime.[36] Agnew's contributions provided several important augmentations to strain theory:

- It highlights that not all crime is related to blocked goal attainment.
- Since youth typically have less power than adults to choose their circumstances, it provides an explanation for why crime peaks in adolescence and young adulthood and then declines with age.
- It has the potential to explain both instrumental and expressive crimes to the extent that crime may be committed to obtain a goal or escape an undesired situation, or out of anger and frustration for being unable to do so.
- It more easily accounts for middle-class criminality, as those at all levels of the social strata experience stress.

Agnew later expanded his theory to specify the different types of strain that may lead to crime:

- Failure to achieve positively valued goals: This is the type of strain most consistent with Merton's conceptualization of strain, although Agnew expanded it to consider nonmonetary as well as short-term goals, including peer approval[37] and just outcomes.[38]
- Removal of positively valued stimuli: Breakups, family divorces, the death of loved ones, and other forms of loss can result in an immense amount of stress. Agnew suggests that it may lead to crime through drug use, attempts at revenge, or efforts to "retrieve the lost stimuli or obtain substitute stimuli."[39]
- Presentation of negative stimuli: Victimization, poor quality relationships, and physically uncomfortable environments can stimulate crime among those looking to escape or cope with the circumstances.

As Agnew continued to develop general strain theory, he suggested that "strains are most likely to result in crime when they (1) are seen as unjust, (2) are seen as high in magnitude, (3) are associated with low social control, and (4) create some pressure or incentive to engage in criminal coping."[40] From this perspective, crime can be addressed through the reduction of strain or an increase in the accessibility of noncriminal coping mechanisms.

BREAKING BAD FROM A STRAIN PERSPECTIVE

AMC's hit show *Breaking Bad* ran for five seasons. Millions of viewers got caught up in the fictional story of Walter White, a high school chemistry teacher with a grim cancer diagnosis who decides to apply his "know-how" to manufacture crystal methamphetamine for his family's financial future. Despite his technical knowledge of chemistry, though, he lacks the knowledge and connections necessary to bring his product to market. His predicament is solved when he recruits former student Jesse Pinkman after learning that he has experience in drug sales. Much of the series is based on their partnership and on the predicaments that arise within Walter's family as a result of his crimes.

Breaking Bad's storyline is highly consistent with the strain perspective. Both Merton's strain theory and Agnew's general strain theory explain Walter's initial motivation—he was in financial straits and experiencing significant sources of nonfinancial stress when he embarked on his illicit activities. Messner and Rosenfeld's institutional anomie theory can account for Walter's risk-taking: Given society's emphasis on financially providing for one's family, he felt that obtaining an influx of funds was the best way that he could care for his loved ones, even when in actuality his endeavors pulled him away from home, caused tension in his marriage, and placed his family at risk. Finally, even with so many sources of "strain" compelling him toward crime, his foray into the crystal methamphetamine industry would not have come to fruition if he had not found someone with the know-how to get his product to market—a detail only accounted for by differential opportunity theory.

Subcultural theories

Embedded within early Chicago School works were references to the presence of conflicting value sets in socially disorganized areas. These works presented few details about these alternative and potentially criminal values, leaving subsequent theorists to fill in the gaps. Subculture theorists do just that: They focus on the subcultural values that develop in socially disorganized areas, typically through the study of gangs and other adolescent peer groups (often referenced as "athletic groups" or "street corner groups" in early criminological works). Cloward and Ohlin defined delinquent subcultures as those "in which certain forms of delinquent activity are essential requirements for the performance of [its] dominant roles."[41]

Delinquent subculture theory

Albert Cohen's "delinquent subculture theory"[42] aligned with strain theorists in recognizing low-income youths' difficulty in obtaining conventional markers of success, but focused attention on the resultant formation of delinquent subcultures. According to Cohen, the success of efforts to obtain upward mobility is contingent on the decisions of gatekeepers such as teachers and business people who hold the power to grant or deny access to others. These gatekeepers value traditionally "middle-class" characteristics such as ambition, personal responsibility, and the acceptance of delayed gratification, whereas lower-class youth are presumed to have limited access to the tools needed to meet these "middle-class measuring rods."

Cohen argued that the pursuit of social mobility in the face of repeated rejection results in psychological stress. To relieve this uncomfortable state, low-income individuals create an oppositional value system that grants status based on the rejection of the values of the system that has rejected them. Unlike Merton's utilitarian argument that crime is often committed as a means to an end, Cohen instead suggests that crime represents a "non-utilitarian, malicious, and negativistic"[43] rejection of middle-class values. Delinquent groups strive for autonomy from mainstream control and value expressions of "short-run hedonism," that is, short-sighted efforts to maximize pleasure.

According to Cohen's framework,[44] not all poor individuals adopt delinquent values. He produced three typologies of response among low-income adolescent males, the population most prone to offending:

1. "College boys" internalize middle-class values, and continue to strive for conventional social mobility.
2. "Corner boys" generally accept middle-class values, but may engage in minor deviant behaviors consistent with the values of their surroundings.
3. "Delinquent boys" experience hostility to their failure to measure up to middle-class standards. They respond through "reaction formation," in which they actively reject middle-class values in favor of a value set that conveys status for criminality.

Focal concerns theory

> [Gangs and other adolescent groups] require a high level of intra-group solidarity; individual members must possess a good capacity for subordinating individual desires to general group interests as well as the capacity for intimate and persisting interaction. ...

> Members possess to an unusually high degree both the *capacity* and *motivation* to conform to perceived cultural norms.
>
> **Miller, 1958[45]**

> Why … is the commission of crimes a customary feature of gang activity? The most general answer is that the commission of crimes by members of adolescent street corner groups is motivated primarily by the attempt to achieve ends, states, or conditions which are valued, and to avoid those that are disvalued within their most meaningful cultural milieu, through those culturally available avenues which appear as the most feasible means of attaining those ends.
>
> **Miller, 1958[46]**

Walter Miller openly critiqued Cohen's analysis as class-centric, advocating for a more culturally relativist approach to understanding criminal behavior among the poor. He suggested that individuals in different areas are exposed to different norms; thus, instead of assuming that "lower-class" values are some kind of response to the middle class, they should be examined on their own merit. Miller suggests that "Lower class culture is a distinctive tradition many centuries old with an integrity of its own."[47] Although rebellion may be one component in shaping what is valued, no society (or subsection thereof) could maintain cohesion based primarily on rebellion, so there must be more to the story.

Miller held that criminal motivations are better understood by speaking directly with offenders. Accordingly, he based his own conclusions on contact with 21 "corner groups" that spanned 3 years. The groups differed in race, age, and stage of adolescence. On the basis of his research, Miller suggests that any given culture is subject to unique "focal concerns," which he defines as "areas or issues that command widespread and persistent attention and a high degree of emotional involvement."[48] Among these corner groups, he identified six lower-class focal concerns. Note that these are not the same as values—these are topics around which the groups orient themselves, but not necessarily things they hold in high regard.

- Trouble: Miller suggested that in the mainstream of the lower class, staying out of trouble was valued similarly to achievement in the middle class. At times though, getting into trouble was accepted as a means of achieving other valued ends, such as the pursuit of excitement. Some groups explicitly valued getting into trouble.
- Toughness: There was a strong premium placed on the presentation of self as "tough," a concept characterized by masculinity, strength, and bravery.
- Smartness: Although intellect is valued in both the middle and lower classes, in the lower class a premium is placed on the ability to use intelligence to get ahead by obtaining material goods or generally outsmarting others. Competitive games of wit are played, as with trading insults as an exercise in "ingenuity, hair-trigger responsiveness, inventiveness, and the acute exercise of mental facilities."[49]
- Excitement: Alcohol, gambling, sexual escapades, and other risky endeavors are valued for the stimulation they provide. Those who value toughness typically also value excitement.
- Fate: Those in the lower class feel little control over their own destiny, so a premium is placed on good luck as a demonstration of the potential for success. Gambling is valued for its simultaneous manifestation of fate, excitement, toughness, and smartness.

- Autonomy: Miller noticed the youth overtly expressing a desire for freedom from external constraints, even as they engaged in activities that invoked those very constraints. Some enlisted in the armed forces, and others ended up incarcerated. Among those who ended up in the correctional system, even as they voiced their disdain for the system they simultaneously viewed themselves as "being cared for," which Miller interpreted as reflective of an underlying desire for dependence.

Contradictory to the traditional framing of gangs as rebellious, Miller suggests that they are actually characterized by a great deal of conformity. Members' primary concern is with the achievement of status within their peer group, which is achieved through conformity; those who behave erratically are shunned. In addition, the values held by gangs conform closely to those held within their immediate communities. Adolescent male peer groups demonstrate two additional focal concerns:

1. Belonging: The male adolescents craved acceptance from their peers, leading to efforts to conform to the values and standards of the group.
2. Status: Although status is valued across socioeconomic classes, within the lower class it is conveyed based on conformity to the peer reference group. Adolescent males place particular value on the appearance of adulthood through displays of toughness, smartness, and autonomy. Status belongs not only to individuals but to groups as well, so that peer groups are conscious of their status relative to other peer groups.

The norms that surround the lower class elevate the costs of showing weakness or backing down from a fight, as doing so would risk both personal and group statuses and, by consequence, one's acceptance within their peer group. Because laws are written based on middle-class values, when the lower class acts in accordance with their own culture, they by consequence break the law.

Theory of delinquent gangs

In an expansion of Cloward's differential opportunity theory, Cloward and Ohlin[50] critique Miller's characterization of the lower class as holding values that are inherently more conducive to crime than those held by the higher classes. Rather, they suggest that all individuals are potentially susceptible to crime regardless of class, but certain social conditions are more conducive to the formation of the following types of delinquent subcultures:

- "Criminal subcultures" value obtaining goods through illegitimate means, whether thievery, fraud, or some other hustle. Legitimate money-making activities are devalued because they do not provide the same opportunity for a "big score." Thus, individuals who stick to conventional means for material success are considered "suckers," and become potential targets for victimization.[50]
- "Conflict subcultures" value toughness. Fighting, unpredictability, and destructiveness are valued because they serve as vehicles for gaining status.
- "Retreatist subcultures" also engage in the hustle (as with the criminal subcultures), but only to support their pursuit of the next high, which may come from "alcohol, marijuana, addicting drugs, unusual sexual experiences, hot jazz, cool jazz. ..."[50]

Cloward and Ohlin held that any given delinquent group may adopt values and activities consistent with any combination of these subcultures.

Research on deviant subcultures

Recent research has furthered the understanding of lower-class culture as it pertains to crime. It has long been recognized that even in the most criminogenic areas, most residents refrain from crime. The work of Elijah Anderson[51] provided a framework for understanding the coexistence of multiple value systems in inner-city communities. According to Anderson, the majority of inner-city residents belong to "decent families" whose members subscribe to traditional middle-class values. Decent families

> value hard work and self-reliance and are willing to sacrifice for their children. Because they have a certain amount of faith in mainstream society, they harbor hopes for a better future for their children, if not for themselves. Many of them go to church and take a strong interest in their children's schooling.[52]

By contrast, other residents subscribe to an oppositional culture that operates according to the "code of the streets," an informal code of conduct based on respect. Anderson suggests this culture has formed due to distrust in the criminal justice system. In an environment where police cannot be relied on to provide protection, residents must take it on themselves to maintain their own security. For these individuals, both safety and self-esteem are derived from the ability to command respect from others, which is done through self-presentation of wealth and a willingness to engage in violence. This is not only consistent with Miller's concepts of status, autonomy, and toughness, but also supports Cohen's contention that deviant subcultures consciously assume an oppositional stance to mainstream values. For Anderson, this opposition is rooted in the perception that the system has failed them. Although Anderson suggested that decent families outnumber those who subscribe to the code of the streets, he also held that decent families in high-crime areas were compelled to subscribe to the code in street interactions to avoid victimization.

The research of Sudhir Venkatesh[53] further revealed the complexity of gang values. On the basis of a multiyear ethnographic study of the Robert Taylor housing project in Chicago, Venkatesh does not dispute gangs' involvement in violence, drug dealing, and extortion. At the same time, he reveals that gang members also play an integral role in maintaining community order. In a space where the police cannot always be relied on to respond to calls, gangs

- Resolve disputes among area residents
- Provide protection for area residents and businesses
- Exact revenge on men who abused women in the neighborhood
- Contribute financially to community events, and to those in need

Thus, even as gangs posed a threat to the broader community through their violence and drug dealing, they also served important institutional functions.

John Hagedorn[54] provides an international perspective on gangs with his multinational study of armed young men. Hagedorn merges a subcultural perspective with critical criminology's acknowledgment of power (see Chapter 8) in identifying oppression as the fundamental commonality in gang formation; thus, his contributions might be labeled "oppression reaction theory." To the extent that gangs assume oppositional values, he identifies at their root a search for a valued identity and meaningful existence that stands independent of the negative messages received from mainstream culture via racism, discrimination, and police brutality and harassment. The resulting "resistance identities"[55] stem from a search for empowerment that may manifest in many ways, including expressive hip-hop and gangsta rap, the adoption of political or nationalist agendas, and/or the more nefarious forms of misogyny and violence that draw the attention of criminologists.

Hagedorn cautions against attempts to categorize delinquent gangs into various subcultures, as they are more fluid and complex than could be reflected in typologies. In his words

> The complex world we live in is not made up of neatly defined groups, some criminal, some political, some cultural. The world of gangs comprises flexible forms of armed groups, some changing from gang to militia to criminal syndicate to political party, or some existing as all types simultaneously.[56]

Hagedorn believes that gangs are likely to be a permanent fixture in areas that contain concentrations of alienated youth. Intervention programs shaped narrowly around recreation or education are important but not sufficient to overcome the effects of oppression. Regarding the permanence of gangs, Hagedorn states that

> The gang is one business that is almost always hiring and may be the only chance many youth have to get a job. But these gangs are not merely economic agents: they develop rituals and ceremonies, a distinctive outlook, and interests of their own. Young people are strongly attracted to and find an identity in these organizations that are deeply rooted in ghettos, barrios, and favelas. Such institutionalized gangs are nearly impossible to destroy, short of totalitarian repression.[57]

Given gangs' resilience but also their fluidity in form and structure, Hagedorn suggests we should not underestimate their capacity as actors in constructive social movements. The key contributions of Hagedorn's work include the following:

- Disadvantage is not a passive state, but rather the result of active exclusion and oppression by the mainstream that must be recognized to fully understand the nature of gangs.
- Adolescent males join gangs in pursuit of a meaningful identity in the face of oppressive circumstances.
- Because the gang structure is not inherently criminal, efforts to reduce criminality should include strategies that empower gang members to initiate and engage in community activities and facilitate their development of positive, meaningful noncriminal identities.

Changing American cities

Some of the observations made by early social structural criminologists continue to be relevant. Crime is not evenly distributed across social space, and crime rates are highest in disadvantaged urban areas, which for the most part continue to be located around city centers. Social ills such as poverty, unemployment, visible signs of disorder, and crime continue to cluster in the disadvantaged neighborhoods. Order maintenance policing and efforts to build collective efficacy are only the most recent manifestations of a social disorganization approach to crime control.

At the same time, there have been some substantial developments that change the context of urban criminality. The poor of the early 1900s had the benefit of more robust social work and social welfare agencies. Incarceration was not a common experience among poor urbanites, with the nation's imprisonment rate remaining in the range of 79–137 per 100,000 from the 1920s to the early 1970s.[58] During the research of Shaw and McKay, factory employment provided residents of poor areas with a vehicle for social mobility. Immigrants were able to work their way "up and out" throughout the 1900s, and in the aftermath of the civil rights movement the many African Americans who had been restricted to disadvantaged areas by segregation, discrimination, and racial violence were increasingly able to do the same. In recent decades, all of these contextual circumstances have undergone dramatic changes as the result of the following processes:

- Deindustrialization: In the 1980s, factories started to shut down due to a combination of automation and outsourcing. The shift from an industrial (factory-based) to a technology- and service-based economy removed the core vehicle for social mobility in disadvantaged communities, which directly contributed to criminal involvement among the unemployed.[59] Hagedorn's research on gangs in Milwaukee found that members were less likely to "age out" of their criminal involvement once the industrial economy had collapsed.[60]
- Reductions in welfare: Recent decades have witnessed a cutback in welfare programs. The impact has been so severe that it has been suggested that the criminal justice system is now one of the primary mechanisms for providing services to dispossessed populations.[61]
- Concentrated disadvantage: As factories shut down, residents of disadvantaged areas had less money to spend at stores and restaurants, causing additional businesses to close. This erosion of local economies propelled the exodus of those who could afford to leave, causing even further damage to the economic base of these neighborhoods. This spiral has resulted in a state of concentrated disadvantage: Those who could not afford to move are now left with few employment opportunities, minimal access to basic services, and no clear path for social mobility. In short, whereas poverty tended to be a transitory experience for urbanites in the early 1900s, individuals are now becoming entrenched in poverty with no clear vehicle out.
- Gentrification: Although many disadvantaged communities still surround urban centers, these neighborhoods are increasingly targets for redevelopment among middle- and upper-class residents looking to move closer to the city center, and city governments hoping to increase their tax base and the general attractiveness of their cities. This "reverse migration" of the upper classes represents a fundamental shift from the process of steady outward city growth described by early Chicago School theorists. The investments brought by gentrification stand to decrease crime by strengthening social institutions, improving physical conditions, and decreasing residential mobility.[62] Critics of gentrification highlight that it only results in the "displacement" of the poor as home values and taxes increase beyond their means. This disrupts social networks and fails to address the underlying social causes of crime, with disadvantaged populations simply pushed to other low-income areas plagued by the same social ills.
- Mass incarceration: Since the early 1970s, a combination of stricter drug enforcement, order maintenance policing, mandatory sentencing, and some states' abolishment of discretionary parole have coalesced to dramatically increase incarceration rates in the United States. The nation's imprisonment rate grew more than fourfold, reaching

a peak of 506 per 100,000 in 2007 and 2008.[63] Overall incarceration rates (which also include jail) reached more than 700 per 100,000. This rate gives the United States the distinction of incarcerating more of its population than any other nation.[64] Most significantly for the social structural perspective, these rates have disproportionately affected disadvantaged urban areas.

MILLION DOLLAR BLOCKS AND THE EFFECTS OF INCARCERATION

The growth of the correctional system has made incarceration so prevalent in some disadvantaged areas that researchers have identified "million dollar blocks," single street blocks for which "more than a million dollars per year are spent to incarcerate and return residents."[65] In their exploration of the spatial distribution of incarceration, Sampson and Loeffler[66] found some Chicago communities had more than eight times the incarceration rate of others. Incarceration further tends to be concentrated by demographic characteristics, particularly age, race, and gender. As of 2006, the demographic breakdown of incarceration rates among 25- to 29-year-olds was as follows:

Incarceration Rates of 25- to 29-Year-Olds by Race and Sex[67]

White female	226 per 100,000
Hispanic female	305 per 100,000
Black female	716 per 100,000
White male	1,685 per 100,000
Hispanic male	3,912 per 100,000
Black male	11,695 per 100,000

The risk of incarceration is not uniform within any given race, varying based on other factors such as class and location. This means that while, for example, there will be black males with far lower rates of incarceration than indicated above, those who live in disadvantaged urban areas will actually experience a more disproportionate rate of incarceration than that reflected on the chart.

Scholars have started to observe detrimental community-level effects of incarceration. No longer seen as just a response to crime, incarceration may also be a contributing factor to its perpetuation. Specifically, incarceration threatens to

- Destabilize social networks and neighborhood institutions due to "coerced mobility," which Todd Clear[68] defines as the forcible removal of residents for a period of incarceration and their subsequent return
- Reduce economic opportunities for those who have been incarcerated,[69] particularly as criminal records become more readily available to potential employers[70]
- Create emotional and financial strain for the families of the incarcerated[71]
- Stigmatize the community, which may discourage investments and damage area businesses[72]

Incarceration rates just saw their first dip after nearly 40 years of steady growth, driven in part by California's response to a Supreme Court order to depopulate its prisons due to unconstitutionally overcrowded positions,[73] and to budgetary constraints facing jurisdictions nationwide.

Summary

- Social structural theorists assume that criminal behavior is rooted in the social conditions of life.
- This perspective tends to focus on neighborhood-level variables to explain the spatial distribution of crime.
- The social structural perspective has its roots in the concept of social ecology, spearheaded by early Chicago School research.
- Early social structural theorists held that the transition to urban life resulted in a state of anomie.
- Emile Durkheim conceptualized urbanization as a shift from mechanical to organic solidarity.
- Ernest Burgess offered that the social ecology of industrialized cities could be conceptualized as five concentric zones, each with its own distinct characteristics.
- Shaw and McKay's social disorganization theory proposed that the social and physical conditions of the transitional zone were responsible for higher crime rates.
- Broken windows theory emphasized the importance of physical signs of disorder, and therefore advocated for law enforcement to take an order maintenance approach.
- Sampson et al. advanced the concept of collective efficacy as a protective factor against social disorganization.
- The strain tradition expanded on Durkheim's concept of anomie to identify specific sources of stress that spawn from disadvantaged urban conditions.
- Merton's strain theory outlined five modes of adaptation that result from the disjunction between socially defined goals and the means to attain them: conformity, ritualism, innovation, retreatism, and rebellion.
- Cloward and Ohlin's differential opportunity theory pointed out that just as there are different levels of access to conventional goal attainment, illegitimate opportunities are also differentially distributed.
- Messner and Rosenfeld's institutional anomie theory held that a cultural emphasis on monetary goals weakens other social institutions, and proposed decommodification as a solution.
- Agnew's general strain theory further expanded the notion of strain to include general life stressors such as breakups and family loss, with the implication that proper coping mechanisms can help decrease crime.
- Subcultural theories examine the subcultural values that result from broader social conditions.
- Cohen's delinquent subculture theory suggested that low-income youth form a consciously oppositional subculture in response to their failure to live up to middle-class measuring rods.
- Miller disagreed with Cohen's characterization of gangs as primarily oppositional in nature, and argued in his theory that the focal concerns of gangs should be identified on their own merit rather than measured according to middle-class standards.
- Cloward and Ohlin's theory of delinquent gangs outlined three types of subcultures: criminal, conflict, and retreatist.
- Elijah Anderson's research supported that most families in disadvantaged communities do not hold criminal values, although they need to abide by the "code of the streets" for their own safety.

- Sudhir Venkatesh's study of gangs in Chicago revealed the complexity of gang members' activities, which included violence and drug dealing as well as more prosocial functions such as providing protection to area residents and contributing financially to community events.
- Hagedorn argued that evaluating gangs from an international perspective reveals the centrality of oppression, racism, and alienation in their formation.
- Over the last several decades, disadvantaged urban populations have been affected by several key developments: deindustrialization, reductions in welfare programs, concentrated disadvantage, gentrification, and mass incarceration.

Questions in review

1. Which of the social structural theories do you think best explains crime?
2. Explain the concept of social disorganization. Do you think Shaw and McKay's social disorganization theory holds relevance in the present day?
3. Describe broken windows theory and its effect on policing.
4. Compare and contrast Merton's strain theory with Agnew's general strain theory.
5. Do you think gentrification is more likely to increase or decrease overall crime rates? Support your answer with information found in this chapter.
6. Identify possible solutions to crime based on each theory presented in this chapter. Do you think these solutions are feasible? Are they likely to be effective?

Practicum

Many faces of gang life

Since the earliest days of the Chicago School, studies of urban crime have focused heavily on gangs as a source of criminal activity. Thrasher's classic study[74] determined that most gangs formed from spontaneous playgroups, whereas subsequent research sought to identify different types of gangs. Although gangs participate in both criminal and non-criminal activities, these studies typically emphasize delinquency as a core component of gang identity and activity.

One brief period of Chicago history challenges the characterization of gangs as inherently criminogenic. In many ways, the formation of the Conservative Vice Lords (CVL) in the 1950s was typical of gangs at the time. Started by friends who met in an Illinois youth reformatory, the CVL began as a recreational group that would host dances to meet women. Its members started to engage in violence to protect its younger members from assaults by other gangs. Recognizing the importance of growth if they hoped to win fights, the CVL focused on growing its membership. Anyone who wanted to join was admitted; for those who refused to join,

> he got his ass whipped right then and there, and everytime we see him we gonna whip his ass 'til he change his mind and say he's gonna be a lord. Eventually they would want to join.[75]

The CVL successfully consolidated many gangs on the west side of Chicago. As they grew, their participation in violence escalated. Fighting became a way to build a reputation, avenge attacks on its members, and obtain desired goods. Members engaged in property crimes, robbing, stealing, and extorting for the things they wanted.

In the 1960s, a strange thing happened. Key leaders of the CVL started to reconsider the gang life. For some, it was a matter of introspection:

> Then I went to thinkin'. What happened to gangs before my gang? I found out they were minus because either they was still doin' life in the pen or were paralyzed or their mothers were takin' them flowers on Memorial Day. So I say, where do I go not to get in this category. [76]

These reflections coalesced with observations of the civil rights movement and a growing awareness of the injustice of their social circumstances. CVL leadership made a conscious decision to reframe the group as a community organization. From that point, they

- Called a truce with former rival gangs and joined forces to participate in social activism
- Used intimidation to discourage other gangs from rioting and other destructive behaviors
- Opened legitimate businesses, including a clothing store and ice-cream parlor
- Obtained a grant from the Rockefeller Foundation to run summer programs for youth
- Organized community cleanup efforts around the slogan "Grass, Not Glass"
- Participated in community planning with businesses including Sears Roebuck
- Hosted an art show, political protests, and a tenant rights group
- Opened two locations for area youth to study and hang out and receive tutoring services

The efforts of the CVL prompted researcher David Dawley to write to Washington:

> There's an untold story in Chicago that ghetto youth are organized and looking for help—"a hand up, not a hand out." This phenomenon, new for gangs and unfamiliar to the community, raises these questions: Can we join with organizations created by ghetto conditions to confront problems of poverty? Is the government willing to work with youth with police records? Is big business prepared to invest in community renewal through direct collaboration with an element whose history is brutal but whose present commitment is honest? [77]

Their efforts resulted in a crime drop in CVL territory at a time when crime was up in other parts of the city. [78]

Despite these significant changes within the CVL, suspicion by local authorities persisted, supported in part by some individual CVL members' continued engagement in crime. In 1969, Chicago's mayor declared a "war on gangs." Business partners began to turn their backs on the CVL, the media stopped covering their initiatives, and police started to pursue its members aggressively. Eventually, the CVL reverted to the entrenched criminal involvement that had characterized its earlier days. Since that time, Chicago has continued to receive national attention for its gang violence, most recently for an increase in homicides in 2012 and early 2013. Much of this violence is concentrated on the south and west sides of the city, including the area where the CVL had engaged in their community efforts several decades ago. [79]

Source: Conservative Vice Lord information based on Dawley, D. (1992/1973). *A nation of Lords: The autobiography of the Vice Lords.* Long Grove, IL: Waveland Press.

Questions

1. Do you see any connection between the description of the CVL and the theories discussed in this chapter?
2. Can community organizations work with gangs to reduce crime, or are gangs inherently criminogenic? Support your answer.
3. If you were the superintendent of police in Chicago, what steps would you take to combat gang violence?

References

1. Shaw, C. R., & McKay, H. (1942). *Juvenile delinquency and urban areas.* Chicago: University of Chicago Press.
2. Wirth, L. (1938). Urbanism as a way of life. *American Journal of Sociology, 44*(1), 1–24.
3. Davis, K. (1955). The origin and growth of urbanization in the world. *American Journal of Sociology, 60*(5), 429–437.
4. Wirth, L. (1938). Urbanism as a way of life. *The American journal of sociology, 44*(1), 1–24
5. Durkheim, E. (1893). Division of labour, crime, and punishment. (M. Thompson Trans.). *De la division du travail social.* Paris, France: Alcan.
6. Park, R. E. (1925). The city: Suggestions for the investigation of human behavior in the urban environment. In R. E. Park, E. W. Burgess & R. D. McKenzie (Eds.), *The city* (pp. 1–46). Chicago: University of Chicago Press.
7. Park, R. E. (1925). The city: Suggestions for the investigation of human behavior in the urban environment. In R. E. Park, E. W. Burgess & R. D. McKenzie (Eds.), *The city* (pp. 1–46). Chicago: University of Chicago Press.
8. Burgess, E. W. (1925). The growth of the city: An introduction to a research project. In R. E. Park, E. W. Burgess & R. D. McKenzie (Eds.), *The city* (pp. 47–62). Chicago: University of Chicago Press.
9. Burgess, E. W. (1925). The growth of the city: An introduction to a research project. In R. E. Park, E. W. Burgess & R. D. McKenzie (Eds.), *The city* (pp. 47–62). Chicago: University of Chicago Press.
10. Burgess, E. W. (1925). The growth of the city: An introduction to a research project. In R. E. Park, E. W. Burgess & R. D. McKenzie (Eds.), *The city* (p. 52). Chicago: University of Chicago Press.
11. Burgess, E. W. (1925). The growth of the city: An introduction to a research project. In R. E. Park, E. W. Burgess & R. D. McKenzie (Eds.), *The city* (p. 54). Chicago: University of Chicago Press.
12. Shaw, C. R., & McKay, H. (1942). *Juvenile delinquency and urban areas.* Chicago: University of Chicago Press
13. Wilson, W. J. (1996). *When work disappears: The world of the new urban poor.* New York: Vintage Books.
14. Becker, H. S. (1999). The Chicago School, so-called. *Qualitative Sociology, 22*(1), 3–12.
15. Becker, H. S. (1999). The Chicago School, so-called. *Qualitative Sociology, 22*(1), 5.
16. Wirth, L. (1928). *The ghetto.* Chicago: University of Chicago Press.
17. Thrasher, F. M. (1927). *The gang: A study of 1,313 gangs in Chicago.* Chicago: University of Chicago Press.
18. Anderson, N. (1923). *The hobo: The sociology of the homeless man.* Chicago: University of Chicago Press.
19. Kelling, G. L., & Wilson, J. Q. (1982). Broken windows: The police and neighborhood safety. *Atlantic Magazine, 249*(3), 29–38.
20. Beckett, K., & Herbert, S. (2010). *Banished: The new social control in urban America.* New York: Oxford University Press.

21. Western, B. (2002). The impact of incarceration on wage mobility and inequality. *American Sociological Review, 67*(4), 526–546.
22. Unless otherwise indicated, information drawn from White, M. D. (2011). The New York City Police Department, its crime-control strategies and organizational changes, 1970–2009. Paper presented at the *Understanding Crime Decline in NYC Conference*, September 23, 2011, New York: John Jay College of Criminal Justice. Retrieved from http://www.jjay.cuny.edu/White.pdf
23. New York City Police Department. (1994). *Reclaiming the public spaces of New York.* New York: Author. As cited in White, M. D. (2011). The New York City Police Department, its crime-control strategies and organizational changes, 1970–2009 (p. 20). Paper presented at the *Understanding Crime Decline in NYC Conference*, September 23, 2011, New York: John Jay College of Criminal Justice. Retrieved from http://www.jjay.cuny.edu/White.pdf
24. Ruderman W. (2012, June 28). Crime report manipulation is common among New York police, study finds. *New York Times.* Retrieved from http://www.nytimes.com/2012/06/29/nyregion/new-york-police-department-manipulates-crime-reports-study-finds.html?_r=0
25. See review in White, M. D. (2011). The New York City Police Department, its crime-control strategies and organizational changes, 1970–2009. Retrieved from http://www.jjay.cuny.edu/white.pdf
26. Margolin, J., & Katersky, A. (2013, August 12). Judge rules NYC's "stop and frisk" unconstitutional, city to appeal. *ABC News.* Retrieved from http://abcnews.go.com/Blotter/judge-rules-nycs-stop-frisk-unconstitutional/story?id=19936326
27. Sampson, R. J., Raudenbush, S. W., & Earls, F. (1997). Neighborhoods and violent crime: A multilevel study of collective efficacy. *Science, 277*, 918–924.
28. Sampson, R. J., Raudenbush, S. W., & Earls, F. (1997). Neighborhoods and violent crime: A multilevel study of collective efficacy. *Science, 277*, 919.
29. Sampson, R. J., Raudenbush, S. W., & Earls, F. (1997). Neighborhoods and violent crime: A multilevel study of collective efficacy. *Science, 277*, 919–920.
30. Merton, R. K. (1938). Social structure and anomie. *American Sociological Review, 3*(5), 672–682.
31. Merton, R. K. (1938). Social structure and anomie. *American Sociological Review, 3*(5), 672–682.
32. Cloward, R. (1959). Illegitimate means, anomie, and deviant behavior. *American Sociological Review, 24*(2), 164–176. Later elaborated in Cloward, R. A., & Ohlin, L. E. (1960). *Delinquency and opportunity: A theory of delinquent gangs.* Glencoe, IL: Free Press.
33. Cloward, R. (1959). Illegitimate means, anomie, and deviant behavior. *American Sociological Review, 24*(2), 164–176. Later elaborated in Cloward, R. A., & Ohlin, L. E. (1960). *Delinquency and opportunity: A theory of delinquent gangs.* Glencoe, IL: Free Press.
34. Messner, S. F., & Rosenfeld, R. (1994). *Crime and the American dream.* Belmont, CA: Wadsworth.
35. Messner, S. F., & Rosenfeld, R. (1994). *Crime and the American dream* (p. 94). Belmont, CA: Wadsworth.
36. Agnew, R. (1985). A revised strain theory of delinquency. *Social Forces, 64*(1), 151–167.
37. Agnew, R. (1985). A revised strain theory of delinquency. *Social Forces, 64*(1), 151–167.
38. Agnew, R. (1992). Foundations for a general strain theory of crime and delinquency. *Criminology, 30*(1), 47–87.
39. Agnew, R. (1992). Foundations for a general strain theory of crime and delinquency. *Criminology, 30*(1), 57.
40. Agnew, R. (2001). Building on the foundation of general strain theory: Specifying the types of strain most likely to lead to crime and delinquency. *Journal of Research in Crime and Delinquency, 38*(4), 319–361.
41. Cloward, R. A., & Ohlin, L. E. (1960). *Delinquency and opportunity: A theory of delinquent gangs.* Glencoe, IL: Free Press.
42. Cohen, A. K. (1955). *Delinquent boys: The culture of the gang.* Glencoe, IL: Free Press.
43. Cohen, A. K. (1955). *Delinquent boys: The culture of the gang* (p. 25). Glencoe, IL: Free Press.
44. Cohen, A. K. (1955). *Delinquent boys: The culture of the gang* (p. 25). Glencoe, IL: Free Press.
45. Miller, W. (1958, Summer). Lower class culture as a generating milieu of gang delinquency. *Journal of Social Issues, 14*, 5–19.
46. Miller, W. (1958). Lower class culture as a generating milieu of gang delinquency. *Journal of Social Issues, 14*, 17.

47. Miller, W. (1958). Lower class culture as a generating milieu of gang delinquency. *Journal of Social Issues, 14*, 19.

48. Miller, W. (1958). Lower class culture as a generating milieu of gang delinquency. *Journal of social issues, 14*, 6.

49. Miller, W. (1958). Lower class culture as a generating milieu of gang delinquency. *Journal of social issues, 14*, 10.

50. Cloward, R.A., & Ohlin, L.E. (1960). *Delinquency and opportunity: A theory of delinquent gangs.* Glencoe, IL: The Free Press.

51. Anderson, E. (1999). *Code of the street: Decency, violence, and the moral life of the inner city.* New York: Norton.

52. Anderson, E. (1994). The code of the streets. *Atlantic Monthly, 273*, 81–94.

53. Venkatesh, S. (2008). *Gang leader for a day: A rogue sociologist takes to the streets.* New York: Penguin Books.

54. Hagedorn, J. M. (2008). *A world of gangs: Armed young men and gansta culture.* Minneapolis, MN: University of Minnesota Press.

55. Hagedorn, J. M. (2008). *A world of gangs: Armed young men and gansta culture* (p.132). Minneapolis, MN: University of Minnesota Press. Hagedorn's application of "resistance identities" is drawn from Manuel Castells.

56. Hagedorn, J. M. (2008). *A world of gangs: Armed young men and gansta culture* (p.132). Minneapolis, MN: University of Minnesota Press. Hagedorn's application of "resistance identities" is drawn from Manuel Castells.

57. Hagedorn, J. M. (2008). *A world of gangs: Armed young men and gansta culture* (p.132). Minneapolis, MN: University of Minnesota Press. Hagedorn's application of "resistance identities" is drawn from Manuel Castells

58. *Sourcebook of Criminal Justice Statistics Online.* (2006). Retrieved from http://www.albany.edu/sourcebook/pdf/t612006.pdf

59. Wilson, W. J. (1996). *When work disappears: The world of the new urban poor.* New York: Vintage Books.

60. Hagedorn, J. (1988). *People and folks: Gangs, crime, and the underclass in a Rustbelt city.* Chicago: Lakeview Press.

61. Comfort, M. (2007). Punishment beyond the legal offender. *Annual Review of Law and Social Science, 3*, 271–296.

62. McDonald, S. C. (1986). Does gentrification affect crime rates? *Crime and Justice, 8* (Communities and Crime), 163–201.

63. Carson, E. A., & Sabol, W. J. (2012). *Prisoners in 2011* (NCJ 239808). Washington, DC: U.S. Department of Justice, Bureau of Justice Statistics.

64. Mauer, M. (1999). *Race to incarcerate.* New York: New Press.

65. Cadora, E., Swartz, C., & Gordon, M. (2003). Criminal justice and health and human services: An exploration of overlapping needs, resources, and interests in Brooklyn neighborhoods. In J. Travis & M. Waul (Eds.), *Prisoners once removed: The impact of incarceration and reentry on children, families, and communities* (pp. 285–312). Washington, DC: Urban Institute Press.

66. Sampson, R. J., & Loeffler, C. (2010). Punishment's place: The local concentration of mass incarceration. *Daedalus, 139*(3), 20–31.

67. Data from Sabol, W. J., Minton, T. D., & Harrison, P. M. (2007). *Prison and Jail Inmates at Midyear 2006* (NCJ No. 217675). Washington, DC: Bureau of Justice Statistics.

68. Clear, T. (2007). *Imprisoning communities: How mass incarceration makes disadvantaged neighborhoods worse.* New York: Oxford University Press.

69. Western, B. (2002). The impact of incarceration on wage mobility and inequality. *American Sociological Review, 67*(4), 526–546. See also Western, B., Petit, B., & Guetzkow, J. (2002). Black economic progress in the era of mass imprisonment. In M. Mauer & M. Chesney-Lind (Eds.), *Invisible punishment: The collateral consequences of mass imprisonment* (pp. 165–180). New York: New Press.

70. Petersilia, J. (2003). *When prisoners come home: Parole and prisoner reentry.* New York: Oxford University Press.

71. For example, Braman, D. (2002). Families and incarceration. In M. Mauer & M. Chesney-Lind (Eds.), *Invisible punishment: The collateral consequences of mass imprisonment* (pp. 117–135). New York: New Press. See also Clear, T. R., Rose, D. R., & Ryder, J. A. (2001). Incarceration and the community: The problem of removing and returning offenders. *Crime & Delinquency, 47*(3), 335–351.

72. Clear, T. R., Rose, D. R., & Ryder, J. A. (2001). Incarceration and the community: The problem of removing and returning offenders. *Crime & Delinquency, 47*(3), 335–351.

73. *Brown, Governor of California, et al. v. Plata et al.*, 131 S. Ct. 1910 (2011).

74. Thrasher, F. (1927). *The Gang*. Chicago: University of Chicago Press

75. Dawley, D. (1992/1973). *A nation of Lords: The autobiography of the Vice Lords* (p. 14). Long Grove, IL: Waveland Press.

76. Dawley, D. (1992/1973). *A nation of Lords: The autobiography of the Vice Lords* (p. 105). Long Grove, IL: Waveland Press.

77. Dawley, D. (1992/1973). *A nation of Lords: The autobiography of the Vice Lords* (p.114). Long Grove, IL: Waveland Press.

78. Dawley, D. (1992/1973). *A nation of Lords: The autobiography of the Vice Lords* (p. 164). Long Grove, IL: Waveland Press.

79. See discussion in Davey, M. (2013, January. 2). In a soaring homicide rate, a divide in Chicago. *New York Times*. Retrieved from http://www.nytimes.com/2013/01/03/us/a-soaring-homicide-rate-a-divide-in-chicago.html?_r=0

chapter six

Social process as a cause of crime

Chapter objectives

After studying this chapter, you should be able to

- Describe the social process approach in explaining criminal behavior
- Discuss the symbolic interaction theories of crime
- Define the basic principles involved in the social process theories of crime causation
- Compare and contrast the different types of control theories of crime causation
- Outline the differential association theory and explain why it is so popular
- Explain the concept of neutralization of criminal behavior
- Describe how labeling theory differs from differential association
- Discuss how social control theories explain crime

Introduction

In this chapter, we examine the use of social process theories to explain criminal behavior. Social process theories assume that everyone has the potential to commit crime and that criminology is not an innate human characteristic. As these theories depend on the processes of interaction between individuals and society, they are also referred to as the interactionist perspectives of crime causation. The major social process theories include differential association, labeling, control, interaction, social learning, and containment.

Social process theorists assume that

- Criminal behavior is a function of a socialization process.
- Criminal behavior is learned in interaction with others and the socialization processes that occur as a by-product of group membership are the primary methods by which the learning occurs.
- Offenders turn to crime as a result of peer group pressure, family problems, poor school performance, legal entanglements, and other situations that gradually steer them to criminal behaviors.
- Anyone can become a criminal.
- The main support of the school of thought stems from the effect of the family on youths who engage in delinquent or violent behaviors.
- There is a linkage between childhood experiences of violence and behavioral problems. In these experiences, children can be victims or eyewitnesses.
- Children who witness family violence are more likely to display diminished social competence and behavioral problems than those who do not.

By socialization, theorists are referring to the process in which an individual's behavior is changed to conform to the standards or expectations of the group involved. Agents of socialization include the family, school, peers, the media, and authorities such as employers. A basic underlying theme of the social process theories is that if these relationships are positive and law-abiding, the individual is not likely to engage in criminal behavior. If they are negative in regard to law-abiding behavior, the individual is likely to turn to crime. The social process school examines four types of control in evaluating human behavior: direct, internal, indirect, and control through needs.

Symbolic interaction

> People act based on symbolic meanings they find within any given situation. We thus interact with the symbols, forming relationships around them. The goals of our interactions with one another are to create shared meaning. Language is itself a symbolic form, which is used to anchor meanings to the symbols.
>
> **R. LaRossa and Donald C. Reitzes, 1993[1]**

> If situations are defined as real, they are real in their consequences. The definition of the situation emphasizes that people act in situations on the basis of how they are defined. Definitions, even when at variance with "objective" reality, have real consequences for people's actions and events.
>
> **William I. Thomas, 1931[2]**

The phrase "symbolic interaction (SI)" was coined by Herbert Blumer in 1937 as he was studying the works of George Herbert Mead. SI theories focus on situations and interactions with society leading up to the crime rather than on the differences or defectiveness of the offenders.[3] Two major crime causation theories based on the concepts of SI are differential association and labeling. Both theories are currently very popular in the United States. These theories look at the process of becoming a criminal.

The SI theories are based on the following assumptions and principles:

- The symbols we learn and use become our social reality.
- We become socialized by the people with whom we associate.
- Individuals' definitions and perceptions of their situations are the sources of their behaviors. (Stated in a different way, the causes of our behavior are based on our interpretation of reality.)
- People act toward things on the basis of the meanings that things have for them.
- The meanings that things have are derived from, or arise out of the social interaction that one has with others.
- The meanings that things have are handled in, and modified through, an interpretative process used by a person in dealing with the things that he or she encounters.

Herbert Blumer summarized SI as follows:

> The meaning of a thing for a person grows out of the ways in which other persons act toward the person with regard to the thing.... Symbolic interactionism sees meanings as social products, as creations that are formed in and through the defining activities of people as they interact.[4]

The criticisms of SI include the following:

- The concepts are not developed into a formal, systematic theory.
- Symbolic interactionist research is often criticized for use of qualitative research methods.
- The theory overestimates the power of individuals to create personal realities.
- The theory does not adequately account for unconscious processes.

Differential association

> According to this theory [differential association] there are two major categories of behavior. There is the reflexive or respondent behavior which is behavior that is governed by the stimuli that elicit it. Such behaviors are largely associated with the autonomic system. On the other hand, there is operant behavior which involves the central nervous system. Examples of operant behavior include verbal behavior, driving a car, and buying a new suit.
>
> **Robert L. Burgess and Ronald L. Akers, 1966[5]**

Edwin Sutherland developed the theory of differential association in an attempt to explain career criminal behavior.[6] As pointed out by Gwynn Nettler and later by Masters and Roberson, "differential association" is not an appropriate title for his theory. "Differential association" sounds as if it refers to people in association and does not refer to who associates with whom. Actually it involves the definition of situations that are differentially associated.[7]

Masters and Roberson state that differential association has been the most influential sociopsychological theory of crime causation in the United States since the 1940s.[8] After Sutherland's death in 1950 and until 1987, Donald Cressey, who was first Sutherland's student and later his colleague and then coauthor of his text on criminology, carried on his work. The text, *Principles of Criminology*, was the standard text in criminology for over 30 years.

Don Gibbons contended that differential association theory's popularity was due in large part to Sutherland's influence on the formation of criminology as a distinct intellectual discipline along with Cressey's ability to explain Sutherland's theory. Unlike some of the other crime causation theories, their theory is easily explained and includes all types of criminal behavior. Gibbons noted as follows:

> The evidence is incontrovertible that Edwin Sutherland was the most important contributor to American criminology to have appeared to date. There has been no other criminologist who even begins to approach his statute and importance. Moreover it is unlikely that anyone will emerge in future decades to challenge Sutherland's position in the annals of this field.[9]

Edwin H. Sutherland's first version of differential association was published in 1937. He continued to revise it in subsequent editions of his textbook on criminology. The last version was published in 1947. Sutherland contended that "all behavior is learned in a social environment." He asserted that criminal behavior is in what is learned, not how it is learned. According to him, we learn both criminal and noncriminal behaviors the same way. Sutherland believed that the criminal is not necessarily different from the noncriminal. He did note that values are important in determining behavior and that certain locations and people are more crime-prone than others. In a 1934 edition of his text, *Principles of Criminology*, Sutherland stated as follows:

> First, any person can be trained to adopt and follow any pattern of behavior which he is able to execute. Second, failure to follow a prescribed pattern of behavior is due to the inconsistencies and lack of harmony in the influences which direct the individual. Third, the conflict of culture is therefore the fundamental principle in the explanation of crime.[10]

His 1934 statement later became the basis of differential association theory. By the term "differential association," Sutherland points out that the content of the patterns presented in associations differ from individual to individual. He does not imply, as some theorists claim, that the mere association with criminals will cause someone to be a criminal. He apparently meant that the content of communications from others is given different degrees of significance depending on the relationship with the person making the verbal or nonverbal communication. Accordingly, the communication from a personal friend would have more effect on our behavior than the communication of a stranger or a television program. Under the same concept, the importance of a communication received from a parent may differ depending on the relationship with the parent and the relationship may change as the child ages.

In the 1939 version of his theory, Sutherland stressed belief that all behavior is learned. In so doing, he moved away from blaming social disorganization, which was popular at the time, and to differential association as the cause of criminal behavior. This movement allowed him to apply the learning process to a broader range of society. The final version of his theory was published in 1947. In the final version, he summarized his theory by stating nine points with point number six being the most important (see sidebar later in section describing the nine points).[11]

Differential association theory is very general in nature. This allows for it to account for most types of criminal behavior. In 1939–1940, Sutherland coined the phrase "white-collar" crime to classify those crimes that are committed by persons in a profession or those individuals who wore white shirts. To a great extent, his work on white-collar crime and attempting to explain it influenced his work on differential association. He noted the following in February, 1940:

> This paper is concerned with crime in relation to business. The economists are well acquainted with business methods but not accustomed to consider them from the point of view of crime; many sociologists are well acquainted with crime but not accustomed to consider it as expressed in business. This paper is an attempt to integrate these two bodies of knowledge. More accurately stated, it is a comparison of crime in the upper or white-collar class, composed of respectable or at least respected business and professional men, and crime in the lower class, composed of persons of low socioeconomic status. This comparison is made for the purpose of developing the theories of criminal behavior, not for the purpose of muckraking or of reforming anything except criminology.... This analysis of the criterion of white-collar criminality results in the conclusion that a description of white-collar criminality in general terms will be also

a description of the criminality of the lower class. The respects in which the crimes of the two classes differ are the incidentals rather than the essentials of criminality.[12]

The general nature of differential association makes it very difficult to test its validity. His propositions are difficult to conceptualize in a manner that would lead to empirical measurement. Many researchers have noted that individuals who associate with criminals are more likely to become criminals. For example, James Short tested a sample of 126 boys and 50 girls at a training school and concluded that there was a strong correlation between delinquent behavior and the association with delinquent peers.[13] Travis Hirschi concluded that boys with delinquent friends were more likely to become delinquent.[14] In sum, studies by Short and Hirschi establish that the validity of differential association would require the researcher to ignore other similarities between the youths involved. For instance, most of the youths involved are probably in the lower socioeconomic groups of society and that fact could have a significant influence on the directions toward deviant behavior that the youth take.

Criticisms of differential association include the following:

- "The theory fails to explain why most people involved in crime become less involved as they grow older." This criticism refers mostly to "street crime." It is an accepted fact that as the ages of these offenders increase they are less involved in criminal behavior. Note that this criticism does not hold true as to the white-collar criminal. As the white-collar criminal tends to advance in his or her profession and therefore is older, they tend to increase their involvement in unacceptable behavior. In other words, unlike the street criminal, the white-collar criminal does not grow out of crime but rather tends to grow into crime.
- "It neglects the fact that there are significant differences in individuals." This criticism may not be valid because of the general nature of the theory; it does not state that an individual will become a criminal. The theory only attempts to explain how an individual progresses toward deviant behavior.
- "The theory seems to exclude the concept of free will." A close reading of the theory does not exclude the concept of free will because the theory does not indicate that the individual is destined to become delinquent.
- "It fails to explain crimes of passion." Although it may not explain crimes of passion, it may explain why individuals take certain courses of action when confronted with a situation involving high personal feelings and/or anger. For example, the child who sees his father beat his mother may be learning that that is acceptable behavior when the child later is situated in a similar confrontation.

EDWIN H. SUTHERLAND'S NINE PRINCIPLES OF DIFFERENTIAL ASSOCIATION[15] WITH AUTHORS' COMMENTS IN BRACKETS

1. "Criminal behavior is learned." (This indicates that criminal behavior is not inherited and that a person who is not already "learned" in crime does not invent criminal behavior, just as a person does not develop computer programs unless he or she has been trained in computer programing. It also rules out biological reasons for crime causation.)

(Continued)

**EDWIN H. SUTHERLAND'S NINE PRINCIPLES OF
DIFFERENTIAL ASSOCIATION[15] WITH AUTHORS'
COMMENTS IN BRACKETS (*CONTINUED*)**

2. "Criminal behavior is learned in interaction with other persons in a process of communications." (The communication referred to in this principle may be verbal or nonverbal. In addition, it is not necessary for the communication to be directed toward the individual receiving it. For example, what nonverbal communication is being transmitted when a young child observes that when riding in an automobile with his father that the father slows to legal speed when a police officer may be in the area but exceeds the speed limit when it is unlikely that a police officer is near?)

3. "The principal part of the learning of criminal behavior occurs within intimate personal groups." (By this principle, Sutherland implies that nonpersonal communications such as movies are relatively unimportant in shaping the behavior of the viewer. What about the child who is a loner and has no friends? If this child substitutes watching television for playtime with friends, in this case would not television messages have a significant influence on the child's learning process?)

4. "When criminal behavior is learned, the learning includes (a) techniques of committing the crime, which are sometimes very complicated, sometimes very simple and (b) the specific direction of motives, drives, rationalizations, and attitudes." (Under this principle, a youth learns the techniques of committing criminal behavior similar to the way a youth on the streets of New York City learns the techniques of playing basketball.)

5. "The specific direction of motives and drives is learned from definitions of the legal codes as favorable or unfavorable." (In some neighborhoods, the individual is surrounded by persons who define the laws as rules of behavior. In others, the individual may be in a neighborhood where many persons' definitions of law are favorable to violations of the law. In many of the neighborhoods, the signals being transmitted are mixed in that some are favorable to law observance and some to violations of the law.)

6. "The person becomes delinquent because of an excess of definitions favorable to violation of the law over definitions unfavorable to violation of law." (Sutherland points out that this principle is the key principle in his theory. According to him, persons become criminal because of contacts with criminal patterns and also because of isolation from noncriminal patterns. As noted by some of his critics, this principle does not explain a scenario in one poor neighborhood in Chicago where two boys lived across the street from each other; one grows up and becomes the mayor of Chicago and the other a career criminal.)

7. "Differential associations may vary in frequency, duration, priority, and intensity." (Sutherland does not provide any precise definition of "intensity" nor does he explain how the associations may vary.)

8. "The process of learning criminal behavior by association with criminal and noncriminal patterns involves all of the mechanisms that are involved in any other learning." (This principle indicates that the learning process is not restricted to the process of imitation.)

9. "Although criminal behavior is an expression of general needs and values, it is not explained by those general needs and values, because noncriminal behavior is an expression." (This principle stands for the position that you cannot explain criminal behavior by general drives and values. A youth may value a fancy automobile. That does not explain why some will work hard at honest labor to get the automobile while others will sell illegal drugs to get the automobile.)

EDWIN HARDIN SUTHERLAND 1883–1950[16]

Edwin Sutherland was born in Gibbon, Nebraska. He grew up and was educated in Ottawa, Kansas, and Grand Island, Nebraska. In 1904, he received his bachelor of arts degree from Grand Island College, where he majored in history with a minor in sociology. After graduation, he taught Latin and Greek history and shorthand for 2 years at Sioux Falls College in South Dakota. During this period, he took a correspondence course in sociology offered by the University of Chicago. He needed the course to meet a requirement to attend their graduate school. He later attended the university and received his PhD in sociology from the University of Chicago in 1913.

After completing graduate studies, Sutherland was appointed as a professor at the University of Minnesota from 1926 to 1929. During this period, his focus was on sociology as a scientific enterprise whose goal was understanding and control of social problems, including crime. It was at the University of Minnesota that he established his reputation as a leading criminologist. In 1930, he accepted a position at the University of Chicago and later moved to the University of Indiana.

Before developing his theory of differential association, Sutherland spent most of his time modifying the central aspects of the social disorganization perspective. Later, Sutherland shifted from sociology to criminology. Several researchers have contended that he switched because of his fear that he might not achieve professional recognition as a sociologist.

In 1939, Sutherland formally presented his theory of differential association in which he relied heavily on the works of Shaw and McKay. Although Sutherland was an extremely brilliant researcher, his students considered him a below-average professor. As one student remarked, it was difficult to listen to Sutherland's lectures because he mumbled.

Sutherland was clearly the most influential American criminologist of the twentieth century. He had a conflict orientation to society. According to Sutherland, an individual has a number of societal values from which he or she can choose from, and the individual's choice is influenced by our associations and situational definitions. In short, we learn to commit crime like we learn to play baseball or basketball.

Differential association reinforcement theory

In everyday life, different consequences are usually contingent upon different classes of behavior. This relationship between behavior and its consequences functions to alter the rate and form of behavior as well as its relationship to many feature of the environment. The

process of operant reinforcement is the most important process by
which behavior is generated and maintained.

Robert L. Burgess and Ronald L. Akers, 1966[17]

Robert Burgess and Ronald Akers developed differential association reinforcement theory
in an attempt to provide a more adequate explanation of the learning process under differential association. They reevaluated Sutherland's theory about differential association
using behaviorism and incorporated the psychological principles of operant conditioning.
Burgess and Akers opined that even nonsocial effects can reinforce criminal behavior.
According to Burgess and Akers, people are first indoctrinated into deviant behavior by
differential association with deviant peers. Then through differential reinforcement, they
learn how to reap rewards and avoid punishment in reference to the actual or anticipated
consequences of given behavior.[18]

The consequences are said to be social and nonsocial reinforcement that further
applies to a criminal's future. They noted that structure can affect a person's differential
reinforcement and that criminal knowledge is gained. Potential criminals often analyze
what they can get out of the crime and what their punishment may be after committing the
crime. After an evaluation, the criminal makes his or her decision. This aspect of Burgess
and Akers's theory included the concept of free will in that the criminal makes a choice
after evaluating the situation.

Differential identification theory

Daniel Glaser used Sutherland's notion of differential association to develop his differential identification theory.[19] According to Glaser, a person pursues criminal behavior to
the extent that he or she identifies himself or herself with real or imaginary persons from
whose perspective his or her criminal behavior appears to be acceptable. The process
leads the individual to an intimate personal identification with lawbreakers and thus
results in criminal behavior. Glaser disagreed with Sutherland in that it was not the frequency or the intensity of association that leads to criminal behavior but the symbolic
process of identification with a person or abstract understanding of what that person
may be like that leads to the behavior. According to Glaser, the role model can consist of
an abstract idea rather than an actual person. Using this concept, a person may identify
with an abstract model of a serial killer without ever having met a serial killer. Glaser
notes that the role of economic conditions, frustrations with one's place in society, learned
moral creeds, or group participation may affect a person's adaption of an abstract or real
role model. For example, Lee Harvey Oswald became infamous for his killing of President
Kennedy. A person who feels that he is neglected and has no place in society could adopt
Oswald as his perceived role model and attempt to become famous by committing a similar act. Glaser's theory could be used to explain the shooting of a U.S. Congresswoman
in Arizona, the theater massacre in Colorado, or the shooting of young school children in
Connecticut.

Labeling theory

The first dramatization of the "evil" which separates a child out
of his group for specialized treatment plays a greater role in making the criminal than perhaps any other experience. It cannot be

emphasized that for the child the whole situation has become different. He now lives in a different world. He has been tagged.

Frank Tannenbaum, 1938[20]

The labeling theory was developed in the early 1960s. It was originally referred to as the societal reaction school. The founders, who advocated the development of the labeling concepts, contended the popular theories of crime causation placed too much emphasis on individual deviance and neglected the reactions of people to this deviance. Frank Tannenbaum contended that we tended to overemphasize the original deviant act as well as the character of the deviant. He challenged the concept that because crime is bad, those who commit crime are also bad.

The development of the labeling perspective can be traced to the early works of Frank Tannenbaum and his 1938 book *Crime and the Community*.[21] Tannenbaum formalized the concept of "dramatization of evil." The concept holds that deviant behavior is not so much a product of the deviant's lack of adjustment to society as it is to the fact that the delinquent has adjusted to a special group and that criminal behavior is the product of a conflict between a group and the community. The conflict results in two opposing views of appropriate behavior. In one view, the community places a "label" on the child and identifies the child as a delinquent. This label results in the child changing his or her self-image and causes other people to react to the label and not the child. Accordingly, the process of labeling persons as criminals or delinquents creates crime.

In support of his theory, Tannenbaum noted that once a youth is arrested and labeled as a criminal, the youth is forced into companionship with other similarly defined youths, the results of which is that the youth is exposed to criminal mores and has a new set of experiences that lead directly to a criminal career.

In the 1960s, as our society was becoming more conscious of racial inequality and civil rights, the issues of the underprivileged members of society was one of the key topics of concern. The social atmosphere promoted by the "Great Society" first by President John Kennedy and later by President Lyndon Johnson helped increase the popularity of the labeling theory. Labeling was accepted as the reason why certain people were more frequently involved in the criminal justice system.

A popular concept used by the labeling theorists is the "looking-glass self." This concept defines the social self as made up of what a person sees others seeing in him or her. Others are a mirror (looking glass) to one's self. According to them, the looking glass is a predictor of future behavior because if a person thinks that others see him as lazy, the person will tend to be lazy. If others tend to see the individual as a criminal, then he or she will assume the part of a criminal. This concept is similar to the "self-fulfilling prophecy" concept.

According to Williams and McShane, the effects of labeling theory on criminology have been substantial. It is responsible for causing criminologists to question the commonly accepted middle-class values that individuals were using in their descriptions of deviance and criminality. In addition, researchers now take a more critical view of criminal justice agencies and the manner in which those agencies process or treat individuals.[22]

The process of making the criminal is, according to the labeling theory, a process of tagging, defining, identifying, segregating, describing, emphasizing, and making conscious and self-conscious. It is a way of stimulating, suggesting, emphasizing, and evoking the very traits that are complained of. The person becomes the thing he or she is described as being. It does not matter whether the valuation is made by those who would punish or by those who would reform. In either case, the emphasis is on conduct that they disapproved of. According to the labeling theorists, the harder individuals work to reform the delinquent, that is, the evil, the greater the evil grows under their hands. The persistent suggestion, with whatever good intentions, works mischief because it leads to bringing out the bad behavior it would suppress. The way out is through a refusal to dramatize the evil. In other words, skip the labeling process because the less said about the delinquent behavior the better. Does this mean that if we ignore the first or primary acts of deviance by a youth that he or she would be less likely to commit additional deviance? Many individuals would argue that by ignoring the primary act we are encouraging the juvenile to commit additional deviant acts.

The basic principles of the labeling theory are the following:

- Society tends to have multiple values with differing degrees of overlap.
- The quality of behavior is determined by the application of societal values to an individual's behavior. The identification of the behavior as deviant occurs because of the reaction to that behavior.
- Deviance exists only because there is a reaction to the behavior.
- Once behavior is perceived and labeled deviant by the social audience, the individual who is responsible for the behavior is labeled as deviant.
- The adverse reaction to behavior and the invocation of the labeling process is more likely to occur when the actor is a member of a less socially powerful class.
- Society tends to observe more closely those whom have been identified as deviants and therefore will find even more deviance in those persons. Subsequent deviant acts are reacted to more quickly and the deviant label more firmly affixed.
- Depending on the strength of an individual's original self-concept, once a person is labeled as deviant, the individual will accept the label as his or her self-identity.
- A person who is labeled as criminal is also perceived to be first and foremost a criminal; individual's other attributes are generally ignored.
- Further deviant behavior (secondary deviance) is a product of living and acting within the deviant label.

The labeling theory has had significant influence on the study of crime causation. It has caused us to reexamine our basic concepts regarding crime and criminals. It has also had its critics. One of the most serious criticisms is that it is not a theory, but a perspective, and that it has no systemic theoretical basis. In addition, like differential association theory, empirical testing of the labeling theory is impossible.

ASSUMPTIONS OF LABELING THEORISTS

- The initial acts of delinquency by an offender are caused by a wide variety of factors.
- Primary deviance is generally considered to be undetected, or not recognized, as deviant by others.
- A deviant is considered as an important key in the process because of the consequences of the label of deviant produces for the labelee.
- The process of moving from primary deviance to secondary deviance is very complex.

- The process of becoming a secondary deviant is based on the connection between the behavior and societal reaction to the behavior.
- The official application of the label of delinquent is dependent on a host of criteria including the behavior itself; the offender's age, sex, race, and social class; and the group's norms.
- The final step is the acceptance by society of the label of deviance applied to the individual.

The labeling theories have generally discussed the effects of formal application of sanctions such as sentences awarded by courts in labeling a person as a criminal. Little attention has apparently been paid to informal sanctions such as the reaction of families, neighbors, and other social groups. Triplett and Jarjoura[23] contend that there is evidence that under certain circumstances, informal social sanctions can worsen the conduct of the individual.

Social control theories

> Control theories of delinquency cover a wide range of topics. Lamar Empey characterizes nineteenth-century and early twentieth-century individualistic theories of delinquency as "control" theories. Travis Hirschi traces the ideas of control theory as far back as Durkheim in the nineteenth century.
>
> **David J. Shoemaker, 2002[24]**

In the 1970s, as labeling theory began to lose popularity and conflict theories became more radical, social control theories gained popularity.[25] The term "control" in social control theories refers to any perspective that tends to control people. Although there are differences between the various control theories, all appear to have one basic principle: People will commit deviant behavior. Whereas most theories ask, "Why do people commit crime?" the control theorist asks, "Why do people obey laws?" Accordingly, the major task of social control theories is their attempt to explain the factors that keep people from committing criminal behavior.[26]

Social control theories may be described as socialization theories. The process of socialization is probably the dominant method by which groups control individuals. We are taught the "right way" to act and to perform. The basic theme of social control theories is that the social bond of an individual to society determines whether or not the individual commits criminal behavior.

The earliest form of social control theory can be traced to Emile Durkheim.[27] Durkheim contended that a society without deviance would be an abnormal society. Durkheim noted that deviance has social utility. Accordingly, deviance helps maintain social order.

Durkheim contended that even punishment plays a role in the maintenance of social solidary. According to him, when the rules of the collective conscience are violated, society responds with repressive sanctions, not for retribution or deterrence, but because those of us who conform will be demoralized. Durkheim noted that when an offender is punished, those of us who are not punished receive the award of "not being punished" because of our "good" behavior.

He contended that it would be a pathological state of society if there were no crime. A society that had no crime would be one in which the constraints of the collective conscience are so rigid that no one could oppose them. In this type of situation, crime would be eliminated, but so would the possibility of any progressive social change because no one would dare deviate from the norm. On a personal level, individual growth could not occur in a child if it was impossible for the child to misbehave. And a child who never did anything wrong would be pathologically overcontrolled. Elimination of misbehavior would also eliminate the possibility of independent growth.

In a perfect society, that is, one without crime or deviance, what would our movies, books of fiction, and television be like? Consider how much of our entertainment involves misconduct or crime. It would be a boring society. In addition, if there were no need for police officers, courts, judges, correctional officers, or school crossing guards a lot of individuals would be without a job.

Social control theorists contend that people's relationships, commitments, values, norms, and beliefs encourage them not to break the law. According to this line of reasoning, if a person's moral codes are internalized and the individual has accepted them and has a stake in their wider community, he or she will voluntarily limit the propensity to commit deviant acts.

The social control theorist is looking to understand the ways in which it is possible to reduce the likelihood of criminality developing in individuals. The theorists do not consider motivational issues. They simply state that human beings may choose to engage in a wide range of activities, unless the range is limited by the processes of socialization and social learning.[28]

SHOULD A PERSON GUILTY OF JAYWALKING RECEIVE THE MAXIMUM ALLOWABLE PUNISHMENT?

Consider the consequences of a society without serious crime. As noted by Emil Durkheim, this would be a pathological state. Using the concept that the most serious crimes should receive the maximum punishments permitted in a society, if aggravated murder is the most serious crime then a person who commits this crime should receive the maximum punishment. But if the society has no serious crime, then would the maximum punishment be reserved for to those individuals who commit minor transgressions such as jaywalking?

EMILE DURKHEIM (1858–1917): THE FIRST SOCIOLOGIST

Emile Durkheim rejected the classical school concepts that humans were free and rational in a contractual society. He focused on society and its organization and development for explanations of criminal behavior. His theories are complex and overlap with different social approaches to criminal behavior.

Emile Durkheim is considered one of the best known and least understood major social thinkers. He was born of Jewish parents in a small French town on the German border. He was schooled in Paris and taught philosophy at various secondary schools in France. Later, he spent a year in Germany studying under the famed experimental psychologist Wilhelm Wundt. After the publication of two articles, he obtained a professorship at the University of Bordeaux. At the university, he taught the first course in a French university on sociology. Later, he received the first doctor's degree awarded by the University of Paris in sociology and an appointment to the faculty at the University of Paris, and he taught there until his death in 1917.

Social bond theory

> The more weakened the groups to which [the person] belongs, the less he depends on them, the more he consequently depends only on himself and recognizes no other rules of conduct than what are founded on his private interests.
>
> **Travis Hirschi, 1969[29]**

One of the more popular control theories is Travis Hirschi's social bond theory. He contended that because of socialization, a bond forms between individuals and the social groups. He contended that when the social bond was weakened or broken, deviance and crime could result.[30] There are four parts of Hirschi's social bond that determine whether or not a person will engage in group conforming behavior that is approved by other members of the group. The parts or types of bonds are the following:

- Attachment: A person's shared interests with others. (By attachment, Hirschi is referring to the ties to people that are important to the individual and to his or her sensitivity to the various options.)
- Commitment: The amount of energy and effort the individual puts into activities with others. (For Hirschi, this is the rational component of the bond. By commitment, he refers to the time and effort or energy that the individual invests in the accepted standards of the group and in the group's ways of living. When there is no commitment to the conventional values of the group, the individual is more likely to commit unacceptable behavior.)
- Involvement: The amount of time the individual spends with members of the group in shared activities. (The more an individual is involved in conventional things, the less the individual is likely to commit unacceptable behavior.)
- Belief: In the shared values and belief in the moral system. (If you have strong beliefs in the shared values and in the moral system, you are less likely to violate them.)

Hirschi's "belief" aspect of his social bond theory distinguishes his social bond theory from the subcultural approaches discussed earlier in Chapter 5. Unlike the subcultural approaches, Hirschi's social bond theory assumes the existence of a common value system within a society or group. The assumption of a common value system implies that the deviant accepts the common values and rules of a society and yet at the same time violates those rules. Hirschi's response is based on the premise that although a person may know that the rules exist, the person just does not care and he or she invests little time in worrying about moral standards.

General theory of crime

> In their search for a universal criminology, Hirschi and Gottfredson
> define crimes as "acts of force or fraud undertaken" in pursuit of
> self-interest. For them, different cultural settings cannot influence
> the causes of crime except by affecting the opportunities and the
> ease with which crimes can occur.
>
> **David Nelken, 2002**[31]

The general theory of crime was developed in the 1990s by Travis Hirschi and Michael Gottfredson. The theory is based on social control theory concepts.[32] The basic premise of the theory is that crime is a natural consequence of unrestrained human tendencies to seek pleasure and avoid pain. And that an offender is neither a diabolical genius of fiction nor an ambitious seeker of the American dream. They see the offender as an individual with little control over his or her desires. According to the theorists, when personal desires conflict with long-term interests, those who lack control will most likely choose the desires of the moment and thus ignore legal restrictions and become involved in crime. Like the social bond theory, the general theory of crime supporters contend that self-control is the key to crime prevention.

Gottfredson and Hirschi differentiate between "criminality" and "crime." Criminality to them refers to the propensity to commit crime, whereas crime refers to an actual act or conduct that violates the law. They note that a propensity to commit a crime (criminality) cannot be acted upon until the opportunity to commit the act exists. They see crime as a by-product of people with low self-control who have high criminogenic propensities coming into contact with illegal opportunities.[33]

Social learning theories

> Modeling or social learning theory emphasizes the point that behav-
> ior may be reinforced not only through actual rewards and punish-
> ments but also through expectations that are learned by watching
> what happens to other people.
>
> **George B. Vold**[34]

Social learning theories were developed in the 1960s but did not become popular until about 1975. There are two social learning theories. One was developed by C. Ray Jeffery, who used the direct application of operant-based learning theories from psychology. This version saw criminal behavior as normal learned behavior and focused on how learning takes place.[35]

The later version of social learning theory was developed in the 1970s by Ronald Akers. Akers examined the social environment in an attempt to explain crime causation. His social learning theory was primarily an extension of Sutherland's differential association. By "learning," the theorists refer to habits and knowledge that develop as the result of the experiences of the individual in entering and adjusting to the environment. They distinguish learning from unlearned or instinctive behavior, which seems to be present in the individual at birth and determined by biology. Albert Bandura contended that all persons have self-regulatory mechanisms and thus reward and punish themselves according to internal standards for judging their own behavior. He concluded that aggression may be inhibited in some people (e.g., high moral standards and religious beliefs); however, these people may still engage in aggressive behavior through the process of disengagement.

Social learning theory is based on the concept that the history of either reward or punishment, as it is associated with criminal behavior, influences its natural continuation. Bandura relied heavily on B.F. Skinner's operant learning theory. He concentrated on researching the causes of violent and aggressive behavior and asserted that not only is learning reinforced through actual rewards and punishments but also that we learn by watching others receive rewards and punishments for certain forms of behavior. According to Bandura, we then imitate or model those behaviors that are rewarded and resist those behaviors that are punished.[36]

Disengagement may result from

- Attributing blame to one's victims
- Dehumanization through bureaucratization, automation, urbanization, and high social mobility
- Vindication of aggressive practices by legitimate authorities
- Desensitization resulting from repeated exposure to aggression in any of a variety of forms

Ronald Akers's social learning theory expanded Sutherland's differential association theory by adding components of operant (voluntary response) and respondent (involuntary response) conditioning. Akers identified four key elements that help shape behavior:

1. The learning of definitions favorable or unfavorable to the law through processes of social interaction
2. Applying one's own attitudes, including orientations, rationalizations, definitions of the situation, and other evaluative aspects of right and wrong
3. The actual or anticipated consequences of engaging in specific behavior
4. Imitation

The concept of imitation or modeling is central to the learning process. Under the social learning concepts, we learn criminal behavior by observing the behavior of others in the context of the social environment.

The learning theories are based on Skinner's operant learning theory. Operant learning theory is concerned with the effect that an individual's behavior has on the environment and the consequences of that effect on the individual. Behavior, therefore, is shaped and maintained by its consequences. According to a learning behavior theorist, we are products of present and past events in our lives. The determination as to whether the frequency of any particular behavior is increased or diminished is based on the contingencies of reinforcement and punishment (aversive stimuli).

The basic principles that learning behavior theorists look at are the following:

- Positive reinforcement
- Negative reinforcement
- Positive punishment
- Negative punishment
- Discriminative stimuli
- Schedules

Reinforcement is considered an event that follows the occurrence of behavior and that alters and increases the frequency of the behavior. Those that directly increase the behavior are positive reinforcers and those that remove something undesirable are negative reinforcers. Punishment is the opposite of reinforcement. Discriminate stimuli do not occur after the behavior, but are present either before or as the behavior occurs. Schedules refer to the frequency with which, and the probability that, a particular consequence will occur. Learning takes place because of the consequences associated with behavior.

Burgess and Akers's differential association reinforcement theory, which is discussed in the section "Differential association reinforcement theory" in this chapter, accepts the six basic principles and adds satiation and deprivation to them. They contend that a stimulus will be more or less reinforcing depending on the individual's current situation. For example, a person who already has money (satiated) will be less reinforced by robbing someone than a person who is impoverished (deprived). Because individuals do not have the same past experiences, their conditioning histories are different. Accordingly, some stimuli that people experience daily will produce different responses in different individuals.

Containment theory

> According to the containment theory, behavior, deviant or conforming, is the result of a struggle between social pressures, social pulls of the milieu, and inner pushes of the individual—all seen in a vertical arrangement.
>
> **Stephen Schafer, 1966**[37]

The containment theory was developed in the 1950s by Walter C. Reckless. Reckless appeared to be troubled by the inability of sociological theories on crime causation to predict which individuals will commit criminal behavior and which ones will not. Reckless also failed to predict which specific individuals would commit criminal behavior. He rationalized this failure by comparing his theory with a biological immune response, noting that only some people who are exposed to a disease catch the disease. Accordingly, not all people who are exposed to situations likely to cause criminal behavior commit crime.[38]

The containment theorists stress that we live in a society that provides a variety of opportunities for conformity or nonconformity. Both illegal and legal opportunities are available and not everyone will choose to commit criminal behavior. Accordingly, the existence of subcultures, the location of goods and services within a city, the population density, and other variables do not adequately explain criminal behavior. According to Reckless, what we need to know is why these phenomena affect some people and not others. That is, why are some individuals immune to such influences?

Walter Reckless attempted to answer this question using his containment theory. He defined the theory as follows:

> The assumption is that there is a containing external social structure which holds individuals in line and that there is also an internal buffer which protects people against deviation of the social and legal norms. The two containments act as defense against deviation from the legal and social norms or as insulation against pressures and pulls—a protection against demoralization and seduction. If there are "causes" which lead to deviant behavior, they are negated, neutralized, rendered impotent, or are paired by the containing buffers.[39]

Reckless formulated two types of containment—outer containment and inner containment. Outer containments are also defined as social pressures and represent the structural buffer in the person's immediate social world. They consist of items such as a presentation of a consistent moral front to the person and institutional reinforcement of his or her norms, goals, and expectations.

Inner containments consist mainly of self-components, such as self-control, good self-concept, ego strength, well-developed superego, high tolerance for frustration, high sense of responsibility, and strong goal orientation. Reckless believed that the inner containments provided the most effective controls on a person. Together, the inner and outer containments work to prevent people from becoming criminals. There are many social pressures that pull and push a person toward criminal behavior and interact with their containments.

Walter Reckless also developed the concept of "categorical risk." The concept is important in describing class variations in criminal involvement. According to Reckless, persons in the lowest socioeconomic group run a greater risk of engaging in common forms of serious criminal behavior because this group generally associates with others of the same socioeconomic group. Reckless also notes that this "lower socioeconomic group" run a greater risk of being suspected of serious crimes and if arrested a greater risk of being prosecuted. If prosecuted, they run a greater risk of being imprisoned. He bases this on the fact that society tends to stereotype individuals based on their socioeconomic class.[40]

WALTER RECKLESS'S CONTAINMENTS

INNER CONTAINMENTS—PERSONAL CONTROLS

- Good self-concept
- Self-control
- Strong ego
- Well-developed conscience
- High tolerance for frustration
- Strong sense of responsibility

OUTER/EXTERNAL CONTAINMENTS

- Institutional reinforcement of goals, norms, and expectations
- Presentation of a consistent moral front to the person
- Provisions for reasonable scope of activity
- Effective supervision and discipline

Techniques of neutralization

> It is our argument that much delinquency is based on what is essentially an unregulated extension of defenses to crimes, in the form of justifications for deviance that are seen as valid by the delinquent but not by the legal system or society at large.
>
> **Gresham M. Sykes and David Matza, 1957**[41]

David Matza and Gresham Sykes contend that delinquents have no commitment either to societal norms or to criminal norms. Instead, delinquents drift in and out of crime. Although delinquents tend to spend most of their time in law-abiding behaviors, they are flexible in their commitment to the values of the dominant society and the majority of them are drifters into criminal activity. Matza and Sykes contend that people do not commit crimes when they are controlled by morals; however, when the morals can be neutralized, the controls lessen and then individuals are more likely to commit criminal actions. Accordingly, people need to neutralize their morals before violating laws they believe in. To explain this concept, Matza and Sykes formulated the techniques of neutralization.[42] The techniques act to lessen the effects of social controls. Those techniques are listed as follows:

- "Denial of responsibility": The delinquent defines himself or herself as lacking responsibility for the behavior in question. The acts are the product of forces beyond the control of the delinquent. The delinquent feels that he or she is being pulled/pushed into situations beyond his or her control. Typical response: "I didn't mean to do it, but … "
- "Denial of injury": There is no harm to victims. For example, auto theft is viewed as borrowing. Gang fighting is seen as a private quarrel and no one else's business. The victim (e.g., insurance company, large company, or government) can easily afford the loss or damage. The delinquent may also feel that his or her behavior does not cause any great harm despite the fact that it runs counter to the law.
- "Denial of the victim": The injury is not wrong in light of the circumstances. The offender is retaliating for a previous act of the victim. The victim deserves the injury or there is no real victim. For example, the victim had it coming to him because the victim was a drug user.
- "Condemnation of the condemners": This technique involves a shift in focus. It is a rejection of the rejecters. For example, to the offender, the police are corrupt, stupid, and brutal. The offender thinks that many condemners are hypocrites and deviants in disguise.
- "Appeal to higher loyalties": The norms of the group or gang are more important than those of society in general. For example, you always help a buddy and never squeal on a friend.

DISCUSSING CRIME CAUSATION WITH FELONS

In 1982, Cliff Roberson, one of the coauthors, was a professor at St. Edwards University in Austin, Texas. He was asked by a representative of a nearby community college to teach a college-level course in criminal justice in a federal prison. When he accepted the assignment, Roberson was under the opinion that he would be teaching a criminology course to the correctional staff at the federal prison.

At his first night in class, he discovered that all 20 plus students were prisoners. This course was part of a program to provide prisoners with an opportunity to obtain an associate's degree during their incarceration. The students were serving sentences for various crimes such as bank robbery, drug trafficking, and tax evasion.

There was a telephone on the wall in the classroom. On the telephone was a panic button that would sound a general alarm in the prison if there was an emergency.

During the first couple of classes, Roberson would stand near the telephone during the class so that the panic button was nearby. Later as the semester progressed, he became more at ease and returned to his customary classroom practice of roaming the classroom during the class.

The students were always well prepared. Without the normal outside influences that are associated with normal college life, the students read and reread their assignments before class. They were very interested in the subject matter and the discussions were very heated. Each had definite opinions about crime causation and how to prevent crime. As the semester progressed and the instructor became more comfortable with the discussions of crime causations with the students, he started asking them questions regarding their involvement in crime. The students (convicted prisoners) were asked if they agreed with certain theories on crime causation and asked how the theories related to any crimes they may have committed. The traditional answer was that they agreed with certain theories, but these theories did not apply in their particular cases because they would then attempt to neutralize their misconduct. For example, one prisoner indicated that he robbed a bank because he knew the bank would not suffer any loss since it was insured, whereas if he robbed a small store, the store owner would suffer a financial loss. Another student indicated that he filed false income tax returns because the federal government had taken his parents' business.

Dramaturgy

All the world is a stage, and all the men and women merely players: They have their exits and their entrances; and one man in his time plays any parts.

William Shakespeare, 1599[43]

Erving Goffman in his book *The Presentation of Self in Everyday Life* introduced the dramaturgy perspective of crime causation.[44] According to Goffman, the individual plays a variety of nearly simultaneous social roles such as student, employee, father, and husband. These roles must be sustained in interaction with others. According to Goffman, social actors present themselves more or less effectively when they are acting out particular roles. Role performances consist of managed impressions. It is through communications, either verbal or nonverbal, that social actors define the situation in which they are involved. Goffman uses the example of a medical doctor. The doctor wears a white coat with a name tag and introduces himself or herself as Dr. Smith. Each choice the doctor makes is in conformity with the doctor's role as a medical healer. The doctor then acts and conveys the message of authority as a doctor. And the doctor acts appropriately.

Goffman sees the discredited or stigmatized individual as acting out his or her role as that individual feels it is appropriate. Accordingly, the delinquent acts out his or her accepted role in society. Goffman also notes that when "normal" people approach someone who has been stigmatized, the normal people expect that the person will conform to stigmatizing behavior. According to Goffman, we judge individuals according to the acting role we expect them to assume. Note that this is very similar to the rationale used by the labeling theorists to explain criminal behavior.

Summary

- Social process theories assume that everyone has the potential to commit crime and that criminology is not an innate human characteristic.
- Because these theories depend on the processes of interaction between individuals and society, the theories are also referred to as the interactionist perspectives of crime causation.
- Social process theorists assume that criminal behavior is a function of a socialization process. Criminal behavior is learned in interaction with others and the socialization processes that occur as a by-product of group membership are the primary methods by which learning occurs. Offenders turn to crime as a result of peer group pressure, family problems, poor school performance, legal entanglements, and other situations that gradually steer them to criminal behaviors. Anyone can become a criminal.
- SI theories focus on situations and interactions with society leading up to the crime rather than on the differences or defectiveness of the offenders.
- The two major crime causation theories based on the concepts of SI are differential association and labeling.
- Edwin Sutherland developed the theory of differential association in an attempt to explain career criminal behavior.
- According to the differential association theory, a person becomes delinquent because of an excess of definitions favorable to violation of the law over definitions unfavorable to violation of law.
- Robert Burgess and Ronald Akers developed differential association reinforcement theory in an attempt to provide a more adequate explanation of the learning process under differential association. They reevaluated Sutherland's theory about differential association using behaviorism and incorporated the psychological principles of operant conditioning.
- Daniel Glaser used Sutherland's notion of differential association to develop his differential identification theory.
- According to Glaser, a person pursues criminal behavior to the extent that he or she identifies himself or herself with real or imaginary persons from whose perspective his or her criminal behavior appears to be acceptable.
- The labeling theory was developed in the early 1960s. It was originally referred to as the societal reaction school. The founders, who advocated the development of the labeling concepts, contended the popular theories of crime causation placed too much emphasis on individual deviance, and neglected the reactions of people to this deviance.
- Frank Tannenbaum contended that we tended to overemphasize the original deviant act as well as the character of the deviant. He challenged the concept that because crime is bad, those who commit crime are also bad.
- A popular concept used by the labeling theorists is the "looking-glass self." This concept defines the social self as made up of what a person sees others seeing in him or her. Others are a mirror (looking glass) to one's self.
- The process of making the criminal is, according to the labeling theory, a process of tagging, defining, identifying, segregating, describing, emphasizing, and making conscious and self-conscious. It is a way of stimulating, suggesting, emphasizing, and evoking the very traits that are complained of.
- The person becomes the thing he or she is described as being.

- The term "control" in the social control theories refers to any perspective that tends to control people.
- Although there are differences between the various control theories, all appear to have one basic principle: People will commit deviant behavior. Whereas most theories ask, "Why do people commit crime?" the control theorist asks, "Why do people obey laws?"
- The earliest form of social control theory can be traced to Emile Durkheim. Durkheim contended that a society without deviance would be an abnormal society. Durkheim noted that deviance has social utility.
- Social control theorists contend that people's relationships, commitments, values, norms, and beliefs encourage them not to break the law.
- One of the more popular control theories is Travis Hirschi's social bond theory. Hirschi contended that because of socialization, a bond forms between individuals and the social groups. He contended that when the social bond was weakened or broken, deviance and crime could result.
- The general theory of crime was developed in the 1990s by Travis Hirschi and Michael Gottfredson. The theory is based on social control theory concepts. The basic premise of the theory is that crime is a natural consequence of unrestrained human tendencies to seek pleasure and avoid pain.
- Social learning theories were developed in the 1960s but did not become popular until about 1975. There are two social learning theories.
- One was developed by C. Ray Jeffery, who used the direct application of operant-based learning theories from psychology. This version saw criminal behavior as normal learned behavior and focused on how learning takes place.
- The later version of the social learning theory was developed mostly in the 1970s by Ronald Akers. Akers examined the social environment in an attempt to explain crime causation. His social learning theory was primarily an extension of Sutherland's differential association.
- The containment theory was developed in the 1950s by Walter C. Reckless. Reckless appeared to be troubled by the inability of sociological theories on crime causation to predict which individuals will commit criminal behavior and which ones will not.
- David Matza and Gresham Sykes contend that delinquents have no commitment either to societal norms or to criminal norms. Instead, delinquents drift in and out of crime. Although delinquents tend to spend most of their time in law-abiding behaviors, they are flexible in their commitment to the values of the dominant society and the majority of them are drifters into criminal activity.
- Erving Goffman introduced the dramaturgy perspective of crime causation. According to Goffman, the individual plays a variety of nearly simultaneous social roles such as student, employee, father, and husband. These roles must be sustained in interaction with others.

Questions in review

1. How does the differential association theory differ from the labeling theory?
2. Which of the social process theories do you think more adequately explains criminal behavior?
3. Explain the role of primary deviance to labeling theorists.
4. How do Burgess and Akers modify Sutherland's differential association theory?
5. Compare and contrast social control and the techniques of neutralization theories.
6. How does Goffman explain criminal behavior?

Practicum

The strange case of Richard Miller

Richard Miller, an FBI special agent, was arrested in 1984 along with two people suspected of being agents of the Soviet KGB. Miller was accused of providing classified documents, including an FBI counterintelligence manual, to the Soviet agents. There was evidence that he demanded for $15,000 cash and $50,000 in gold for this information. Miller, who had eight children and was faced with financial difficulties, was alleged to be having an affair with the female agent, and was preparing to travel with her to Vienna at the time of his arrest.

According to various news accounts, Miller occasionally took 3-hour "lunches" at the 7-Elevens near his Los Angeles FBI office, gorging himself on stolen candy bars while reading comic books. He was alleged to have cheated his own uncle by selling a muscle-relaxant device he had patented and skimmed cash from bureau coffers meant for one of his informants. The media reported that Miller also ran auto-registration checks and searched FBI criminal indexes for a local private investigator at $500 per search. Before his arrest, Miller was considered a very religious person with a conservative political ideology and had been an FBI special agent for almost 20 years. Miller is reported to have stated that his relationship with a Russian woman spy was "the dumbest thing I did in my whole life." The female Soviet spy alleged in an interview that Miller had initiated the affair and had forced himself upon her. In 1982, a psychologist had examined Miller and told the FBI that he was emotionally unstable and should be nurtured along in some harmless post until retirement.

At trial, Miller pleaded innocent, and after 11 weeks of testimony, a mistrial was declared. At a second trial, he was found guilty of espionage and bribery. During his trials, Miller claimed that his actions were because of his attempts to infiltrate the KGB as a double agent. This claim was rejected by the jury. He was sentenced to two consecutive life terms and 50 years on other charges. This conviction was overturned by an appellate court on the grounds that the U.S. District judge erred in admitting polygraph evidence during the trial. He was retried a third time and received a 20-year prison sentence that was later reduced to 13 years.[45]

Questions regarding the Miller case

1. Does any of the crime causation theories examined in this chapter or in earlier chapters explain why Miller, a 20-year FBI special agent, would commit espionage and bribery?
2. Should the fact that he was tried by three separate trials have any effect on the length of punishment he should have received?
3. If you were a researcher studying crime causation, what questions would you ask Miller if you had the opportunity to interview him after he has been released from prison?

References

1. LaRossa, R., & Reitzes, D. C. (1993). Symbolic interactionism and family studies. In P. G. Boss, W. J. Doherty, R. LaRossa, W. R. Schumm, & S. K. Steinmetz (Eds.), *Sourcebook of family theories and methods: A contextual approach* (pp. 135–163). New York: Plenum Press.
2. Thomas, W. I. (1931). *The unadjusted girl* (p. 12). Boston: Little, Brown.

3. Sanders, W. B. (1983). *Criminology*. Reading, MA: Addison-Wesley.
4. Blumer, H. (1969). *Symbolic interaction* (pp. 4–5). Englewood Cliffs, NJ: Prentice-Hall.
5. Burgess, R. L., & Akers, R. L. (1966, Fall). A differential association-reinforcement theory of criminal behavior. *Social Problems, 14*, 128–147.
6. Sutherland, E. H. (1977). The differential association theory. In S. Schafer & R. D. Knudten (Eds.), *Criminological theory*. Lexington, MA: Lexington Books.
7. Nettler, G. (1978). *Explaining crime* (2nd ed.). New York: McGraw-Hill. See also Masters, R., & Roberson, C. (1990). *Inside criminology*. Englewood Cliffs, NJ: Prentice-Hall.
8. Masters, R., & Roberson, C. (1990). *Inside criminology* (p. 201). Englewood Cliffs, NJ: Prentice-Hall
9. Gibbons, D. (1978). *The criminological enterprise* (p. 65). New York: Macmillan.
10. Sutherland, E. H. (1934). *Principles of criminology* (2nd ed., pp. 54–55). Philadelphia: Lippincott.
11. Sutherland, E. H., & Cressey, D. (1978). *Criminology* (10th ed., pp. 80–82). Philadelphia: Lippincott.
12. Sutherland, E. H. (1940). White collar criminology. *American Sociological Review, 5*(1), 1–2. [Because of the age of the article, the American Sociological Association stated permission was not needed to quote sections of the article.]
13. Short, J. S. (1960). Differential association as a hypothesis: Problems of empirical testing. *Social Problems, 8*, 14–15.
14. Hirschi, T. (1969). *Causes of delinquency* (p. 95). Berkeley, CA: University of California Press.
15. Sutherland, E. H., & Cressy, D. R. (1978). *Criminology* (10th ed.). Philadelphia: Lippincott.
16. The Crime Theory Box on Edwin Sutherland was originally printed in DiMarino, F., & Roberson, C. (2013). *An introduction to white collar and corporate crime*. Boca Raton, FL: CRC Press.
17. Burgess, R. L., & Akers, R. L. (1966, Fall). A differential association-reinforcement theory of criminal behavior. *Social Problems, 14*, 128–147.
18. Burgess, R. L., & Akers, R. L. (1966, Fall). A differential association-reinforcement theory of criminal behavior. *Social Problems, 14*, 129
19. Glaser, D. (1960). Differential association and criminologist. *Social Problems, 8*, 6–14.
20. Tannenbaum, F. (1938). *Crime and the community* (pp. 19–20). Boston: Ginn.
21. Tannenbaum, F. (1938). *Crime and the community*. Boston: Ginn.
22. Williams, F. P., III, & McShane, M. D. (1994). *Criminological theory* (2nd ed., p. 141). Englewood Cliffs, NJ: Prentice-Hall.
23. Triplett, R. A., & Jarjoura, G. R. (1994). Theoretical and empirical specification of a model of informal labeling. *Journal of Quantitative Criminology, 10*, 246–271.
24. Shoemaker, D. J. (2002). *Theories of delinquency* (p. 207). Oxford, England: Oxford University Press.
25. Empey, L. T. (1978). *American delinquency: Its meaning and construction*. Homewood, IL: Dorsey.
26. Hirschi, T. (1969). *Causes of delinquency*. Berkeley, CA: University of California Press.
27. Durkheim, E. (1895). *The rules of the sociological method*. (S. A. Solovay & J. Mueller, Trans.). New York: Free Press.
28. Reiss, A. J. (1951). Delinquency and the failure of personal and social controls. *American Sociological Review, 16*, 196–207.
29. Hirschi, T. (1969). *Causes of delinquency* (p. 16). Berkeley, CA: University of California Press.
30. Hirschi, T. (1969). *Causes of delinquency*. Berkeley, CA: University of California Press.
31. Nelken, D. (2002). Comparing criminal justice. In M. Maguire, R. Morgan, & R. Reiner (Eds.), *The Oxford handbook of criminology* (3rd ed., pp. 174–228). Oxford, England: Oxford University Press.
32. Gottfredson, M., & Hirschi, T. (1990). *A general theory of crime*. Stanford, CA: Stanford University Press.
33. Gottfredson, M. R., & Hirschi, T. (2003). A general theory of crime. In F. Cullen, & R. Agnew (Eds.), *Criminological theory: Past to present* (pp. 240–253). Los Angeles: Roxbury.
34. Vold, G. B. (1958). *Theoretical criminology* (p. 207). Oxford, England: Oxford University Press.
35. Williams, F. P., III, & McShane, M. D. (2004). *Criminological theory* (4th ed., pp. 217–218). Columbus, OH: Pearson.
36. Bandura, A. (1973). *Aggression: A social learning approach*. Englewood Cliffs, NJ: Prentice Hall.

37. Schafer, S. (1966). *Theories in criminology: Past and present philosophies of the crime problem* (p. 224). New York: Random House.
38. Reckless, W. C. (1967). *The crime problem* (4th ed.). New York: Appleton-Century Crofts.
39. Reckless, W. C. (1970). Containment theory. In M. Wolfgang, L. D. Savitz, N. B. Johnston (Eds.), *The sociology of crime and delinquency* (2nd ed., pp. 402–403). New York: John Wiley.
40. Shur, E. M. (1969). *Our criminal society: The social and legal sources of crime in America* (p. 39–40). Englewood Cliffs, NJ: Prentice-Hall.
41. Matza, D. (1964). *Delinquency and drift.* New York: Wiley. See also Sykes, G. M., & Matza, D. (1957). Techniques of neutralization. *American Sociological Review*, 22, 664–671.
42. Matza, D. (1964). *Delinquency and drift.* New York: Wiley. See also Sykes, G. M., & Matza, D. (1957). Techniques of neutralization. *American Sociological Review*, 22, 664–671.
43. Shakespeare, W. (1599). *As you like it.* Act II, Scene 7, line 139. Retrieved January 26, 2013, from www.poets.org/viewmedia.php/prmMID/15740
44. Goffman, E. (1959). *The presentation of self in everyday life.* Garden City, NY: Doubleday.
45. Howe, R. W. (1993). *Sleeping with the FBI: Sex, booze, Russians and the saga of an American counter-spy who couldn't.* Washington, DC: National Press Books.

chapter seven

Integrated theories

Chapter objectives

After studying this chapter, you should be able to

- Explain why developmental theories were popular during the 1980s and 1990s
- Describe how developmental theorists examine offending from an early age to adulthood
- Understand the key concepts of the integrated cognitive antisocial potential theory
- Explain how the developmental propensity theory views offending
- Distinguish between the social development model and the dual pathways theory
- Discuss the network theory
- Explain the distinguishing feature of multifactor theories
- Describe the key arguments of control balance theory
- Analyze the implications of differential coercion theory for criminal justice policy
- Explain the contribution of Le Banc's generic control theory

Introduction

In this chapter, we examine those theories that integrate and expand upon the arguments of other theories to provide more robust explanations of crime. Integration involves the linking and synthesizing of different theories of crime causation in an attempt to discover why individuals commit crime or antisocial behavior. Integrative theories vary in their scope. For example, although some focus on particular types of behavior or offenders in social process modeling, others may focus on why most individuals desist from offending as they age or how individuals develop. They can generally be divided into two categories based on their emphasis: (1) developmental theories, which prioritize explanations of change over time within individual offenders and (2) multifactor theories, which focus on building an explanation of crime that crosscuts different layers of analysis.

Developmental theories of offending

Developmental theories of criminology were popular in the 1980s and 1990s. One reason for their popularity in those two decades is attributed to the enormous volume and significance of longitudinal research on offending that was published during that period.

Developmental theories of criminology are concerned with the following:

- The development of offending and antisocial behavior from birth to death
- The influence of risk and protective factors at different ages
- The effects of life events on the course of development[1]

The developmental theories examined in this section include the general theory or "super traits" theory of Robert Agnew, the developmental propensity theory of Lahey and Waldman, the adolescence-limited/life-course-persistent theory of Moffitt, the interactional theory of Thornberry and Krohn, and the age-graded informal social control theory of Sampson and Laub.

Traditional criminological theories are generally focused on explaining differences in offending between individuals such as trying to explain why lower-class boys commit more offences than boys from more affluent families. Developmental theories are focused on explaining the differences in offending rates of individuals over a period, for example, why does an individual commit more criminal acts at a certain age than he or she commits at a different age?

Developmental theories investigate the prevalence of offending at different ages. Because the theories are interested in the differences of an individual at different ages, research is generally conducted using longitudinal studies, for example, the Cambridge Study in Delinquent Development, which was a prospective longitudinal survey of over 400 London males from age 8 to 48.

CAMBRIDGE STUDY IN DELINQUENT DEVELOPMENT 1961–1981

The Cambridge Study in Delinquent Development was a longitudinal survey of 411 males. Data collection was started in 1961 when the boys were at ages 8 and 9. The boys in 1961 were living in a working-class neighborhood in London. They were almost all white Caucasians. There were only 12 boys who were black. The boys were interviewed and tested in their schools when they were aged about 8, 10, and 14. They were interviewed in the Cambridge Research Center around ages 16, 18, 21, and 24. During the study, 1 boy died and 22 were eventually missing. At age 21, only those who were convicted delinquents were reinterviewed.[2]

According to the researchers, the most important predictors, at age 8–10, of later offending (whether measured by convictions or by self-reports) fell into six categories of theoretical constructs:

1. Antisocial child behavior, including troublesomeness, dishonesty, and aggressiveness
2. Hyperactivity-impulsivity-attention deficit, including poor concentration, restlessness, high daring (risk taking), and psychomotor impulsivity
3. Low intelligence and low school achievement
4. Family criminality, including convicted parents, delinquent older siblings, and siblings with behavior problems
5. Family poverty, including low family income, large family size, and poor housing
6. Poor parenting, including harsh and authoritarian discipline, poor supervision, parental conflict, and separation from parents

The researchers concluded that offending was only one element of a much larger syndrome of antisocial behavior that tends to persist over time. For example, the boys who were convicted up to age 18 (most commonly for offenses of dishonesty, such as burglary and theft) were significantly more deviant than the nonoffenders on almost every factor that was investigated at that age.[3]

An important life event that encouraged desistance was moving out of London. The researchers noted that the reported offending of the men decreased after they and their families moved out of London, possibly because of the effect of the move in breaking up delinquent groups. One interesting conclusion of the study was that marriage to a good woman is one of the best treatments for male offending. Another conclusion was that the consequences of offending may, as a result of a learning process, lead to changes in antisocial tendency or in the cost–benefit calculation. Their final conclusion was that the Cambridge Study shows that the types of acts that lead to convictions (principally, crimes of dishonesty) are only components of a larger syndrome of antisocial behavior.[4]

Some of the developmental theories assume that a latent trait—a "master trait"—influences behavioral choices across times and situations while other development theories do not. All developmental theories maintain that although a criminal career may be initiated at any time, it is almost always begun in childhood. Moreover, as noted earlier, to understand an individual's criminal career requires longitudinal studies.

Desisting issues according to developmental theories

For some offenders, their desistance from antisocial behavior is abrupt. For others, it is a slow process. A primary question examined by these theorists is "Do offenders desist from offending because they are psychologically healthy and healthy youths respond adaptively to changing contingencies?" What about the individuals who are not involved in antisocial behavior? Some of the theorists contend that it is probable that they are individuals who exhibit excessive guilt feelings when considering antisocial behavior and have an excessive fear of the negative consequences of nonconformity.

Developmental theories in general

Developmental theories aim to explain the development of antisocial behavior, the risk and protective factors most salient at different ages and at different stages. Developmental theories offer many advantages because of their dynamic nature. They generally integrate and consider sociological, psychological, and biological factors as a coherent whole. From a research point of view, the theorists tend to follow the same individuals over long periods rather than relying on quick convenient samples. The longitudinal studies help identify characteristics that lead to the onset of, persistence of, and desistance from crime in the same individuals. Developmental theories point out that human life is characterized by dynamism and people can change at any time. They tend to support the same kind of family-based nurturant strategies supported by biosocial and social- and self-control theories.

"Developmental life-course theories focus on human development and how individual and social factors interact in different ways and at different development stages to influence individual propensity for criminal behavior."
Source: New Zealand, Ministry of Justice (March 2009) Statistical Brief: Theories of Crime Causation, available online at http://www.justice.govt.nz/justice-sector/drivers-of-crime/documents/spb-theories-on-the-causes-of-crime

General theory or "super traits" theory

In Robert Agnew's "super traits theory," he lists five life domains that contain possible crime-generating factors: personality, family, schools, peers, and work. To Agnew, the latent traits of low self-control and irritability are super traits. The neurological and endocrine changes during adolescence temporarily increase irritability/low self-control among adolescents who limit their offending to that period, while for those who continue to offend irritability/low self-control is a stable characteristic of their life.[5] Agnew is also considered a strain theorist because of his writing in which he contends that strains caused by negative relationships increase the likelihood for anger and frustration. According to Agnew, many youths react to the strain by performing acts of delinquency. Agnew's views on the causes of crime may be summed up in one sentence: Law-breaking behavior is a coping mechanism that enables those who engage in it to deal with the socioemotional problems generated by negative social relations.[6]

Age-graded informal social control theory

The key concept in Sampson and Laub's age-graded informal social control theory is the strength of bonding to family, peers, schools, and, later, adult social institutions such as marriages and jobs. Sampson and Laub primarily attempt to explain why people do not commit offenses, on the assumption that why people want to offend is unproblematic presumably caused by hedonistic desires and that offending is inhibited by family bonding activities that keep parents and children in harmony, ensuring they share the same goals and attitudes within the family.[7]

Sampson and Laub's theory is basically a social control theory extended into adulthood to include adult bonds. Sampson and Laub assume that crime and other forms of deviance result, in part, from weak or broken bonds to society. According to them, people who bond well with conventional others build social capital. Social capital acts as a store of positive relationships in social networks built on norms of reciprocity and trust developed over time upon which the individual can draw for support. Sampson and Laub see life as a series of transitions that may change a person's life trajectory in prosocial directions, which the researchers labeled turning points.

The theory is based on informal social control that is age graded. The strength of bonding to family, peers, schools, and adult social institutions such as marriage increases as the age of the individual increases. In other words, as we grow older, our bonds to our social institutions increase and thus we are less likely to deviate from accepted norms. The child who is offended based on his or her hedonistic desires is now inhibited by the stronger bonds of adult social institutions.

A notable difference between social control theory and age-graded informal social control theory is that the latter acknowledges the role of both state dependence (social control processes) and population heterogeneity (self-control) in the continuity of delinquent behavior. According to Sampson and Laub, the cumulative continuity of disadvantage is not only a result of stable individual differences in criminal propensity, but a dynamic process whereby childhood antisocial behavior and adolescent delinquency foster adult crime through the severance of adult social bonds. They describe a mixed theory in which the relationship between past and present offending is only partially mediated by informal social control variables.[8]

**COMPARISON OF THE GENERAL THEORY OF CRIME
AND AGE-GRADED LIFE-COURSE THEORY**

The general theory of crime and the age-graded life-course theory are considered disparate explanatory models of the development of criminal behavior. They explain that lack of self-control does not require crime to exist and that self-control can be modified by opportunities and other constraints. The general theory of crime assumes that although the individual's personality (i.e., the characteristic of self-control) remains stable through time, the relationship between self-control and crime is amenable to change. Conversely, age-graded life-course perspective posits that both continuity and change exist throughout the life course and that modifications in individual behavior may occur through new experiences or social circumstances.[9]

Age-graded life-course theory appears to be a viable explanation of how change occurs in the lives of some individuals. Self-control appears to be a trait that exists on a continuum; it can be directly modified and does not consistently predict crime and imprudent behavior. It is also noted that low self-control does not preclude the later likelihood of job or relational attachments among formerly persistent offenders. The researchers who contend that the two theories are capable of being linked in a side-by-side fashion through the use of the common construct of attachment also suggest that empathy may be critical to the development of an attachment relationship.[10]

Dual pathways theory

Terrie Moffitt's dual pathway developmental theory contends that the vast majority of youths who offend during adolescence mature and desist as they grow older. There are, however, a small number of them who continue to offend in adulthood. The latter group is referred to by her as the life-course-persistent offenders (LCPs). According to Moffitt, the LCPs are individuals who begin offending before puberty and continue well into adulthood. Generally, they start offending earlier than those offenders who later desist (adolescent-limited offenders [ALs]) and the LCPs offend later. According to Moffitt, LCPs have higher rates of antisocial potential (AP) because of neuropsychological and temperamental deficits that are manifested in low IQ, hyperactivity, inattentiveness, negative emotionality, slow heart rate, and low impulse control.

Those offenders who desist as they mature are referred to as adolescent-limited offenders because their delinquent acts are limited to the adolescence time span in their lives. The ALs have a different developmental history that places them on a prosocial trajectory that is temporarily derailed at adolescence. Moffitt views adolescent antisocial behavior as adaptive because it offers delinquents opportunities to gain valuable resources they could not otherwise obtain. In the case of LCPs, however, stable antisocial characteristics precede the development of temporary antisocial characteristics. The ALs may need to associate with delinquent peers to initiate delinquency. Accordingly, there is little or no genetic influence involved with ALs.

The main factors that encourage offending by the LCPs include cognitive deficits, an undercontrolled temperament, hyperactivity, poor parenting, disrupted families, teenage parents, poverty, and low socioeconomic status. While genetic and biological factors, such as a low heart rate, are important, Moffitt fails to discuss neighborhood factors, but assumes that the neuropsychological risk of the LCPs interacts multiplicatively with disadvantaged environments, for example, poor neighborhoods.

Moffitt does not propose that neuropsychological deficits and disadvantaged environments influence an underlying construct such as antisocial propensity; rather, she suggests that neuropsychological and environmental factors are the key constructs underlying antisocial behaviors. The main factors that encourage offending by the ALs are the "maturity gap" (their inability to achieve adult rewards such as material goods during their teenage years) and peer influence (especially from the LCPs). Consequently, the ALs stop offending when they enter legitimate adult roles and can achieve their desires legally. The ALs can easily stop because they have few neuropsychological deficits.

Note that there can be labeling effects of "snares" such as a criminal record, incarceration, drug or alcohol addiction, and (for girls) unwanted pregnancy, especially for the ALs. However, the observed continuity in offending over time is largely driven by the LCPs. Moffitt focuses primarily on the development of offenders and does not attempt to explain why offenses are committed. However, she notes that the presence of delinquent peers is a critical situational influence on ALs.

Decision making involving criminal opportunities is rational for the ALs who weigh likely costs against likely benefits. According to Moffitt, it is a different story for the LCPs (who largely follow well-learned "automatic" behavioral repertoires without thinking). She sees the LCPs as mainly influenced by utilitarian motives, whereas the ALs are influenced by teenage boredom. Because the LCPs are strongly committed to an antisocial lifestyle, adult life events such as getting a job or getting married are of little importance to them. ALs desist naturally as they age into adult roles.

Network theory

Thornberry and Krohn advocated the thesis that desistance from criminal behavior was caused by changing social influences such as stronger family bonding, protective factors such as high intelligence and school success, and intervention programs. Accordingly, they contend that criminal justice processing has an effect on future offending. Later, Thornberry extended this theory to explain the intergenerational transmission of antisocial behavior. He suggested that the parent's prosocial or antisocial bonding, structural adversity, stressors, and ineffective parenting mediated the link between the parent's and the child's antisocial behavior. Thornberry and others tested these ideas in the Rochester Intergenerational Study and concluded that parental stress and ineffective parenting were the most important mediating factors.

The interactional theory of Thornberry and Krohn particularly focuses on factors encouraging antisocial behavior at different ages. They do not propose types of offenders but suggest that the causes of antisocial behavior vary for children who start at different ages.

At the earliest ages (birth to 6), the three most important factors are as follows:

1. Neuropsychological deficit and difficult temperament (e.g., impulsiveness, negative emotionality, fearlessness, and poor emotion regulation).
2. Parenting deficits (e.g., poor monitoring, low affective ties, inconsistent discipline, and physical punishment).
3. Structural adversity (e.g., poverty, unemployment, welfare dependency, and a disorganized neighborhood). They also suggest that structural adversity might cause poor parenting.

Neuropsychological deficits are less important for children who start antisocial behavior at older ages. For children at ages 6–12, neighborhood and family factors are particularly important. For children at ages 12–18, school and peer factors dominate. Thornberry and

Krohn suggest that deviant opportunities, for example, gangs and deviant social networks are important for children at ages 12–18.

Thornberry and Krohn see the late starters (ages 18–25) as having cognitive deficits such as low intelligence and poor school performance but state that the later starters were protected from antisocial behavior at earlier ages by a supportive family and school environment. The later starters find it harder to make successful transitions to adult roles such as employment and marriage.

A distinctive feature of their theory is its emphasis on reciprocal causation. If the child's antisocial behavior results in coercive responses from parents and rejection by peers, the antisocial behavior is more likely to continue in the future. The theory does not identify a single key construct underlying offending but suggests that children who start offending early tend to continue because of the persistence of neuropsychological and parenting deficits and structural adversity. The researchers also predict that late starters will show more continuity over time than earlier starters because the late starters have more cognitive deficits. Apparently, Thornberry and Krohn see that early starters and late starters are likely to continue to commit antisocial acts.

ROCHESTER INTERGENERATIONAL STUDY

The Rochester Youth Development Study is a longitudinal investigation regarding the development of antisocial behavior, including delinquency and drug use, in juveniles. The study began in 1988 with 1000 adolescents living in the Rochester, New York area. The youths and their parents were interviewed about topics including their family relationships, peers, gang membership, delinquency, drug use, and education. The panel members were interviewed 12 times between 1988 and 1997. In addition, data were collected from the official records of police, schools, and social service agencies.

As discussed later in this section, the oldest biological children in the original sample of adolescents were the focal subjects of a new phase of the study. By this time, most of the subjects were in the age range of 24–26 years. Data were collected via videotaped observations of parent–child interactions, parent interviews, child interviews, and official records. Many of the topics were the same as those in the original study, with special emphasis on parenting behaviors and parent–child interactions. This new phase of the study focused on transmission of antisocial behavior across generations, examining both continuities and discontinuities in these behaviors.[11] The researchers concluded that the number of risk factors was a better predictor of child outcomes than any specific single risk factor or characteristic of the child.

In 1999, a companion intergenerational study was begun. The study focused on the oldest biological children in the third generation of these families and in 2013 began the 15th year of annual assessments of the child's growth and development. The study had two primary aims. The first was to investigate intergenerational continuity in drug use, delinquency, and related problem behaviors and to identify key mediating processes that help account for the observed level of continuity. The second was to investigate intergenerational discontinuity, or intergenerational resilience, and identify the moderating influences that help children born to parents with a history of antisocial behavior avoid involvement in the drug use, delinquency, and related problem behaviors.[12]

(Continued)

ROCHESTER INTERGENERATIONAL STUDY (*CONTINUED*)

The latter study is most often cited for its findings regarding substance abuse. For example, the findings indicate that there is intergenerational continuity in drug use for generation-two daughters, but not sons. That use by generation-three individuals was significantly influenced by both generation-two mothers and generation-one grandmothers. However, for children of generation-two fathers, neither prior generation's substance use was significantly related to use by generation-three individuals. There was some indication that the absence of an effect from generation-two fathers to generation-three drug use was due to the number of nonresident fathers in the sample.[13]

Integrated cognitive antisocial potential theory

David Farrington developed a theory, which is identified as the integrated cognitive antisocial potential (ICAP) theory. The theory is based on the concept that a person's AP determines whether or not the individual will commit deviant acts.

AP is a person's risk or propensity to engage in crime, and cognition is the thinking or decision-making process that turns potential into actual process. Their key construct is antisocial propensity, which tends to persist over time and has a wide variety of behavioral manifestations, reflecting the versatility and comorbidity of antisocial behavior.

Individuals are grouped into long-term and short-term AP. Individuals in the long-term AP group tend to come from poor families; to be poorly socialized, low on anxiety, impulsive, and sensation seeking; to have low IQ; and to fail in school. Individuals in the short-term AP group may suffer deficits, which may temporarily increase their AP in response to certain situations or inducements. The consequences of offending, however, may change a short-term AP into long-term AP over time. The level of a person's AP, which varies over time based on both social and individual reasons, determines whether a person desists from offending.

Farrington contends that numerous crime theories, alternative hypotheses about causes of crime, and often unsystematic methods of testing them contribute to confusion about the causes of crime and about how to intervene effectively.

Social development model

The social development model developed by Richard Catalano and J. David Hawkins is a general theory of antisocial behavior. In their theory, the researchers attempt to explain key elements of the "criminal career" such as onset and persistence. The key tenets of the social development model take on a holistic, multidomain approach to explaining behavior, drawing on aspects of individuals, their immediate environment (which includes the parents and peers), and the broad social structure. The social development model compares key general overarching principles and anchors individuals to a progression through social institutions (e.g., elementary school, high school) and across multiple developmental stages. The theory is an expansive and ambitious framework for explaining the development and continuance of antisocial behavior. The theory hypothesizes that a social bond consisting of attachment to conventional others, commitment to conventional lines of action, and belief in the conventional moral order inhibits the initiation of drug use and delinquency. This social bond results from a social process involving four constructs:

1. Opportunities for involvement in conventional activities and interactions with conventional others
2. The degree of involvement and interaction
3. The skills to participate in these involvements and interactions
4. The rewards one perceives as forthcoming from performance in conventional activities and interactions[14]

The theory also hypothesizes that the existing normative consensus makes conventional modes of action preferable to illegal ones in that if other things are equal, conventional paths of action are chosen over illicit ones. The theory recognizes that illicit paths of action exist and can provide rewards when the conventional socialization process breaks down. This breakdown occurs when people are denied the opportunity to participate in conventional life, when their skills are inadequate for conventional performance to produce rewards, or when the environment fails to reward them consistently for effective conventional performance.

Catalano and Hawkins did not accept the concepts asserted by strain theorists that the lack of such opportunities leads directly to deviant behavior as an alternative means of achieving desired legitimate goals. Catalano and Hawkins contend that the youths must encounter opportunities for such involvement. The perception or the youths' recognition that these opportunities exist cannot be assumed and must be viewed as problematic for youths, especially when they enter new settings, such as in making the transition from home to elementary school or from elementary school to middle or junior high school or from middle or junior high school to high school.

Catalano and Hawkins state that the availability of such opportunities is likely to vary in association with macrolevel conditions in society such as economic prosperity with meso- and microlevel conditions such as educational policies that affect the availability of alternative education programs in a community or the use of ability tracking within schools and with microlevel variables such as the individual place of residence that helps to determine the likelihood that an individual will encounter conventional people with whom he or she can interact.

Opportunities for interaction with conventional others, and opportunities for involvement in conforming activities, in conjunction with willingness to participate in these interactions and involvements, affect the degree of interaction with conventional others and involvement in conventional activities. This causal ordering differs from the ordering of variables in Hirschi's control theory in which attachment predicts commitment and commitment in turn predicts involvement. This model also diverges from Hirschi's control theory in that Hirschi does not specify interaction with conventional others as an encounter opportunity for such involvements.

Developmental propensity theory

The developmental propensity theory was developed by Benjamin Lahey and Irwin D. Waldman.

Lahey and Waldman use a developmental propensity model to explain the origins of conduct problems and delinquency during childhood and adolescence. Rather than dividing individuals into groups that desist from antisocial behavior as they age and those who continue to offend, Lahey and Waldman propose a continuum of development trajectories rather than two categories of individuals. In their research, however, they do not address adult life events or attempt to explain desistance in adult years.

Their model seeks to explain why there are multiple developmental trajectories for conduct problems from school-entry age through adolescence. According to Lahey and Waldman, the answer lies in an individual's propensity toward conduct problems and the environmental factors that either foster or inhibit an individual from expressing his or her antisocial tendencies. The key construct according to them is antisocial propensity that tends to persist over time and has a wide variety of behavioral manifestations that reflect the versatility and comorbidity of antisocial behavior. The key factors that contribute to antisocial propensity are low cognitive ability (especially verbal ability) and three dispositional dimensions. Lahey and Waldman considered these factors to have a genetic basis.

Lahey and Waldman's three dispositional dimensions were the following:

1. Sympathetic response to others
2. Negative emotional response to threat, frustration, and loss
3. Positive response to novelty and risk transact with the environment to influence risk for conduct disorder

Multifactor theories of crime

Alongside developmental theories, "multifactor theories" of crime—sometimes named integrated or "general" theories—have gained prominence in recent decades. Rather than focusing narrowly on individual, social, or situational explanations of crime, multifactor theorists integrate all three layers of analysis into a single unified theory that draws from, and expands upon, existing theories. Thus, each of these theories attempts to account for patterns pertaining to the following:[15]

- The criminal: The individual who engages in the criminal behavior
- The crime: The criminal event
- Criminality: Rates of crime on a societal scale

From the perspective of multifactor theorists, no theory is complete without successfully accounting for all the three phenomena.

Control balance theory

> Deviant behavior is interpreted as a device, or maneuver, that helps people escape deficits and extend surpluses of control.
>
> **Charles R. Tittle, 1995[16]**

Charles Tittle's control balance theory suggests that individuals are prone to commit crime when they experience a surplus or deficit of control. He suggests that three factors converge to determine any given individual's risk for criminality: their desire for autonomy, physical and psychic needs, and their perceived "control ratio." For Tittle, "control" refers to any situation in which people are curtailed from the full realization of their desires or impulses.[17] Those who experience either a deficit or surplus of control will be prone to different types of offending.

When individuals experience a "control deficit," that is, they feel they are subject to more control than they exert, they become predisposed to crimes in pursuit of rectifying the imbalance. The greater the perceived deficit of control, the more motivated individuals will become to counterbalance it, or at least this is true up to the point where they are so heavily controlled that they see no opportunity to alter their situation. So, for example, he suggests that a hungry person may be motivated to steal food, but if they are ridiculed for their need, they will be "doubly motivated" to engage in assault or theft to rectify "their feeling of debasement."[18] Tittle suggests that control deficits help to explain predatory crimes. On the other hand, those who experience a "control surplus"—those who exercise more control than that to which they are subject—will develop a taste for extending their control over others. The greater their surplus, the less understanding they will have for the position of others, and the more ruthless their actions will become.

Tittle believes that his framework can explain overall social patterns of offending. For example, he suggests that people tend to gain power as they age, so their forms of crime are likely to shift from those characteristic of power deficits to power surpluses. Similarly, his theory can help to explain racial differences in crime: To the extent that ongoing racial inequality results in whites more often holding positions of power, their criminality will tend to reflect power surpluses. On the other hand, blacks—particularly those who bear the brunt of economic as well as racial inequality—will be more prone to crimes stemming from power deficits.

He also argues that control balance theory can explain the situational component of offending. In other words, why does crime manifest in particular times and places? He suggests that crime will only result when the person perceives that the crime will empower them, either to rectify a control deficit or to extend a control surplus. Thus, crime is unlikely to occur unless an individual perceives a criminal opportunity to exert power in pursuit of their needs or desires.

Differential coercion theory

> Chronic criminals are made, not born. They emerge from a developmental process that is punctuated by recurring, erratic episodes of coercion. They become both the recipients and perpetrators of coercion, entrapped in a dynamic that propels them along a pathway toward chronic criminality.
>
> **Mark Colvin, 2000[19]**

Mark Colvin published a book introducing his differential coercion theory in 2000.[20] He suggests that criminal behavior is a function of the coercion to which individuals are subject. Coercion can take many forms, including (actual or threatened) force, intimidation, or the removal of social supports, along with economic or social pressures that feel outside of the individual's control.[21] Furthermore, it can vary along two dimensions. "Degrees of coerciveness" range from noncoercive to highly coercive. "Degrees of consistency" range from highly consistent to highly erratic. Based on where individuals' experiences fall along these two dimensions, the control to which they are subject will take one of the following forms:

- Type 1: Consistent, noncoercive
- Type 2: Erratic, noncoercive
- Type 3: Consistent, coercive
- Type 4: Erratic, coercive

According to Colvin, those who are subject to highly coercive, highly erratic control are at the greatest risk for serious predatory criminal behavior. The level of coercion makes them aware that they are at the losing end of a power imbalance. Being subject to coercive control arouses feelings of humiliation, anger, hostility, and defiance, which in turn tend to weaken social bonds. Those emotional responses, coupled with their exposure to the modeling of coercive behavior, contribute to the desire to obtain power over others. At the same time, the erratic nature of the punishments to which they are subject weakens their perceived control over their own life outcomes, feeding low self-control and self-responsibility. This combination of low self-control, negative emotions, weak social bonds, and desire to exercise control over others produces a volatile mix that renders the subject ripe to engage in predation.

By contrast, Colvin suggests that crime is the least likely among those who have been subject to consistent, noncoercive control. This form of control offers consistent incentives for prosocial behavior and firm but fair correction for deviance. The consistency of outcomes helps the individual feel in control of their own fate and supports their internalization of social norms. These individuals lack exposure to models of coercive behavior.

Other combinations of the two dimensions produce different criminal outcomes. Erratic, noncoercive control is consistent with lax, permissive environments. Individuals are not consistently awarded for prosocial behavior, and punishments for deviance are applied only sporadically. This produces individuals who are unmotivated to achieve prosocial goals and have few reasons to resist the temptation to engage in deviant behavior. They may be more prone to lying, manipulation, experimentation with pleasurable forms of deviance, and other forms of nonpredatory crime.

Those who experience consistent, coercive control may initially abstain from deviant behavior, but only due to a fear of punishment, not due to the internalization of social norms. They also develop anger and weakened social bonds. As a result, when the controls are loosened—for example, when a person from a highly repressive household strikes out on their own—it shifts them to a context more akin to Type 4, where they may act out on their anger.

Colvin uses this framework to critique contemporary criminal justice policies in the United States. He suggests that the nation's heavy-handed punishments are both highly coercive and erratic due to idiosyncrasies in enforcement. Wealthy offenders are sometimes able to evade punishment, which feeds a sense of unfairness and lack of personal control among those who bear the brunt of the punishment. He suggests that the coercive nature of prison is evident in that it

- Weakens social bonds to those on the outside
- Enmeshes inmates into a violent subculture
- Places inmates in physical state of insecurity
- Reduces inmates' capacity for self-control by placing them in a circumstance where all decisions are made for them and they have little autonomy

In addition, probation and parole places offenders under increased scrutiny and subjects them to the "whims of police and parole officers who at any time can send them back into the system."[22] Colvin concludes that such practices are destined to be counterproductive.

CRIMINAL JUSTICE AND COERCION

From the early 1970s onward, the correctional system in the United States has been characterized by increasingly harsher sentences. The nation now imprisons a greater portion of its population than any other nation in the world. The United States is also one of the few countries to retain the death penalty. Proponents of harsh sentencing argue that these policies are necessary to deter crime.

Although crime has dropped in the last 20 years, the United States still has a murder rate about three to six times higher than that of other nations.[23] Part of the reason for this failure may be the lack of certainty of punishment for any given crime—as of 2007, the clearance rate for murder and manslaughter was only 61.2%,[24] with less serious crimes having far lower rates of detection and arrest. Even for those who are caught, the experience of incarceration does not seem to have the desired impact: In the last national study on recidivism, 67.5% of offenders were rearrested within 3 years of their release from prison.[25]

Consider this information in light of Colvin's argument. Does he make a point about the erratic, coercive nature of imprisonment, or do you think there are other processes at work that are contributing to the relative failure of incarceration to reduce crime? What changes are needed to increase the effectiveness of our system?

Generic control theory

In a series of works, Marc Le Blanc[26] introduced the propositions of his generic control theory. He works in the tradition of social control theory, which holds as central the question of what makes people obey the law (see Chapter 6), but branches off from the work of Travis Hirschi and others to compose a more comprehensive set of theoretical propositions that operate at all of the requisite layers of analysis.

Le Blanc proposed four categories of social control mechanisms that mediate the effects of "environment" and "setting." He describes them as follows:

- Bonding: Mechanisms of social cohesion at the community or interpersonal levels
- Unfolding: A community's or individual's natural progression toward a desirable state
- Modeling: Patterns of opportunity to observe prosocial behavior and identify pathways to prosocial success
- Constraining: Direct and indirect restraints on behavior, including external constraints and the internalization of social norms

Le Blanc's Explanatory Variables for Criminals, Crime, and Criminality

	Individual Level	Situational Level	Societal Level
Environment	The individual's social status (location in the social structure)	Community control	Social structure, including the mobility of the population and the socioeconomic status of the community
Setting	The individual's biological capacity	Personal control	The physical condition of the community, which may be more or less conductive to crime or social control
Bonding	Bonds to other individuals	Routine activities	Cohesiveness among members of the community

(Continued)

Le Blanc's Explanatory Variables for Criminals, Crime, and Criminality (*Continued*)

	Individual Level	Situational Level	Societal Level
Unfolding	Allocentrism, or "the movement away from the natural egocentrism of the individual" (p. 233)	Self-control	"The growth and development of a community toward a desirable state" (p. 242)
Modeling	Models of prosocial behavior are available	Occasions	The availability of prosocial success relative to access to criminal opportunities
Constraining	Personal relationships that provide support for prosocial behavior and disincentive for deviant behavior	Guardianship	The presence of organizations and institutions that encourage conformity and punish deviance

At the individual level, crime is most likely to occur if prosocial models are lacking, social bonds are strained, constraints are insufficient, and deviant models present. Le Blanc stresses that the relationships among variables are highly synergistic. For example, the natural process of unfolding facilitates the development of strong social bonds, while strong social bonds also facilitate the process of unfolding.

Criticisms of the multifactor approach include the following:

- The causal processes described by any given theory are so varied, complex, and/or broad that they are difficult to test.
- The theories are so expansive in scope that they offer few realistic policy implications.
- In some cases, the theories draw so heavily upon existing theoretical arguments that they offer little new to our understanding of crime.

Summary

- Developmental theories of criminology were popular in the 1980s and 1990s. Their popularity in those two decades is attributed to the enormous volume and significance of longitudinal research on offending that was published during that period.
- The developmental theories of criminology are concerned with the development of offending and antisocial behavior from birth to death, the influence of risk and protective factors at different ages, and the effects of life events on the course of development.
- Developmental theories are focused on explaining the differences in offending rates of individuals over a period of time. For example, why does an individual commit more criminal acts at a certain age than he or she commits at a different age?
- In Robert Agnew's super traits theory, he lists five life domains that contain possible crime-generating factors: personality, family, schools, peers, and work. To Agnew, the latent traits of low self-control and irritability are "super traits."
- A notable difference between social control theory and age-graded informal social control theory is that the latter acknowledges the role of both state dependence and population heterogeneity in the continuity of delinquent behavior.
- Terrie Moffitt's dual pathway developmental theory contends that the vast majority of youths who offend during adolescence mature and desist as they grow older.

- Moffitt does not propose that neuropsychological deficits and disadvantaged environments influence an underlying construct such as antisocial propensity; rather, she suggests that neuropsychological and environmental factors are the key constructs underlying antisocial behaviors.
- The key concept in Sampson and Laub's age-graded informal social control theory is the strength of bonding to family, peers, schools and, later, adult social institutions such as marriages and jobs.
- Thornberry and Krohn advocated the thesis that desistance from criminal behavior was caused by changing social influences such as stronger family bonding, protective factors such as high intelligence and school success, and intervention programs. Accordingly, they contend that criminal justice processing has an effect on future offending.
- David Farrington developed a theory identified as the ICAP theory. The theory is based on the concept that a person's AP determines whether or not the individual will commit deviant acts.
- The social development model developed by Richard Catalano and J. David Hawkins is a general theory of antisocial behavior. In their theory, the researchers attempt to explain key elements of the "criminal career" such as onset and persistence.
- Lahey and Waldman use a developmental propensity model to explain the origins of conduct problems and delinquency during childhood and adolescence. Rather than dividing individuals into groups that desist from antisocial behavior as they age and those who continue to offend, Lahey and Waldman propose a continuum of development trajectories rather than two categories of individuals.
- Multifactor theories integrate and expand on arguments from existing theories to produce "general theories" that can account in variations of crime at the individual, situational, and social levels.
- Charles Tittle's control balance theory suggests that individuals will be more prone to crime when experiencing control deficits or surpluses.
- According to control balance theory, crime will only take place if individuals perceive that it will enhance their level of control, either to counteract a deficit or to expand a surplus.
- Colvin's differential coercion theory proposes that crime is most likely to occur among those who are subject to erratic, coercive control. Alternatively, crime is least likely to be committed by those who experience consistent, noncoercive control.

Questions in review

1. How do the developmental theorists explain antisocial behavior?
2. Why do some youths outgrow antisocial behavior?
3. What are the notable differences between social control theory and age-graded informal social control theory?
4. List the five life domains identified by Agnew.
5. What is the key concept in Sampson and Laub's age-graded informal social control theory?
6. Explain Terrie Moffitt's dual pathway developmental theory.
7. According to Charles Tittle's control balance theory, crime is most likely to arise under what circumstances?
8. Explain differential coercion theory's argument against current criminal justice policies. Do you agree with the argument? Explain your answer.

Practicum

Ted Bundy[27]

Ted Bundy, one of the most prolific serial killers of all time, was born in Philadelphia to a 22-year-old unwed mother on November 24, 1946, although due to the stigma of single parenthood at that time, he was told that his mother was his "sister," and his grandparents his "parents." He and his mother moved to Washington State when he was still a young child. His mother met and fell in love with the man who would become his stepfather. By all accounts, it was a stable household: His stepfather was a Boy Scout leader, his mother a secretary, and he had four half-siblings for whom he often babysat without complaint. During his childhood, there were few signs of what he would become, although he was picked up twice "for suspicion of auto theft and burglary."[28] He was shy and teased "mercilessly"[29] in middle school, but by high school he was reasonably popular, and his best friends were leaders in student politics. He maintained a B average in school, and his mother considered him smart and destined for college.

Bundy went on to study at the University of Puget Sound, and then transferred to the University of Washington, where he met and fell in love with Stephanie Brooks. Although they had fun on dates, Stephanie became concerned that Bundy did not have any real future—he was likable but some considered him a schemer, and Stephanie suspected that he used people and may have lied to her. Bundy was so devastated when Stephanie broke up with him that his grades dropped and he ultimately dropped out of school. Shortly afterward, he returned to Philadelphia to look into his roots, at which time he confirmed his suspicion that his "sister" was actually his mother. He worked his way back to the West Coast and tried to reconnect with Stephanie in 1969, but she was unreceptive. One author observed, "Had she accepted him back at that point, some of his humiliation might have been tempered."[30]

After Stephanie's second rejection, an odd thing happened—unlike the initial breakup, this time he seemed spurred back onto the right track, at least on the surface. He was busy and high achieving during this period. He returned to school to study psychology at the University of Washington, where he became primarily an A student. In a letter of recommendation, a professor wrote in part that

> He is exceedingly bright, personable, highly motivated, and conscientious. He conducts himself more like a young professional than a student. He has the capacity for hard work and because of his intellectual curiosity is a pleasure to interact with.[31]

At one point, he worked for Seattle's Crime Prevention Advisory Commission, though he resigned when he failed to secure the position of director. He volunteered at a crisis hotline where he was well regarded. He was becoming active and well connected in Republican political circles, even working for the Governor's reelection campaign, serving as a driver for a candidate for lieutenant governor, and then becoming an assistant to the chairman of the Washington State Republican Party. He applied and was accepted to law school. Throughout this period he was dating a woman with a young son, and by all accounts they had a happy relationship.

These details make it all the more striking that in late summer 1973, while on a business trip, he sought out Stephanie. She flew to Seattle to see him in September, and the two talked marriage as he wined and dined her. Things suddenly took a turn, though—by December of that year, after 6 years of infatuation with Stephanie, Bundy became cold and evasive toward her, "uninterested, almost hostile."[32] He stopped calling or writing, did not respond to a letter she sent, and then hung up on her when she called. It has been speculated that his 4 years of "success" were a ploy to seduce and then get revenge on Stephanie.

Shortly thereafter is when women began disappearing. They were often taken from on or near college campuses. In some instances, they were attacked in their own beds; in others, Bundy feigned disability with a cast or crutches and asked the women for help to lure them near his car. Interestingly, they all bore a striking resemblance to Stephanie—the victims were young Caucasian women with fair complexions, slender builds, and long hair parted in the middle.[33] (Bundy denied any symbolism to this profile, suggesting that the only thing they held in common was that they were attractive young women.) When the bodies were discovered or victims survived his attacks, the injuries were horrific—women were bludgeoned, brutally sodomized, strangled, and in some cases bitten.

Bundy ultimately confessed to at least 36 murders across several states, although at one point he indicated that his count was much higher. A look into his past reveals scattered instances of lying, theft, and scheming, but also periods marked by genuine popularity, intelligence, and high achievement. A psychiatric assessment did not reveal any signs that he was "psychotic, neurotic, the victim of organic brain disease, alcoholic, addicted to drugs, suffering from a character disorder or amnesia, and [he] was not a sexual deviant."[34] There is a chance that he began committing murders before 1973—a 9-year-old went missing from near his home when he was 15, and two women from Seattle were bludgeoned, one to death, in 1966—but it is impossible to know for sure. What is known is that he committed a series of murders from 1973 until his first arrest in 1975, and then again after escaping prison until he was ultimately caught, convicted, and executed for murder in the state of Florida.

Questions regarding Ted Bundy

1. Can any of the developmental theories in this chapter explain Ted Bundy's crimes?
2. Analyze Ted Bundy's life from the perspective of control balance theory. Does the theory offer any insight into his crimes? Explain your answer.
3. How would a differential coercion theorist analyze Ted Bundy's life?

References

1. Farrington, D. P. (2002). Developmental criminology and risk-focused prevention. In M. Maguire, R. Morgan, & R. Reiner (Eds.), *The oxford handbook of criminology* (pp. 657–701). New York: Oxford.
2. Farrington, D. P., & West, D. J. (1981). The Cambridge study in delinquent development. In S. A. Mednick, & A. E. Baert (Eds.), *Prospective longitudinal research*. Oxford: Oxford University Press.
3. Farrington, D. P. (1988). Studying changes within individuals: The causes of offending. In M. Rutter (Ed.), *Studies of psychosocial risk* (pp. 158–183). Cambridge, MA: Cambridge University Press.
4. Farrington, D. P. (1989). Later adult life outcomes of offenders and non-offenders. In M. Brambring, F. Losel, & H. Skowronek (Eds.), *Children at risk: Assessment, longitudinal research, and intervention* (pp. 220–244). Berlin: De Gruyter.
5. Robert. A. (2002). Crime causation, sociological theories. In J. Dressler (Ed.), *Encyclopedia of crime and justice* (Vol. 1, pp. 324–334). New York: Boston.
6. Robert. A. (1985). Social control theory and delinquency: A longitudinal test. *Criminology, 23*(1), 47–61.
7. Sampson, R. J., & Laub. J. H. (1992). Crime and deviance in the life-course. *Annual Review of Sociology, 18*, 63–84.

8. Laub, J. H., & Sampson. R. J. (1993). Turning points in the life-course: Why change matters to the study of crime. *Criminology, 31*(3), 301–325.

9. Rebecca, S. K. (1999). Building the foundation for a side-by-side explanatory model: A general theory of crime, the age-graded life-course theory, and attachment theory. *Western Criminology Review, 1*(2). Retrieved August 21, 2013, from http://wcr.sonoma.edu/v1n2/katz.html

10. Rebecca, S. K. (1999). Building the foundation for a side-by-side explanatory model: A general theory of crime, the age-graded life-course theory, and attachment theory. *Western Criminology Review, 1*(2). Retrieved August 21, 2013, from http://wcr.sonoma.edu/v1n2/katz.html

11. Thornberry, T. P., Krohn, M. D., Smith, C. A., Lizotte, A. J., & Porter, P. K. (2003). Causes and consequences of delinquency: Findings from the Rochester youth development study (pp. 11–46) In T. P. Thornberry, & M. D. Krohn (Eds.), *Taking stock of delinquency: An overview of findings from contemporary longitudinal studies* (pp. 11–46). New York: Kluwer Academic/Plenum Publishers and Thornberry, T. P., & Krohn, M. D. (2001). The development of delinquency: An interactional perspective. In S. O. White (Ed.), *Handbook of youth and justice* (pp. 289–305). New York: Plenum.

12. As reported on the University of Maryland's Department of Criminal Justice website. (2012). *Early adolescences.* Retrieved August 30, 2013, from http://www.ccjs.umd.edu/projectprofile/1082

13. Andrews, J. A., Hops, H., Ary, D. V., Tildesley, T., & Harris, J. (1993). Parental influence on early adolescent substance use: Specific and nonspecific effects. *Journal of Early Adolescence, 13,* 285–310.

14. Catalano, R. F., & David Hawkins, J. (1986, November). *The social development model: A theory of antisocial behavior.* Paper presented at the Safeco Lectureship on Crime and Delinquency, School of Social Work, University of Washington, Seattle, Washington. Retrieved August 21, 2013, from https://www .ncjrs.gov/pdffiles1/Digitization/124878NCJRS.pdf

15. Jean Pinatel, as cited in Le Blanc, M. (1997). A generic control theory of the criminal phenomenon: The structural and dynamic statements of an integrative multilayered control theory. In T. P. Thornberry (Ed.), *Developmental theories of crime and delinquency* (pp. 215–285). New Brunswick, NJ: Transaction Publishers.

16. Tittle, C. R. (1995). *Control balance: Toward a general theory of deviance* (p. 142). Boulder, CO: Westview Press.

17. Tittle, C. R. (1995). *Control balance: Toward a general theory of deviance* (p. 143). Boulder, CO: Westview Press.

18. Tittle, C. R. (1995). *Control balance: Toward a general theory of deviance* (p. 178). Boulder, CO: Westview Press.

19. Colvin, M. (2000). *Crime and coercion: An integrated theory of chronic criminality* (p. 1). New York: St. Martin's Press.

20. Colvin, M. (2000). *Crime and coercion: An integrated theory of chronic criminality* (p. 1). New York: St. Martin's Press.

21. Colvin, M. (2000). *Crime and coercion: An integrated theory of chronic criminality* (p. 5). New York: St. Martin's Press.

22. Colvin, M. (2000). *Crime and coercion: An integrated theory of chronic criminality* (p. 143). New York: St. Martin's Press.

23. United Nations. (2009). *International Homicide Statistics.* Retrieved August 12, 2012, from http:// www.unodc .org/documents/data-and-analysis/IHS-rates-05012009.pdf

24. Federal Bureau of Investigation. (2007). *Crime in the United States, 2007.* Retrieved August 1, 2013, from http://www2.fbi.gov/ucr/cius2007/offenses/clearances/index.html

25. Langan, P. A., & Levin, D. J. (2002). *Recidivism of prisoners released in 1994.* (NCJ 193427). Washington, DC: Bureau of Justice Statistics.

26. Le Blanc, M. (1997). A generic control theory of the criminal phenomenon: The structural and dynamic statements of an integrative multilayered control theory. In T. P. Thornberry (Ed.), *Developmental theories of crime and delinquency* (pp. 215–285). New Brunswick, NJ: Transaction Publishers.

27. Information drawn from Rule, A. (2000/1980). *The stranger beside me.* New York: W.W. Norton and Company.

28. Information drawn from Rule, A. (2000/1980). *The stranger beside me* (p. 24). New York: W.W. Norton and Company.
29. Information drawn from Rule, A. (2000/1980). *The stranger beside me* (p. 23). New York: W.W. Norton and Company.
30. Information drawn from Rule, A. (2000/1980). *The stranger beside me* (p. 28). New York: W.W. Norton and Company.
31. Cited in Rule, A. (2000/1980). *The stranger beside me* (p. 30). New York: W.W. Norton and Company.
32. Information drawn from Rule, A. (2000/1980). *The stranger beside me* (p. 51). New York: W.W. Norton and Company.
33. Information drawn from Rule, A. (2000/1980). *The stranger beside me* (p. 78). New York: W.W. Norton and Company.
34. Information drawn from Rule, A. (2000/1980). *The stranger beside me* (p. 192). New York: W.W. Norton and Company.

chapter eight

Theories of critical criminology

Chapter objectives

After studying this chapter, you should be able to

- Identify and describe the subareas of critical criminology
- Explain the differences between mainstream and critical criminology
- Differentiate among the concepts of "legally defined crimes," "true crimes," and "criminalization"
- Describe the historical development of critical criminology
- Identify and explain the key concepts and arguments of culture conflict theory
- Explain the contributions of Willem Bonger
- Identify and define the key concepts in feminist theory
- Distinguish between the contributions of left idealists and left realists
- Compare and contrast culture conflict, Marxist, and feminist criminology
- Identify the policy implications of culture conflict, Marxist, and feminist criminology
- Describe the contributions of peacemaking criminology
- Identify the weaknesses of the critical perspective

Introduction

This chapter introduces the critical perspective of criminology. The perspective is primarily concerned with inequality as it relates to crime and justice. Rather than focusing on individual traits or immediate social conditions, critical theorists "zoom out" to take a "macrosocial approach": they examine the relationship between crime and society's overall structure, specifically in regard to the distribution of wealth, power, and other resources. "Critical criminology" encompasses the following subareas:

- "Conflict criminology" focuses on power differences among groups, generally defined as those formed around different cultures, subcultures, or interests.
- "Marxist criminology" is primarily concerned with the distribution of economic wealth in capitalist societies and its subsequent impact on crime, law, and law enforcement practices.
- "Feminist criminology" examines power differences in terms of gender. It includes efforts to better understand women's experiences with crime, victimization, and the criminal justice system.
- "Peacemaking criminology" is more concerned with society's responses to crime than its underlying causes, advocating that correctional strategies should be designed to "do the least harm."

While the specifics vary, all of these theorists share a common interest in the power dynamics that underlie crime, criminal law, and the criminal justice system. They

provide an important complement to other theories addressed in this book, as they illuminate the inequalities that pervade issues of crime and justice. This chapter addresses
the distinguishing features of critical criminology; the radical criminology movement
of the 1960s and 1970s; and the subareas of conflict, Marxist, feminist, and peacemaking
criminology.

Critical and mainstream criminology: A comparison

> Criminal law … is a direct expression of the ruling class; it is con-
> cerned with the protection of their property and the consolidation
> of their political power. The "real" function of policing is political
> rather than the control of crime per se.

Young, 1986[1]

While the subareas of critical thought are clearly distinct from one another, they share key
underlying assumptions:

- Society is composed of groups with differing priorities, cultures, and interests.
- These groups vary in their access to political power, which in turn shapes their relative ability to influence the law.
- The law tends to protect the interests and values of those in power and work to the
  relative detriment of others.

Unlike theorists who uncritically assume that the law reflects broad moral consensus,
critical theorists subscribe to the conflict model of law: They believe that those in power
write laws to maintain their position of advantage while systematically subjugating the
norms, values, and/or best interests of others. To these theorists, acts become labeled as
"criminal" in the context of a broader sociopolitical struggle.

Critical criminologists accuse mainstream theorists of being misguided in their
efforts to explain and prevent violations of criminal law, as these violations are not an
accurate representation of social harm. Critical theorists launch three critiques against the
approach taken by most mainstream criminologists. First, they note that criminal law has
a tendency to overlook the harmful actions of the powerful. Second, the law will tend to
"overcriminalize" behaviors of disadvantaged populations. Third, a focus on law violators
overlooks the macrosocial conditions that underlie much lower-class criminality.

Critical theorists argue that mainstream criminologists' uncritical acceptance of
the legal definition of "crime" only serves to perpetuate stereotypes about who criminals are, which distracts from the more substantial injustices perpetrated every day by
those in power. This perspective holds that it is absurd to focus solely on those who
break the law without also trying to understand other forms of exploitive, uncom-
passionate, or otherwise harmful behavior. For example, what insight can be gained
by studying prostitutes without also studying those who would allow young women
and men, often underage, to be exploited by pimps and johns? Similarly, why expend
efforts to understand why people would steal, rob, and burglarize, without also trying
to understand why others would allow the poor to go without having their most basic
needs met? From the critical perspective, all forms of social harm are fair game in the
study of crime.

A macrosocial perspective on inequality

While other theorists—specifically those in the social structural tradition—acknowledge the concentration of crime in disadvantaged communities, they nonetheless maintain a narrow focus on immediate social conditions as an explanation for that crime. Critical theorists argue that we need to take a step back to see the real cause of crime, which is the inequality that causes disadvantaged neighborhoods to exist in the first place. In this broader social context, the crimes of the poor take on new meaning. Rather than being seen as responses to "disorganized" neighborhood conditions, critical theorists suggest that much lower-class crime can be understood as efforts to

- Improve their position of power
- Obtain otherwise unobtainable resources
- Express their frustration or anger at their position of disadvantage

Key concepts in critical criminology

> In accepting the state and legal definition of crime, the scope of analysis [in traditional criminology] has been constrained to exclude behavior which is not legally defined as "crime" (for example, imperialism, exploitation, racism and sexism) as well as behavior which is not typically prosecuted (for example, tax-evasion, price-fixing, consumer fraud, government corruption, police homicides, etc.). The most serious crimes against the people ... have been neglected.
>
> **Tony Platt, 1974[2]**

Critical criminologists point out that a focus on "legally defined crimes"—behaviors that violate criminal laws—overlooks a broad array of "true crimes": the wide range of socially harmful behaviors that may or may not be legally defined as "criminal," and that are more equitably distributed throughout society. Critical theorists note that since the ruling class holds the power to shape criminal law, the law will tend to overlook their harmful behaviors and leave the disadvantaged to bear the brunt of the stigma and punishment of the criminal justice system. Specifically, critical criminologists note the tendency for the criminal justice system to systematically

- Assign low penalties to white-collar crimes, including those that are more harmful to society than many street offenses
- Punish corporate crimes through corporate fines rather than criminal penalties for the individuals responsible
- Enforce laws most stringently against disadvantaged populations

These inequalities pathologize "street offenders" while often turning a blind eye to the harmful acts of the powerful, as when businesses release potentially fatal toxins into the air and water supply, fail to take precautions for their workers' safety, or cut corners in ways that may put consumers at risk.

THINKING LIKE A CRITICAL CRIMINOLOGIST

In 2009, Jason Theus Cunningham walked into a Las Vegas branch of Bank of America, put a semiautomatic pistol to a teller's head, and demanded money.[3] He was apprehended by officers who found the loaded weapon and $2700 from the robbery in his car.[4] Cunningham was sentenced to 10 years in prison and 5 years of supervised release for his crime.[5]

In 2013, the U.S. Department of Justice sued Bank of America for allegedly lying to investors, making false statements, and failing to perform due diligence in regard to risky mortgages, resulting in an estimated $100 million in losses to investors.[6] The alleged behavior was described by New York Attorney General Eric Schneiderman as "a key cause of the housing collapse that crashed [the United States] economy."[7] The civil action allows the government to issue fines in an effort to recoup the loss of any wrongdoing.[8]

How would a critical criminologist view these two cases and their outcomes?

Given their recognition that not all socially harmful behaviors are legally defined as criminal, critical theorists expand their focus of study to include "criminalization," or the process by which select acts come to be legally identified as "criminal." Since the critical perspective broadens the scope of criminology to include not just the behavior of the criminalized but also the process and effects of criminalization, critical criminologists spend as much time studying "law-makers" as "law-breakers." They ask questions such as

- Why do some socially harmful acts become criminalized, while others do not?
- By what process does this criminalization occur?
- What are the effects of criminalization?
- What types of "true crimes" evade the process of criminalization?
- What are the nature and scope of harms that result from the "true crimes" of the powerful?

THE HOMELESS: CRIMINALS OR VICTIMS?

In Barak and Bohm's work on homelessness,[9] they observe that the homeless are often criminalized by laws against loitering, panhandling, or trespassing in public parks after hours.[10] The authors suggest that this approach overlooks that the homeless "are more victims than perpetrators,"[11] both for their vulnerability to street crimes and for their role as "victims of structural forces and government policies that subject them to all forms of abuse, neglect, and dehumanization."[12]

Barak's later work[13] documents the many ways that homelessness can be equated with victimization. Some people are driven into homelessness by traditional forms of victimization, as with those who flee circumstances of child abuse, neglect, or domestic violence without anywhere to go. Homelessness also increases the risk of subsequent victimization based on the inherent vulnerability of those without shelter to attacks by street criminals or other homeless individuals.[14] The circumstances of the homeless subject them to "numerous indecencies, indignities, and obscenities" that attack their sense of self-worth and negatively affect their overall well-being.[15] The homeless can also be seen as victims of society's "true crimes," as with the unwillingness to provide adequate resources for those struggling with addiction, mental illness, or access to shelter, and as victims of an economic structure that has widened the gap between rich and poor and rendered housing prices out of reach for many.[16]

Barak and Bohm argue that efforts to criminalize the homeless are misguided and counterproductive. Instead, they advocate for policies that provide for the welfare of the disadvantaged. Barak advocates for a "nonrepressive and humane"[17] approach to homelessness that uses public–private partnerships to connect victims to shelter, food programs, and other much-needed resources.

Conflict theories

Conflict theories provide the foundation for the other forms of critical criminology discussed in this chapter. These theories developed alongside the social structural perspective in the early to mid-1900s as an alternative explanation for the concentration of crime in poor, often immigrant urban communities. Rather than focusing on immediate social conditions, conflict criminologists view crime as the outcome of broader group dynamics. They observe that society is composed of a number of groups with varying beliefs, norms, and interests. When two or more groups clash, the more powerful of them will use the law to enforce their will on others, resulting in the criminalization of the less powerful. The most prominent conflict theorists are Thorsten Sellin, George Vold, and Austin Turk.

Culture conflict theory

Thorsten Sellin was the first of the conflict criminologists. In 1938, he published a well-known work that outlined different types of conflicts that are likely to arise when one cultural group holds the power to govern others. According to Sellin, "primary culture conflict" was likely to occur whenever[18]

- Two normatively different cultures border one another.
- The laws of one cultural group extend into the territory of another.
- Members of one cultural group migrate to the territory of another.

In each of these circumstances, people are rendered "criminal" simply by engaging in behaviors that are consistent with their culture, but which place them at odds with criminal law.

While primary culture conflict can directly result in crime, Sellin indicates that this is rare, pointing to evidence that first-generation immigrants have lower overall crime rates than subsequent generations. He attributes the spike in crime among immigrant's children to the "secondary culture conflict"[19] that arises when subcultures form as a result of disadvantaged social conditions, as when the poor are exposed to the "disorganizing" influences of urban poverty.[20] While this is highly consistent with the arguments of the social structural school (see Chapter 5), it differs slightly in its attention to the macrostructural group dynamics that underlie the creation of disorganized areas.

Group conflict theory

> The whole political process of law making, law breaking, and law enforcement becomes a direct reflection of deep-seated and fundamental conflicts between interest groups and their more general struggles for control of the police power of the state.
>
> **George Vold, 1958[21]**

In 1958, George Vold published a work that expanded conflict theory to include conflicts among groups who may share a common culture but clash over other interests. According to Vold,

- Groups form based on the common needs and interests of their members.
- Groups are constantly forming and disbanding depending on how well they meet their members' needs.
- Group conflict arises when "the interests and purposes [the groups] serve ... overlap, encroach on one another, and become competitive."[22]
- Conflict often serves to "intensify the loyalty of the group members to their respective groups."[23]

Vold suggests that such conflicts have only two possible resolutions: conquest or compromise. Since the more powerful group has little incentive to compromise, the subordinate group must fight for some kind of leverage to defend its interests. Examples of such efforts include the civil rights and antiwar movements.

Theory of normative-legal conflict

Austin Turk[24] recognized that conflict between two groups with contrasting value sets is not inevitable—plenty of groups manage to get along despite their differences. To better understand the specific circumstances that result in group conflict, he asked the following: Under what circumstances are people most likely to conflict with authority figures (such as the police)? Also, when conflict does arise, what factors influence whether it results in the criminalization of one of the parties?

To help answer these questions, Turk draws a distinction among three types of norms:

1. Cultural norms: Those generally claimed or articulated within a culture
2. Social norms: Those actually reflected in behavior within the culture
3. Legal norms: Those that have been codified into law

Turk observes that "talk" does not always equal "action"—people's actions do not always match their stated beliefs, nor are the laws always in line with the values held within a given society. Groups will sometimes culturally denounce, or even outlaw, certain behaviors even as they continue to engage in them.

According to Turk, conflict is most likely to arise when

- Both authorities and those without legal power genuinely believe in and abide by the stated norms of their respective cultures, but the norms clash between the two groups.
- The disempowered group is highly organized but lacks the sophistication to conceal their violation of legal norms.
- Authorities lack the sophistication to gain compliance without resorting to forceful means.

In other words, conflicts arise when each party is solidly grounded in their norms, and both parties lack the sophistication to navigate the norm differences more subtly. Turk suggests these conflicts are most likely to result in the criminalization of the subordinate group if the norms personally held by police are aligned with the legal norms that they are tasked with enforcing.

Radical criminology movement

Critical criminology has early roots in the "utopian socialists, anarchists, and Marxists"[25] of the 1800s and earlier, but it most directly stems from conflict and labeling theories, both of which expanded the scope of criminology to include processes of criminalization and societal responses to deviance.[26] These theoretical foundations converged with the social movements of the 1960s and 1970s to inspire a strain of radical criminology that catapulted the maturation of Marxist and feminist criminology into full-fledged schools of thought.

Birth of radical criminology

In the 1960s and 1970s, the convergence of the civil rights, antiwar, and counterculture movements—and the resulting clashes between protesters and police—fed growing distrust in the government and the desire for social change.[27] These movements inspired some liberal criminologists to pursue radical critiques of inequality in the criminal justice system. These criminologists were diverse in their specific perspectives[28] and used different terms to describe themselves, including "conflict," "critical," and "radical,"[29] but held in common some key details. They all

- Questioned official definitions of crime
- Called for a human rights definition of crime[30] that included the harmful acts of the powerful, including "corporate violence and terrorism"[31]
- Placed an emphasis on action, not just research or theory, in pursuit of social justice[32]

The radical criminologists viewed mainstream criminology as complicit in the oppression of people by the state.[33] Mainstream theorists were accused of becoming corrupted by the "lure of research grants, travel, prestige, and other benefits"[34] for conducting government research, which was also seen as stifling creativity and work on controversial issues.[35]

The critiques of radical criminologists were not well received by government or university officials. Early radical criminologists found themselves fired, denied tenure, and otherwise marginalized in the field.[36] Still, they left their mark: The work that resulted from the movement contributed significantly to the literature on racism, sexism, classism, and other inequalities in relation to the justice system. The movement was a catalyst for work in the areas of Marxist and feminist criminology, both of which remain prominent threads in criminology today.

RISE AND FALL OF UC BERKELEY'S SCHOOL OF CRIMINOLOGY

Many of the early radical criminologists were professors in UC Berkeley's School of Criminology. The School opened in 1949 to serve as a professionalized training program for leaders in law enforcement.[37] It shifted toward a more liberal, academic

(Continued)

RISE AND FALL OF UC BERKELEY'S SCHOOL OF CRIMINOLOGY (*CONTINUED*)

orientation in the late 1950s,[38] but it was not until the social movement of the 1960s and 1970s that a small subset of professors began to embrace a truly radical approach to their work. While most professors in the department remained moderate liberals, the context surrounding Berkeley, including the well-known "People's Park" protest and the subsequent clash between protesters and police,[39] provided the fuel for it to become a hotbed for critical thought.

The radical criminologists at Berkeley designed courses with Marxist and anticolonialist perspectives and actively advocated for an expansion of the definition of crime to encompass "sexism, racism, imperialism, and exploitation," with the goal of developing "new perspectives toward crime and criminological issues based on an understanding of human rights and social liberation, rather than on property rights of the privileged and the punitive coercion of the oppressed segments of the population."[40] They organized a "Union of Radical Criminologists" and created a dedicated academic journal to support the development of ideas in this new branch of criminology.[41]

The political radicalization within the School was met with disdain from other professors who supported an orientation toward professionalized training.[42] Radical professors were denied tenure, including one who was chided by the chancellor for his political activity and another denied due to his authorship of radical works. In 1972–1973, committees at UC Berkeley recommended that the School be dismantled because its graduate program had become "too academic" (vs. professional) and its undergraduate program too unstructured due to its emphasis on contemporary social issues. Liberals began to distance themselves from the radicals who were drawing negative attention to the School, deepening internal political divides. The School was ultimately dismantled in 1976.

The New Criminology

The 1973 publication of Taylor, Walton, and Young's *The New Criminology*[43] helped to clarify the foundation of radical criminology and increase the legitimacy of the movement. The authors critiqued traditional criminology as stagnant due to criminologists' loyalty to disjointed camps such as psychology, biology, rational choice, and social learning. According to the authors, this tendency was a barrier to achieving a more holistic understanding of crime. To help resolve this issue, they proposed an integration of components of choice, social structural, and social process theories with the contributions of radical criminology. They argued that any criminological theory should account for the following:

- The criminal act: The offensive behavior that elicits a negative response from others
- Social reaction: The reception of, and response to, the offensive behavior by others
- Political economy: The macrosocial "context of inequalities of power, wealth, and authority"[44] that provides the broader framework in which the crime and reaction are embedded
- Social psychology: The thought processes that underlie the behaviors of the offender and their audience within the context of their social circumstances

The work was intended as a blueprint for theorists looking to meld critical and mainstream criminology.

Critical theories in the present day

Critical theories have come a long way toward mainstream acceptance since the days of firings and tenure denials. They are now widely acknowledged as an important complement to mainstream criminology. The American Society of Criminology (ASC), a national professional organization for criminologists, instituted a "Division of Critical Criminology" in 1990, and critical criminologist William Chambliss served as ASC's president in 1988.[45] Still, the two schools of thought continue to exist at arms' length: Mainstream criminology continues to favor heavily positivistic and microsocial examinations of crime, whereas critical criminologists continue to favor macrosocial analyses and critical examinations of state power.

Marxist theories

> Distress due to poverty gives the worker only the choice of starving slowly, killing himself quickly or taking what he needs where he finds it—in plain English—stealing. And it is not surprising that the majority prefer to steal rather than to starve to death or commit suicide.
>
> **Friedrich Engels, 1958[46]**

> The part played by economic conditions in criminality is preponderant, even decisive. This conclusion is of the highest importance for the prevention of crime … where crime is the consequence of social and economic conditions, we can combat it by changing those conditions.
>
> **Willem Bonger, 1916[47]**

Karl Marx is known for his procommunist writings and activism. Marx held that "capitalist" economies—those characterized by private ownership of businesses and free market competition—were inherently exploitive of the working class, and that the only solution to the ills of capitalism was a communist revolution. While Marx wrote minimally about crime, his ideas have appealed to those critical of state power and concerned about patterns of class inequality. Marxist criminologists assume that

- The economy is the central organizing factor in all social relations.
- Capitalist economies foster inequality between the "bourgeoisie" (owners of the means of production) and "proletariat" (working class).
- Law is used in capitalist systems to protect the wealth and privilege of the bourgeoisie and maintain the oppression of the proletariat.

Early roots of Marxist criminology

Willem Bonger is often identified as the first "Marxist criminologist" for his book *Criminology and Economic Conditions*, first published in 1905. Bonger believed that capitalism has the following effects:

- It encourages "egoism," or self-interest, over a commitment to the common good.
- It provides businesses with an incentive to suppress the wages of employees on one hand, and inflate the cost of goods on the other, both of which widen the gap between the rich and poor.
- The resulting inequality has a demoralizing effect on the poor, who must contend with unsatisfying work, substandard housing, and low-quality education.

Bonger argued that this state of affairs is inherently criminogenic as one person's advantage can only come at the cost of others. Capitalism thus breeds crime among the rich and poor. Among the wealthy, it encourages predatory, exploitive, and competitive behavior among entrepreneurs and business owners who have incentive to exploit laborers, cheat customers, and engage in other unsavory business practices. The working class may in turn be driven to alcohol, prostitution, and other forms of debasement to cope with the stress of their class position.

Consistent with Marx, Bonger viewed the overthrow of capitalism as the only solution to these ills. In its place, he encouraged a system of "socialism," or community ownership of the means of production. He believed that this different economic structure would foster altruism, remove the incentive for exploitation, and all but eliminate the crime that stems from social disadvantage.

KARL HEINRICH MARX (1818–1883)[48]

Karl Marx was born in Trier, Prussia (now Germany). At the age of 17, Marx began his academic studies in law at the University of Bonn, but over time he came to focus more heavily on philosophy (particularly the work of Hegel), history, and economics. Marx demonstrated a consistent interest in grand theorizing, and only two years into his studies wrote to his father of his efforts "to elaborate a philosophy that would cover the whole field of law."[49] By 1841, when he graduated with his doctorate from the University of Jena, he had developed a reputation as a gifted philosopher.

Much of Marx's adult life was lived in exile as a result of his growing involvement in revolutionary politics. His time in Prussia ended in 1843 when he resigned as editor of a liberal newspaper that was subject to government suppression. From there he moved to Paris, where his political leanings intensified. In 1845, he was expelled at the request of the Prussian government in response to his authorship of two anti-Prussian articles. He eventually settled in London, where he continued his involvement in Communist organizations and his writing.

While in the present day communism remains poorly regarded for its association with repressive governments, Marx's work continues to have a lasting legacy in the field of sociology for its contribution to the theoretical analysis of economics, and capitalism in particular, as it relates to the human condition. Mainstream sociologists often recognize Marx, along with Emile Durkheim and Max Weber, as one of the "fathers of sociology."

Law, Order, and Power

William Chambliss and Robert Seidman propose a theory of crime that combines elements of conflict theory and Marxism. In their 1971 book *Law, Order, and Power*, they suggest that both political and economic arrangements shape the distribution of power among groups, which in turn affects the probability that any given group will have their values reflected in law.[50] In Chambliss' future works, he went on to argue that[51]

- The inevitable tensions that stem from capitalism encourage the bourgeoisie to criminalize the proletariat in an effort to maintain social control.
- As conflicts increase, the penal law will expand.

- Laws will not be equally enforced, allowing the members of the ruling class to more readily break the law without consequence.
- Crime is a natural and rational response to class position among the alienated proletariat.

Chambliss also argues that in many instances officers' tendency to enforce the laws more stringently against the powerless is simply a rational response to social realities. Criminal charges against the poor and otherwise disadvantaged are more likely to be quickly processed through the justice system, whereas those with political and economic resources are more likely to fight charges against them. Chambliss, as with other Marxist criminologists, suggests that the only solution to this state of affairs is the replacement of capitalism with a socialist economy.[52]

Left idealism

Early Marxist criminologists have been critiqued for taking a "left idealist" approach characterized by sympathy for the working class and contempt for those in power. Left idealists tend to minimize the harmful behaviors of the working class on the basis that such behaviors are simply the logical outgrowth of people's life circumstances under capitalism. While left idealism holds some popular appeal for its focus on economic inequality, the primary concern is that it provides few realistic ideas for changing society short of a revolution. Idealists largely hold "that crime ... cannot be eliminated unless there is a revolutionary transition from capitalism to socialism."[53]

Left realism

"Left realists" share left idealists' concern for the working class, but differ in two important ways. First, they acknowledge the real harms that stem from working class crime. Second, they use the arguments of left idealism to form attainable, realistic social policies (short of revolution) that may lessen crime by reducing inequality. For example, in a discussion of inner city violence, DeKeseredy makes the following policy recommendations:[54]

- Implement job creation and training programs.
- Increase the minimum wage.
- Provide government-sponsored day care.
- Provide housing assistance.
- Teach entrepreneurial skills to high school students.
- Form partnerships among schools, businesses, and government agencies.
- Provide universal health care.

While these proposals are not aimed at "social control" in the traditional sense, each of these steps would lessen social inequality, which in turn would be expected to reduce crime.

Criticisms of a Marxist approach to criminology include that it

- Ignores "evidence for the existence of substantial consensus about major crime categories"[55]
- Minimizes the very real harms of lower-class criminality[56]

- Fails to account for individual differences in crime
- Overromanticizes communism, and in doing so fails to explain the persistence of crime within socialist economies
- Is unable to account for substantial differences in crime rates among capitalist nations

Feminist criminology

> Patriarchal power relations shape gender differences in crime, pushing women into crime through victimization, role entrapment, economic marginality, and survival needs.

Jennifer Schwartz and Darrell Steffensmeier, 2007[57]

> To understand crime, we must comprehend how gender, race, and class relations are part of all social existence.… Crime operates subtly through a complex series of gender, race, and class practices.

James Messerschmidt, 1997[58]

Throughout recorded history and across cultures, males have committed the majority of crimes. Despite this pervasive trend, few mainstream criminologists consider the role of gender in criminality. The few early researchers who studied female offending assumed essentialist differences between males and females, as with Lombroso's work on the anthropomorphic characteristics of female offenders.[59]

Research has supported that the motivations and contexts of female criminality often differ from those of males. Relative to offenses committed by males, those perpetrated by women are[57]

- More often committed in contexts of abuse and exploitation
- More often committed with others, in the role of accomplice
- Less often violent, and less likely to involve a weapon
- More likely to be committed out of need

Females more frequently have "blurred boundaries" between victimization and offending,[60] as with women who are victimized by human trafficking and forced into prostitution, or those who murder their abusive spouses out of fear for their lives.

Feminists point to two key theoretical questions that remain unaddressed by mainstream criminology.[61] First, traditional criminology fails to address the "generalizability problem": Do the theoretical arguments apply equally to male and female criminality?[62] Second, most criminologists do not account for the "gender ratio problem": Why are women less likely than men to commit crime, and why do men tend to have greater involvement in crime?[63] Criminologists who claim the objectivity and universal applicability of their theories in actuality generally ignore female criminality and the role of gender in crime among both men and women and exclude the perspectives and experiences of women.[64] Feminists thus critique mainstream criminology as "androcentric," or male centered, to the detriment of a comprehensive understanding of crime.

Schwartz and Steffensmeier argue that any gendered theory of offending should be able to account for four factors:[65]

1. The organization of gender (differences in norms, moral development, social control, and relational concerns, as well as reproductive, sexual, and other physical differences)
2. Access to criminal opportunity (underworld sexism, differences in access to skills, crime associates, and settings)
3. Motivation for crime (differences in taste for risk, self-control, cost–benefits, stressful events, and relational concerns)
4. The context of offending (differences in the circumstances of particular offenses, such as setting, victim–offender relationship, and use of weapons)

Feminist criminologists hold a wide array of perspectives, but they share in common their concern with the generalizability and gender ratio problems. Some of the different perspectives include the following:[66]

- "Liberal feminism" is primarily concerned with patterns of discrimination against women, which supporters of this perspective feel can be overcome through social and legal reform.
- "Marxist feminism" suggests that gender oppression is integrally entwined within the capitalist structure, and accordingly argues for a complete restructuring of society.
- "Radical feminism" argues that men have an innate tendency toward domination and control and thus advocates female empowerment and the eradication of female dependency on males.

Feminist theorists differentiate between sex and gender. They use the term "sex" to refer to the physical differentiation of males and females, whereas "gender" refers to social constructs of masculinity and femininity—the many traits, behaviors, and other markers that have become culturally associated with each sex. They observe that sex differences pertain primarily to physical development, hormones, and the ability to bear children. By contrast, gender has a more pervasive effect on social roles and relationships. Within this framework, "patriarchy," or male domination, is seen as a primary source of social inequality. In some cases patriarchy entails the systematic exclusion of women from positions of power. It can also refer to more subtle effects, such as valuing masculine traits more highly than feminine traits. Finally, patriarchy can entail the acceptance of males' experiences as the "norm," with women's experiences portrayed as special cases or anomalies.

Feminists argue that the concept of patriarchy has broad applicability in criminology, having shaped women's experiences with crime and victimization in a variety of ways. For example, until the activism of "second-wave feminism," which spanned the 1960s and 1970s, the crimes of domestic violence and sexual assault were often not taken seriously.[67] Women's lower pay and higher rates of poverty shape their risk for financially motivated crimes such as prostitution. Depending on the nature of the offense, women may be treated more harshly or leniently at sentencing.

More recently, "third-wave feminism," beginning around 1980, has called attention to the different effects of gender oppression based on "intersectionality," that is, the manner in which age, race, religion, and other characteristics overlap to shape women's and men's unique gendered experiences. This more nuanced understanding of identity and differ-ence has helped researchers illuminate women's varied experiences.

GENDER ENTRAPMENT[68]

On the basis of interviews conducted with female offenders at Rikers Island, Beth Richie identified six common pathways to female criminality:

1. Women held hostage: These women were in abusive situations that they felt they could not leave for fear of their lives. In multiple cases, the abuser ultimately killed their child, and the women were arrested for their failure to intervene.
2. Projection and association: These women were arrested for crimes against men that were not their abusers, but that were fed by their experiences as victims.
3. Sexual exploitation: These women were arrested for illegal sex work, and in many cases had been coerced into the trade by their abusive partners.
4. Fighting back: These women were serving time for property destruction committed in the context of fighting back against their abusers.
5. Poverty: The women were detained for property offenses that were committed out of financial need, or due to coercion from the men with whom they were involved.
6. Addiction: The women sometimes turned to drugs as a way of dealing with the stress of victimization.

On the basis of these findings, Richie concluded that many women behind bars experienced what she terms "gender entrapment": a situation in which they are unable to safely change or avoid their problematic social situation or position, but are ultimately criminalized for their response to those conditions. An example is a woman who feels unable to leave an abusive situation, but is then held criminally liable for coerced or retaliatory crimes that stem from that abuse.

Power-control theory

In a series of articles, John Hagan and associates outlined a Marxist feminist explanation of gender differences in crime. They work from the assumption that crime is most likely to be committed by those who exercise the most power and are subject to the least control.[69] On this basis, they argue that gender differences in crime can be attributed, in part, to sons being subject to less parental control than daughters. They posit that the difference will be most pronounced within patriarchal families, in which the mother has the least power and the daughter will be subject to the most control.[70] As families move toward egalitarianism, mothers gain power, and daughters become subject to control more commensurate with that of sons.

Structured action theory

James Messerschmidt is a theorist and researcher firmly couched in "third-wave feminism." In his structured action theory,[71] he argues that the meanings of race, class, and gender can vary in different contexts. In some contexts, the expectations placed upon people can lead to crime, as when people break the law to

- Conform to others' expectations of their race, class, or gender, as with men who engage in violence to "prove" their masculinity
- Challenge the social constraints of their race, class, or gender, as with women who break the law when retaliating against a domestic abuser
- Defend or achieve a privileged position, as with corporate heads that engage in deceptive practices to maintain an advantage in the marketplace

Criticisms of feminist criminology include that it

- Overemphasizes the role of gender relative to other factors that affect male and female criminality, such as class status
- Too quickly discounts the explanations for crime patterns offered by mainstream criminology

Peacemaking criminology

> What is required, in our work as criminologists, is not only an academic literature and a professional organization, but ways of thinking, speaking, and writing that foster peace.
>
> **Richard Quinney, 1993**[72]

> Let us begin with a fundamental realization: no amount of thinking and no amount of public policy have brought us any closer to understanding and solving the problem of crime. The more we have reacted to crime, the farther we have removed ourselves from any understanding and any reduction of the problem.
>
> **Richard Quinney, 1991**[73]

Peacemaking criminologists argue that the only legitimate goal in responding to crime should be the reduction of human suffering. They believe that traditional punishments are, in themselves, a form of violence that perpetuate harm rather than alleviate it, and thus implicate traditional criminology and criminal justice as being rooted in "mean-mindedness."[72] They characterize the criminal justice system's use of coercion and force as wars of convenience that victimize those who are already socially marginalized,[74] pointing out that society is most likely to criminalize and condemn those who lack social connections, even as the more harmful acts of the socially connected are readily forgiven.[75]

In the place of this harmful and arbitrary system they advocate a "nonviolent criminology,"[73] or, at the very least, responses to crime that "do the least harm" and take the well-being of victims into account. They support interventions that focus on reparation and understanding over those based in retribution or incapacitation. Since this perspective contends that all crime starts from a place of human suffering, it also holds that crime reduction strategies should

- Start from a place of compassion
- Avoid vengefulness
- Extend beyond the criminal justice system, as with providing "quality education for children, physical and mental health services, family support programs, employment and job security, and the allocation of resources for the reduction of poverty"[72]

Hal Pepinsky[76] describes peacemaking criminology as developing along three threads:

1. The "religious and humanist traditions" draw heavily on the concepts of Buddhism. They focus on the oneness and connectedness of humans and challenge the conception of criminals as something other than ourselves.
2. "Feminist traditions" explore mechanisms for reducing gender-based violence and propagating a peaceful world.
3. "Critical peacemaking" focuses on identifying the harms of the traditional "us versus them" approach to criminal justice.

Johan Galtung has posited two ways of conceiving of peace: "negative peace," defined as the "absence of violence and war," and "positive peace," which refers to the presence of "not what the government should prevent, but what government or the society should provide—*justice* ... not just criminal justice, but also political, economic, and social justice."[77] Elias has suggested that our system, more often built around a war mentality—"war on crime," "war on drugs"—is antithetical to both forms of peace.[78]

Policy implications of peacemaking criminology

> To adopt alternative crime policies, we'd have to pursue crime control that really reduces crime rather than merely overseeing it. We'd have to stop manipulating or blaming victims, and take victimization (criminal and otherwise) seriously. We'd have to reject "democracy for the few" in favor of a more just political economy.
>
> **Robert Elias, 1991[79]**

Peacemaking criminologists advocate for policy changes that range from restorative justice to radical nonintervention. Some examples of practices that are consistent with peacemaking criminology include[80]

- Restorative justice programs: Interventions that aim to repair the harm stemming from the crime, or, where such reparation is not possible, to "bring together the various stakeholders to craft a mutually agreeable solution."[81] For example, arrangements could be made for a vandal to clean up the damage he or she caused, or for a burglar to pay the victim for damages and property loss. In the case of a violent crime, a negotiated outcome might include an apology, payment for medical treatment, and/or involvement by the offender in violence-reduction campaigns.
- Victim–offender reconciliation program (VORP): This strategy brings the offender(s) and victim(s) in front of a mediator to determine an appropriate outcome. The approach aims to satisfy the victim and help the offender take responsibility for their crime and support the healing of both parties.
- Family group conferencing: Similar to VORP, this strategy involves a negotiation of outcomes, but it includes relatives of the victim(s) and offender(s) in the process.
- Victim–offender panels: In some cases where it might not be appropriate to bring together victim and offender, the offender(s) may be asked to meet with victims of similar types of offenses, as when drunk drivers are ordered to meet with victims of drunk-driving accidents.

Peacemaking criminology has been critiqued on the basis that its policy recommendations may not be practical, particularly in regard to serious offenses.

Summary

- Critical criminology takes a macrosocial approach to crime.
- There are four subcategories of critical criminology: conflict, Marxist, feminist, and peacemaking.
- Critical criminology is concerned with the distribution of power as it relates to crime, criminal law, and criminal justice.
- Critical criminologists assume that society is composed of groups with differing cultures and interests. The group that holds the most power to shape the law will be able to mold it to their best interests.
- This perspective rejects the consensus view of law.
- Critical criminologists point out that the definition of "crime" used by mainstream criminologists captures only a small subset of socially harmful behavior, or "true crimes."
- Critical criminologists are as concerned with criminalization—the process by which certain actions come to be legally defined as "criminal"—as with crime itself.
- Conflict theorists describe the concentration of crime in disadvantaged communities as the outcome of group processes.
- Thorsten Sellin's culture conflict theory posits that primary culture conflict is likely to occur when one cultural group overlaps with the legal jurisdiction of another. Secondary culture conflict arises when the disempowered cultural group is subject to economic disadvantage and the social conditions that result. While both types of conflict can result in crime, Sellin viewed it as most likely to stem from secondary culture conflict.
- George Vold expanded the concept of "conflict" to include groups bonded for reasons other than culture.
- Austin Turk theorized about the circumstances most likely to result in conflict and criminalization. He held that where norms are divergent and strongly held by both groups conflict will be most likely. Disempowered groups high in organization but lacking in sophistication are the most vulnerable to criminalization.
- The social movements of the 1960s and 1970s converged with the existence of conflict and labeling theories and fed a movement of radical criminology that questioned official definitions of crime, called for a new definition founded in human rights, and placed heavy emphasis on action in pursuit of social justice.
- The radical criminology movement spurred the maturation of Marxist and feminist criminology as prominent threads of study.
- Taylor, Walton, and Young's 1973 work *The New Criminology* advocated for the formation of theories that integrate components of both mainstream and radical criminology. Specifically, they believed that any holistic criminological theory would be able to explain the criminal act, the social reaction to the act, the broader political–economic context, and the role of social psychology.
- Critical criminology is more accepted by mainstream criminologists than was once the case, although they still represent distinct (and in some ways incompatible) strains of thought.

- Marxist criminologists are concerned with the inequitable distribution of wealth, particularly the gap between the bourgeoisie and proletariat in capitalist economies.
- Willem Bonger is often identified as the first "Marxist criminologist." He argued that capitalism encourages crime by fostering egoism and inequality in society and its demoralizing effects on the poor.
- William Chambliss used a Marxist framework to explain the concentration of both crime and criminalization among the poor.
- Left idealism is a Marxist perspective that minimizes the harm of lower class criminality and promotes revolution as the only true solution to crime.
- Left realism shares concern for the working class, but holds that meaningful reforms are possible within the capitalist structure. Policy recommendations typically aim to reduce inequality, as with job programs and housing assistance.
- Feminist criminologists critique mainstream criminology as androcentric and for its failure to address the generalizability problem and gender ratio problem.
- Feminists distinguish between sex and gender, and implicate patriarchy in shaping gendered experiences of crime, victimization, and justice.
- Types of feminist criminology include liberal, Marxist, and radical feminism.
- The feminist movement is often considered to have taken place in three waves. The second wave of feminism helped call attention to domestic and sexual violence against women. The third wave of feminism emphasizes that women's and men's experiences—including their experiences of criminality, victimization, and criminalization—vary depending on other characteristics such as age and race.
- Hagan's power-control theory holds that gender differences in crime are most pronounced in patriarchal families in which daughters are subject to greater control than sons. As families become more egalitarian, the control exercised over daughters and sons will equalize, thus reducing gender differences in crime.
- James Messerschmidt proposed his structured action theory to explain how gender, race, and other characteristics can affect individuals' behavior by shaping others' expectations of them.
- Peacemaking criminology argues that traditional punishments are forms of violence that perpetuate harm rather than alleviating it. They believe that peace can be achieved only through peace, and the criminal justice system should thus be rooted in compassion rather than vengefulness.
- Strains of peacemaking criminology include religious/humanist, feminist, and critical perspectives.
- Peacemaking criminology is consistent with restorative justice, VORPs, and family group conferencing.

Questions in review

1. How does critical criminology differ from the other theories that you have studied in this course?
2. Explain the difference between "crime" and "criminalization."
3. Compare and contrast the contributions of Marxism and feminism.
4. Identify and describe criminal justice practices that are consistent with peacemaking criminology.
5. Which of the theories in this chapter do you think offers the most to our understanding of crime and criminalization, and why?

Practicum

Bangladesh factory deaths: Who is responsible?

The Bangladesh clothing industry has become the subject of international scrutiny for sweatshop conditions, low pay, and insufficient safety precautions that endanger the life and health of employees. Concern over these conditions peaked in April 2013, when more than 1,100 workers were killed and another 1,900 were injured in the collapse of the Rana Plaza garment factory in Dhaka, Bangladesh.[82] The day before the collapse, inspection teams had noted cracks in the building's structure: While other businesses in the building closed due to the safety concerns, the garment factory owners decided to stay open.[83] This was not the first or the last incident to call attention to unsafe work conditions at factories in the nation. Consider the following incidents:

- In 2005, at least 64 people were killed in a garment factory collapse.[84]
- In December 2010, a fire at a garment factory killed more than 20 people.[85]
- In November 2012, more than 100 people were killed in a fire at a clothing factory. Despite the identification of "high-risk" conditions at the factory in 2011, at the time of the fire there were insufficient fire exits, and the response to the blaze was slowed by its location.[86]
- In May 2013, at least eight people were killed in a fire at a clothing factory.[87]
- In October 2013, at least nine people were killed in a fire at a clothing factory.[88]

Most if not all of the above cases took place in Bangladesh factories that supplied Western retailers. While some of these retailers have agreed to support safety improvements, progress has been slow.[89] For example, in 2012, efforts to improve safety conditions within the Bangladesh garment industry were stymied when two large American retailers refused to pay higher prices to support the measures.[90]

The owners of the factories argue that they cannot afford appropriate security measures without the support of their customers, even with many of their employees making only the minimum wage of $37 a month.[91] One such owner explained,

> Look, we make a particular brand of polo shirt, which they pay us
> $15 to make and they sell for $150. We only make five percent on that
> by the time we pay the bank, the workers and compliance costs....
> There is a tremendous pressure to maintain the minimum level of
> compliance [with safety standards] ... with those costs not every fac-
> tory can afford to maintain that level.[92]

The business owners are afraid that if they raise prices to increase factory safety the retailers that compose their customer base will simply go elsewhere. Similarly, the Bangladesh government may be reluctant to enforce stringent safety standards for fear that it would hinder one of the nation's largest industries.[93]

Despite the unsafe work conditions, about four million people work in the garment factories in Bangladesh.[94] Most of the employees (85%) are women.[95] The work is valued as it provides a steady paycheck that can assist with the support of large families and presents a desirable alternative to farm or domestic positions.[96] The availability of factory work for women, with the independence and financial support it provides, may also have contributed to a reduction in forced marriages.[97]

Questions regarding the Bangladesh factory deaths

1. What connections do you see between the work conditions in Bangladesh factories and the arguments of conflict, Marxist, and feminist theorists?
2. Can any of the theories from previous chapters help explain these deaths?
3. In cases like this, who (if anyone) should be accountable: The head of the garment factories? The corporations that contract with them? Consumers who buy the products?
4. Who (if anyone) should be punished for deaths that result from unsafe work conditions? What would be an appropriate punishment?

References

1. Young, J. (1986). The failure of criminology: The need for a radical realism. In R. Matthews & J. Young (Eds.), Abridged from *Confronting crime* (pp. 9–30). London: Sage. (Republished chapter 40 (pp. 442–452) in J. Muncie, E. McLaughlin & M. Langan (Eds.). (1996). *Criminological perspectives: A reader*. Thousand Oaks, CA: Sage. p. 445).
2. Platt, T. (1974). Prospects for a radical criminology in the United States. *Crime and Social Justice, 1*, 2–10.
3. United States Attorney's Office, District of Nevada. (2010, Feb. 2). Felon who robbed local Bank of America in August 2009 sentenced to 10 years in prison. Retrieved February 2, 2010, from http://www.justice.gov/usao/nv/news/2010/02022010.html
4. United States Attorney's Office, District of Nevada. (2010, Feb. 2). Felon who robbed local Bank of America in August 2009 sentenced to 10 years in prison. Retrieved February 2, 2010, from http://www.justice.gov/usao/nv/news/2010/02022010.html
5. United States Attorney's Office, District of Nevada. (2010, Feb. 2). Felon who robbed local Bank of America in August 2009 sentenced to 10 years in prison. Retrieved February 2, 2010, from http://www.justice.gov/usao/nv/news/2010/02022010.html
6. United States Department of Justice. (2013, Aug. 6). Department of Justice sues Bank of America for defrauding investors in connection with sale of over $850 million of residential mortgage-backed securities. Retrieved August 6, 2013, from http://www.justice.gov/opa/pr/2013/August/13-ag-886.html
7. United States Department of Justice. (2013, Aug. 6). Department of Justice sues Bank of America for defrauding investors in connection with sale of over $850 million of residential mortgage-backed securities. Retrieved August 6, 2013, from http://www.justice.gov/opa/pr/2013/August/13-ag-886.html
8. United States Department of Justice. (2013, Aug. 6). Department of Justice sues Bank of America for defrauding investors in connection with sale of over $850 million of residential mortgage-backed securities. Retrieved August 6, 2013, from http://www.justice.gov/opa/pr/2013/August/13-ag-886.html
9. Barak, G., & Bohm, R. M. (1989). The crimes of the homeless or the crime of homelessness? On the dialectics of criminalization, decriminalization, and victimization. *Contemporary Crises, 13*, 275–288.
10. Barak, G., & Bohm, R. M. (1989). The crimes of the homeless or the crime of homelessness? On the dialectics of criminalization, decriminalization, and victimization. *Contemporary Crises, 13*, 275–288.
11. Barak, G., & Bohm, R. M. (1989). The crimes of the homeless or the crime of homelessness? On the dialectics of criminalization, decriminalization, and victimization. *Contemporary Crises, 13*, 284.
12. Barak, G., & Bohm, R. M. (1989). The crimes of the homeless or the crime of homelessness? On the dialectics of criminalization, decriminalization, and victimization. *Contemporary Crises, 13*, 284.
13. Barak, G. (1991). Homelessness and the case for community-based initiatives: The emergence of a model shelter as a short-term response to the deepening crisis in housing. In H. E. Pepinsky & E. Quinney (Eds.), *Criminology as peacemaking* (chap. 4, pp. 47–68). Bloomington: Indiana University Press.

14. Barak, G. (1991). Homelessness and the case for community-based initiatives: The emergence of a model shelter as a short-term response to the deepening crisis in housing. In H. E. Pepinsky & E. Quinney (Eds.), *Criminology as peacemaking* (chap. 4, p. 49). Bloomington: Indiana University Press.

15. Barak, G. (1991). Homelessness and the case for community-based initiatives: The emergence of a model shelter as a short-term response to the deepening crisis in housing. In H. E. Pepinsky & E. Quinney (Eds.), *Criminology as peacemaking* (chap. 4, p. 49). Bloomington: Indiana University Press.

16. Barak, G. (1991). Homelessness and the case for community-based initiatives: The emergence of a model shelter as a short-term response to the deepening crisis in housing. In H. E. Pepinsky & E. Quinney (Eds.), *Criminology as peacemaking* (chap. 4, p. 49). Bloomington: Indiana University Press.

17. Barak, G. (1991). Homelessness and the case for community-based initiatives: The emergence of a model shelter as a short-term response to the deepening crisis in housing. In H. E. Pepinsky & E. Quinney (Eds.), *Criminology as peacemaking* (chap. 4, p. 55). Bloomington: Indiana University Press.

18. Sellin, T. (1938). *Culture conflict and crime* (p. 63). New York: Social Science Research Council.

19. Sellin, T. (1938). *Culture conflict and crime* (p. 105). New York: Social Science Research Council.

20. Sellin, T. (1938). *Culture conflict and crime* (p. 104). New York: Social Science Research Council.

21. Vold, G. (1958). *Theoretical criminology* (pp. 208–209). New York: Oxford University Press.

22. Vold, G. (1958). *Theoretical criminology* (p. 205). New York: Oxford University Press.

23. Vold, G. (1958). *Theoretical criminology* (p. 206). New York: Oxford University Press.

24. Turk, A. (1969). *Criminality and legal order.* Chicago: Rand McNally.

25. Greenberg, D. F. (1993). *Crime and capitalism: Readings in Marxist Criminology* (p. 1). Philadelphia: Temple University Press.

26. Greenberg, D. F. (1993). *Crime and capitalism: Readings in Marxist Criminology* (p. 3). Philadelphia: Temple University Press.

27. Cardarellli, A. P., & Hicks, S. C. (1993). Radicalism in law and criminology: A retrospective view of critical legal studies and radical criminology. *Journal of Criminal Law & Criminology, 84*(3), 502–553.

28. Cardarellli, A. P., & Hicks, S. C. (1993). Radicalism in law and criminology: A retrospective view of critical legal studies and radical criminology. *Journal of Criminal Law & Criminology, 84*(3), 520.

29. Cardarellli, A. P., & Hicks, S. C. (1993). Radicalism in law and criminology: A retrospective view of critical legal studies and radical criminology. *Journal of Criminal Law & Criminology, 84*(3), 521.

30. Cardarellli, A. P., & Hicks, S. C. (1993). Radicalism in law and criminology: A retrospective view of critical legal studies and radical criminology. *Journal of Criminal Law & Criminology, 84*(3), 513.

31. Schwartz, M. D., & DeKeseredy, W. S. (1991). Left realist criminology: Strengths, weaknesses, and the feminist critique. *Crime, Law, and Social Change, 15,* 51–72.

32. Cardarellli, A. P., & Hicks, S. C. (1993). Radicalism in law and criminology: A retrospective view of critical legal studies and radical criminology. *Journal of Criminal Law & Criminology, 84*(3), 514.

33. Smart, C. (1990). Feminist approaches to criminology or postmodern woman meets atavistic man. In A. Morris & L. Gelsthorpe (Eds.), Abridged from *Feminist perspectives in criminology* (pp. 71–84). Milton Keynes: Open University Press. (Republished as chapter 41 (pp. 453–465) in J. Muncie, E. McLaughlin & M. Langan (Eds.). (1996). *Criminological perspectives: A reader.* Thousand Oaks, CA: Sage. p. 453).

34. Platt, T. (1975). Prospects for a radical criminology in the USA. In I. Taylor, P. Walton & J. Young (Eds.), *Critical criminology* (chap. 3, pp. 95–112). London: Routledge & Kegan Paul.

35. Platt, T. (1975). Prospects for a radical criminology in the USA. In I. Taylor, P. Walton & J. Young (Eds.), *Critical criminology* (chap. 3, p. 100). London: Routledge & Kegan Paul.

36. Cardarellli, A. P., & Hicks, S. C. (1993). Radicalism in law and criminology: A retrospective view of critical legal studies and radical criminology. *Journal of Criminal Law & Criminology, 84*(3), 534.

37. Schauffler, R., & Hannigan, M. (1974). Criminology at Berkeley: Resisting academic repression, part 2. *Crime and Social Justice, 2,* 42–47.

38. Platt, T., & Shank, G. (1976). Editorial: Berkeley's School of Criminology, 1950–1976. *Crime and Social Justice, 6,* 1–3.

39. Miller, A. H. (1972). People's park: Dimensions of a campus confrontation. *Politics & Society, 2,* 433–457.

40. Schauffler, R. (1974). Criminology at Berkeley: Resisting academic repression. *Crime and Social Justice, 1,* 58–61.

41. Platt, T., & Shank, G. (1976). Editorial: Berkeley's School of Criminology, 1950–1976. *Crime and Social Justice, 6,* 1–3.

42. Schauffler, R. (1974). Criminology at Berkeley: Resisting academic repression. *Crime and Social Justice, 1,* 58–61.

43. Taylor, I., Walton, P., & Young, J. (1973). *The new criminology: For a social theory of deviance.* London: Routledge & Kegan Paul.

44. Taylor, I., Walton, P., & Young, J. (1973). *The new criminology: For a social theory of deviance* (p. 270). London: Routledge & Kegan Paul.

45. Cardarellli, A. P., & Hicks, S. C. (1993). Radicalism in law and criminology: A retrospective view of critical legal studies and radical criminology. *Journal of Criminal Law & Criminology, 84*(3), 502–553.

46. Engels, F. (1993). The demoralization of the English working class. In F. G. David (Ed.), *Crime and capitalism: Readings in Marxist criminology* (chap. 2, pp. 48–50). Philadelphia: Temple University Press. (Reprinted from Friedrich Engels (1958), *The condition of the working class in England.* W.O. Henderson and W.H. Chaloner (Trans. and Eds.). Oxford: Basil Blackwell, pp. 48, 130, 145–156, 149, 242–243).

47. Bonger, W. (1916). Criminality and economic conditions. Abridged from *Criminality and economic conditions* (pp. 402–405, 667–672). London: Heinemann. (Republished chapter 5 (pp. 40–46) in J. Muncie, E. McLaughlin & M. Langan (Eds.). (1996). *Criminological perspectives: A reader.* Thousand Oaks, CA: Sage. p. 44).

48. Based on Blumenberg, W. (1998). *Karl Marx: An illustrated biography* (D. Scott, Trans.). London: Verso.

49. Based on Blumenberg, W. (1998). *Karl Marx: An illustrated biography* (D. Scott, Trans., p. 25). London: Verso.

50. Chambliss, W. J., & Seidman, R. (1971). *Law, order, and power.* Reading, MA: Addison-Wesley.

51. Chambliss, W. J. (1975). Toward a political economy of crime. *Theory and Society, 2*(1), 149–170.

52. Chambliss, W. J. (1975). Toward a political economy of crime. *Theory and Society, 2*(1), 153.

53. Schwartz, M. D., & DeKeseredy, W. S. (1991). Left realist criminology: Strengths, weaknesses, and the feminist critique. *Crime, Law, and Social Change, 15,* 51–72.

54. Dekeseredy, W. (2003). Left realism on inner-city violence. In M. D. Schwartz & S. E. Hatty (Eds.), *Controversies in critical criminology* (chap. 3, pp. 29–41). Cincinnati, OH: Anderson Publishing.

55. Greenberg, D. F. (1976). On one-dimensional Marxist criminology. *Theory and Society, 3,* 611–621.

56. Greenberg, D. F. (1976). On one-dimensional Marxist criminology. *Theory and Society, 3,* 612.

57. Schwartz, J., & Steffensmeier, D. (2007). The nature of female offending: Patterns and explanation. In R. Zaplin (Ed.), *Female offenders: Critical perspective and effective interventions* (2nd ed., Chap. 2, pp. 43–75). Boston: Jones & Bartlett.

58. Messerschmidt, J. W. (1997). *Crime as structured action: Gender, race, class, and crime in the making* (p. 3). Thousand Oaks, CA: Sage.

59. Lombroso, C., & Ferrero, W. (1895). *The female offender.* New York: D. Appleton and Company.

60. Miller, J., & Mullins, C. W. (2006). The status of feminist theories in criminology. In F. Cullen, J. P. Wright, & K. Blevins (Eds.), *Taking stock: The status of criminological theory* (Vol. 15, pp. 217–249). In series Advances in Criminological Theory. F. Adler and W. Laufer (series Eds.). Piscataway, NJ: Transaction.

61. Daly, K., & Chesney-Lind, M. (1988). Feminism and criminology. *Justice Quarterly, 5*(4), 497–538.

62. Daly, K., & Chesney-Lind, M. (1988). Feminism and criminology. *Justice Quarterly, 5*(4), 514.

63. Daly, K., & Chesney-Lind, M. (1988). Feminism and criminology. *Justice Quarterly, 5*(4), 515.

64. See Miller, J., & Mullins, C. W. (2006). The status of feminist theories in criminology. In F. Adler, & W. Laufer (Series Eds.) & F. Cullen, J. P. Wright, & K. Blevins (Eds.), *Taking stock: Vol. 15. The status of criminological theory. Advances in criminological theory* (pp. 217–249). Piscataway, NJ: Transaction Publishers.

65. List quoted verbatim from Schwartz, J., & Steffensmeier, D. (2007). The nature of female offending: Patterns and explanation. In R. Zaplin (Ed.), *Female offenders: Critical perspective and effective interventions* (2nd ed., Chap. 2, pp. 43–75). Boston: Jones & Bartlett.

66. Based on Simpson, S. S. (1996). Feminist theory, crime, and justice. In P. Cordella & L. Siegel (Eds.), *Readings in contemporary criminological theory* (chap. 21, pp. 319–339). Boston: Northeastern University Press.

67. Adapted from Morash, M. (2006). *Understanding gender, crime, and justice.* Thousand Oaks, CA: Sage; and Van Wormer, K., & Bartollas, C. (2007). *Women and the criminal justice system* (2nd ed.). Boston: Allyn & Bacon.

68. Based on Richie, B. (1996). *Compelled to crime: The gender entrapment of battered, black women.* New York: Routledge.

69. Hagan, J., Gillis, A. R., & Simpson, J. (1985). The class structure of a gender theory of delinquency toward a power-control theory of common delinquent behavior. *American Journal of Sociology, 90*(6), 1151–1178.

70. Hagan, J., Simpson, J., & Gillis, A. R. (1987). Class in the household: A power-control theory of gender and delinquency. *American Journal of Sociology, 92*(4), 788–816.

71. Messerschmidt, J. W. (1997). *Crime as structured action: Gender, race, class, and crime in the making.* Thousand Oaks, CA: Sage Publications.

72. Quinney, R. (1993). A life of crime: Criminology and public policy as peacemaking. *Journal of Crime and Justice, 16*(2), 3–9.

73. Quinney, R. (1991). The way of peace: On crime, suffering, and service. In H. E. Pepinsky & R. Quinney (Eds.), *Criminology as peacemaking* (pp. 3–13). Bloomington: University of Indiana Press.

74. Pepinsky, H. (1997). What is peacemaking? In B. D. MacLean & D. Milovanovic (Eds.), *Thinking critically about crime.* Vancouver, WA: Collective Press.

75. See Pepinsky, H. (1997). What is peacemaking? In B. D. MacLean & D. Milovanovic (Eds.), *Thinking critically about crime* (pp. 109–114). Vancouver, WA: Collective Press.

76. Pepinsky, H. E. (1991). Peacemaking in criminology and criminal justice. In H. E. Pepinsky & E. Quinney (Eds.), *Criminology as peacemaking* (chap. 20, pp. 299–327). Bloomington: Indiana University Press.

77. Elias, R. (1991). Crime control as human rights enforcement. In H. E. Pepinsky & R. Quinney (Eds.), *Criminology as peacemaking* (chap. 17, pp. 251–262). Bloomington: University of Indiana Press.

78. Elias, R. (1991). Crime control as human rights enforcement. In H. E. Pepinsky & R. Quinney (Eds.), *Criminology as peacemaking* (chap. 17, pp. 251–252). Bloomington: University of Indiana Press.

79. Elias, R. (1991). Crime control as human rights enforcement. In H. E. Pepinsky & R. Quinney (Eds.), *Criminology as peacemaking* (chap. 17, p. 255). Bloomington: University of Indiana Press.

80. Based on Fuller, J. (2003). Peacemaking criminology. In M. D. Schwartz & S. E. Hatty (Eds.), *Controversies in critical criminology* (chap. 7, pp. 85–96). Cincinnati, OH: Anderson Publishing.

81. Based on Fuller, J. (2003). Peacemaking criminology. In M. D. Schwartz & S. E. Hatty (Eds.), *Controversies in critical criminology* (chap. 7, p. 89). Cincinnati, OH: Anderson Publishing.

82. Liljas, P. (2013, Sept. 16). In Bangladesh, Rana Plaza victims still await compensation. *Time.* Retrieved September 16, 2013, from http://world.time.com/2013/09/16/in-bangladesh-rana-plaza-victims-still-await-compensation/

83. Manik, J. A., & Yardley, J. (2013, Apr. 24). Building collapse in Bangladesh leaves scores dead. *New York Times.* Retrieved April 24, 2013, from http://www.nytimes.com/2013/04/25/world/asia/bangladesh-building-collapse.html?_r=0

84. Manik, J. A., & Yardley, J. (2013, Apr. 24). Building collapse in Bangladesh leaves scores dead. *New York Times.* Retrieved April 24, 2013, from http://www.nytimes.com/2013/04/25/world/asia/bangladesh-building-collapse.html?_r=0

85. Manik, J. A., & Bajaj, V. (2010, Dec. 14). Bangladesh factory fire kills at least 20. *New York Times.* Retrieved December 14, 2010, from http://www.nytimes.com/2010/12/15/world/asia/15bangladesh.html

86. Bajaj, V. (2012, Nov. 25). Fatal fire in Bangladesh highlights the dangers facing garment workers. *New York Times*. Retrieved November 25, 2013, from http://www.nytimes.com/2012/11/26/world/asia/bangladesh-fire-kills-more-than-100-and-injures-many.html

87. Campbell, C. (2013, May 9). Bangladesh: Eight killed in factory fire; collapse toll hits 1,000. *Time*. Retrieved May 9, 2012, from http://world.time.com/2013/05/09/latest-bangladesh-garment-factory-disaster-spotlights-continuing-safety-concerns/

88. Smith, A. (2013, Oct. 9). Nine die in fire at Bangladesh factory with links to Western clothing brands. *NBC News*. Retrieved October 9, 2013, from http://worldnews.nbcnews.com/_news/2013/10/09/20883238-nine-die-in-fire-at-bangladesh-factory-with-links-to-western-clothing-brands?lite

89. *Huffington Post*. (2013, May 20). Bangladesh factory safety accord: At least 14 major North American retailers decline to sign. Retrieved May 20, 2013, from http://www.huffingtonpost.com/2013/05/17/bangladesh-factory-safety-accord_n_3286430.html

90. Kavoussi, B. (2012, Dec. 5). Walmart rejected proposal to protect Bangladesh factories against fire. *Huffington Post*. Retrieved December 5, 2012, from http://www.huffingtonpost.com/2012/12/05/walmart-bangladesh-factory-fire_n_2244891.html

91. Campbell, C. (May 9, 2013). Bangladesh: Eight killed in factory fire; Collapse toll hits 1,000. *Time*. Retrieved from http://world.time.com/2013/05/09/latest-bangladesh-garment-factory-disaster-spotlights-continuing-safety-concerns/

92. Quoted in Uddin, S., & Newland, J. (2013, May 25). Bangladeshi garment factory owners on defensive, fear losing 'lifeline.' *NBC News*. Retrieved May 25, 2013, from http://worldnews.nbcnews.com/_news/2013/05/25/18297608-bangladeshi-garment-factory-owners-on-defensive-fear-losing-lifeline?lite

93. Manik, J. A., & Yardley. (April 24, 2013). Building collapse in Bangladesh leaves scores dead. *The New York Times*. Retrieved from http://www.nytimes.com/2013/04/25/world/asia/bangladesh-building-collapse.html?_r=0

94. Uddin, S. (2013, May 26). Bangladesh factory collapse: Why women endure danger to make clothes for the West. *NBC News*. Retrieved May 26, 2013, from http://worldnews.nbcnews.com/_news/2013/05/26/18447688-bangladesh-factory-collapse-why-women-endure-danger-to-make-clothes-for-the-west?lite

95. Uddin, S. (2013, May 26). Bangladesh factory collapse: Why women endure danger to make clothes for the West. *NBC News*. Retrieved May 26, 2013, from http://worldnews.nbcnews.com/_news/2013/05/26/18447688-bangladesh-factory-collapse-why-women-endure-danger-to-make-clothes-for-the-west?lite

96. Uddin, S. (2013, May 26). Bangladesh factory collapse: Why women endure danger to make clothes for the West. *NBC News*. Retrieved May 26, 2013, from http://worldnews.nbcnews.com/_news/2013/05/26/18447688-bangladesh-factory-collapse-why-women-endure-danger-to-make-clothes-for-the-west?lite

97. Uddin, S. (2013, May 26). Bangladesh factory collapse: Why women endure danger to make clothes for the West. *NBC News*. Retrieved May 26, 2013, from http://worldnews.nbcnews.com/_news/2013/05/26/18447688-bangladesh-factory-collapse-why-women-endure-danger-to-make-clothes-for-the-west?lite

chapter nine

American system of justice

Chapter objectives

After studying this chapter, you should understand and be able to explain

- The constitutional basis of the U.S. justice system
- How laws are legislated and adjudicated
- The nature, responsibilities, and interrelationships of the local, state, and federal court systems
- The responsibilities and functioning of appellate and supreme courts at the state and federal levels
- The nature, jurisdictions, and interrelationships of various local, state, and federal law enforcement agencies
- The nature and functioning of the correctional system at the local, state, and federal levels.
- The fundamental principles of various criminological theories
- How criminological theories affect criminal justice policymaking in the United States

Introduction

Having witnessed the various abuses of power possible through the laws and courts in a monarchy, America's Founding Fathers were determined to avoid the duplication of a legal system with such explicit potential to further the aims of those in power. Given that the initial waves of colonization of what would become the United States came mostly from England, it is not particularly surprising that the U.S. legal system draws heavily on the traditions of English common law. Yet in the process of seeking a fresh start in the New World, those colonists almost immediately began modifying their legal traditions. As early as 1636, the leaders of the Plymouth Colony, in codifying the first written laws set down on American shores, deliberately departed from English traditions in certain respects. From creating the concept of civil marriage (under English law marriage was possible only through the church) to granting property rights to widows and changing the rules governing property inheritance to establishing a formal recording system for titles, mortgages, and other conveyances of property, the colonists took advantage of the opportunity to build a legal system in much the same manner as they were building their settlements—from bare ground up.[1]

Often the popular perception is that abuses of the legal system were at the behest of the Crown, to maintain the power of the monarch and extend his (or her) power. Although there is some degree of truth to this notion—the king's Court of Star Chamber was extensively abused by Charles I, for example, and as a result abolished in 1641—the truth is more prosaic. The English legal system of the eighteenth century with which the colonists would have been familiar was corrupt, ineffective, and heavily weighted against the poor. The magistrates, who headed the courts and formed the core of the judiciary, were by law unpaid. The intent was for the post to be filled by propertied men to minimize their susceptibility to bribery. Yet, the actual result was exactly the opposite. Because the magistrate was permitted by law to keep bail money, some had people arrested without cause simply to generate income from bail. Despite the unpleasant, demanding, and sometimes outright dangerous nature of these positions, the power associated with them was also a powerful draw.[2]

In creating a plan of government, the framers of the Constitution established responsibility for the creation of laws, established a system for the adjudication of those laws, and—primarily through the Bill of Rights—imposed specific protections for citizens within the legal system.

The Constitution, the law, and the courts

Once the issue of balancing power between the state and national governments was resolved by the replacement of the Articles of Confederation with the Constitution, the next act of the framers was to address in greater detail the rights of the people. Certain specific protections were built into the body of the Constitution, such as the prohibitions on suspension of habeas corpus, bills of attainder (essentially, a declaration of guilt and summary sentence against a person or group of persons, without benefit of trial), and *ex post facto* (retroactive) laws found in Section 9 of Article I.[3]

The power to draft and pass laws, including criminal statutes, is reserved to Congress by Article I, Section 8. As it happens, the language in this regard is (perhaps surprisingly) relatively vague. The last of the 18 Enumerated Powers is "To make all Laws which shall be necessary and proper for carrying into Execution the foregoing Powers, and all other Powers vested by this Constitution in the Government of the United States, or in any Department or Officer thereof."[4] In point of fact, far more criminal statutes are found at the state and local levels than the federal; Section 9 specifically lists areas in which Congress is to enact laws: bankruptcy, "counterfeiting the Securities and current Coin of the United States," and "Piracies and Felonies committed on the high Seas, and Offences against the Law of Nations."[5] These are highly specific and relatively rare offenses (bankruptcy being a civil, not criminal, matter).

The only court specifically established by the Constitution is the U.S. Supreme Court, in Article III. Article III additionally directs in Section 2 that all criminal trials other than impeachment must be before a jury and must take place in the state in which the crime was committed. Section 3 clearly defines treason (historically a handy hook upon which a sovereign could hang a charge against his opponents) and further specifies that a conviction requires the testimony of two witnesses to the same act or a confession in open court. The power to create courts below the Supreme Court is allocated to Congress, directly as one of the Enumerated Powers in Article I, Section 8, and obliquely in Article III, Section 1.[6] Because today the federal judiciary is established and new courts are not being created, in practice Congress controls the federal court system in three principal ways: It determines the number and assignment of federal judges, approves or denies presidential appointments to the federal bench, and appropriates the budgets of the entire federal judiciary.[7]

But while the bulk of the Constitution itself thus addresses the functions of the branches of government and their interrelationships, as well as the relationship between state and federal powers, the Bill of Rights was focused squarely on the relationship between the government and the governed. In fact, the Preamble to the Bill of Rights opens by declaring, "The Conventions of a number of the States, having at the time of their adopting the Constitution, expressed a desire, in order to prevent misconstruction or abuse of its powers, that further declaratory and restrictive clauses should be added: And as extending the ground of public confidence in the Government, will best ensure the beneficent ends of its institution."[8] Four of the ten amendments address a citizen facing arrest or prosecution for criminal acts: IV (prohibition of unreasonable searches and seizures), V (Due Process clause), VI (speed trial by jury and rights to counsel and to confront witnesses), and VIII (prohibition of excessive bail and cruel and unusual punishments).

Sources of law

Two broad categories of law (enshrined in statutes) exist: public and private (or civil). Public laws are the province of the state (in this context meaning the government generally) and set out both standards of conduct and punitive measures, which the state is entitled to take against those who violate those standards. Naturally, both the determination of guilt or innocence under such statutes and the imposition of penalties (whether they are the deprivation of freedom through imprisonment, the deprivation of property through fines and/or the confiscation of nonfinancial possessions, or even the deprivation of life in the case of capital crimes) are governed by the U.S. Constitution. The three categories of public law are criminal, constitutional, and administrative.

Civil law, such as the Uniform Commercial Code, regulates the interactions of individuals and legal entities such as corporations—hence the alternative name "private law." It is divided into tort law (disputes between individuals), property law (governance of the ownership and transfer of real property), contract law (disputes over fulfillment of contractual obligations), and family law (divorce and child custody). Trust law is sometimes added as a fifth category.

In some cases, the government does become involved in the arena of civil law. For example, the U.S. Patent and Trademark Office serves as a neutral registry of intellectual property, which may be the subject of infringement claims (tort law). In addition, it is federal law that establishes the standards on which intellectual property infringement claims are judged. But while criminal statutes governing intellectual property rights do exist and are enforced by the U.S. Department of Justice,[9] such disputes are generally civil matters, with a successful plaintiff typically rewarded with monetary damages, disgorgement of profits, and/or an injunction against further use of the infringed intellectual property.

Administrative law, while public rather than civil, often blurs the lines between the two categories. This area of the law addresses the interpretation and enforcement of government regulations. Because of the highly technical nature of many areas of government policy, Congress frequently passes legislation that mandates the broad outlines of regulation but leaves detailed rule-making to the responsible agency. Although these rules have the force of law, in some cases their violation carries civil rather than criminal penalties.

The focus of this discussion, however, is criminal law, the aspect of public law probably best known to most citizens. It is important to note that because the state has the potential to impose such substantial penalties, proof in a criminal trial must meet the standard of "beyond a reasonable doubt." For civil matters, the standard is only "preponderance of the evidence." In some noteworthy cases, criminal defendants have been acquitted only to be sued in civil court and lose. One of the most publicized instances was the trial of O. J. Simpson for the murders of Nicole Brown Simpson and Ronald Goldman on June 12, 1994. Despite what seemed to be damning physical evidence against him, Simpson was acquitted of two counts of first-degree murder on October 3, 1995. One year later, the trial in a wrongful death suit filed by the Brown and Goldman families opened, and on February 4, 1997, the jury found for the plaintiffs and awarded $8.5 million in compensatory damages.[10]

Public laws derive from several primary sources. The first and most significant is the U.S. Constitution, and at the state level the relevant state constitution. The Constitution is the most significant because no law—federal or state—may contravene it; for this reason, it is sometimes referred to as the "supreme law of the land."[11] Responsibility for the review of such conflicts falls to the federal court system (established, remember, by Congress) and ultimately to the U.S. Supreme Court (expressly established by the Constitution). Most state constitutions mimic the U.S. Constitution in many ways. Although a state constitution may grant that state's citizens additional rights over and above those ensconced in the U.S. Constitution, it may not place any limitations on those rights guaranteed by it.

Statutes are enacted by Congress or by a state legislature. The relevant executive authority—the president or governor—may veto a law, subject to override by a supermajority of the legislature. In addition, the courts are a potential check on legislative action should a law conflict with constitutional protections. In the arena of statutes, the relationship between the state and federal governments is reversed: State laws may be more restrictive than federal laws, subject of course to constitutional limits.

For example, the District of Columbia (which is not actually a state, but the comparison is nonetheless valid) in June 1976 passed a ban on handguns and severely restricted other firearms, far exceeding federal laws on the matter. After years of lawsuits and abortive action by Congress, the issue finally came before the U.S. Supreme Court, which struck down the ban. However, the District still maintains strict requirements for registration and background checks, as well as a ban on semiautomatic weapons.[12] Similarly, in the wake of the December 2012 New Haven, Connecticut school shooting, the state of New York passed an "assault weapon" ban.[13]

On the other hand, federal law preempts state law under certain circumstances. Constitutionally, there are three forms of preemption. "Conflict preemption" occurs when a state law directly contradicts a federal law. That is, if it is impossible for a citizen to comply with both the state and federal statutes, the federal law is supreme.[14]

"Express preemption" results from a federal statute specifically stating that it is superior to state law. However, this occurs only when Congress is exercising one of its constitutional authorities. The complication has been that as society and laws become more complex, determining the exact circumstances of preemption has sometimes been difficult. In 1974, the Employee Retirement Income Security Act included a provision to preempt all state laws related to "any employee benefit plan," except for state regulation of "insurance, banking, or securities." It should be readily apparent how a law that can involve annuities, life insurance, investments, and other financial instruments could easily come into conflict with state laws in these areas, and the result has been a steady string of court cases.

Finally, "implied preemption" is interpreted by the courts. It results from a determination that a given federal statute was intended to "occupy the field" and govern all aspects of a particular area of the law. The National Labor Relations Act, for example, has been held to be the final word in all aspects of labor unions, preempting any state action in this area.

A recent source of well-publicized conflict over preemption has been state-level legalization of marijuana (medical or otherwise). Although Colorado and Washington legalized recreational marijuana use based on the outcome of state referenda in the 2012 election cycle, the U.S. Drug Enforcement Administration (DEA) maintains cannabis as a Schedule I controlled substance under the Controlled Substances Act, meaning it has among other criteria "no currently accepted medical use in the United States."[15]

Three additional sources contribute to the body of law in varying degrees. Regulations, rules, and orders are part of the body of administrative law, which has already been addressed. Although relatively uncommon and outside the scope of traditional criminal justice, criminal penalties can be and sometimes are assessed.

The most noteworthy recent such case involves the energy company BP. As a result of the 2010 Deepwater Horizon disaster, BP entered guilty pleas to 12 felony charges (most related to the deaths of workers on the rig, but one of them obstruction of Congress) and two misdemeanors. It was assessed $4.5 billion in fines as well as 5 years of probation and a requirement for two independent monitors to oversee the company's ethics and safety performance for 4 years. Of the total, $1.256 billion represents a criminal fine; the remaining amount will be distributed to the National Fish and Wildlife Foundation ($2.4 billion), the National Academy of Sciences ($350 million), and the Securities and Exchange Commission (a civil penalty of $525 million). However, the company is also liable for civil damages under the Clean Water Act, and in the event of a finding of gross negligence could see the penalty quadrupled to $21 billion.[16] (All of this is separate and apart from litigation and claims settlements in the civil law arena.)

Regulations, rules, and orders are typically established to supplement the broad directions established by legislative actions. Agencies often have responsibility for highly technical matters (consider the Food and Drug Administration, the Federal Communications Commission, or the Environmental Protection Agency). Because of the high level of technical expertise required to deal with these rules, many agencies have administrative judges or tribunals that operate in much the same fashion as traditional courts. In some sense, these functions incorporate aspects of both the legislative and judicial branches. Ultimately, however, all are answerable to action by Congress (or the appropriate state legislature, as states also have such agencies) and to review by the U.S. Court of Appeals.[11]

The next category is the executive order. Presidential executive orders are best known, but a governor is the chief executive of his or her state and may similarly issue an executive order. These orders are law, although they cannot block or contradict Congressional action. (This would violate the separation of powers.) Naturally, they are also subject to judicial review of their constitutionality.

Many executive orders are almost "housekeeping" in the sense that they provide direction to federal agencies but do not (at least directly) impact the public at large. For example, on May 17, 2012, President Obama issued a presidential memorandum (similar to an executive order) directing federal agencies to implement the Prison Rape Elimination Act of 2003. The memorandum established what agencies were affected—it specifically included private contractors handling detention for federal agencies—and established timelines for implementation.[17]

In other cases, executive orders can have tremendous and far-reaching impact. A particularly notorious one is Executive Order 6102, issued by President Franklin Roosevelt on April 5, 1933. This order essentially outlawed the possession of gold above a value of $100 "by individuals, partnerships, associations, and corporations" and required all gold in public possession to be surrendered to the Federal Reserve. (An exception was granted for collectible gold coins.)[18] This order remained in effect until it was reversed by a subsequent executive order issued by President Gerald Ford on December 31, 1974—a period of over 40 years.

Finally, though it is a relatively rare and somewhat obscure case, a treaty may serve as a source of law. Once ratified by the Senate, a treaty obliges the federal government to enforce the provisions it contains. Had the United States adopted the Kyoto Protocol in 1997, for example, it would have been bound to enact regulations to reduce its domestic greenhouse gas emissions to meet the standards of the treaty.[19]

Society and human activity give rise to so many different situations and circumstances that to codify all the necessary laws would be simply impossible. Instead, the American system of law derived from that of England, which in turn had evolved over the centuries and possessed a huge body of "common law." Common law is not made up of legislated statutes; it is instead the accumulation of decisions made in similar cases that guide the adjudication of current ones.

So important is common law to the American legal system, in fact, that respect for it is a fundamental principle. The formal name for this principle is *stare decisis*, which translated from Latin means "to stand by things decided." A portion of the opinion issued in *Planned Parenthood of Southeastern Pennsylvania v. Casey*, 505 U.S. 833 (1992), sums up *stare decisis* admirably:

> The obligation to follow precedent begins with necessity, and a contrary necessity marks its outer limit. With Cardozo, we recognize that no judicial system could do society's work if it eyed each issue afresh in every case that raised it.... Indeed, the very concept of the rule of law underlying our own Constitution requires such continuity over time that a respect for precedent is, by definition, indispensable.... At the other extreme, a different necessity would make itself felt if a prior judicial ruling should come to be seen so clearly as error that its enforcement was for that very reason doomed.[20]

This passage encompasses both the sanctity of precedent—the body of previously decided case law—and the importance of recognizing when an existing precedent is no longer appropriate in current circumstances. *Plessy v. Ferguson*, 163 U.S. 537 (1896), established the principle of "separate but equal" in regard to racial segregation; it took half a century and an evolution of attitudes toward race for this principle to be overturned by *Brown v. Board of Education*, 347 U.S. 483 (1954), but nevertheless there finally came a time when that precedent had to be set aside.

Precedent has value to the legal system in a number of important ways. First, it is an obstacle to arbitrary or prejudiced action by a judge. Certainly the ideological makeup of the appellate courts at various times does affect opinions on politically sensitive issues to some degree. While we expect and hope that judicial opinions will be based on a careful examination of case history and sober legal scholarship—and generally they are—the weight of precedent channels rulings into a fairly narrow range.

Second, there is a tremendous practical effect: It saves judges and courts the trouble of "reinventing the wheel" with every case that comes before them. It is not only possible but expected that a case will be decided in much the same manner as previous cases with similar facts and circumstances.

This, in turn, gives us a legal system that evolves rather than changing abruptly. It lends the American justice system stability and predictability—any good attorney can easily research the precedent relevant to a given case, and citizens can transact business with confidence in the legal foundation that governs their actions.

Finally, *stare decisis* promotes equality and fairness. In much the same manner that it restrains arbitrary acts by judges, precedent requires all people in similar situations to be treated similarly, regardless of race, wealth, power, or any other consideration. The transparency it brings to the operation of the law gives citizens faith in their legal system.

Precedent is most significant in the realms of civil and constitutional law. It has less significance for criminal law because criminal statutes are straightforward, so these cases present fewer situations that are not clearly covered by existing law. However, constitutional considerations are extremely significant for "procedural law"—the aspect of criminal law that governs the investigation, arrest, trial, and incarceration of the accused, as opposed to defining what acts are illegal.

Despite the emphasis the American legal system places on precedent, however, there are significant limitations to its application. First, in deciding a case, a court need only look at the legal principles applied in relevant previous cases. This is the "holding"; the Latin term is *ratio decidendi* (literally, "the reason for the decision"). The observations, reasoning, and opinions—collectively referred to as *obiter dicta* ("things said by the way")—expressed in a ruling may be informative, but they are extraneous to the holding itself and do not carry the weight of precedent.

Second, as should be clear by now, a previous case stands as precedent for a current one only if both have substantially similar facts—that is, they are "analogous." Otherwise, they are "disanalogous" or "distinguished," and reliance on such faulty precedent can undermine the validity of a decision.

Third, many decisions—especially in those cases that involve complex or controversial issues—are not unanimous. Precedent requires only consideration of the "majority" opinion; any "concurring" or "dissenting" opinions are not binding.

The final limitation on *stare decisis* is procedural. The only precedent that applies to a matter under consideration is the decision of the "highest" court "within that jurisdiction." In ruling on a case, a Missouri circuit court, for example, is not bound by precedent established by the California Supreme Court. This results in an even higher degree of uniformity in the application of precedent.

Although this last restriction might seem to be a simple principle, it is not always so straightforward. Following are the rules that apply:

- A state supreme court must honor its own prior decisions on matters of state law and those of the U.S. Supreme Court in regard to federal law. It is not bound by decisions on federal law rendered by a U.S. District Court or a U.S. Circuit Court of Appeals, though in practice decisions by the appellate court do receive careful consideration.
- State appellate courts are bound by the decisions of the state or U.S. Supreme Court for issues of state law and federal law, respectively, and by their own prior decisions "if" the state's supreme court has not previously addressed the matter.
- State trial courts must honor prior decisions of the state or U.S. Supreme Court in matters of state law and federal law, respectively, and of a state appellate court for issues on which the state supreme court has not ruled.
- All federal courts are bound by decisions of the U.S. Supreme Court, as is the Supreme Court itself—except that the high court can modify or outright overrule its previous decisions.
- Federal appellate courts are bound by their own prior decisions, but only within that circuit, not by those of other circuits. (In practice, the opinions rendered by other circuits may receive close consideration.) Because cases before these appellate courts are rarely heard by the entire bench of judges (referred to as the court sitting *en banc*) but instead a smaller number called a "panel," the court *en banc* can reverse or overrule any decision by a panel.
- Federal district courts are bound by the appellate court only for the circuit in which they reside. However, the district court's own prior decisions are not binding.

The rules governing application of *stare decisis* may seem tortuous, but they preserve the lines of authority within the various court systems (the structure of which we will examine next). This hierarchy is important to maintaining the consistent evolution of precedent.

Jurisdictions and court systems: Local and state

The most common manifestation of local court systems is in municipalities. However, municipal systems overwhelmingly deal with relatively minor crimes (misdemeanors) and matters that are not generally thought of as truly "criminal" such as traffic and other ordinance violations. For that reason, they may be considered along with state systems, which do the lion's share of the U.S. judicial system's criminal prosecution work.

These trial courts are of two types: courts of "general jurisdiction" and courts of "limited jurisdiction" (sometimes referred to as "special jurisdiction"). The limited jurisdiction court typically handles only the preliminary stages of felony cases but is the sole venue for misdemeanors and ordinance violations. In civil matters, cases heard by these courts generally have a relatively low maximum monetary liability (though not necessarily so low as to constitute only a "small claims" court). Limited jurisdiction courts may have jurisdiction over an entire county or may be limited to a smaller area—municipal courts are frequently limited jurisdiction. The term "special jurisdiction" is usually applied when the court, in fact, has a specific and specialized area of jurisdiction: a workers' compensation or water court, for example.[21]

Naming conventions and exact organization vary from state to state. To offer a few examples, Arizona's general jurisdiction court is the Superior Court, and it has two limited jurisdiction courts: Justice of the Peace and Municipal. Tennessee has four different general jurisdiction courts—Circuit, Chancery, Criminal, and Probate—plus three limited jurisdiction courts: Juvenile, Municipal, and General Sessions. Rhode Island is at the other end of the spectrum, having a single general jurisdiction court (Superior) but six limited jurisdiction courts: Workers' Compensation, District, Family, Probate, Municipal, and Traffic Tribunal. Georgia has eight different limited jurisdiction courts, including municipal courts in Columbus and Atlanta, and New York has three general jurisdiction and seven limited jurisdiction systems.[22]

Courts with the titles "Superior," "Circuit," and "District" are often general jurisdiction courts, but this does not hold true everywhere—in several states, the District Court is actually limited jurisdiction. It is best to research specifics rather than making any assumptions in regard to specific state court systems. In addition, most refer to the highest appeals court as the Supreme Court just as the federal government does, but not all—in New York, supreme courts are the primary trial courts and the highest appellate court (known generically as a "court of last resort"; all those below it are "intermediate appellate courts") is the Court of Appeals.[23]

Appellate courts are universally distinguished by having an odd number of judges, compared to juries of 6 or 12 members. Most commonly seen is a seven-member panel, found in 28 states and Puerto Rico; 16 states have five members, and five have nine members (mimicking the federal structure). Oklahoma is the lone standout, with a five-member Court of Criminal Appeals but nine justices sitting on the Supreme Court. It is worth noting that rarely does the entire bench hear a case. Far more commonly, a smaller panel—three judges is common—will hear routine cases to process the caseload more efficiently.[24]

Jurisdictions of general jurisdiction courts also vary from state to state. Some use the county as the judicial district, though this is more common in large states—California is an example. The majority have districts (or circuits) composed of multiple counties, with apportionment being on the basis of either geography or population.

Jurisdictions and court systems: Federal

The basis of the federal judiciary is the system of district courts. The system is divided into 94 federal judicial districts, with each state, the District of Columbia, and Puerto Rico having one or more districts. Relatively sparsely populated states like Wyoming or Utah have a single district; others may have two (e.g., the Northern and Southern in Iowa or the Eastern and Western in Missouri, Arkansas, Wisconsin, or Michigan) or more (the Northern, Southern, Eastern, and Western in Texas and California).[25] The district courts are the federal trial courts and hear both criminal and civil cases; each district also has a separate bankruptcy court.

As previously demonstrated, jurisdiction over most criminal cases is at the state or local level. For federal statutes to apply, there must be extenuating circumstances that create federal jurisdiction (e.g., unless the offense in question is peculiarly federal—the prohibition on counterfeiting currency). The most common of these circumstances arises when a criminal crosses state lines. As the Constitution specifies that criminal trials must be held in the state where the offense was committed, "but when not committed within any State, the Trial shall be at such Place or Places as the Congress may by Law have directed,"[26] the interstate nature of the crime creates a situation in which trial in a federal setting is appropriate. Kidnapping is a common example; if the offense takes place within the borders of a single state, it will probably be tried at the state level, but once the kidnapper crosses into another state in the course of the crime, he or she is almost certainly bound for federal court upon apprehension.

In the case of nonphysical crimes, communication methods often create federal jurisdiction. Mail fraud is the sending of materials or information intended to defraud another through the U.S. postal system (directly using a federal system, of course), but given the nature of telephone and particularly Internet systems, any electronic communication method is likely to break the tripwire of federal jurisdiction. Particular forms of fraud, such as violation of securities laws, typically land in federal court. Although most states have their own securities laws that date to the early twentieth century, since the establishment of the Securities and Exchange Commission in the wake of the 1929 stock market crash, the pursuit of these offenses has generally been a federal interest.

Today it is usually possible to establish a legal basis for federal jurisdiction for nearly any crime. A murderer who never leaves his hometown but used the Internet to research methods of killing or disposing of the body used an interstate telecommunications system in the planning of the crime. Perhaps he purchased the murder weapon with a credit card, once again using interstate telecommunications and also drawing funds from a financial institution probably located in another state. But in practice, federal resources are limited just as those of any other judicial system, and unless there is a pressing need for federal prosecution, a routine crime will likely be left in the hands of state authorities.

Over the past decade, two distinct categories of crime have come to dominate the federal court system. According to the Bureau of Justice Statistics, of 95,891 cases concluded in a U.S. district court in 2009, 33.1% were drug-related and 30.3% were immigration-related.[27] Given these proportions, it should not be surprising that the five districts along the U.S.–Mexico border—the Southern District of California, the Districts of Arizona and New Mexico, and the Western and Southern Districts of Texas—were the source of over half of all arrests by federal law enforcement in 2009.[28] Considering arrests rather than prosecutions and looking at arrests solely by the U.S. Marshal Service, in 2009, 16.9% were drug-related and 46.3% were immigration-related. Besides supervision violations at 13.3%, no other category—including violent, property, and weapon crimes—exceeded single digits.[29] This gives a clear indication of where federal criminal enforcement and prosecution efforts currently lie.

Appellate courts and the appeals process

The American legal system contains an inherent recognition that the judicial process may be imperfect for any number of reasons: A convicted defendant has the option to appeal the conviction should he or she so choose. This may be accomplished in one of two ways: a direct appeal or an indirect appeal.

We will first consider the "indirect appeal," which is less common and simpler (but is also typically the appellant's last resort). An indirect appeal is accomplished by a petition of habeas corpus. The principle of *habeas corpus* (Latin for "you have the body") arises from English common law and dates at least to the Magna Carta of 1215. The term is essentially a demand to either produce "the body" (i.e., release an individual held in custody) or provide legal justification of continued incarceration. It was long a defense against the arbitrary detention of, for example, political enemies of the monarch either for no reason or on the basis of trumped-up charges.

Today, habeas corpus underlies the restriction on how long law enforcement may detain an individual without filing charges. For decades, there was a general consensus that the limit was from 24 to 72 hours, though this was hardly an absolute standard (and, obviously, allowed much leeway for potential abuse). The U.S. Supreme Court took the first steps toward placing limits in 1975 with its ruling in *Gerstein v. Pugh*, 420 U.S. 103 (1975). The case challenged Florida's standards for bringing an arrestee before a judge for an initial review of the evidence against him (the process of "arraignment"), and the high court agreed that "the Constitution clearly requires at least a timely judicial determination of probable cause as a prerequisite to pretrial detention."[30] However, that opinion did not proffer a more precise definition of "timely."

It was not until 1991 that the court, ruling in *County of Riverside v. McLaughlin*, 500 U.S. 44 (1991), actually established a hard standard. Examining the arraignment policies of Riverside County, California, in response to a class action suit, the justices ruled that "the County's regular practice exceeds the 48-hour period we deem constitutionally permissible."[31] With that stroke of the pen, an opinion was issued that set a standard to which every jurisdiction in America must now adhere.

A habeas corpus petition does not pose any direct challenge to the grounds of the conviction (as, we shall see, a direct appeal does). However, because it requires the state to justify the appellant's incarceration, it implicitly calls into question the conviction and requires its reexamination. In theory, there are no time limitations on filing a habeas corpus petition, but because the practice has been subject to abuse by inmates in the past, Supreme Court rulings have placed limits on these petitions, and Congress has also acted to restrict them, particularly with time limits in the event the appellate is demonstrably engaging in deliberate delay of the process.[32]

A "direct appeal" is a challenge of the legal reasoning on which the conviction is based or—more commonly in criminal cases—on a procedural issue. Many well-known Supreme Court cases (and plenty that are less well known) have arisen from challenges to convictions on Fourth or Fifth Amendment grounds. Yet interestingly, the U.S.

Constitution does not offer any right of appeal, although all states provide one, some by a provision in the constitution and others by statute.[33] Unlike with a habeas corpus petition, there are also fairly strict time limits for the filing of a direct appeal, typically a matter of months.

The Fifth Amendment guarantee of due process has commonly been used as a basis for the right to appeal, as due process presumably requires a fair trial and an appeals process is the only means of ensuring one. However, the Supreme Court has never ruled that an appeal is constitutionally mandated. In the late nineteenth century, the majority opinion in *McKane v. Durston*, 153 U.S. 684 (1894), stated that "review by an appellate court of the final judgment in a criminal case, however grave the offense of which the accused is convicted, was not at common law, and is not now, a necessary element of due process of law."[34] Over a century later, the court has not yet diverted from that position. Nevertheless, procedural rules at both the state and federal levels now establish a set number of appeals (which might explain why the Supreme Court has not felt any urgency to rule on the issue).

Such is the volume of appeals that a specialized appellate court system exists in the federal system and each state system, as previously outlined. By definition, an appellate court exercises a greater level of authority than a trial court as it has the ability to reverse the decisions of the trial court, or order it to review a conviction based on guidance from the appellate court (an act known as "remanding"). Of course, it may also uphold (affirm) the trial court decision.

It is important to understand the outcome of a successful appeal by a defendant. Reversal of a conviction does not exonerate the appellant and set him free. Rather, the defendant must be retried absent any excluded evidence or avoiding whatever procedural error might have been committed. One of the most famous appeals that ultimately reached the Supreme Court was *Miranda v. Arizona*, 384 U.S. 436 (1966), which resulted in the well-known Miranda warning regarding the rights to silence and legal counsel when interrogated by the police. The appellant, Ernesto Miranda—convicted of the kidnap and rape of a mentally challenged woman—was retried, this time absent the now-barred confession he had made under interrogation. Nevertheless, the result was a second conviction and a prison sentence of more than 20 years.

Specific rules for the appellate process vary from jurisdiction to jurisdiction. More important to this overview is an understanding of the basic rights of appellants. Somewhat ironically, given that it has never explicitly affirmed the right to appeal, the Supreme Court has over the years built up a body of precedent that establishes protections for defendants who file an appeal.

The first, set down in *Griffin v. Illinois*, 351 U.S. 12 (1956), requires indigent defendants to be given trial transcripts. These documents are crucial to reviewing the trial process. Defense counsel might have raised an objection that was improperly overruled, for example, or for that matter failed to object when he or she should have.

This leads to the next fundamental right, which is that an indigent defendant must not only have counsel but have competent and effective counsel at no cost in the appeal process. (Poor performance by a court-appointed defense attorney has been the basis of more than a few appeals over the years.) This was established in *Douglas v. California*, 372 U.S. 353 (1963).

However, this should not be construed as the entitlement to a seemingly endless parade of appeals marching steadily up the appellate chain, all at government expense. The *Douglas* decision referred specifically to "the *one and only* [emphasis in the original] appeal an indigent has," but a decade later in *Ross v. Moffitt*, 417 U.S. 600 (1974), the high court outlined the practical limits of this right:

> A defendant in respondent's circumstances is not denied meaning-
> ful access to the State Supreme Court simply because the State does
> not appoint counsel to aid him in seeking review in that court, since
> at that stage, under North Carolina's multi-tiered appellate system,
> he will have, at the very least, a transcript or other record of the
> trial proceedings, a brief in the Court of Appeals setting forth his
> claims of error, and frequently an opinion by that court disposing of
> his case, materials which, when supplemented by any *pro se* submis-
> sion that might be made, would provide the Supreme Court with an
> adequate basis for its decision to grant or deny review under its stan-
> dards of whether the case has "significant public interest," involves
> "legal principles of major significance," or likely conflicts with a pre-
> vious Supreme Court decision.[35]

An appellant is unlikely, in other words, to lack resources to file subsequent appeals once the initial one has been made. The likelihood that grounds for substantially new arguments not broached initially will exist in follow-on appeals is low.

Finally, an appellant should not have to fear retribution by the state should he suc-
cessfully appeal. Bear in mind that an appeal only means a new trial, and should a second conviction occur the defendant could be at risk of heavier punishment. Although this might seem far-fetched, the Supreme Court ruled that precisely this had happened on two notable occasions. In *North Carolina v. Pearce*, 395 U.S. 711 (1969), an appellant who was convicted again following his appeal received a heavier sentence, and in *Blackledge v. Perry*, 417 U.S. 21 (1974), a successful appellant faced a more serious charge at his retrial.[32]

Counterintuitive though it might be, an appeal need not wait until a conviction has been handed down. Once the trial is complete but before a verdict is rendered, a defendant can file an "interlocutory appeal." Such appeals are limited in scope; they must address procedural issues that pose constitutional violations. Some examples are listed below:

- Imposition of excessive bail (*Stack v. Boyle*, 342 U.S. 1 (1951))
- Double jeopardy (*Abney v. United States*, 431 U.S. 651 (1977))
- An involuntary plea of guilty
- Presentation of evidence that was the result of an impermissible search or seizure or an unlawful arrest
- Entry of a confession that is coerced or other information similarly obtained from the defendant in violation of the right against self-incrimination
- Failure by the prosecution to provide the defendant with evidence that would support his or her defense
- Failure to provide effective legal counsel
- Failure to provide a speedy trial
- Unconstitutional selection and empanelment of a jury[32]

Although appeals are typically thought of as the province of defendants, it is possible in limited circumstances for the prosecution to enter an interlocutory appeal. The most common reason (and one covered by federal statute) is to contest the "suppression" (exclusion from presentation at trial) of certain evidence when that suppression impedes the prosecution's case.

A final feature of the appeals process is the "harmless error." There will be cases in which the appellate court agrees with the argument posed by the appellant and agrees that the trial court made a procedural error, yet does not reverse the conviction. Although these must be considered carefully, if it is clear that the error in question did not affect the outcome of the trial, the appellate court will issue a ruling of harmless error.

The standard, however, is fairly high. In *Chapman v. California*, 386 U.S. 18 (1967), the prosecutor mentioned over and over during the closing argument that the defendant had refused to testify, and the trial judge permitted it. The Supreme Court ruled that those comments could well have prejudiced the jury, overturning the conviction. In *Connecticut v. Johnson*, 460 U.S. 73 (1983), the judge gave flawed instructions to the jury regarding a fairly technical issue of the law, telling them that they could infer the guilt of the defendant since he had been charged with a specific intent crime, when in fact it was the responsibility of the prosecutor to prove intent. That conviction was also reversed. As minor as these mistakes might seem, they rose beyond the level of a harmless error and could reasonably be assumed to have tainted the outcome of the trial.[32]

Supreme courts and judicial review

The U.S. Supreme Court has become inextricably linked in the minds of most citizens with decisions regarding constitutionality—a determination of whether a statute (i.e., an act of the legislative branch), an executive order (an act of the executive branch), or the ruling of a lower court (which can establish precedent) is consistent with the U.S. Constitution. On the surface this seems consistent with the systems of "checks and balances" established by the Constitution. Yet, you may be surprised to learn that the U.S. Constitution nowhere provides for this process, which is called "judicial review."

Article III, which addresses the judicial branch, contains three sections and a grand total of 369 words. Section 1 establishes the Supreme Court and assigns Congress the power to establish lower courts, requires "good behavior" on the part of all judges, and mandates that they be compensated. Section 3 explicitly defines treason, specifies the grounds for conviction of treason, and forbids "Corruption of Blood," the practice of punishing family members of a person found guilty of treason.

Section 2 establishes the powers of the judicial branch, defining the authority of the Supreme Court. Brief as it is, it is worth repeating those words verbatim here.

> The judicial Power shall extend to all Cases, in Law and Equity, arising under this Constitution, the Laws of the United States, and Treaties made, or which shall be made, under their Authority;— to all Cases affecting Ambassadors, other public Ministers and Consuls;—to all Cases of admiralty and maritime Jurisdiction;— to Controversies to which the United States shall be a Party;—to Controversies between two or more States;—between a State and Citizens of another State;—between Citizens of different States;— between Citizens of the same State claiming Lands under Grants of different States, and between a State, or the Citizens thereof, and foreign States, Citizens or Subjects.
>
> In all Cases affecting Ambassadors, other public Ministers and Consuls, and those in which a State shall be Party, the Supreme Court shall have original Jurisdiction. In all the other Cases before

mentioned, the Supreme Court shall have appellate Jurisdiction, both as to Law and Fact, with such Exceptions, and under such Regulations as the Congress shall make.[36]

As you can see, there is no mention of reviewing the constitutional validity of acts by the legislative or executive branches, nor even of trial or lower appellate courts except in the specific areas enumerated, which are fairly esoteric except for litigation between citizens of different states.

How, then, did the principle of judicial review originate? The first step in this direction was the Judiciary Act of 1789, which fulfilled the Congressional responsibility to establish the federal court system. In Section 13 of that law, language was included directing that the Supreme Court would "have power to issue … writs of mandamus, in cases warranted by the principle and usages of law, to any courts appointed, or persons holding office under the authority of the United States."[37] (*Mandamus* is a Latin term meaning "we command," and a writ of mandamus is an order directing some entity (which can be an individual or other legal entity such as a corporation, a government agency including another court, or a government official) to perform a specific act).

The issuance of a writ of mandamus is a necessary part of the appellate process, so that authority does not necessarily constitute judicial review. Scholars have since speculated on the intent of the framers of the Constitution. One school of thought is that as the concept of judicial review was not included in the language of Article III, the framers did not intend the courts to have that power, which seems simple enough. Yet another school of thought holding essentially the opposite position is that judicial review was not explicitly included because the division of powers established by the Constitution made it so obviously necessary as to require no enumeration. A final possibility—which it is frankly difficult to take seriously—is that no one thought Congress would ever pass legislation not authorized by the enumerated powers.[38]

Notes taken by James Madison during the Constitutional Convention indicate that of the 55 delegates, only 11 ever expressed an opinion on judicial review at all. Two opposed it, nine favored it, and James Wilson went so far as to specifically state that the courts should be empowered to overturn any piece of "unjust" legislation, whether federal or state. In addition, more than half of the original 13 states authorized judicial review at the state level.[39]

The landmark case in the concept of judicial review is *Marbury v. Madison*, 5 U.S. 137 (1803). The specifics of the case, however, do not establish the most inspiring basis for this principle. John Adams, a Federalist, lost the 1800 election to Thomas Jefferson. In early 1801, the outgoing Congress passed the Judiciary Act of 1801 (not to be confused with the original Judiciary Act of 1789) and created seats for 58 new judges. On March 3, 1801, the night before Jefferson's inauguration, John Marshall—secretary of state under Adams but already named to replace Chief Justice John Jay when Jay refused reappointment to the bench in January 1801—affixed the official seal to the judges' commissions. The next day he instructed James Madison, the new secretary of state, not to deliver 17 of the commissions. One of those was for William Marbury. Marbury promptly sued, asking the court to issue a writ of mandamus against Madison requiring him to deliver Marbury's commission.

John Marshall—who was obviously deeply involved in the whole affair that led to the suit and by today's standards would be forced to recuse himself from the case—wrote the opinion in this case. Beyond the ethical conflict, Section 13 of the original Judiciary Act makes it clear that Marbury petitioned the wrong court and invoked an incorrect statute (and possibly both), yet Marshall forged ahead and ruled on the case, treating the suit as valid. He overturned Section 13 of the Judiciary Act of 1789 as unconstitutional on the rationale that Congress had expanded the judiciary's authority beyond what was permitted by Article III, resulting in the dismissal of Marbury's suit for lack of jurisdiction.

At the state level, supreme courts function much more frequently in the typical role as the court of last resort in the appellate process, though they are certainly the body called upon to rule on any conflicts between a statute and the state's constitution. As with the U.S. Supreme Court, state supreme courts do not automatically hear all appeals; they must issue a *writ of certiorari*. These courts also typically become involved when a lower appellate court has failed to resolve a matter. As an example, the Supreme Court of New Jersey states on its homepage that it "decides appeals from the lower courts and cases in which a panel of appellate judges has disagreed on one or more issues on appeal.... The Court may agree to hear an appeal because it presents legal issues of great importance to the public or because the issue is the subject of separate, conflicting appellate opinions."[40] This is a good summary of the typical standards used by state supreme courts.

Law enforcement agencies: Local

The courts are responsible for the trial process—determining the guilt or innocence of a defendant—and for the sentencing of those convicted. But enforcement of the laws starts in the local community with the agencies charged with preventing crime, investigating those that occur, and identifying and apprehending the parties presumed responsible to bring them before the court system for judgment.

The 2008 Census of State and Local Law Enforcement Agencies conducted by the Bureau of Justice Statistics in September 2008 and issued in July 2011 identified 17,985 state and local agencies, the vast majority of them police departments (12,501) and sheriff's offices (3,063). In total, these agencies used 1,133,000 full-time personnel (765,000 of them sworn officers) and roughly 100,000 part-time personnel (44,000 of them sworn officers).[41]

We will consider the state of Alabama as an example of typical law enforcement organization. Police departments have jurisdiction within the corporate limits of a municipality (city or town) as well as a defined area outside those limits. (American Indian reservations have tribal police forces with jurisdiction within the reservation's boundaries.) The chief of police is appointed by the municipal government. Sheriff's offices have jurisdiction within the bounds of a specific county. As a practical matter to most efficiently use resources, enforcement activity within municipalities is left to the appropriate police force, but in some cases, such as an extremely small police force, the sheriff's office may provide support. (Odd as it may seem, over 2000 local agencies have only a single full-time employee.)[42] In some areas of the country, municipalities have elected to combine the police force and sheriff's department into a single entity. The sheriff is elected to a 4-year term, is answerable to the county commission, and is authorized to appoint a chief deputy.

Alabama has a number of specific qualifications for deputy sheriffs, which are typical for jurisdictions across the country:

- At least 21 years of age
- Normal vision (or correctable to normal standards)
- Normal hearing
- U.S. citizen and citizen of the state
- Valid driver's license for the state in question
- No mental, emotional, or physical conditions likely to negatively affect job performance
- No criminal record

- No religious or moral objection to the use of force, including lethal force, in the course of duty
- Pass the civil service examination (not mandatory in all Alabama police departments)
- Successfully achieve all training standards (the relevant version of the Peace Officer Standards and Training, or POST, requirements)
- Pass a background investigation (which in many jurisdictions extends to immediate family members as well)[43]

Although we might feel that we have a solid grasp of the functions of local law enforcement, an actual detailed list is surprisingly long. The first function is the most obvious and direct: the maintenance of public order and safety. An Alabama statute enumerates the following responsibilities for police departments and sheriff's offices within the state: "To take reasonable precautions against disruptions of the peace, to apprehend or prevent criminal behavior, to create procedures for dealing with law violations, to pursue general approaches to the crime problem (deterrence, incarceration, or rehabilitation), and to inform the public and enlist public support."[44] In addition to criminal statutes, police officers are tasked with enforcing various municipal codes and ordinances, most designed to regulate businesses and prevent public nuisances. Local agencies may also assist federal or state agencies with security details for various dignitaries.

Another substantial component of this public order and safety responsibility is traffic control. This covers a wide range of activity, including assisting motorists; escorting processions, caravans, and oversized loads; directing traffic; monitoring vehicle speeds; issuing traffic citations; responding to, investigating, documenting, and reporting motor vehicle accidents; and notifying next of kin in the event of fatalities.

The next major function—less glamorous, less public, but vitally important—is communication and reporting. Communication systems operate both within and among local agencies, as well as to agencies of other states and the federal government. This information flow involves not only criminal activity but also severe weather and civil defense events. The reporting function involves feeding accurate data into local, state, and federal systems, the best known of which is probably the National Criminal Information Center. These interconnected systems aid in the identification and apprehension of criminals whose activities may cross many jurisdictional and state boundaries. The compilation of statistical data enables agencies to identify patterns of crime that aid enforcement, such as determining the best geographical assignment of resources based on where crime is most frequently occurring.

The third function is investigation. Although the public order and safety function is predominantly a mandate to prevent crime, crimes will inevitably occur. State laws typically mandate the investigation of all felonies; the requirement for misdemeanors varies, and there may be other specific statutory requirements—Alabama law, for example, requires the investigation of "all" juvenile crimes.[45] The internal investigation of officers when necessary is included in this function.

The next function is arrest. An arrest may be made when an officer personally observes the commission of a crime. This is the basis of a traffic citation, which is actually a summons to appear in court and answer a misdemeanor charge (though most people simply pay the fine, thereby admitting guilt). Most arrests, however, are made based on a "warrant." This is an order from a judge or magistrate who is satisfied based on the evidence presented that an individual has committed a specific crime and therefore directs their detention.

The arrest function leads inevitably to the next: booking and detention. Defendants are held in city or county jails while awaiting and standing trial if they are unable to post bail or bail is denied. During this time, the police department or sheriff's office is responsible for their custody, control, and care.

Officers also provide assistance to the courts. This function includes the obvious—acting as a bailiff, who maintains security and order in the courtroom—but extends as well to supervising those convicts who have been paroled, returning fugitives who have fled the state, and transporting prisoners. Of course, the normal course of duty will frequently require an officer to provide testimony at trial. In addition, sheriff's offices have the responsibility for service of subpoenas, notices, orders, and writs for both government and civil matters. They enforce judgments and handle the confiscation and disposition of property when necessary (e.g., the sheriff's auction of homes and other property to recover delinquent taxes).

The incarceration of offenders is also a law enforcement function (we discuss the correctional system specifically later in the chapter). In the majority of jurisdictions, municipal jails do not hold offenders with sentences longer than 1 year; this is similarly the case for many county jails, such as Harris County, Texas, which contains the city of Houston.[46] However, some states, such as Louisiana, have programs under which sheriffs may choose to house state inmates in their jails if they have unused bed space and be compensated by the state for doing so.

Local law enforcement agencies are the frontline defense against crime, responsible for investigating the vast majority of criminal offenses across the United States. Although the details will vary somewhat across the nearly 18,000 jurisdictions, the broad responsibilities are the same.

Law enforcement agencies: State

Each state has its own law enforcement agency. The terms "state police" and "highway patrol" are frequently used interchangeably, but this is an oversimplification. In some states, the highway patrol is a separate agency, and investigative functions are assigned to a state bureau of investigation, which may or may not be part of the state police force. In some states, the path to service as a state bureau of investigation agent starts as a uniformed trooper; in others, it is possible to directly apply to the bureau.

A total of 22 states have separate bureaus of investigation.[42] Colorado, for example, has a separate Colorado Bureau of Investigation chartered in 1967 to "assist local, county, and state criminal justice agencies through the provision of professional investigative and forensic laboratory systems."[47] In California, the Bureau of Investigation was not created until 2012 and is an adjunct of the Attorney General's office.[48] The Kansas Bureau of Investigation is similarly part of the Attorney General's office rather than the state police, though it dates to 1939.[49] Louisiana, on the other hand, is one of the states that have a bureau of investigation that is part of the state police force.[50]

The main function of the state police force is to patrol the roads and highways outside municipalities, with emphasis on interstate and U.S. highways. (The patrol of smaller side roads is typically the function of the sheriff's office.) These state agencies also handle the investigation of criminal activity that tends to span larger areas, which is why some states have a narcotics enforcement agency that is either independent or part of the state police organization. The state police force may also fulfill specialized functions, such as providing security details for the governor.

At both the local and state levels, there are also hundreds of "special jurisdiction" agencies—a total of 1733 in 2008. The largest share is represented by university, college, and school district police forces (508, 253, and 250, respectively). Other large public facilities, such as state government buildings, public hospitals, or public housing complexes, may have independent forces.[42]

Transportation systems and facilities may also have separate agencies. New York City's Metropolitan Transportation Authority Police is one of the best known, along with the Port Authority of New York and New Jersey Police, which was brought to the forefront of public attention when 37 of its officers were killed on September 11, 2001 because of the agency's responsibility for the World Trade Center complex.[51]

At the state level are various natural resource enforcement agencies, including 56 fish and wildlife conservation authorities, 124 park and recreational agencies, and others charged with the enforcement of boating or environmental laws or the protection of forest or water resources. Six levee districts nationwide also fall into this category.

Finally, 54 special enforcement agencies are found at the state level. These are responsible for alcohol and tobacco, agricultural, narcotics, gaming, and racing laws.[42]

Law enforcement agencies: Federal

The 2008 Bureau of Justice Statistics survey of federal law enforcement agencies published in June 2012 counted about 120,000 full-time law enforcement officers (defined as those authorized to make arrests and carry firearms) manning 73 agencies.[52] The nation's oldest agency, dating to the Judiciary Act of 1789, is the U.S. Marshals Service. Section 27 of the act authorized a marshal for each district to be appointed for a 4-year term and further authorized those marshals to appoint deputies as necessary. The primary enumerated authority in Section 28 was the execution of "federal judicial writs and process," though Section 27 broadly assigned the power to "execute throughout the district, all lawful precepts directed to him, and issued under the authority of the United States."[53]

However, the Marshals Service is far from the largest federal agency. Only four agencies had more than 10,000 officers as of September 2008: U.S. Customs and Border Protection (CBP, 36,863), the Federal Bureau of Prisons (FBOP or more commonly BOP, 16,835), the Federal Bureau of Investigation (FBI, 12,760), and U.S. Immigration and Customs Enforcement (ICE, 12,446). (The Marshals Service had 3313 full-time officers.)[52] Following the creation of the Department of Homeland Security (DHS) and the reorganization that resulted, 45.5% of all federal officers now belong to an agency that falls under DHS; a third (33.1%) fall under the Department of Justice.

The FBI is tasked "to protect and defend the United States against terrorist and foreign intelligence threats and to enforce the criminal laws of the United States."[54] Although the mention of "foreign intelligence threats" might seem odd if one assumes that these would be the province of the Central Intelligence Agency, it is not a law enforcement agency and is not authorized by law to conduct operations within the United States. The FBI mission is divided into three national security priorities—terrorism, counterintelligence, and cybercrime—and five criminal priorities—public corruption, civil rights, organized crime, white-collar crime, and violent crime and major thefts.[55]

Two agencies with related missions are ICE and U.S. CBP. ICE was formed by a 2003 merger of the U.S. Customs Service and the Immigration and Naturalization Service. It is the "principal investigative arm of the U.S. Department of Homeland Security … and the second largest investigative agency in the federal government." Its mission is "to promote homeland security through the criminal and civil enforcement of federal laws governing border control, customs, trade, and immigration."[56] CBP has "a priority mission of keeping terrorists and their weapons out of the U.S. It also has a responsibility for securing the border and facilitating lawful international trade and travel while enforcing hundreds of U.S. laws and regulations, including immigration and drug laws."[57] In general terms—keeping in mind that there is a certain degree of overlap between ICE and CBP—CBP is responsible for manning the ports of entry (e.g., CBP personnel perform customs checks at international airports) and through the Border Patrol for monitoring the border away from the ports of entry. ICE is concerned primarily with the issuance of visas and other immigration management tasks, and through its Enforcement and Removal Operations with identifying, apprehending, and, in some cases, detaining those illegally in the United States; providing a judicial review process; and deporting those not authorized to remain in the country.

The DEA was established (by an executive order issued by President Richard Nixon, not legislatively) in July 1973 to centralize the efforts of United States to combat the international drug trade. Its mission is to "enforce the controlled substances laws of the United States," to bring individuals and organizations involved in the "growing, manufacture, or distribution of controlled substances appearing in or destined for illicit traffic in the United States" before the justice system, and "to recommend and support non-enforcement programs aimed at reducing the availability of illicit controlled substances on the domestic and international markets."[58]

Although these represent some of the best-known federal law enforcement agencies, there are many that are much more obscure or poorly understood. The popular perception of the U.S. Secret Service focuses on the presidential protective detail, for example, but the primary responsibility of the agency is the pursuit of currency and financial crimes. Some agencies are highly specialized: the U.S. Mint Police, the U.S. Park Police and Rangers (two separate agencies under the National Park Service), the Bureau of Alcohol, Tobacco, Firearms and Explosives, or the U.S. Capitol Police. Some are adjuncts of cabinet-level departments: the Bureau of Diplomatic Security (Department of State), the Pentagon Force Protection Agency (Department of Defense), or the National Nuclear Security Administration (Department of Energy). Finally, there are many that would not normally be thought of as having gun-carrying officers: the U.S. Postal Inspection Service, the U.S. Fish and Wildlife Service, the Internal Revenue Service Criminal Investigation division, the Veterans Health Administration, the Bureau of Indian Affairs, or the Bureau of Land Management.[52]

The correctional system

Once an individual is convicted of a crime and sentenced, he or she must be remanded to an agency that will take responsibility for the offender's custody, control, and care. We have already discussed briefly the function of municipal and county jails in housing defendants during the trial process, as well as those sentenced to relatively short sentences through local courts. (Those accused of federal crimes, incidentally, are held by the U.S. Marshals Service until such time as they are acquitted or sentenced.)

State correctional systems incarcerate by far the majority of offenders. In 2011—the last year for which comprehensive statistics are currently available—the state inmate count was 1,382,418 compared to 216,362 for the federal system.[59]

The BOP incarcerates all federal offenders. It was originally established in 1930 to oversee the 11 federal facilities that existed at the time. The agency currently manages 119 facilities in addition to residential reentry centers and home-based confinement programs. As of this writing, BOP manages about 219,000 offenders, of which 81% are housed in institutions directly operated by the Bureau and the balance are in privately operated contract facilities or local jails.[60]

Among the states, California long held the lead in inmate headcounts. Its system reached a point of such critical overcrowding that on May 23, 2011, the U.S. Supreme Court affirmed the ruling of a lower court that ordered the state of California to reduce its inmate population to no more than 137.5% of design capacity.[59] This level represented a capacity of about 110,000 prisoners; its headcounts that year and the prior 2 years were 149,569 in 2011, 165,062 in 2010, and 171,275 in 2009. California moved to comply by passing two laws that year intended to reduce its inmate population.[59]

Even before California was under pressure to cut its headcount, Texas was rapidly catching up. In 2009, Texas had an average population of only 26 inmates lower than California (171,249) and took the lead in 2010 with 173,649 compared to California's 165,062. The gap widened still further in 2011 even though Texas saw a decrease to 172,224. Of all the U.S. states, only three—Florida is the third, with a low of 103,055 and a high of 104,306 during those 3 years— have six-digit inmate populations. The prize for smallest population goes to North Dakota with 1423 in 2011.[59]

With the budgetary constraints that have developed since the 2008 recession—states are constitutionally required to balance their budgets—and only a relatively few areas of discretionary spending available for cuts, the corrections systems in most states are under financial pressure. There have been two primary approaches to addressing this challenge.

The first has been increased reliance on alternatives to traditional incarceration. We will explore several here, some more commonly used than others.

Because relatively harsh sentencing guidelines and minimum sentence requirements have been put in place over the past three decades in an attempt to curb the nation's drug problem, much of the explosion in prison populations has been produced by drug offenders. All 50 states now have what are called "drug courts," though none exist in the federal system. These programs are highly focused on resolving drug dependency issues and generally require participation in a drug treatment program and/or counseling, random urine testing, and regular reports to a parole officer. Their use is restricted to nonviolent offenders with little criminal history. A defendant does not have the option of drug court; he or she must be referred by the prosecutor or judge, and often a guilty plea is a prerequisite. Successful completion of the treatment program results in no further punishment and, in many cases, removal of the offense from the defendant's record, but failure generally means jail time.[61]

Existing options can be more widely used, which has been the point of many "early release" programs designed to cut prison populations. Probation already provides a high level of supervision for an offender released into the community including employment requirements, drug testing, and counseling for substance abuse or mental health when necessary, and the option to return an offender to prison should he or she fail to meet all requirements. For those who require a somewhat higher level of supervision, there is the halfway house. Already often used for offenders transitioning back into the community following a long sentence, this system requires the offender to remain at the halfway house except when at work. As the level of security is much lower, costs are likewise substantially less.[62]

A third option growing in popularity (thanks primarily to technological advances that provide reliable confirmation of offender location) is home confinement (commonly called "house arrest") combined with electronic monitoring for enforcement. Participants in such a program are permitted to leave home only for necessary activities such as work or school, and often must frequently contact a probation officer and, if appropriate, undergo drug testing.[63]

Another trend in alternative sentencing has been a focus on restitution to victims and to the community in general. Fines have long been imposed, and in some cases may be combined with prison time. However, the traditional structure of fines—a fixed amount or range for a given offense—lacks equity. At one end of the spectrum, for a wealthy individual most such fines represent a pittance, or at least an amount so small as to represent no real deterrent or penalty. At the opposite end, for the poor the fine may be so large in relative terms that jail is the only option. A more progressive option is the so-called "day fine," which is proportionate to the offender's daily income. In this way, it is both fair and a meaningful punishment regardless of wealth or poverty.

A fine may or may not be combined with restitution, which is a requirement to compensate a victim (or the community, if the offense has no direct victim) for losses caused by the crime. Medical expenses and property losses are the most common. Another variation on restitution to the community is community service: unpaid work performed for the good of the community or a civic organization. Probably the most progressive version of this approach is restorative justice, which features such innovations as collaborative sentencing that includes the victim, the offender, and even members of the community in addition to justice system officials. Restitution and when appropriate victim–offender mediation may also be included as part of this process, and community service is frequently a component as well.[64]

Just as drug courts attempt to address the source of the crime (addiction), when appropriate, an approach that emphasizes mental health treatment over punishment may be used. Mental health courts mirror the drug court system, only with a focus on treating mental health issues and developing life skills. Similarly, sex offenders may be placed in a specialized probation program that places limits on their activities (registration, bars from living or working near schools, prohibitions on Internet use, and the like) and mandates therapy and counseling. Because of the serious nature of these offenses, treatment is often performed in a secure facility (albeit not a traditional prison), and diversion to probation programs of this type frequently only follows completion of a traditional prison sentence.[65]

Alternative sentencing programs can offer many advantages in the area of cost. The option of a conventional prison sentence is still available should an offender fail to meet the program requirements, and the likelihood of achieving a long-term resolution of a substance abuse or mental health problem is at least as great as what is likely to be achieved through traditional incarceration. The inclusion of restitution provisions and the ineligibility of habitual offenders tend to make these options more palatable to victims and to the community as a whole.

Theories of criminology and criminal justice policy

Given how inextricably crime has been an element of human society throughout recorded history, it should come as no surprise that scholars have long attempted to explain why crime occurs and by extension how it can be prevented (and should be addressed). Criminological theories can be grouped into several major categories. We examine (briefly, by necessity) the theories in each of these categories, look at a representative theory in more detail, and then consider their general impact on the criminal justice policies promulgated by government.

The rational theories view crime as a choice, and in this regard are essentially updates of the classical theory that originated in the late eighteenth century. These include lifestyle theory (Hindelang, Gottfredson, and Garofalo), cognitive theory (Walters and White), and routine activities theory (Cohen and Felson). These theories embrace deterrence to encourage a potential criminal to choose lawful actions over criminal ones.

Deterrence, in turn, has three elements. "Certainty" is the perceived likelihood that criminal activity will be detected and punished. "Celerity" is how soon after the actual crime that punishment is imposed. "Severity" is the harshness or degree of punishment.

Of the three, certainty is the most important. Severity must be carefully judged, as rational theories hold that while punishment that is too mild will not have sufficient deterrent effect, unjustly harsh punishment will lead to more—not less—crime.[66]

The routine activities theory dates to 1979. It proposes three elements that must be present for a criminal act to occur: a motivated offender, a suitable target, and a lack of capable guardians. This theory, which was intended to explain the substantial increase in crime from 1960 to 1980, looked carefully at the social patterns that had developed during that time—the "routine activities" of the theory's name. Changes such as more women in the workforce meant more homes unoccupied during the day, and the migration away from urban centers decreased the presence of close friends and family in the area who might help keep watch over a home. In addition to deterrence, routine activities theory called for "target hardening," measures such as alarm systems, neighborhood watch programs, and more sophisticated locks that would reduce the number of opportunities for crime.

Other scholars assumed that criminals were born, not made, giving rise to the biological theories. These include "criminal born" man and woman (Lombroso), somatotyping (Sheldon), XYY chromosome, sociobiology, and differential conditionality (Eysenck).

Older biological theories often have some disturbing overtones, as they rely on assumptions of fundamental physiological differences that make criminals "different." It is important to remember that racism, sexism, and even Nazi persecution of the Jews and Slavic ethnic groups were based on pseudoscientific certainty that these groups were biologically inferior. Lombroso's theory, for example, referred to the "atavistic" man, the "criminal born" of his theory's name.

Later variations looked at biological factors revealed by newer research; the XYY chromosome theory, for example, proposed that males with two Y chromosomes are "super-males" with proportionately greater tendencies to aggression and violence. The 1992 movie *Alien 3* featured this theory as a central plot point; the movie's events take place on a prison planet populated by "double-Y chromos," male criminals so violent as to be considered unredeemable. There is, however, virtually no scientific support for this theory, and in any event the XYY disorder is rare—too rare to account for the vast majority of criminal acts.

Current versions of biological theory take into account environmental interaction, placing much less emphasis on biological factors. Because this is a departure from the primacy of biological factors in causing criminal behavior, the entire school of pure biological theory can be considered all but discredited.[67]

The next movement beyond biological science was into psychological and psychiatric theories. This school has many component theories, divided into three subgroups. Social learning theories include modeling and imitation (Bandura), differential association (Sutherland), differential identification (Glaser), differential reinforcement (Jeffery and Akers), and social learning (Akers). There are two different psychoanalytic theories, one from Freud (the founder of psychoanalysis) and another by Warren and Hindelang. Finally, moral development theories include moral development theory (Kohlberg) and criminal personality theory (Yochelson and Samenow).

At their heart, all of these theories are based on an assumption that either mental illness (psychoanalytic theories) or personality defects (social learning and moral development theories) cause criminal behavior. This being the case, the deterrence on which rational theories rely are useless, because the criminal is not making a rational choice (or by some theories, any choice at all). The proper response to a criminal act, then, is therapy and treatment of the underlying problem.[68]

Sociological theories came to prominence in the 1950s. Because middle-class values were so predominant in America and criminal activity was so foreign to those values, criminologists looked for potential sources of those "deviant" values. There are many different sociological theories, and they can be broken into subgroups in more than one manner. The simplest is to distinguish social structure theories from social process theories.

Social structure theories include social disorganization and anomie theory (Durkheim) (both of which date from the turn of the century), strain theory (Merton), general strain theory (Agnew), culture conflict theory (Sellin), subculture of delinquency theory (Cohen), differential opportunity (Cloward and Ohlin), lower-class focal concerns (Miller), high delinquency areas (Shaw and McKay), and subculture of violence theory (Wolfgang and Ferracuti).

An overview of these theories will be necessarily broad and general, but each takes a specific perspective on the development of modern society and its role in causing criminal behavior. Social disorganization theory, for example, looked at the rapid changes taking place around the turn of the century—including large waves of immigration and urbanization of the population—that were beginning to fundamentally reshape the American social order. The theory's assumption, which is difficult not to see as grounded in discomfort with the nature of those changes, is in its simplest terms that a loss of social order—that is, social disorganization—leads to antisocial behavior. Anomie, strain, and general strain theories point to the characteristics of modern industrial societies that cause people to feel isolated from those around them (anomie and alienation) and that do not provide equal opportunity for people to achieve the goals generally valued by society (prosperity foremost among them). Frustrated by what they perceive as an inability to achieve those goals through accepted means, some will turn to criminal acts instead.

It is easy to see the notions of wealth, class, and social justice that underlie these theories. In the early twentieth century, it was the lower class laborer who struggled to make enough to get by and had no hope of attaining an education or accumulating enough money to achieve financial independence. In the 1960s and 1970s, it was the disadvantaged inner-city youth with no hope of a better life.

The various subculture theories—which above all stemmed from mid-century notions of middle-class values—in essence explain criminal behavior as learned. That learning may come from social norms modeled in parts of lower class society (keep in mind the assumed superiority of the middle, and presumably upper, classes in these theories) or from membership in a subculture of delinquent youth. The widespread existence of youth gangs in inner cities was one piece of evidence underpinning these theories.

Social process theories include labeling theories (tagging, primary and secondary deviance, the developmental career model, and radical nonintervention) and social control theories (containment, social bond, techniques of neutralization, and low self-control). Labeling theories propose that individuals who are "tagged" as criminals accept that definition, leading to a self-reinforcing cycle in which society reacts to and treats those individuals as criminals, driving them to associate with people who are like them who model more criminal behavior. (If you are wondering what prompts the initial act that leads to the label of criminal, it is a valid question.) In his Developmental Career Model, Howard Becker proposed that no act is by definition deviant (i.e., in the mind of the person committing that act); rather, society or "the system" impose definitions of deviance. As the criminal progresses further into criminal habits, his perspective on what constitutes deviant behavior gradually changes and departs more and more from social norms.[69]

Social control theories start from a novel assumption: Every person has the desire or at least willingness to commit criminal acts, so the proper question is why people do "not" commit crimes. This is where the existence of social controls comes into play, and its proponents assume that the more positive social connections (family, friends, career, and organizations) a person has the less likely they are to commit a crime because that inherent desire is overridden by the desire to conform to social norms.

There are actually two perspectives on social control. One (macrosocial) emphasizes the formal mechanisms in society: the criminal justice system, influential groups who strongly influence social norms, government, and so forth. The "microsocial" perspective argues that acceptance by friends, family, and other peers is more important.

Finally, there are Marxist, feminist, and other critical theories. These include the social reality of crime (Quinney), conflict theory (Turk), adolescent frustration (Greenberg), liberation theory (Adler), opportunity theory (Simon), power-control theory (Hagan), and instrumental theory (Schwendinger) in addition to Marxism and feminism.

These theories tend to place the criminal justice system in the context of broader social theories. Marxist theory, for example, considers the entire criminal justice system to be a tool of the bourgeoisie (the ruling class) to help maintain control of the proletariat (the working class or masses). It separates crime into two categories: crimes of domination and repression, which are committed by the bourgeoisie against the proletariat, and crimes of accommodation and resistance, which are committed by the proletariat against the bourgeoisie (or the capitalist system in general). The glaring shortcoming of this approach— namely, how to categorize crimes committed by one member of the proletariat against another—should be obvious, to say nothing of the fact that crime still occurs in socialist societies. (Marxist theory assumes capitalism to be the cause of all crime.)

Feminist theory assumes crime to be driven by two primary factors: Men commit crimes to exert power over women, or they commit them to show their masculinity and live up to social assumptions of gender roles. Critical theory moves away from the absolute positions of Marxist theory, but still holds that crime is the result of imbalances in power and wealth. For this reason, it views capitalist societies as particularly prone to crime.[70]

You may have already recognized that the realist theories have primarily driven modern criminal justice policy. Deterrence and punishment have been emphasized. This has led to such responses as imposing stiffer penalties for the possession of "crack" cocaine than for the powder form of the drug (which have since been rescinded) to answer the rapid spread of the drug in the 1980s and the violence that accompanied it, or the legislation of "three strikes" rules. However, unintended consequences sometimes follow. The long list of minimum-sentence guidelines for most drug offenses led to a swelling prison population, which has squeezed budgets and is now causing the early release of prisoners or measures to avoid incarceration at all, such as the policy of Harris County, Texas, to issue citations rather than make arrests for possession of personal use quantities of marijuana. Concern for the sentence that would result under the "three strikes" rule sometimes leads a prosecutor not to bring a case against a given defendant at all.

Elements of other theories have crept into policy, both directly and indirectly. Diversion to various forms of substance abuse or mental health treatment programs (albeit in secure facilities) recognizes the role addiction or mental illness plays in some crimes. Outside the criminal justice system, government initiatives to provide jobs, training, and education to disadvantaged segments of the population or to reform the nature of public housing complexes are responses to assumptions about the social and economic motivations behind other crimes.

It seems likely that given the incredible variety of human behavior and circumstances, no single theory is adequate to explain every crime. Integrated and development life course theories blend components of multiple theories in recognition of the fact that more often than not, the causes of criminal behavior are highly complex.

Summary

America's criminal justice system evolved out of a respect for many of the fundamental components of the English legal system combined with a determination to curb the excesses of its monarchy and prevent the infringement of government on the rights of the people. Today, we have a multitiered court system at the municipal, state, and federal levels, paired with a similarly multitiered appellate system to ensure that miscarriages by the trial court systems can be remedied. Atop it all sits the U.S. Supreme Court, monitoring the constitutionality of the actions of the legislative and executive branches and the lower courts.

Thousands of separate law enforcement agencies at the local level maintain public order and safety, investigate crimes, and apprehend suspects. At the federal level, dozens of highly specialized agencies focus on areas of specific federal responsibility (immigration control and currency fraud) and those that require greater resources than can be mustered on the local level (counterintelligence, counterterrorism, and combating international drug trade).

State and federal correctional systems house and attempt to rehabilitate and transition back into society those convicted of crimes. All of these elements combine into a whole that is staggeringly complex and requires the efforts of millions of men and women unified and coordinated in working toward a common goal.

Practicum

1. As part of a proposed ban on assault weapons, a public interest group petitions Congress to also make illegal their possession by anyone who purchased such a weapon between the expiration of the 1994 assault weapons ban and the effective date of the new statute. What would this specific aspect of the law be called, and what prohibits such laws?

2. When Congress passes a law that addresses a highly technical field of knowledge, such as environmental policy, does the legislation contain every detailed rule? Why or why not? If not, where do the detailed rules originate?

3. Is the conflict between the 2012 legalization of recreational marijuana use by Colorado and Washington and its continued prohibition by federal law an example of conflict preemption? Why or why not? If it is not, what form of preemption might exist? Why?

4. Because of the principle of *stare decisis*, American laws tend to change gradually and slowly rather than radically and quickly. Do you think this is a positive effect of respect for precedent? Why or why not?

5. The U.S. Constitution contains no express requirement for an appeal in a criminal case. However, the Due Process Clause is often cited in justifying appeals. How do you think the Due Process Clause serves as a basis for the right to appeal?

6. Give an example of a procedural error that might give rise to a successful interlocutory appeal by a criminal defendant.

7. Although we might assume that every crime is investigated, this is not the case. For what types of crimes do local jurisdictions normally mandate investigation? Why do law enforcement agencies not investigate all crimes?

8. Give two reasons that the FBI is tasked by law with the lead responsibility for domestic counterterrorism and counterintelligence operations.

9. Identify two strengths and two weaknesses of alternative sentencing compared to traditional incarceration. How might alternative sentencing programs be viewed and accepted by the general public?
10. Do you think the public today is more or less willing to accept at least the partial validity of various criminological theories that shift any blame for criminal acts away from the criminal himself than it would have been in 1980? Why?

Resources

Bureau of Justice Statistics, http://bjs.ojp.usdoj.gov
United States Courts, http://www.uscourts.gov/FederalCourts/UnderstandingtheFederalCourts/FederalCourtsInAmericanGovernment.aspx
Directory of Law Enforcement Agencies Series, University of Michigan, http://www.icpsr.umich.edu/icpsrweb/ICPSR/series/169
Criminological Theory Summaries, University of Wisconsin at Eau Claire, www.uwec.edu/patchinj/crmj301/theorysummaries.pdf

References

1. Olson-Raymer, G. Criminal laws. (2012). *The Evolving Colonial Criminal Justice System* [lecture]. Arcata, CA: Humboldt State University, Department of History.
2. Olsen, K. (1999). *Daily life in 18th-century England* (pp. 207–208). Westport, CT: Greenwood Publishing Group.
3. Constitution of the United States. (1787). Washington, DC: National Archives. Retrieved January 18, 2013, from http://www.archives.gov/exhibits/charters/constitution_transcript.html
4. Constitution of the United States. (1787). Washington, DC: National Archives. Retrieved January 18, 2013, from http://www.archives.gov/exhibits/charters/constitution_transcript.html
5. Constitution of the United States. (1787). Washington, DC: National Archives. Retrieved January 18, 2013, from http://www.archives.gov/exhibits/charters/constitution_transcript.html
6. Constitution of the United States. (1787). Washington, DC: National Archives. Retrieved January 18, 2013, from http://www.archives.gov/exhibits/charters/constitution_transcript.html
7. Federal Courts & Congress. (2013). *Understanding the federal courts*. Washington, DC: Administrative Office of the U.S. Courts. Retrieved January 18, 2013, from http://www.uscourts.gov/FederalCourts/UnderstandingtheFederalCourts/FederalCourtsInAmericanGovernment.aspx
8. Preamble to the Bill of Rights, Constitution of the United States. (1789). Washington, DC: National Archives. Retrieved January 18, 2013, from http://www.archives.gov/exhibits/charters/bill_of_rights_transcript.html
9. Office of Policy and External Affairs. (2012, December 6). Domestic IP enforcement. *IP Law & Policy*. Washington, DC: U.S. Patent and Trademark Office. Retrieved February 2, 2013, from http://www.uspto.gov/ip/global/enforcement/domesticip.jsp
10. Linder, D. O. (2009). *The O. J. Simpson trial. Famous American trials*. Kansas City, MO: University of Missouri at Kansas City School of Law. Retrieved February 2, 2013, from http://law2.umkc.edu/faculty/projects/ftrials/simpson/simpsonchron.html
11. Brill, R. (2009). *Sources of law [course material]*. Kent, OH: Kent State University School of Law. Retrieved February 3, 2013, from http://www.kentlaw.edu/faculty/rbrill/classes/BrillTortsF2009Eve/CoursePages/courseinfo/orient2hndout.pdf
12. Smith, M., & Carliner, L. (2008, June 26). A history of D.C. gun ban. *The Washington Post*. Retrieved February 3, 2013, from http://www.washingtonpost.com/wp-dyn/content/article/2007/07/17/AR2007071700689.html

13. The Associated Press. NY passes first US gun control law since massacre. *National Public Radio*. Retrieved January 15, 2013, from http://www.npr.org/templates/story/story.php?storyId=169389350

14. Marchant, R. (2003, May). Federal Preemption of State Law. *Constitutional highlights, III*(1). Wisconsin Legislative Reference Bureau. Retrieved February 4, 2013, from http://legis.wisconsin.gov/lrb/pubs/consthi/03consthiIII051.htm

15. Office of Diversion Control. (2012, September). *Definition of controlled substance schedules.* Washington, DC: U.S. Department of Justice, Drug Enforcement Administration. Retrieved February 4, 2013, from http://www.deadiversion.usdoj.gov/schedules/index.html#list

16. Reddall, B., & Gardner, T. (2013, January 29). Judge okays BP plea, $4 billion penalty in Gulf oil spill. *Reuters* (U.S. edition). Retrieved February 5, 2013, from http://www.reuters.com/article/2013/01/29/us-bp-spill-idUSBRE90S0WL20130129

17. Obama, B. (2012, May 17). *Presidential memorandum: Implementing the Prison Rape Elimination Act.* Washington, DC: The White House. Retrieved February 5, 2013, from http://www.whitehouse.gov/the-press-office/2012/05/17/presidential-memorandum-implementing-prison-rape-elimination-act

18. Roosevelt, F. D. (1933, April 5). *Executive order 6102: Requiring gold coin, gold bullion, and gold certificates to be delivered to the government.* Washington, DC: The White House. Retrieved February 5, 2013, from http://www.presidency.ucsb.edu/ws/index.php?pid=14611

19. Kyoto Protocol. (2012). *New York: United Nations framework convention on climate change.* Retrieved February 6, 2013, from http://unfccc.int/kyoto_protocol/items/2830.php

20. Stare Decisis. (2010). Legal Information Institute. *Cornell University Law School.* Retrieved February 6, 2013, from http://www.law.cornell.edu/wex/stare_decisis

21. Rottman, D. B., & Strickland, S. M. (2006, August). *State Court Organization, 2004* (p. 7). Washington, DC: Bureau of Justice Statistics, Office of Justice Programs, U.S. Department of Justice.

22. Rottman, D. B., & Strickland, S. M. (2006, August). *State Court Organization, 2004* (pp. 40–42). Washington, DC: Bureau of Justice Statistics, Office of Justice Programs, U.S. Department of Justice.

23. Rottman, D. B., & Strickland, S. M. (2006, August). *State Court Organization, 2004* (pp. 7, 40–42). Washington, DC: Bureau of Justice Statistics, Office of Justice Programs, U.S. Department of Justice.

24. Rottman, D. B., & Strickland, S. M. (2006, August). *State Court Organization, 2004* (p. 7). Washington, DC: Bureau of Justice Statistics, Office of Justice Programs, U.S. Department of Justice.

25. Geographic Boundaries of United States Courts of Appeals and United States District Courts [map]. (2012). Washington, DC: Administrative Office of the U.S. Courts. Retrieved January 18, 2013, from http://www.uscourts.gov/uscourts/images/CircuitMap.pdf

26. Constitution of the United States. (1787). Washington, DC: National Archives. Retrieved January 18, 2013, from http://www.archives.gov/exhibits/charters/constitution_transcript.html.

27. Motivans, M. (2011, December). *Federal justice statistics, 2009* (p. 9). Washington, DC: Bureau of Justice Statistics, Office of Justice Programs, U.S. Department of Justice.

28. Motivans, M. (2011, December). *Federal justice statistics, 2009* (p. 4). Washington, DC: Bureau of Justice Statistics, Office of Justice Programs, U.S. Department of Justice.

29. Motivans, M. (2011, December). *Federal Justice Statistics, 2009* (p. 2). Washington, DC: Bureau of Justice Statistics, Office of Justice Programs, U.S. Department of Justice.

30. Stewart, P. (1975, February 18). *Gerstein v. Pugh et al.* Washington, DC: Supreme Court of the United States. Retrieved February 7, 2013, from http://scholar.google.com/scholar_case?case=206345582594072284&hl=en&as_sdt=2,19&as_vis=1

31. Sandra, D. O'C. (1991, May 13). *County of Riverside v. McLaughlin.* Washington, DC: Supreme Court of the United States. Retrieved February 7, 2013, from http://www.law.cornell.edu/supct/html/89-1817.ZO.html

32. Spohn, C., & Hemmens, C. (2012). *Courts: A text/reader* (2nd ed., p. 496). Thousand Oaks, CA: Sage.

33. Spohn, C., & Hemmens, C. (2012). *Courts: A text/reader* (2nd ed.). Thousand Oaks, CA: Sage, p. 496.

34. John., M. H. (1894, May 14). *McKane v. Durston.* Washington, DC: Supreme Court of the United States. Retrieved February 7, 2013, from http://www.law.cornell.edu/supremecourt/text/153/684

35. Rehnquist, W. (1974, June 17). *Ross et al. v. Moffitt*. Washington, DC: Supreme Court of the United States.
36. Constitution of the United States. (1787). Washington, DC: National Archives. Retrieved January 18, 2013, from http://www.archives.gov/exhibits/charters/constitution_transcript.html
37. United States Congress. (1789). Judiciary Act. *Annals of Congress, 1st Congress, 1st Session* (p. 2,245). Retrieved February 8, 2013, from http://memory.loc.gov/cgi-bin/ampage?collId=llac&fileName=002/llac002.db&recNum=484
38. Linder, D. (2012). Judicial review. *Exploring constitutional law*. Kansas City, MO: University of Missouri at Kansas City Law School. Retrieved February 8, 2012, from http://law2.umkc.edu/faculty/projects/ftrials/conlaw/judicialrev.htm
39. Linder, D. (2012). Judicial review. *Exploring constitutional law*. Kansas City, MO: University of Missouri at Kansas City Law School. Retrieved February 8, 2012, from http://law2.umkc.edu/faculty/projects/ftrials/conlaw/judicialrev.htm
40. New Jersey Judiciary (2013). Supreme Court of New Jersey. *New Jersey Courts*. Retrieved February 8, 2013, from http://www.judiciary.state.nj.us/supreme/index.htm
41. Reaves, B. A. (2011, July). *Census of state and local law enforcement agencies, 2008* (pp. 1–2). Washington, DC: U.S. Department of Justice, Office of Justice Programs, Bureau of Justice Statistics.
42. Reaves, B. A. (2011, July). *Census of state and local law enforcement agencies, 2008* (p. 2). Washington, DC: U.S. Department of Justice, Office of Justice Programs, Bureau of Justice Statistics.
43. Local Government Records Commission (2011, November 2). *Local law enforcement agencies: Functional analysis & records disposition authority* (pp. 1–2). Montgomery, AL: Alabama State Records Commission.
44. Local Government Records Commission (2011, November 2). *Local law enforcement agencies: Functional analysis & records disposition authority* (pp. 1–3). Montgomery, AL: Alabama State Records Commission.
45. Local Government Records Commission (2011, November 2). *Local law enforcement agencies: Functional analysis & records disposition authority* (pp. 1–4). Montgomery, AL: Alabama State Records Commission.
46. Moran, C. (2010, March 30). Harris Co. to release 20 jail inmates to ease crowding. *Houston Chronicle*. Retrieved February 8, 2013, from http://www.chron.com/news/houston-texas/article/Harris-Co-to-release-20-jail-inmates-to-ease-1613117.php
47. State of Colorado. (2013). About. *Colorado Bureau of Investigation*. Retrieved February 8, 2013, from http://www.colorado.gov/cs/Satellite/CDPS-CBIMain/CBON/1251621964719
48. California Department of Justice. (2013). Bureau of Investigation. *Services & Information*. Office of the Attorney General. Retrieved February 8, 2013, from http://oag.ca.gov/bi
49. State of Kansas. (2013). History. *Kansas Bureau of Investigation*. Retrieved February 8, 2013, from http://www.accesskansas.org/kbi/about/history.shtml
50. Department of Public Safety & Corrections. (2010). Sections of Louisiana State Police. *Louisiana State Police Public Safety Services*. Retrieved February 8, 2013, from http://www.lsp.org/sections.html
51. Smithsonian Institution, (2002). Port Authority police memorial. *September 11: Bearing Witness to History*. Retrieved February 8, 2012, from http://amhistory.si.edu/september11/collection/record.asp?ID=51
52. Reaves, B. A. (2012, June). *Federal law enforcement officers, 2008* (p. 1). Washington, DC: U.S. Department of Justice, Office of Justice Programs, Bureau of Justice Statistics.
53. U.S. Marshals Service. (2013). Oldest Federal Law Enforcement Agency. *History*. Washington, DC: U.S. Department of Justice, U.S. Marshals Service. Retrieved February 9, 2013, from http://www.usmarshals.gov/history/oldest.htm
54. Federal Bureau of Investigation. (2013). What we investigate. *About Us*. Washington, DC: U.S. Department of Justice, Federal Bureau of Investigation. Retrieved February 9, 2013, from http://www.fbi.gov/about-us/investigate/what_we_investigate
55. Federal Bureau of Investigation. (2013). What we investigate. *About Us*. Washington, DC: U.S. Department of Justice, Federal Bureau of Investigation. Retrieved February 9, 2013, from http://www.fbi.gov/about-us/investigate/what_we_investigate

56. Immigration and Customs Enforcement. (2013). Overview. *About ICE*. Washington, DC: U.S. Department of Homeland Security, Immigration and Customs Enforcement. Retrieved February 9, 2013, from http://www.ice.gov/about/overview/

57. Customs and Border Protection. (2013). Overview. *About CBP*. Washington, DC: U.S. Department of Homeland Security, Customs and Border Protection. Retrieved February 9, 2013, from http://www.cbp.gov/xp/cgov/about/

58. Drug Enforcement Administration. (2013). DEA mission statement. *About*. Washington, DC: U.S. Department of Justice, Drug Enforcement Administration. Retrieved February 9, 2013, from http://www.justice.gov/dea/about/mission.shtml

59. Carson, E. A., & Sabol, W. J. (2012, December). *Prisoners in 2011*. Washington, DC: U.S. Department of Justice, Office of Justice Programs, Bureau of Justice Statistics.

60. Federal Bureau of Prisons. (2013). *About the bureau of prisons*. Washington, DC: U.S. Department of Justice, Federal Bureau of Prisons. Retrieved February 9, 2013, from http://www.bop.gov/about/index.jsp

61. Families Against Mandatory Minimums. *Alternatives to incarceration fact sheet* (p. 2). Washington, DC: Families Against Mandatory Minimums Foundation. Retrieved July 8, 2011 and February 9, 2013, from http://www.famm.org/repository/files/alternatives%20in%20a%20nutshell%207.30.09%5B1%5Dfinal.pdf

62. Families Against Mandatory Minimums. *Alternatives to incarceration fact sheet* (pp. 2–3). Washington, DC: Families Against Mandatory Minimums Foundation. Retrieved July 8, 2011 and February 9, 2013, from http://www.famm.org/repository/files/alternatives%20in%20a%20nutshell%207.30.09%5B1%5Dfinal.pdf

63. Families Against Mandatory Minimums. *Alternatives to incarceration fact sheet* (p. 3). Washington, DC: Families Against Mandatory Minimums Foundation. Retrieved July 8, 2011 and February 9, 2013, from http://www.famm.org/repository/files/alternatives%20in%20a%20nutshell%207.30.09%5B1%5Dfinal.pdf

64. Families Against Mandatory Minimums. *Alternatives to incarceration fact sheet* (pp. 3–4). Washington, DC: Families Against Mandatory Minimums Foundation. Retrieved July 8, 2011 and February 9, 2013, from http://www.famm.org/repository/files/alternatives%20in%20a%20nutshell%207.30.09%5B1%5Dfinal.pdf

65. Families Against Mandatory Minimums. *Alternatives to incarceration fact sheet* (p. 4). Washington, DC: Families Against Mandatory Minimums Foundation. Retrieved July 8, 2011 and February 9, 2013, from http://www.famm.org/repository/files/alternatives%20in%20a%20nutshell%207.30.09%5B1%5Dfinal.pdf

66. Akers, R. L., & Sellers, C. S. (2004). *Criminological theories: Introduction, evaluation, and application* (4th ed.). Los Angeles: Roxbury Publishing.

67. Akers, R. L., & Sellers, C. S. (2004). *Criminological theories: Introduction, evaluation, and application* (4th ed.). Los Angeles: Roxbury Publishing.

68. Akers, R. L., & Sellers, C. S. (2004). *Criminological theories: Introduction, evaluation, and application* (4th ed.). Los Angeles: Roxbury Publishing.

69. Akers, R. L., & Sellers, C. S. (2004). *Criminological theories: Introduction, evaluation, and application* (4th ed.). Los Angeles: Roxbury Publishing.

70. Akers, R. L., & Sellers, C. S. (2004). *Criminological theories: Introduction, evaluation, and application* (4th ed.). Los Angeles: Roxbury Publishing.

chapter ten

Criminal activity: Types, severity, and social impact

Chapter objectives

After studying this chapter, you should understand and be able to explain

- The basic categories of crimes with examples of each
- How the severity of crimes has traditionally been assessed
- Factors mitigating the severity of a crime under both common and modern law
- The general nature of the insanity defense
- How precedent has treated the tradeoff between severity and diminished constitutional rights
- How the public views the relative severity of a variety of crimes
- The general trends in crime in the U.S. over the past several years

Introduction

History has demonstrated that collectively criminals are an enterprising and creative lot. As new technologies, new financial tools, and new social conditions arise, they find completely new ways to steal, defraud, injure, or kill or update old tricks to give them new life. In recent times, this has been nowhere more evident than with the development of computer technology and the growth of the Internet: As we will see in the next chapter, law enforcement agencies are fighting a generally losing battle against cybercriminals in an "arms race" of cybercrime techniques that always seems to favor the criminals.

In this chapter, we consider two of the predominant categories of crime: violent crime and property crime. We consider their impacts on society—economic and otherwise—and delve into the complexities of determining to what degree one crime may be worse than another, especially for constitutional purposes. Weighing the interests of the government to investigate, arrest, prosecute, and punish criminals against the rights of citizens and how the severity of a crime may impact that determination is a question that has challenged the nation's courts for many years. We also see how the general public perceives the relative severity of various crimes.

Finally, we examine trends in crime over the past decade or so to gain insight into how criminal activity in our society is evolving. We also look at how the costs of crime prevention may be objectively weighed against the benefits provided.

Types of crimes

As part of its responsibilities as the senior national law enforcement agency for the United States, the Federal Bureau of Investigation (FBI) annually compiles statistics on criminal activity nationwide in its Uniform Crime Report (UCR). Collecting data from dozens upon dozens of jurisdictions requires imposing a high degree of standardization, providing a convenient opportunity to consider types of criminal activity as classified by the FBI.

The UCR uses two major classifications: violent crime and property crime. Violent crime is subdivided into murder, forcible rape, robbery, and aggravated assault. Property crime consists of burglary, larceny-theft, motor vehicle theft, and arson.[1] Some authorities add two additional classes: business- and government-related crimes and drug abuse, drug trafficking, and organized crime.[2] In this text, we separately consider business- and government-related crimes in Chapter 11 and drug-related crimes in this chapter.

In addition to the major categories analyzed in the UCR, violent crimes also include kidnapping, domestic violence (including child abuse and elder abuse), stalking, extortion, hate crimes, and terrorism. For property crimes, additional categories include receiving stolen property, fraud, forgery and counterfeiting, blackmail, identity theft, and computer crime.

Naturally, some crimes blur or cross the lines between neat categories. Carjacking, for example, is arguably both a property and a violent crime. (Most authorities tend to treat carjacking as a violent crime, much as robbery is a violent crime whereas burglary is a property crime, the difference being that the victim is confronted by the criminal and faced with the potential of bodily harm.) Many financial crimes such as fraud and forgery cross the lines into business-related crime, depending on who is affected and how the offense is perpetrated. Through the course of our discussion, we rely on the category assignments for various crimes embraced by the majority of authorities.

Severity of crimes

The division of criminal acts into property and violent crimes is only the first step. It should be obvious from the start that the severity of a crime has great significance. In more formal legal terms, severity is based on the number and type of aggravating factors. While some crimes are by nature more severe than others—murder significantly outweighs petty theft, for example—even the same crime can have a tremendous range of severity in its execution. The man who hits and kills a pedestrian while driving because he was not paying attention has not committed a crime comparable to the man who sexually assaults, strangles, and dismembers a 7-year-old girl, even though in both cases a human life has been ended untimely, and most would argue that the two crimes deserve very different treatment in sentencing.

Yet even more significantly, the question of severity can reach even into constitutional issues, substantially magnifying its impact. A question that has repeatedly reached the appellate courts is whether First and Fourth Amendment issues can turn on severity. A good example of this distinction is found in *Brinegar v. United States* (338 U.S. 160, June 27, 1949).

To provide the necessary background, in March 1947, Brinegar was arrested for smuggling 13 cases of liquor into Oklahoma, which was a dry state until 1959, from Missouri. The officers who conducted the vehicle stop did so based on the knowledge of one, Malsed of the state's Alcohol Tax Unit, who had previously arrested Brinegar for liquor smuggling, had observed him loading liquor into vehicles in Missouri on multiple occasions, and "knew him to have a reputation for hauling liquor."[3] Malsed recognized both Brinegar and his vehicle, and both officers testified that the vehicle appeared to be heavily loaded. After speeding up as he passed the officers' parked car, Brinegar was pulled over after a chase of about a mile and under questioning admitted to having liquor in the car. The constitutional issue was whether the officers had probable cause to conduct the chase and vehicle stop, which subsequently led to Brinegar's admission of transporting contraband. The court ultimately upheld the search, referring extensively to *Carroll v. United States* (267 U.S. 132) in determining that it did not violate the unreasonable search prohibition of the Fourth Amendment.[4]

It is the dissenting opinion of Justice Robert Jackson, however, that is relevant to our discussion of severity. He notes in part in his dissent,

> [Brinegar's] automobile was one of his "effects," and hence within the express protection of the Fourth Amendment. Undoubtedly the automobile presents peculiar problems for enforcement agencies, is frequently a facility of the perpetration of crime, and an aid in the escape of criminals. But if we are to make judicial exceptions to the Fourth Amendment for these reasons, it seems to me they should depend somewhat upon the gravity of the offense. If we assume, for example, that a child is kidnapped and the officers throw a roadblock about the neighborhood and search every outgoing car, it would be a drastic and undiscriminating use of the search. The officers might be unable to show probable cause for searching any particular car. However, I should candidly strive hard to sustain such an action, executed fairly and in good faith, because it might be reasonable to subject travelers to that indignity if it was the only way to save a threatened life and detect a vicious crime. But I should not strain to sustain such a roadblock and universal search to salvage a few bottles of bourbon and catch a bootlegger.[5]

Clearly, severity plays a real and very significant role in determining how far constitutional boundaries may be pushed, at least for Justice Jackson.

The problem, as UCLA law professor Eugene Volokh points out, is that severity is something that must be interpreted, and interpreted over and over again in case after case. Addressing the *Brinegar* case, he notes that while Jackson apparently considers alcohol smuggling to be a petty crime, "alcohol causes many deaths, many crimes, and much other harm. Today, for instance [Volokh was writing in 2004], alcohol use is implicated in 100,000 deaths each year, including likely about 10,000 deaths of victims other than the drinkers themselves."[6] Jackson referred in his example to the life of one child being at stake; Brinegar's crime contributed (albeit indirectly and fractionally) to the deaths of thousands, although under Oklahoma law at the time it was a misdemeanor. Severity is obviously a relative thing.

Finding common crimes and classes of crime that provoke widespread disagreement over severity is easy. Illegal drugs, for example, have received extensive media attention given the decriminalization of marijuana for medical purposes (or, more recently, for recreational use) by several states. Some advocate for the legalization of marijuana while others would like to see even stiffer penalties for drug crimes. In 1986, in a reaction to the perceived epidemic of crack cocaine, federal drug statutes imposed a 100-to-1 sentencing disparity for possession of crack versus powder cocaine. (The statutory minimum 10-year sentence was imposed at 50 or more grams of crack compared to 5 kg—5000 g—of powder cocaine.) This disparity was reduced to 18 to 1 by the Fair Sentencing Act of 2010, but it shows how public perception of differences in severity can extend even to different versions of the same drug.[7]

White-collar crime is another example. The armed robber who steals $500 from a convenience store at gunpoint will often be sentenced more harshly than the broker who steals $5 million through securities fraud. Does the use of a firearm and thereby the creation of risk of bodily harm to one or more people outweigh the financial harm imposed? Current sentencing patterns say that it does, but many would disagree. Copyright infringement (piracy) has also been the subject of much debate. Although from a legal standpoint the matter is fairly clear-cut, many members of the public find it hard to become exercised about these crimes when "big corporations" are the ones perceived as suffering the vast majority of the financial harm.

In exploring the legal impact of severity, Volokh presents four options. The first is to simply eliminate all distinctions based on severity. There are only a handful of U.S. Supreme Court cases that have traveled any distance down this path. The first was *Mincey v. Arizona* (437 U.S. 385, June 21, 1978). Following a narcotics raid on an apartment in which an undercover police officer was killed, homicide detectives conducted an extensive 4-day search of the residence without a warrant while the offender was hospitalized and also questioned him despite his serious condition and despite repeated requests to cease interrogation until legal counsel was present. The Arizona Supreme Court subsequently overturned the assault and murder convictions but upheld the narcotics conviction, in essence making warrantless search of a homicide scene acceptable given the severity of the crime. The U.S. Supreme Court rejected this assumption, ruling that none of the exigency exceptions to the Fourth Amendment had been met and that the simple fact that a homicide had been committed did not create a special circumstance.[8]

In *New Jersey v. T. L. O.* (469 U.S. 325, January 15, 1985), the court upheld the search of a student's purse that turned up marijuana, paraphernalia, a large amount of cash, and documents indicating that the student was dealing marijuana. The search had been prompted when a teacher discovered the then-14-year-old defendant smoking in the restroom. The assistant vice principal searched her purse after the student denied that she had been smoking or in fact smoked at all, finding cigarettes and rolling papers; the rolling papers prompted him to search her purse further since they are commonly associated with marijuana use. In addition to confirming the expanded rights of school officials to perform searches on students under their control in a school environment, the court also refused to make any distinction based on the severity of the suspected offense.[9]

Finally, in the First Amendment case *Branzburg v. Hayes* (408 U.S. 665, June 29, 1972), the court ruled that "the First Amendment does not relieve a newspaper reporter of the obligation that all citizens have to respond to a grand jury subpoena and answer questions relevant to a criminal investigation."[10] More significantly for this discussion, the justices refused to "create a First Amendment journalists' privilege that was sensitive to the severity of the crime being investigated," stating that "considering whether enforcement of a particular law served a 'compelling' governmental interest, the courts would be inextricably involved in distinguishing between the value of enforcing different criminal laws" and "would be making a value judgment that a legislature had declined to make, since in each case the criminal law involved would represent a considered legislative judgment, not constitutionally suspect, of what conduct is liable to criminal prosecution."[6]

The typical standard applied in Fourth and especially First Amendment cases is whether the government's interest is "compelling," meaning the potential harm to the public good clearly outweighs any harm to an individual's rights. To refer once more to *Brinegar*, stopping a kidnapping and possible murder warrants an intrusion into privacy far more than does stopping 13 cases of liquor from crossing state lines illegally. But severity can also be used as an argument for additional restraint in constitutional matters rather than less: As Volokh puts it, "the more severe the crime, the more we want to convict the guilty, but the more we also want to avoid convicting the innocent."[6]

The *Branzburg* opinion focused on a key distinction about judging the severity of a crime: "The task of judges, like other officials outside the legislative branch, is not to make the law but to uphold it in accordance with their oaths."[11] By this reasoning, the courts can never weigh in on severity; rather, that task is left to legislatures, which can enshrine such judgments in statute and are elected representatives of the people.

The second option Volokh proposes is to use objective characteristics of crimes to create rules based on severity. The most common distinction made under this philosophy is between violent and property crimes. The Supreme Court applied the Fourth Amendment in *Tennessee v. Garner* (471 U.S. 1, March 27, 1985) to hold that law enforcement may not fire at a fleeing suspect except when "the suspect threatens the officer with a weapon or there is probable cause to believe that he has committed a crime involving the infliction or threatened infliction of serious physical harm." In *Garner,* an officer had shot and killed a man suspected of committing a burglary; the court held that this violated the reasonableness standard of the Fourth Amendment's prohibition against search and seizure.[12]

The same standard has generally been applied to sentencing. Simply put, the death penalty is considered an appropriate response to taking the life of another and not much more, save particularly heinous crimes such as child rape and those that have the potential to place at risk thousands or even millions, such as espionage and treason. The Supreme Court expressly stated in *Coker v. Georgia* (433 U.S. 584, June 29, 1977) that imposing the death penalty for rape is a violation of the Eighth Amendment prohibition against excessive punishments, even though Coker had multiple prior convictions for capital crimes.[13]

Volokh proposes several potential distinctions along these lines: violent versus property crimes, victim versus victimless crimes, reckless versus negligent conduct, and negligent versus nonnegligent conduct.[14] But even these supposedly bright lines can be clouded. What crimes are truly victimless? Some characterize drug dealing as victimless, while others point to those who suffer directly or indirectly as a result. The term also begs the question of why an act has been criminalized if no one suffers as a result. (Certainly there have been acts that were criminalized despite having no true victims; the various Jim Crow and antimiscegenation laws in the southern U.S. before the civil rights movement are a good example, but these statutes had an entirely fallacious basis from the beginning.)

Even such a principle as treating child rape as a capital crime but adult rape as a noncapital crime seems obvious when viewed from one perspective but makes less sense in the converse: Who wants to be the one to tell an adult victim of rape that what happened to her was less traumatic, less serious, and all in all worthy of less punishment than the rape of someone who might be 5 or 10 years younger? Rutgers law professor Sherry Colb expressed it thus in evaluating a Louisiana court's 2003 sentence of death for a child rapist:

> It is arbitrary … to treat child rape as qualitatively more heinous than the "rape of an adult woman," for death penalty purposes. To do so minimizes the devastation of rape for women, because it suggests that although the rape of one category of people is bad enough to call for execution, adult women do not qualify—as a matter of constitutional law—for inclusion in that category.[15]

(The Louisiana statute in question, dating to 1995, permits a sentence of death for the rape of a child under 12 years of age.)

Volokh's third option is to distinguish severity but to do so on the basis of the statutory categorization of the crime, as that categorization is a product of legislative action, rather than on the basis of objective characteristics.[16] This removes the onus from the courts and allows judges to rely on existing statutes. For example, while precedent has established that the constitutional right to jury trial does not apply to petty crimes, distinguishing exactly what constitutes a "petty crime" is rather more challenging.

The Supreme Court was faced with this issue in *Duncan v. Louisiana* (391 U.S. 145, May 20, 1968). Gary Duncan was convicted of simple battery and sentenced to 60 days in the parish jail and a fine of $10. He did not receive a jury trial, however, because the Louisiana constitution permitted jury trials only for offenses punishable by death or imprisonment at hard labor. Duncan's appeal reached the Supreme Court, which in the course of acknowledging that "petty offenses were tried without juries both in England and in the Colonies, and have always been held to be exempt from the otherwise comprehensive language of the Sixth Amendment's jury trial provisions" noted that "the boundaries of the petty offense have always been ill-defined, if not ambulatory."[17] Outlining contemporary judicial standards, the opinion pointed out that "in the federal system, petty offenses are defined as those punishable by no more than six months in prison and a $500 fine" and that "in 49 of the 50 States, crimes subject to trial without a jury, which occasionally include simple battery [the crime at issue in the case], are punishable by no more than one year in jail."[18]

As it happened, *Duncan* was fairly straightforward since Louisiana law dictated a sentence of up to 2 years for simple battery, and the court reversed the conviction. But in exploring the boundaries of petty crime, the justices noted that drawing those boundaries "falls on the courts" "in the absence of an explicit constitutional provision" and "where the legislature has not addressed itself to the problem." They continue by stating that "it is necessary to draw a line in the spectrum of crime, separating petty from serious infractions. This process, although essential, cannot be wholly satisfactory, for it requires attaching different consequences to events which, when they lie near the line, actually differ very little."[19]

Using statutory maximum penalties to distinguish petty crimes seems fairly straightforward. As Volokh points out, "After all, if the legislature didn't think some offense was worth making a felony, how can the government argue that the offense is serious enough to justify special relaxation of the Fourth Amendment rules?"[20] But the "events which … lie near the line" invoked by the justices in *Duncan* rear their collective head to once more complicate the seemingly simple. "Distribution of child pornography and of newspaper articles based on material that someone leaked in violation of a felony trade secret law would have to be treated equally," Volokh explains, and "so would the fleeing rapist and the fleeing thief of products that are worth more than the felony theft threshold."[21]

However, this standard does create the potential for abuse. Assuming that felony offenses warrant a lower level of constitutional protection that benefits the government's enforcement efforts, legislatures might be tempted to reclassify certain crimes from misdemeanors to felonies. It might seem that such moves would create a public outcry, but that is not a reliable assumption. This is particularly true when there is actually strong public support for curbing such offenses. For validation, we need only consider the previously discussed disproportionate treatment of crack cocaine compared to powder cocaine in the 1980s or the sweeping powers conveyed by the Patriot Act, which was passed in the wake of 9/11.

The final option is to distinguish severity case by case based on evaluation by the court. This has happened on a number of occasions, one of the most notable being the determination that child pornography does not enjoy First Amendment protection because of its association with the sexual exploitation of children. Existing precedent in sentencing has generally expected judges to give strong consideration to the severity of the crime at issue.

This might seem a fair and reasonable approach, and indeed it is often used in the U.S. justice system, but it too has flaws. The first is that when the judgment of severity is rendered after the fact by a judge, it provides little in the way of guidance for either law enforcement officers or citizens, who do not routinely conduct detailed studies of legal precedent.

Having judges in hundreds of federal, state, and local jurisdictions making case-by-case determinations of severity is likely to lead to significant variations in outcomes, especially given the differences in community opinion toward certain classes of crimes in various parts of the country. Moreover, the public perception that judges are simply arbitrarily applying their personal standards is more likely with so much variation, even if that perception is inaccurate, and would undermine overall confidence in the system.

By now it should be clear that assessing severity is no simple matter, not when the full range of possible criminal conduct is considered. Removing or affirming constitutional protections based on severity is an issue of significant gravity as well. Yet, finding a consistently fair, objective basis for determining severity is fraught with complications. This is true regardless of whether the task is entrusted to the courts or to the legislatures.

Assessing the severity of specific criminal acts

Although contemplating the severity of broad classes of crimes is complicated, the body of American jurisprudence has evolved extensive and detailed rules for assessing specific criminal acts. Although in some cases there is significant variation in laws at the federal and state levels, in several portions of this discussion, we consider the Model Penal Code (MPC). Dating from 1962 but modified periodically since, the MPC was created by the American Law Institute (ALI) "to stimulate and assist legislatures in making a major effort to appraise the content of the penal law by a contemporary reasoned judgment" and to assist in the "revision and codification of the substantive criminal law of the United States."[22] Because it has influenced so much of the American penal code, it is a useful substitute for attempting to pursue every minor distinction from jurisdiction to jurisdiction, although we will consider some significant differences between the existing statutes and the MPC.

Douglas Colbert, a professor at the University of Maryland Francis King Carey School of Law, defines crime as "an act or omission and its accompanying state of mind, which if duly shown to have taken place, will incur a formal and solemn pronouncement of the moral condemnation of the community."[23] The first factor we will consider is the defendant's state of mind.

Under the MPC, there are four states of mind. From least serious to most serious, they are negligence, recklessness, knowledge, and purpose. These states determine the level of culpability ("moral blameworthiness") on the part of the defendant and may be associated with the conduct, circumstances, or outcome of the act. Unless the statutory definition of a given crime specifies the nature of culpability, under the MPC, a minimum of recklessness is required for a crime to take place.[24] Moreover, culpability must be demonstrated for each of the three factors (conduct, circumstances, and outcome).[25]

There are a number of general defenses available to a defendant, which may either reduce the degree of culpability or exculpate the accused entirely. The first is self-defense. Although fairly clear-cut, there are subtleties involved. The aggressor is not entitled to self-defense except in two situations. If the aggressor makes a good faith effort to withdraw from the confrontation (or announces that intent to the other party if withdrawal is currently impossible), he is then entitled to self-defense should the other party continue aggression. Also, should the victim escalate the level of force involved in the confrontation without giving the aggressor the opportunity to withdraw, then the aggressor also gains the right to self-defense.[26]

Another potential defense is duress. A crime committed as a result of a third party's threat of harm or actual use of force (whether against the defendant or his family) is excusable (but not justifiable, although the effect for the defendant is the same). However, the threat of harm must be immediate, not future—that is, if the defendant would have the opportunity to take steps to mitigate the threat, there is no defense of duress. Also, duress may not be used as a defense for homicide.[27]

Duress is caused by a human actor; there is a related defense of necessity. Necessity arises from a physical or natural force. To be a defense, the harm must be imminent and severe; the harm that results from the crime must be less severe than that the natural force will inflict; the defendant's intent must have been to avoid more serious harm; there must have been no better alternative; and the physical force that threatens harm must not have been caused by the defendant. The simple example offered by Colbert is that of a person committing trespass by taking shelter from a severe storm in a barn. So long as no property is damaged, the defendant can assert the rule of necessity as a defense. Interestingly, a penniless (but not starving) man who claimed necessity as a defense for stealing groceries was unsuccessful. There are, after all, a number of options for those unable to buy food.[27]

Finally, we come to the various mental capacity defenses popularly known as the insanity defense. To first address the question of a more limited and temporary defect of mental capacity, intoxication can be a defense in those crimes that require knowledge or intent, assuming that intoxication was sufficient to prevent the formation of the necessary mental state (and that intoxication was not a deliberate attempt to create a defense).

There are several rules for invoking the defense of insanity. The first, used in 1843 in England, was the McNaughton Rule. It was named for Edward McNaughton, who killed the prime minister's secretary because he believed that the prime minister was conspiring against him. He was acquitted by reason of insanity, although he was institutionalized for the remainder of his life. In response to public outcry over the acquittal, Queen Victoria ordered the creation of a standardized (and stricter) test for insanity. (Courts had previously attempted more vague determinations, such as whether a defendant knew the difference between good and evil or recognized what he had done.)

The resulting rule required the jury to decide, based on medical testimony from expert witnesses, whether the defendant had a mental defect such that he "could not … know the nature and quality of the act he was doing or, if he did know it, that he did not know what he was doing."[28] (Note the "or" in the language; a defendant need meet only one of the conditions to be judge insane.) This standard was accepted in both the United Kingdom and the United States and today remains the legal standard for insanity in almost half of U.S. states.

A less structured alternative used by some states was the Irresistible Impulse Test. Under it, if a defendant was unable to control his actions generally or conduct himself in accordance with the law specifically because of mental illness, then he was legally insane. In some jurisdictions, both the McNaughton Rule and Irresistible Impulse Test are used; a defendant need only meet the conditions of one.[29]

In 1954, a federal appellate judge attempted to update the insanity determination during the review of the 1953 conviction of Monte Durham for housebreaking. What resulted was the Durham Rule, the broadest definition of insanity ultimately adopted by only a few states. Under it, a crime must have been caused by some defective or diseased mental condition, and it must be established that the crime would not have occurred otherwise. Essentially, the defense required a diagnosis from a psychiatric professional rather than the presentation of a collection of symptoms alleged to be the product of mental illness. In practice, different psychiatrists might assign different diagnoses to the same defendant, which created confusion for juries. The Durham Rule was abandoned after being overturned in the D.C. Circuit Court of Appeals in 1972 (*United States v. Brawner*, 471 F.2d 969, 153 U.S. App. D. C. 1). It was so broad that it had successfully been used as a defense by drug addicts, compulsive gamblers, and alcoholics.[29]

Following the vacation of the Durham Rule, the ALI updated the MPC in 1972 to add a rule for insanity defenses. Also known as the "substantial capacity test," it requires proof that the defendant lacked the "substantial capacity [as distinguished from total capacity] either to appreciate the criminality of his conduct or to conform his conduct to the requirements of the law." Because it was derived from the *Brawner* decision, it became known as the Brawner Rule.[30] Essentially, the Brawner Rule combines the McNaughton Rule (because of a mental defect, the defendant lacked knowledge of what he was doing or of right and wrong), and the Irresistible Impulse Test (because of a mental defect, the defendant lacked the ability to control his actions) into a single standard. Although this standard is not easy for a jury to assess, especially in the face of competing testimony from defense and prosecution expert witnesses, at present it is used in about half of U.S. states.

The most recent update to the insanity defense came in 1984 with the Insanity Defense Reform Act, part of the Comprehensive Crime Control Act signed by President Ronald Reagan. (Ironically, the man who attempted to assassinate Reagan, John Hinckley, Jr., was acquitted by reason of insanity.) The federal standard for insanity became "clear and convincing evidence" that "the defendant, as a result of a severe mental disease or defect, was unable to appreciate the nature and quality or the wrongfulness of his acts" at the time he committed the crime. The Act also added sentencing guidelines for mentally ill defendants.[30]

To conduct a practical examination of the various mitigating or aggravating circumstances that can affect the adjudged severity of a crime, let us consider homicide. First, understand that in legal terms, homicide is not necessarily murder, although in popular usage the two are often interchangeable. The English common law definition of homicide was that one had caused the death of a living human being when death occurred within a year and a day of the homicidal act. (Today, it is rare to find any statute of limitations associated with homicide, so the "year and a day" rule is now mostly a historical curiosity.) Common law recognized murder, voluntary manslaughter, and involuntary manslaughter; the imposition of degrees on murder offenses is a modern creation.

Criminal homicide is that which has no justification or excuse, as already discussed. Murder is unlawful killing with malice aforethought—that is, with premeditated deliberate intent. In legal terms, "malice" exists when the defendant had the intent to kill or to cause serious bodily injury, acts with such recklessness as to demonstrate wanton disregard for human life, or had the intent to commit a felony during which the death of another resulted.[31]

Manslaughter is homicide committed without malice aforethought. Voluntary manslaughter occurs when the defendant kills intentionally but does so because of adequate provocation and "in the heat of passion"—that is, without having enough time to "cool off" and judge the situation rationally. Involuntary manslaughter results from negligence or as an adjunct to the commission of a nonfelony crime.[31]

This begs the question of what the law considers "adequate provocation." Common law enumerated specific mitigating and nonmitigating circumstances. Mitigating events included mutual combat (dueling), illegal arrest, aggravated assault or battery, the commission of a serious crime against a close relative, or a husband discovering a wife in the act of adultery (*in flagrante delicto*). Nonmitigating events were discovering adultery (not by observing the act), observing a fiancée being unfaithful, trivial battery, or words, regardless of how offensive they might be.[31]

Today, the standards are less direct. Most jurisdictions instruct a jury that circumstances are mitigating if they would cause a reasonable person to act out of passion rather than rational decision making and if in the time that elapsed between the provocation and the homicidal act a reasonable person would have been unable to "cool off." (Some jurisdictions exclude the cooling-off period entirely; no time must elapse after provocation for mitigation to voluntary manslaughter.) As with common law, both the MPC and most statutes do not consider words alone adequate provocation, although there have been a few exceptions to this in case law.[31]

As to degrees of murder, most willful, deliberate, premeditated murders qualify as first-degree murder. (Keep in mind that in this context the word "deliberate" means that the defendant took time to think about his act, not that it was intentional—that is the meaning of "willful.") If the defendant instead is demonstrated to have had intent to cause serious physical harm rather than death but in the event killed his target, this will normally be second-degree murder. Similarly, acting with extreme recklessness and thereby causing death is treated as second-degree murder: The defendant should have known that his actions had a strong likelihood of harming others and acted with flagrant disregard for the safety of others.[31]

The line between second-degree murder and involuntary manslaughter is determined by the difference between recklessness and negligence. A defendant who is negligent in legal terms should have recognized that his act could cause harm but was not aware. As an example, if an individual engages in horseplay with a gun he knows is loaded and the weapon discharges and kills another, he is guilty of second-degree murder—he knew the dangers of a loaded gun and chose to act recklessly. Had he thought the gun was unloaded, he would instead be guilty of involuntary manslaughter.[31]

The MPC standards are generally similar, although they do not recognize degrees of murder. Murder occurs when an individual purposefully, knowingly, or recklessly (refer back to the four degrees of culpability discussed at the beginning of this section) causes the death of another, assuming no excusing, justifying, or mitigating factors. Reckless murder is an offense, though a jury may consider reckless manslaughter as an alternative. The MPC presumes "extreme recklessness" for homicide resulting from the commission of a felony. Murder and reckless murder are first-degree felonies, carrying a minimum sentence of 1–10 years and a maximum of life imprisonment. (As of 2009, the ALI withdrew capital punishment as an option under the MPC.) What common law calls involuntary manslaughter is negligent homicide under the MPC. It is a third-degree felony with a minimum sentence of 1–2 years and a maximum of 5 years.[31]

Manslaughter under the MPC results from reckless homicide (with recklessness distinguished from extreme recklessness by a lack of extreme indifference) or mitigating circumstances. What common law calls adequate provocation the MPC refers to as "extreme mental or emotional disturbance" (EMED), assuming the cause of the EMED meets the reasonable person standard, and provocation is not necessarily required, although there is no provision for a cooling-off period. Unlike under common law, EMED can be found to have been caused by words alone. Proving EMED is the responsibility of the defense, but only a preponderance of the evidence is required, not beyond a reasonable doubt.[31]

As this examination of the standards for murder and manslaughter should make clear, the intricacies of drawing lines between degrees of severity that translate to significant differences in sentences are many and complex. Often it is the responsibility of the jury to navigate these muddy statutory waters, even when making such challenging determinations as sanity versus insanity. But these distinctions are important ones in keeping our system of justice fair and effective.

Public perceptions of crime severity

The criminal justice system should—at least to most people—be a reflection of a society's values and, as put into practice by government at various levels, an extension of the will of the people. As we are examining distinctions based on the relative severity of various crimes, it would be helpful to ascertain how the public at large perceives this issue. As it happens, the Bureau of Justice Statistics published in June 1985 a research project on this very subject—at this point not yet replicated—titled the National Survey of Crime Severity (NSCS).

The NSCS was compiled based on data collected in a 6-month period in 1977 from 60,000 respondents. Although a total of 204 crimes were rated in the survey, each respondent assessed only 25 crimes. This methodology did produce some anomalies. For example, the survey included four versions of planting a bomb in a public building: one in which 20 people are killed, one in which one person is killed, one in which one person is injured but requires no medical treatment, and one in which 20 people are injured but required no medical treatment. Although the first version (20 casualties) scored the highest of all 204 crimes, at 72.1, the scoring of the last two versions was counterintuitive: The scenario in which 20 people were injured scored lowest, at 30.5, whereas the scenario in which only one person was injured scored 33.0.[32]

Nevertheless, overall respondents tended to hold similar views about the severity of various crimes. However, the researchers did note some specific demographic trends. Members of nonwhite racial groups tended to assign generally lower scores than whites. Older respondents assigned higher severity scores to high-dollar-value thefts than did younger ones. Those who had been crime victims assigned higher scores overall than nonvictims. Gender did not appear to be a significant determinant; the scoring patterns of men and women showed no statistically significant divergence.[33]

Not surprisingly, violent crimes were considered more severe than property crimes. It also seems that the vulnerability of the victim plays some role in the perception: A child killed by his or her parent rated 47.8 compared to a husband stabbing his wife to death (39.2) and a wife's murder of her husband (27.9). Bearing in mind that these survey responses date from over 35 years ago and that social views of certain crimes have changed, what some today call "victimless crimes" were taken very seriously. Operating a narcotics ring rated higher at 33.8 than a skyjacking (32.7), and selling heroin rated higher at 20.6 than raping a women when her injuries did not require hospitalization (20.1).[34]

In reviewing some of the ratings, similar crimes and different versions of the same crime will be compared side by side to provide insight into what factors respondents considered aggravating and to what degree. (We have already seen four versions of planting a bomb in a public building.) The highest score, 72.1, went to planting a bomb in a public building that kills 20 people. (It would be intriguing to see how this crime is viewed today in the wake of 9/11 and a heightened awareness of terrorism.) The lowest score, 0.2, went to a person under 16 years of age playing "hooky" from school.[35]

Rape and Sexual Assault

A man forcibly rapes a woman; she dies of her injuries	52.8
A man forcibly rapes a woman; she requires hospitalization	30.0
A man forcibly rapes a woman; no physical injury occurs	25.8
A man forcibly rapes a woman; her injuries require medical treatment but not hospitalization	20.1
A man drags a woman into an alley and tears her clothing but flees before physically injuring or sexually assaulting her	16.9
A man runs his hands over the body of a female victim, then runs away	5.1
A man exposes himself in public	4.7
A person makes an obscene phone call	1.9

Forcible rape with resultant death had the second-highest severity rating on the survey. The higher rating for rape with no physical injury (25.8) compared to rape causing injuries that require medical treatment but not hospitalization (20.1) is an apparent anomaly. In another sign of contemporary values, two persons willingly engaging in a homosexual act was one of the 204 listed crimes, although respondents gave it a rating of only 1.3.

Kidnapping

A man tries to entice a minor into his vehicle for immoral purposes	25.2
A person kidnaps a victim; the victim is returned unharmed after a $1000 ransom is paid	24.5
A person kidnaps a victim	21.2

It is curious that a straightforward kidnapping was rated lower than one in which it is specified that the victim is returned unharmed. Presumably the ransom was the aggravating factor.

Armed Robbery

A person robs a victim at gunpoint; the victim resists and is shot to death	43.2
A person robs a victim of $1,000 at gunpoint; the victim is wounded and requires hospitalization	21.0
A person robs a victim of $10 at gunpoint; the victim is wounded and requires hospitalization	17.9
A person robs a bank at gunpoint during business hours, stealing $100,000; no one is injured	17.7
A person robs a victim of $1,000 at gunpoint; the victim is wounded and requires medical treatment but not hospitalization	16.5
A person robs a victim of $10 at gunpoint; the victim is wounded and requires medical treatment but not hospitalization	15.7
A person armed with a lead pipe robs a victim of $10; the victim is injured and requires hospitalization	13.3
A person robs a victim of $1,000 at gunpoint; no physical injury occurs	9.7
A person robs a victim of $10 at gunpoint, no physical injury occurs	9.4
A person armed with a lead pipe robs a victim of $1,000; no injury occurs	9.0
A person armed with a lead pipe robs a victim of $10; no injury occurs	7.5
A person armed with a lead pipe robs a victim of $10; the victim is injured and requires medical treatment but not hospitalization	7.1

Once again, the higher rating for armed robbery of $10 with a nonfirearm when no injury occurs versus medical treatment without hospitalization is an anomaly of the survey methodology.

Robbery, Burglary, and Auto Theft	
A person using force robs a victim of $1,000; the victim is physically injured and requires hospitalization	16.8
A person using force robs a victim of $1,000; the victim is physically injured and requires medical treatment but not hospitalization	16.6
A person breaks into a bank at night and steals $100,000	15.5
A person steals property worth $10,000 from outside a building	10.9
A person breaks into a department store, forces open a safe, and steals $1,000	9.7
A person breaks into a school and steals equipment worth $1,000	9.7
A person walks into a museum and steals a painting worth $1,000	9.7
A person breaks into a home and steals $1,000	9.6
A person steals an unlocked car and sells it	8.0
A person using force robs a victim of $1,000; no physical injury occurs	8.0
A person trespasses in a railroad and steals tools worth $1,000	7.9
A person steals $1,000 worth of merchandise from a store counter	7.6
A person breaks into a department store and steals merchandise worth $1,000	7.3
A person breaks into a public recreation center, forces open a cash box, and steals $1,000	6.9
A person steals property worth $1,000 from outside a building	6.9
A person using force robs a victim of $10; the victim is injured and requires medical treatment but not hospitalization	6.7
A person steals $1,000 worth of merchandise from an unlocked car	6.6
A person using force robs a victim of $10; no physical injury occurs	5.1
A person snatches a handbag containing $10 from a victim on the street	4.9
A person steals an unlocked car and later abandons it undamaged	4.4
A person robs a victim; the victim is injured but not hospitalized	4.4
A person breaks into a public recreation center, forces open a cash box, and steals $10	4.3
A person attempts to break into a home but runs when a police car approaches	4.2
A person attempts to break into a car but runs when a police car approaches	3.6
A person steals property worth $100 from outside a building	3.6
A person breaks into a department store, forces open a cash register, and steals $10	3.3
A person picks a victim's pocket of $10	3.3
A person attempts to rob a victim but runs when a police car approaches	3.3
A person breaks into a building and steals property worth $10	3.2
A person breaks into a home and steals $100	3.1
A person forces open a cash register in a department store and steals $10	3.1
A person breaks into a school and steals $10 worth of supplies	3.1
A person steals property worth $50 from outside a building	2.9
A person breaks into a department store and steals merchandise worth $10	2.8
A person trespasses in a city-owned storage lot and steals equipment worth $10	2.2
A person steals $10 worth of merchandise from a store counter	2.2
A person steals property worth $10 from outside a building	1.7
A person breaks into a parking meter and steals $10 worth of nickels	1.6
A person trespasses in a railroad yard and steals a lantern worth $10	1.4

The ratings of this extensive list of (mostly) property crimes contain no real surprises. The value of property stolen, whether a break-in was required, the degree of threat to the victim, and injury sustained by the victim all seem to factor into the severity rating.

Assault	
A person intentionally injures a victim, resulting in the victim's death	35.6
A person intentionally injures a victim; the victim requires hospitalization	11.9
A man beats a stranger with his fists; the victim requires hospitalization	11.8
A person threatens to seriously injure a victim	9.3
A person intentionally hits a victim with a lead pipe; the victim requires medical treatment but not hospitalization	8.9
A person intentionally injures a victim; the victim requires medical treatment but not hospitalization	8.5
A person intentionally hits a victim with a lead pipe; the victim does not require medical treatment	7.9
A person beats a victim with his fists; the victim is injured but does not require medical treatment	7.3
A person beats a victim with his fists; the victim requires hospitalization	6.9
A person beats a victim with his fists; the victim requires medical treatment but not hospitalization	6.2
A person intentionally shoves a victim; no medical treatment is required	1.5

We see another minor anomaly in bare-handed assault requiring hospitalization (6.9) versus no medical treatment (7.3).

Assault with a Deadly Weapon	
A person stabs a victim to death	35.7
A person intentionally shoots a victim with a gun; the victim requires hospitalization	24.8
A person intentionally shoots a victim with a gun; the victim requires medical treatment but not hospitalization	19.0
A person stabs a victim with a knife; the victim requires hospitalization	18.0
A person intentionally shoots a victim with a gun; the victim is slightly injured but does not require medical treatment	17.8
A person stabs a victim with a knife; the victim requires medical treatment but not hospitalization	17.1
A person attempts to kill a victim with a gun; the weapon misfires and the victim is not injured	16.4
A person stabs a victim with a knife; the victim requires no medical treatment	11.8
A person intentionally hits a victim with a lead pipe; the victim requires hospitalization	10.4
A person intentionally hits a victim with a lead pipe; the victim requires medical treatment but no hospitalization	8.9
A person intentionally hits a victim with a lead pipe; the victim requires no medical treatment	7.9

Drug Offenses

A person runs a narcotics ring	33.8
A person sells heroin to others for resale	20.6
A person smuggles heroin into the country	19.5
A person smuggles marijuana into the country for resale	10.5
A person illegally sells barbiturates to others for resale	10.3
A person sells marijuana to others for resale	8.5
A person uses heroin	6.5
A person has some heroin for his own use	5.4
A person takes barbiturates for his own use without a prescription	1.5
A person has some barbiturates for his own use without a prescription	1.4
A person smokes marijuana	1.4
A person has some marijuana for his own use	1.3

Heroin was one of the most dangerous drugs available at the time the survey was conducted, and attitudes toward it compared to marijuana and barbiturates are notable—19.5 versus 10.5 for smuggling heroin into the country as opposed to marijuana. The severity tiers from "kingpin" to street-level dealer to user are also fairly clear-cut.

Domestic Violence

A parent beats his young child with his fists; the child dies as a result	47.8
A man stabs his wife; she dies as a result	39.2
A woman stabs her husband; he dies as a result	27.9
A parent beats his young child with his fists; the child requires hospitalization	22.9
A man beats his wife with his fists; she requires hospitalization	18.3
A teenage boy beats his mother with his fists; she requires hospitalization	15.9
A teenage boy beats his father with his fists; he requires hospitalization	7.9

It would seem that the respondent's perception of the victim's vulnerability plays a key role in assessing severity; note the successive approximate 10-point drops from a child killed by a parent to a wife killed by a husband to a husband killed by a wife. Note also the substantial difference between a mother beaten by her teenage son and a father: half the severity value. (It would be interesting to see how a 35-year difference in attitudes toward gender might modify these responses today.)

Malfeasance by a Public Official

A legislator takes a bribe of $10,000 from a company to vote for a law favoring that company	16.9
A county judge takes a bribe to grant a lighter sentence to a criminal	15.7
A legislator takes a bribe from a company to vote for a law favoring that company	13.9
A police officer takes a bribe to not interfere with an illegal gambling operation	12.0
A government official intentionally hinders a criminal investigation	10.0
A police officer knowingly makes a false arrest	9.6
A public official takes $1,000 of public money for personal use	9.4
A city official takes a bribe from a company for assistance in obtaining a city contract for the company	9.0[36]

Once again, we should be cautious in reading too much into these severity ratings given the age of the survey data. However, as a gauge of general trends, it probably remains a valid indicator. A link to the entire study is provided in the "Resources" section of this chapter; you may choose to compare responses in detail to gain a clear understanding of what the general public considers the aggravating factors for different classes of crimes.

Depravity scale

Both mitigating and aggravating factors contribute to the court's perception of the severity of a given crime, as we have seen. As it happens, many aggravating factors have been formalized into statute or sentencing guidelines in many jurisdictions. For example, causing "physical, emotional, or financial torture to [a] victim or [the] victim's family" is an aggravating factor in both capital and noncapital crimes in 19 states; causing the death of multiple victims, in 23 states; and performing or commissioning a contract killing, in 29 states. But the most widely used aggravating factor, found in 34 states, is the commission of a crime that is "heinous, atrocious, cruel, depraved, wanton, vile, [or] outrageous."[37]

Unfortunately, there is a certain degree of subjectivity to these adjectives that leaves them open to interpretation. This has been recognized in more than one court decision. In *Gregg v. Georgia* (428 U.S. 153, July 2, 1976), the presiding judge had instructed the jury that one of the justifying criteria for imposing the death penalty would be their determination that the crime was "outrageously and wantonly vile, horrible, and inhuman." A death sentence was returned. The Supreme Court upheld the sentence, but in the majority opinion Justice Potter Stewart noted, "It is, of course, arguable that any murder involves depravity of mind or an aggravated battery." He continues, however, "But this language need not be construed in this way, and there is no reason to assume that the Supreme Court of Georgia will adopt such an open-ended construction."[38]

In *Walton v. Arizona* (497 U.S. 639, June 27, 1990), a defendant had been convicted of first-degree murder and sentenced to death based in part on Arizona's standard that an offense committed "in an especially heinous, cruel, or depraved manner" represented an aggravating factor. While again upholding the sentence, the court acknowledged that "In this case there is no serious argument that Arizona's 'especially heinous, cruel, or depraved' aggravating factor is not facially vague," and furthermore praised "a definition that would limit Oklahoma's 'especially heinous, atrocious, or cruel' aggravating circumstance to murders involving 'some kind of torture or physical abuse'" that was discussed in another case, *Maynard v. Cartwright.*[39]

Finally, the use of such language was condemned in the ruling overturning a death sentence in *Godfrey v. Georgia* (446 U.S. 420, May 19, 1980). The majority opinion noted that

> the validity of the petitioner's death sentences turns on whether, in light of the facts and circumstances of the murders that he was convicted of committing, the Georgia Supreme Court can be said to have applied a constitutional construction of the phrase "outrageously or wantonly vile, horrible, or inhuman in that [they] involved … depravity of mind …." We conclude that the answer must be no. The petitioner's crimes cannot be said to have reflected a consciousness materially more "depraved" than that of any person guilty of murder.[40]

Clearly a more objective standard is required.

The Forensic Panel, an independent research group, began conducting research in 1998 with the intent of creating "a standardized methodology for distinguishing the worst of crimes in any given legal case." By 2001, the group identified 24 factors proposed as objective determinants of a crime's depravity—hence the name Depravity Scale.[37]

The intent is to ultimately weight each of the various standards to further refine the precision of the scale. To accurately group different aggravating behaviors, researchers also associated those behaviors with several psychiatric diagnoses including antisocial personality disorder, psychopathy, sadism, sexual sadism, and antisocial personality disorder by proxy. Standards were deliberately constructed to be applicable to the widest possible range of crimes: "'Intent to maximize damage,' for example, is applicable to the planting of a computer virus as much as it is to a mass casualty terror plot."[37]

Though the Depravity Scale standards are not yet finalized, some examples of proposed standards include the following:

- Intent to cause permanent physical disfigurement
- Targeting victims who are not merely physically vulnerable, but helpless
- Exploiting a close and trusting relationship to the victim
- Prolonging the duration of a victim's physical suffering
- Exceptional degree of physical harm; amount of damage
- Influencing depravity in others to destroy more
- Falsely implicating others, knowingly exposing them to wrongful penalty and the stress of prosecution
- Disrespect for the victim after the fact[37]

It can be hoped that general acceptance of objective standards like these will aid in consistent and constitutionally valid application of aggravating factors in sentencing.

Property crime and its social impact

In attempting to quantify the social impacts of crime, it is perhaps easier to begin with property crime. The losses created by property crime are, after all, predominantly economic, so assigning firm values to material impacts is easier. It is important to remember that direct costs are only a portion of a crime's social impact. Indirect costs spread throughout society much like the ripples from a stone dropped into a pond, decreasing the more an individual is removed from the victim.

The first and most easily quantified costs are direct tangible costs. The value of property lost to crime and/or the cost to replace it is obviously the first. Additional property may also be damaged in the course of the crime: Consider the thief who breaks out a car window to gain access and steal packages from the back seat, for example. Yet, there are direct costs that are more challenging to quantify from a research standpoint, mostly because they tend to arise after the crime event itself. A crime victim may have to take time from work to deal with filing a criminal complaint, participating in the criminal justice process, having property repaired, or dealing with insurance claims. In some cases, a victim may suffer serious mental anguish even from a property crime, possibly impacting his or her productivity or even interfering with his or her ability to work for a time.

Even as we consider direct costs, however, the metaphorical ripples begin to spread. Many people carry insurance, after all, so property crime losses are often reimbursed at least partially. However, these insurance claims impact other policyholders as well, contributing to increased premiums. Although probably miniscule in the context of a single crime, taken collectively property crimes can have significant financial impacts even on those who never become victims.

The first level of indirect costs comes in the form of the criminal justice system, financed primarily by tax revenues and therefore once again spread across society. Law enforcement agencies, court systems, correctional systems, and all the various adjuncts have substantial costs, and high rates of crime directly drive those costs. More crime means a need for more police officers, more prosecutors and public defenders, more jail and prison beds, more probation officers, and so forth.

A secondary and less visible set of indirect costs result as citizens take steps to protect themselves, possibly out of concern that law enforcement does not have sufficient resources to adequately protect them. Billions of dollars are spent annually on alarm systems and monitoring, security camera systems, armored car services, security guards, improved locks and other security measures, and even firearms. Citizens spend directly on their own homes, vehicles, and other property; businesses spend even more, and of necessity build those additional costs into their pricing, passing them along to consumers.

The third and final set of factors is even more rarefied and intangible. Money spent by a state government on a new prison, a municipality on additional police officers, or even a citizen on a new alarm system represent opportunity costs. Without knowing what potentially beneficial programs or other purposes those funds might have supported, we cannot even begin to quantify the social impact. Would a local department store have hired an additional employee if not for the need to install security cameras and the losses it sustains from shoplifting? Would state government have put additional funds toward education or health care had it not been forced to allocate tens of millions of dollars to provide additional beds for inmates? Money spent in response to crime is not an investment in the future; it is remedial. Even the best inmate rehabilitation program or drug court system is only correcting problems.

Crime also contributes to a vicious cycle in many cases. Consider a neighborhood that suffers a steadily increasing rate of property crime. Even if violent crime is relatively rare, it can be expected that many residents will venture away from home less and less, especially at night, out of a combination of a desire to protect their property and a sense that they run the risk of falling victim to violent crime. Those who are able—in most cases the most affluent residents—will begin to move away. The number of vacant properties will increase, contributing to more frequent and more varied crimes. (Abandoned houses may become "drug dens" or "crack houses," for example.) The neighborhood will, in short, slowly decay.

(Interestingly, a 1995 study conducted using 1970 and 1980 census and crime data for Baltimore found that increased rates of assault and murder resulted in declining home "values," whereas increased rates of burglary seemed to produce increased home "vacancy rates."[41])

Finding examples of recent and completed research into the costs of crime in the literature is challenging. Much data from the U.S. government is collected either infrequently or on an ongoing basis, as is the case with the National Crime Victimization Survey, begun in 1973 and conducted annually by the Bureau of Justice Statistics. Much of what is available deals extensively with the costs of violent crime. That being the case, to consider some concrete numbers we will transition our discussion to violent crime.

Violent crime and its social impact

Violent crime brings with it an entire set of additional direct and indirect costs. Some degree of property damage or loss often accompanies violent crimes, of course, but the most significant direct cost is medical care. Even more than with property crimes, these costs tend to be shifted to society at large, since either health insurance or government programs such as Medicaid and Medicare and charity hospital systems tend to pay the bulk of them. The mental health costs associated with violent crime are much more significant, as are the impacts of psychological trauma.

Social costs in terms of criminal justice system involvement are also higher for violent crime. This is a function of both the more extensive investigative and prosecutorial efforts and the longer sentences in higher-security facilities typically required for violent offenses. Violent crimes also do not lend themselves well to alternative programs such as drug courts that reduce criminal justice costs because of public safety concerns—violent offenders are often specifically excluded from nearly all such programs, in fact.

David A. Anderson, an economics professor, conducted one of the most authoritative studies on the cost of crime, publishing his results in October 1999. Professor Anderson updated his study and published those results in the journal *Foundations and Trends in Microeconomics* in 2012. However, in some cases, his data sources were a few years older.

Anderson calculates an aggregate direct and indirect cost of crime in the United States at $3.126 trillion of which $1.561 trillion represents "transfers" from victims to criminals, leaving a net cost of $1.655 trillion or $5284 per capita. To put these numbers into context, the 2012 U.S. gross domestic product was calculated at $16.6334 trillion.[42] The high-level breakdown of these costs (excluding transfers) includes $646 billion for crime-induced production, $253 billion in opportunity costs, and $756 billion in risks to life and health.[43] We now consider each category in detail.

"Crime-induced production" represents "goods and services that would be obsolete in the absence of crime" and totals $646,327,000,000. About half, $300 billion, is spent on private anticrime measures such as security guards; alarm systems; and locks, vaults, and safes. The detailed breakdown is as follows:[44]

Police protection	$113,469 million
Drug trafficking	$84,367 million
Corrections	$81,233 million
Federal agencies	$76,084 million
Computer viruses and security	$53,113 million
State and local judicial and legal services	$42,442 million
Prenatal exposure to cocaine and heroin	$39,946 million
Security systems	$36,441 million
Federal drug control programs	$28,282 million
Medical care for victims	$22,704 million
Security guards and patrol services	$20,239 million
Driving Under the Influence conviction costs to drivers	$14,252 million
Locks, safes, vaults, and locksmiths	$9,426 million
Recovery from vandalism	$8,251 million
Small arms and small arms ammunition	$5,335 million
Protective fences and gates	$3,487 million
Armored car services	$2,524 million
Safety lighting	$1,955 million
Investigation services	$1,920 million
Replacements due to arson	$702 million
Theft insurance (less indemnity)	$68 million
Nonlethal personal defense products	$45 million
Mothers Against Drunk Driving	$42 million

"Opportunity costs" comprise predominantly lost productivity, although these costs include some components that may be both surprising and amusing: $164.5 billion on lost time spent locking and unlocking locks and looking for lost keys (shown in the table as "Time spent securing assets") and $2.389 billion on time spent on the crimes themselves. The detailed breakdown is as follows:[45]

Time spent securing assets	$164,495 million
Criminals' lost workdays in prison	$69,749 million
Criminals' lost workdays planning and executing crimes	$2,389 million
Victims' lost workdays	$14,700 million
Time spent on neighborhood watches	$1,352 million

"Value of risks to life and health" are based on what is known as the "value of a statistical life" (VSL) of $10.05 million and a calculated cost of $74,679 for nonfatal injuries. (The VSL calculation is based on "studies of wage-risk trade-offs made in the labor market" and does not presume to assign a dollar value to human life.)[46] Those costs are as follows:[47]

Value of lost life	$653,509 million
Value of injuries	$102,646 million

The other portion of crime costs is transfers, a euphemism for property and money "transferred" from victims to criminals as a result of criminal acts. The reason transfers are separated is because they are not a "net burden" to society. As Anderson explains the underlying rationale, "Although the purchase of stolen goods often substitutes for the purchase of legal goods, it is also likely that the antecedent theft will lead to an equivalent purchase of legal goods because the victims will replace what they have lost. Thus, it is likely that replacement purchases by victims in the legal market offset legal purchases foregone due to the availability of stolen goods."[48] Transfers break down as follows:[49]

Occupational fraud	$761,635 million
Unpaid taxes	$293,915 million
Health insurance fraud	$183,554 million
Retail fraud	$143,432 million
Telemarketing fraud	$54,875 million
Mail fraud	$51,055 million
Insurance fraud (other than health insurance)	$40,000 million
Shoplifting	$12,380 million
Personal theft	$6,819 million
Household burglary	$5,173 million
Motor vehicle theft	$5,096 million
Coupon fraud	$1,294 million
Business burglary	$1,052 million
Robbery	$727 million

As an examination of these figures will show, what are perceived as serious property crimes (such as robbery, household and business burglary, and auto theft) are actually on the low end of economic losses. Rather, it is the traditional "white-collar" crimes that carry hefty price tags. This should not be particularly surprising, of course, since these crimes tend to be sophisticated, sometimes months or years in duration, and perpetrated by those with extensive knowledge in relevant areas.

Accurately establishing the direct and indirect costs of crime have significance far beyond academic curiosity or government statistics. A simple example involves determining whether increased spending on some component of the criminal justice system is worthwhile from an economic standpoint. Anderson points to prior research that indicates that a 1% increase in police activity produces a 1% reduction in the economic impact of crime (as distinct from a 1% decrease in crime rates). Based on his 2012 study, a 1% increase in policing would cost approximately $1.13 billion, whereas a 1% reduction in the economic impact of crime would produce a benefit of approximately $15.42 billion.[50]

Some authorities have proposed that a similar calculus drives criminal activity. That is, criminals compare the economic value of the transfers produced by their crimes to the costs of committing those crimes and potential arrest, conviction, and punishment. As Anderson explains,

> A rational cost calculation by a potential criminal would include the opportunity cost of time spent planning and carrying out crimes, the cost of fencing operations, and the expected value of time spent in prison. If the marginal crime is similar to the average crime, assuming rationality and full information, the total value of the criminals' gains—loot and psychic benefits—will approximate the value of time and resources devoted to crime.[51]

The weakness of this theory, of course, is whether criminals make—even unconsciously—rational economic decisions along these lines. Personal opinions either way aside, this question has been objectively evaluated. Anderson surveyed 219 offenders from a county jail and a medium security state prison in 2002. Although the sample size was small, the results provided a strong indication: "When their crimes were committed, 77 percent of the inmates either did not think about apprehension or punishment, thought there was no risk of apprehension, or had no idea of the likely punishment if they were convicted. Marginal analysis on the part of criminals could not be performed accurately under any of these circumstances."[52] It would appear that economic analysis may be a valuable part of public discourse on the use of government resources, but altering the economic calculus of crime is unlikely to be an effective counter to the activity of criminals themselves.

U.S. crime trends

To see the general trends in major crime categories, we examine UCR data from the FBI. We also consider some limited anecdotal data going back somewhat further provided by the 2012 Anderson study that illuminates the complexities in taking simple positive or negative percentages at face value.

First, we present a few words on methodology: The FBI collects its data from law enforcement agencies across the country and utilizes the data from those that report at least 6 months in a given year. It also reserves the right to exclude outliers: "When the FBI determines certain variables have created unusual fluctuations in the data, those data are excluded from the trend tabulations."[53] In addition, the agency excluded certain data sets from the 2012 UCR for a variety of reasons:

- Arson data was not used unless the reporting agency submitted data for all 12 months of the year.
- Data from agencies that the FBI judges have not followed UCR guidelines for offense reporting are excluded.
- In two jurisdictions (Rochester, MN and Chicago, IL), the methodology used by local agencies for collecting forcible rape data did not comply with UCR guidelines, so their data for both forcible rape and violent crime (of which forcible rape is a subset) were excluded.
- For the Madison, Wisconsin jurisdiction, "The FBI determined that the agency's data were over-reported," so its data were excluded.[54]

With those considerations in mind, following are the year-over-year percentage changes for the past 4 years in the occurrences of violent crime, property crime, and four major subsets of each.[55]

	Violent Crime	Murder	Forcible Rape	Robbery	Aggravated Assault
2008–2009	−4.4	−10.0	−3.3	−6.5	−3.2
2009–2010	−6.0	−4.2	−5.0	−10.0	−4.1
2010–2011	−4.0	−1.3	−3.8	−3.9	−4.1
2011–2012	+1.2	+1.5	−0.3	+0.6	+1.7
	Property Crime	Burglary	Larceny-Theft	Motor Vehicle Theft	Arson
2008–2009	−6.1	−2.5	−5.3	−18.7	−8.2
2009–2010	−2.7	−2.0	−2.4	−7.4	−7.6
2010–2011	−0.6	+0.4	−0.7	−3.2	−4.7
2011–2012	−0.8	−3.6	Negligible	+1.3	−1.2

However, a decrease in occurrence rates does not necessarily equate to a decrease in the cost of crime. For example, Anderson notes that from 2004 to 2008 personal thefts decreased from 14.2 million annually to 12.3 million, yet the economic loss to victims rose from $5.7 billion to $6.8 billion when both amounts are adjusted for inflation to 2012 values.[56] Similarly, intentionally set structural fires increased to approximately 27,500 in 2010, a 3.8% increase over 2009. The cost of property losses actually decreased to $585 million, a decline of 14.5%, yet civilian deaths increased by 17.7%.[56]

Anderson does caution against assuming that the crime costs calculated in his 1999 study can always be directly compared to those in the 2012 study. Although in some cases previous data sources were used (simply adjusted for inflation if no new data collection had taken place in the interim), in others the sources changed. In others, the agencies used as data sources changed their data collection methods.[56]

Still, in some areas, some broad comparisons can be made. From 1995 to 2010, violent crime dropped sharply: 10.02 million occurrences annually to 3.8 million. Violent crime similarly decreased substantially: 29.5 million occurrences annually to 14.8 million. The costs of combating drug trafficking, arson losses, and robbery losses also fell significantly during the same period.[56]

As we have already seen, however, a decrease in frequency does not necessarily mean a decrease in cost. Substantial increases were seen in medical costs incurred by victims, financial losses from workdays lost due to crime, and vandalism repair. Given the high rates of health-care cost inflation, the increase in medical costs comes as no surprise. The greater cost of lost workdays could be attributed to a few different factors, but a major one is the increase in worker productivity, particularly, thanks to technology in the period under consideration. As for vandalism, the source of higher costs is difficult to discern; it could be the result of more severe incidents or some other less obvious factor. Nevertheless, during that time, the per capita cost of crime fell from $5842 per American to $5284, a decrease of roughly 9.5%.[56]

Summary

Even young children understand intuitively that certain wrongs are worse than others, and people tend to react with innate revulsion to certain crimes—those that involve harm to a child or a pregnant mother (consider the Laci Peterson murder), particularly when a parent is accused of the crime (consider Caylee Anthony), or those committed with an excessive level of brutality.

Yet as the examination of case history regarding statutory language like "heinous," "cruel," "atrocious," "depraved," and others reveals, questions of sentencing or even limitations on constitutional rights that pend on the severity of a given crime must have a more objective basis. The Depravity Scale is the best example of an attempt to create a set of objective factors for assessing severity.

Although it might seem callous to place dollar values on such intangible results of crime as pain and suffering, decisions of governance and the allocation of tax resources must have an objective basis as well. Research such as that conducted by Anderson that assesses the economic impact of crime makes it possible to create realistic cost versus benefit analyses to guide such decisions. There are, in short, numerous sound reasons for objectively judging both the severity and the social impact of crime.

Practicum

1. What are three examples of property crime aside from those mentioned in the text?
2. What are three examples of violent crime aside from those mentioned in the text?
3. In his dissent to *Brinegar v. U.S.*, Justice Jackson wrote that saving a kidnapped child was worth fairly significant infringements on Fourth Amendment rights whereas stopping a smuggler with a dozen cases of liquor was not. Given the substantial number of deaths and significant degree of social harm caused by alcohol, do you agree? Why or why not?
4. The standards of the insanity defense have changed repeatedly over the decades. What do you consider to be a reasonable standard and why?
5. Do you think the death penalty is justifiable for any crimes that do not involve the death of a victim? Why or why not?
6. Common law refuses to recognize any form of verbal offense as "adequate provocation" to mitigate murder, but there have been a few instances in recent jurisprudence that permitted it. Do you feel this is appropriate? Why or why not?
7. Explain your understanding of the distinctions between negligence and recklessness.
8. In the NSCS, the offense of a legislator accepting a $10,000 bribe to vote in a manner favorable to the bribing company received a significantly higher severity rating (16.9) than the same offense with no dollar value specified (13.9). Why do you think this is the case?

Resources

Bureau of Justice Statistics National Crime Victimization Survey, http://www.bjs.gov/index
.cfm?ty=dcdetail&iid=245
Bureau of Justice Statistics National Survey of Crime Severity, http://www.bjs.gov/content/pub/
pdf/nscs.pdf
Federal Bureau of Investigation Uniform Crime Reports, http://www.fbi.gov/about-us/cjis/ucr
David A. Anderson's 2012 Cost of Crime study, http://www.centre.edu/cost_of_crime.pdf

References

1. Mueller, R. S., III. (2013). Table 4: January to December 2011–2012 offenses reported to law
   enforcement by state by city 100,000 and over in population. *Preliminary Annual Uniform Crime
   Report, January–December, 2012*. Washington, DC: Federal Bureau of Investigation. Retrieved
   July 3, 2013, from http://www.fbi.gov/about-us/cjis/ucr/crime-in-the-u.s/2012/preliminary-
   annual-uniform-crime-report-january-december-2012
2. Reid, S. T. (2011, March). *Crime and criminology* (pp. 188–189). New York, NY: Oxford
   University Press. Retrieved July 3, 2013, from http://www.oup.com/us/pdf/reid/Reid_
   Chapter7.pdf
3. Rutledge, W. B. (1949, June 27). *Brinegar v. United States* [majority opinion]. Washington, DC:
   Supreme Court of the United States. Retrieved July 3, 2013, from http://www.law.cornell.edu/
   supct/html/historics/USSC_CR_0338_0160_ZO.html
4. Rutledge, W. B. (1949, June 27). *Brinegar v. United States* [majority opinion]. Washington, DC:
   Supreme Court of the United States. Retrieved July 3, 2013, from http://www.law.cornell.edu/
   supct/html/historics/USSC_CR_0338_0160_ZO.html
5. Jackson, R. H. (1949, June 27). *Brinegar v. United States* [dissenting opinion]. Washington, DC:
   Supreme Court of the United States. Retrieved July 3, 2013, from http://www.law.cornell.edu/
   supct/html/historics/USSC_CR_0338_0160_ZD.html
6. Volokh, E. (2004, October 20). Crime severity and constitutional line-drawing. *Virginia Law
   Review, 90*, 1957, 1959–1960. Retrieved July 3, 2013, from http://www2.law.ucla.edu/volokh/
   severity.pdf
7. Editorial staff (2011, June 29). Reducing unjust cocaine sentences. *The New York Times*. Retrieved
   July 3, 2013, from at http://www.nytimes.com/2011/06/30/opinion/30thu3.html?_r=0
8. Stewart, P. (1978, June 21). *Mincey v. Arizona*. Washington, DC: Supreme Court of the United
   States. Retrieved July 3, 2013, from http://www.law.cornell.edu/supct/html/historics/
   USSC_CR_ 0437_0385_ZS.html
9. White, B. R. (1985, January 15). *New Jersey v. T. L. O.* Washington, DC: Supreme Court of
   the United States. Retrieved July 3, 2013, from http://www.law.cornell.edu/supct/html/
   historics/USSC_CR _ 0469_0325_ZS.html
10. White, B. R. (1972, June 29). *Branzburg v. Hayes*. Washington, DC: Supreme Court of the United
    States. Retrieved July 3, 2013, from http://www.law.cornell.edu/supct/html/historics/
    USSC_CR_0408_ 0665_ZS.html
11. White, B. R. (1972, June 29). *Branzburg v. Hayes* [majority opinion]. Washington, DC: Supreme
    Court of the United States. Retrieved from http://www.law.cornell.edu/supct/html/historics/
    USSC_CR_0408_0665_ZO.html
12. White, B. R. (1985, March 27). *Tennessee v. Garner*. Washington, DC: Supreme Court of the
    United States. Retrieved from http://supreme.justia.com/cases/federal/us/471/1/case.html
13. White, B. R. (1977, June 29). *Coker v. Georgia*. Washington, DC: Supreme Court of the
    United States. Retrieved from http://www.law.cornell.edu/supct/html/historics/USSC_
    CR_0433_0584_ZS.html
14. Volokh, p. 1968.
15. Colb, S. F. (2003, September 10). Is capital punishment too harsh for rapists? A Louisiana
    jury sentences a child's rapist to death. Retrieved from http://writ.corporate.findlaw.com/
    colb/20030910.html

16. Volokh, p. 1971.
17. White, B. R. (1968, May 20). *Duncan v. Louisiana.* Washington, DC: Supreme Court of the United States. Retrieved from http://www.law.cornell.edu/supct/html/historics/USSC_CR_0391_0145_ZO.html
18. White, B. R. (1968, May 20). *Duncan v. Louisiana.* Washington, DC: Supreme Court of the United States. Retrieved from http://www.law.cornell.edu/supct/html/historics/USSC_CR_0391_0145_ZO.html
19. White, B. R. (1968, May 20). *Duncan v. Louisiana.* Washington, DC: Supreme Court of the United States. Retrieved from http://www.law.cornell.edu/supct/html/historics/USSC_CR_0391_0145_ZO.html
20. Volokh, p. 1973.
21. Volokh, p. 1974.
22. The American Law Institute Council. (1962). *Model penal code.* Philadelphia, PA: The American Law Institute. Retrieved from http://www.ali.org/index .cfm?fuseaction=publications.ppage&node_id=92
23. Colbert, D. (2010). *Criminal law* (p. 4) [course outline]. Baltimore: University of Maryland Francis King Carey School of Law. Retrieved from https://www.google.com/url?sa=t&rct=j&q=&esrc=s&source=web&cd=4&ved=0CFgQFjAD&url=http%3A%2F%2Fwww.law.umaryland.edu%2Fstudents%2Flife%2Forgs%2Fsba%2Fdocuments%2Foutlines%2Fcrimlaw%2Fcrimlaw_colbert .doc&ei=C6IGUqjJCsLV2AWngYGQBQ&usg=AFQjCNEemOSEHTdvufFupG4A0W3BTlJbXg&sig2=JteSf75lktoVUTO8TW_-Pw&bvm=bv.50500085,d.aWc&cad=rja
24. Colbert, D. (2010). *Criminal law* (p. 1) [course outline]. Baltimore: University of Maryland Francis King Carey School of Law. Retrieved from https://www.google.com/url?sa=t&rct=j&q=&esrc=s&source=web&cd=4&ved=0CFgQFjAD&url=http%3A%2F%2Fwww.law.umaryland.edu%2Fstudents%2Flife%2Forgs%2Fsba%2Fdocuments%2Foutlines%2Fcrimlaw%2Fcrimlaw_colbert .doc&ei=C6IGUqjJCsLV2AWngYGQBQ&usg=AFQjCNEemOSEHTdvufFupG4A0W3BTlJbXg&sig2=JteSf75lktoVUTO8TW_-Pw&bvm=bv.50500085,d.aWc&cad=rja
25. Colbert, D. (2010). *Criminal law* (p. 8) [course outline]. Baltimore: University of Maryland Francis King Carey School of Law. Retrieved from https://www.google.com/url?sa=t&rct=j&q=&esrc=s&source=web&cd=4&ved=0CFgQFjAD&url=http%3A%2F%2Fwww.law.umaryland.edu%2Fstudents%2Flife%2Forgs%2Fsba%2Fdocuments%2Foutlines%2Fcrimlaw%2Fcrimlaw_colbert .doc&ei=C6IGUqjJCsLV2AWngYGQBQ&usg=AFQjCNEemOSEHTdvufFupG4A0W3BTlJbXg&sig2=JteSf75lktoVUTO8TW_-Pw&bvm=bv.50500085,d.aWc&cad=rja
26. Colbert, D. (2010). *Criminal law* (p. 2) [course outline]. Baltimore: University of Maryland Francis King Carey School of Law. Retrieved from https://www.google.com/url?sa=t&rct=j&q=&esrc=s&source=web&cd=4&ved=0CFgQFjAD&url=http%3A%2F%2Fwww.law.umaryland.edu%2Fstudents%2Flife%2Forgs%2Fsba%2Fdocuments%2Foutlines%2Fcrimlaw%2Fcrimlaw_colbert .doc&ei=C6IGUqjJCsLV2AWngYGQBQ&usg=AFQjCNEemOSEHTdvufFupG4A0W3BTlJbXg&sig2=JteSf75lktoVUTO8TW_-Pw&bvm=bv.50500085,d.aWc&cad=rja
27. Colbert, D. (2010). *Criminal law* (p. 2) [course outline]. Baltimore: University of Maryland Francis King Carey School of Law. Retrieved from https://www.google.com/url?sa=t&rct=j&q=&esrc=s&source=web&cd=4&ved=0CFgQFjAD&url=http%3A%2F%2Fwww.law.umaryland.edu%2Fstudents%2Flife%2Forgs%2Fsba%2Fdocuments%2Foutlines%2Fcrimlaw%2Fcrimlaw_colbert .doc&ei=C6IGUqjJCsLV2AWngYGQBQ&usg=AFQjCNEemOSEHTdvufFupG4A0W3BTlJbXg&sig2=JteSf75lktoVUTO8TW_-Pw&bvm=bv.50500085,d.aWc&cad=rja
28. The "insanity defense" and diminished capacity. (2012). Legal Information Institute. *Cornell Law School.* Retrieved from http://www.law.cornell.edu/background/insane/insanity.html
29. Lee, S. (2010). The Durham standard. *The history of the insanity plea.* Fredericksburg, VA: University of Mary Washington. Retrieved from http://insanityplea.umwblogs.org/standards/the-durham-standard/
30. The "insanity defense" and diminished capacity. Legal Information Institute. *Cornell Law School.* Retrieved from http://www.cornell.edu/background/insane/insanity.html
31. Colbert. University of Maryland. Retrieved from http://www.law.umaryland.edu/students/life/orgs/sba/outlines.html

32. Wolfgang, M. E., Figlio, R. M., Tracy, P. E., & Singer, S. I. (1985, June). *The national survey of crime severity* (pp. vi–vii). Philadelphia: The Center for Studies in Criminology and Criminal Law, The Wharton School, University of Pennsylvania. Retrieved from http://www.bjs.gov/content/pub/pdf/nscs.pdf

33. Wolfgang, M. E., Figlio, R. M., Tracy, P. E., & Singer, S. I. (1985, June). *The national survey of crime severity* (p. vi). Philadelphia: The Center for Studies in Criminology and Criminal Law, The Wharton School, University of Pennsylvania. Retrieved from http://www.bjs.gov/content/pub/pdf/nscs.pdf

34. Wolfgang, M. E., Figlio, R. M., Tracy, P. E., & Singer, S. I. (1985, June). *The national survey of crime severity* (p. vi). Philadelphia: The Center for Studies in Criminology and Criminal Law, The Wharton School, University of Pennsylvania. Retrieved from http://www.bjs.gov/content/pub/pdf/nscs.pdf

35. Wolfgang, M. E., Figlio, R. M., Tracy, P. E., & Singer, S. I. (1985, June). *The national survey of crime severity* (pp. vi, x). Philadelphia: The Center for Studies in Criminology and Criminal Law, The Wharton School, University of Pennsylvania. Retrieved from http://www.bjs.gov/content/pub/pdf/nscs.pdf

36. Wolfgang, M. E., Figlio, R. M., Tracy, P. E., & Singer, S. I. (1985, June). *The national survey of crime severity* (pp. vi–x). Philadelphia: The Center for Studies in Criminology and Criminal Law, The Wharton School, University of Pennsylvania. Retrieved from http://www.bjs.gov/content/pub/pdf/nscs.pdf

37. Welner, M. (2006). Classifying crimes by severity: From aggravators to depravity. *The Forensic Panel*, 3. Retrieved from https://depravityscale.org/depscale/documents/classifying-crimes-welner.pdf

38. Stewart, P. (1976, July 2). *Gregg v. Georgia* [majority opinion]. Washington, DC: Supreme Court of the United States. Retrieved from http://www.law.cornell.edu/supct/html/historics/USSC_CR_0428_0153_ZO.html

39. White, B. R. (1990, June 27). *Walton v. Arizona* [majority opinion]. Washington, DC: Supreme Court of the United States. Retrieved from http://www.law.cornell.edu/supct/html/88-7351.ZO.html

40. Stewart, P. (1980, May 19). *Godfrey v. Georgia* [majority opinion]. Washington, DC: Supreme Court of the United States. Retrieved from http://supreme.justia.com/cases/federal/us/446/420/case.html

41. Taylor, R. (1995, May). The impact of crime on communities. *Annals of the American Academy of Political and Social Science, 539.* Cited by Shapiro, E. (1999, August). *Cost of crime: A review of the research studies* (p. 11). St. Paul, MN: Minnesota House of Representatives Research Department. Retrieved from http://www.house.leg.state.mn.us/hrd/pubs/costcrime.pdf

42. Bureau of Economic Analysis (2013, July 31). *National income and product accounts*. Washington, DC: Department of Commerce. Retrieved from http://www.bea.gov/newsreleases/national/gdp/gdpnewsrelease.htm

43. Anderson, D. A. (2012). The cost of crime. *Foundations and Trends in Microeconomics, 7*(3), 249. Retrieved from http://www.centre.edu/cost_of_crime.pdf

44. Anderson, D. A. (2012). The cost of crime. *Foundations and Trends in Microeconomics, 7*(3), 244–245. Retrieved from http://www.centre.edu/cost_of_crime.pdf

45. Anderson, D. A. (2012). The cost of crime. *Foundations and Trends in Microeconomics, 7*(3), 247–248. Retrieved from http://www.centre.edu/cost_of_crime.pdf

46. Anderson, D. A. (2012). The cost of crime. *Foundations and Trends in Microeconomics, 7*(3), 236. Retrieved from http://www.centre.edu/cost_of_crime.pdf

47. Anderson, D. A. (2012). The cost of crime. *Foundations and Trends in Microeconomics, 7*(3), 248. Retrieved from http://www.centre.edu/cost_of_crime.pdf

48. Anderson, D. A. (2012). The cost of crime. *Foundations and Trends in Microeconomics, 7*(3), 223. Retrieved from http://www.centre.edu/cost_of_crime.pdf

49. Anderson, D. A. (2012). The cost of crime. *Foundations and Trends in Microeconomics, 7*(3), 249. Retrieved from http://www.centre.edu/cost_of_crime.pdf

50. Anderson, D. A. (2012). The cost of crime. *Foundations and Trends in Microeconomics, 7*(3), 251. Retrieved from http://www.centre.edu/cost_of_crime.pdf

51. Anderson, D. A. (2012). The cost of crime. *Foundations and Trends in Microeconomics, 7*(3), 252. Retrieved from http://www.centre.edu/cost_of_crime.pdf

52. Anderson, D. A. (2012). The cost of crime. *Foundations and Trends in Microeconomics, 7*(3), 252. Retrieved from http://www.centre.edu/cost_of_crime.pdf

53. Mueller, R. S., III. (2013). Table 3 data declaration. *Preliminary Annual Uniform Crime Report, January–December, 2012.* Washington, DC: Federal Bureau of Investigation. Retrieved from http://www.fbi.gov/about-us/cjis/ucr/crime-in-the-u.s/2012/preliminary-annual-uniform-crime-report-january-december-2012/tables/table_3_percent_change_for_consecutive_years_2012.xls/@@template-layout-view?override-view=data-declaration

54. Mueller, R. S., III. (2013). *Table 4 data declaration. Preliminary Annual Uniform Crime Report, January–December, 2012.* Washington, DC: Federal Bureau of Investigation. Retrieved from http://www.fbi.gov/about-us/cjis/ucr/crime-in-the-u.s/2012/crime-in-the-u.s.-2012/tables/4tabledatadecoverviewpdf/table_4_crime_in_the_united_states_by_region_geographic_division_and_state_2011-2012.xls/@@template-layout-view?override-view=data-declaration

55. Mueller, R. S., III. (2013). Table 3: January to December 2011–2012 percent change for consecutive years. *Preliminary Annual Uniform Crime Report, January–December, 2012.* Washington, DC: Federal Bureau of Investigation. Retrieved from http://www.fbi.gov/about-us/cjis/ucr/crime-in-the-u.s/2012/preliminary-annual-uniform-crime-report-january-december-2012/tables/table_3_percent_change_for_consecutive_years_2012.xls

56. Anderson, D. A. (2012). The cost of crime. Foundations and Trends in *Microeconomics, 7*(3). Retrieved from http://www.centre.edu/cost_of_crime.pdf

chapter eleven

Government- and business-related crimes

Chapter objectives

After studying this chapter, you should understand and be able to explain

- The nature of wrongdoing by government agencies and individuals within the government
- How individuals and governments commit fraud against the government
- The nature of modern cybercrime and the organizations that perpetrate it
- The legal complications involved in combating terrorism and why terrorism falls into a gray area between law enforcement and warfare
- How law enforcement handles criminal violations by corporations
- The nature of white-collar crime
- The nature and history of organized crime in the United States

Introduction

Crime at its most basic level is committed by an individual against an individual. In the broadest sense, crime dates to prehistoric man, although in the absence of any mutually agreed (or societally imposed) code of conduct from a strict semantic standpoint a "crime" cannot be committed. (Remember, an act that is unethical or immoral is not necessarily illegal.) However, the earliest set of laws—the Code of Hammurabi, dating to approximately 1780 bc—includes extensive regulations governing commerce, down to setting the rental rates for oxen, carts, ferries, and freight boats and the reimbursements for very specific damages to such rented property.[1] Judging from the number of statutes governing business matters, this must have been an area with substantial potential for conflict.

Of course, once governments were established to impose and maintain order (in part through the creation and enforcement of laws), it became necessary to finance their operations. As time progressed and governments became increasingly sophisticated, they began purchasing goods and services; later still, they began to make various types of largesse available to certain members of the public, particularly the disadvantaged. All of this created the need for additional laws and opportunities for criminal acts: avoiding taxes or other financial obligations, selling substandard or overpriced goods to the government, or obtaining benefits under false pretenses.

Today, the blurred lines that exist between governments and so-called nonstate actors have created the possibility of criminal acts sponsored (directly or indirectly) by governments. Terrorism by nonstate actors has also opened a Pandora's box of legal complexities related to how national governments deal with such acts.

In this chapter, we consider the spectrum of government- and business-related crimes. That includes crimes committed against the government both by individual and corporate actors and by individuals within the government. We also consider crimes defined by various standards as "white-collar crime." As recent events such as the 2010 Deepwater Horizon oil spill have demonstrated, even corporations can be accused of crimes. Finally, we consider two areas of criminal activity that might at first glance seem only marginally relevant: cybercrime and organized crime. Cybercrime targets predominantly governments and businesses, and organized criminal activity often uses legitimate or semilegitimate business fronts for money laundering and other purposes.

Government misconduct and whistle-blowing

It was the English historian Lord John Acton who gave us the aphorism about power and corruption in 1887, although his original quote is often shortened: "Power tends to corrupt, and absolute power corrupts absolutely. Great men are almost always bad men...."[2] Leaving aside his judgments regarding great men, it should be no surprise to anyone that those with access to power will occasionally abuse it. This sad fact is not limited to tyrants and dictators; although the pillaging of national wealth by the likes of Saddam Hussein made headlines, most government misconduct takes place at much lower levels.

A criminal act by someone within the government (and acting in an official capacity or using their authority for illegitimate ends) nearly always has one of two ends: money or power. Criminal pursuit of power is the stuff of movies and novels, but in the United States at least this motive is actually rare.

The quintessential example of a power-related crime is the Watergate scandal. To summarize the events, in June 1972, three men were arrested for the burglary of the Democratic National Committee Washington office, housed in the Watergate office complex. The point of the break-in, it turned out, was actually to plant listening devices in the office. One of the men, James McCord, was subsequently revealed to be on the payroll of the Nixon reelection campaign. In addition, $25,000 in campaign funds had been paid to one of the burglars. E. Howard Hunt, formerly of the Central Intelligence Agency (CIA), and G. Gordon Liddy, formerly of the Federal Bureau of Investigation (FBI), were indicted, tried, and convicted for assisting the break-in by guiding the burglars through radio from a hotel across from the Watergate building.

The investigation would ultimately result in the prosecution of four senior Nixon administration officials for perjury and obstruction of justice: John Ehrlichman, Nixon's chief advisor on domestic policy; John Dean, a White House legal advisor; H. R. Haldeman, Nixon's chief of staff; and Richard Kleindienst, the Attorney General. In addition, former Secretary of Commerce (and at the time of the break-in a main Nixon fund-raiser) Maurice Stans was linked to the funds paid to the burglar. The *Washington Post*, which had run most of the lead coverage of the scandal, contended that the White House had threatened and harassed the paper, and it was subsequently learned that the day after the newspaper broke the story, Nixon and Haldeman explored how they might have the CIA exert pressure on the FBI to pursue the investigation less zealously.[3]

It is far more common to see those in government attempt to use their office or position to enrich themselves than to garner power, however. At the most basic level, this can be, for example, the law enforcement officer who accepts a bribe or takes some of the cash discovered in a raid, or the bureaucrat who accepts a payment or other bribe to "smooth" (or ignore) a licensing, regulatory, or similar process. But all too often, it seems as though the most substantial crimes are committed by those with significant power.

A high-profile example of this type of government misconduct is former Illinois governor Rod Blagojevich, sentenced to 14 years in prison for 18 counts of corruption. His most publicized misdeed was the virtual auctioning of the U.S. Senate seat vacated by President Barack Obama.[4] However, Blagojevich engaged in what one journalist described as seeking "financial gain in nearly every element of government work, from picking members of state commissions to signing legislation." Other significant allegations included proposed financial compensation of one sort or another in return for approving racetrack-related legislation, releasing grant money to a school, and funding a hospital.[5]

There is no shortage of examples of public officials using their power to build wealth. In 1888, the Kentucky treasurer, James Williams Tate, vanished shortly before the $150,000 in state funds he had embezzled came to light. James "Jimmy" John Walker, mayor of New York City, resigned in 1932 to avoid impeachment and prosecution for corruption, and Vice President Spiro T. Agnew left the Nixon administration in 1973 as part of a deal to avoid federal prosecution for bribery and extortion committed while he had been a county executive and governor in Maryland.

Some officials were clever enough to make it through their entire political career without getting caught. Harold G. Hoffman, a congressman and governor of New Jersey, confessed posthumously (through a letter deposited with his daughter) to embezzling $300,000 from a bank and as much as $50,000 a month as commissioner of motor vehicles. Chicago mayor William Hale Thompson died in 1944, and when two of his safe deposit boxes were opened, they turned up $1.5 million in cash. Illinois secretary of state Paul Powell died in 1970 in a hotel room with his personal secretary (who was not, needless to say, his wife); subsequent investigation revealed the proceeds of a long career of bribery and kickbacks, including $200,000 in coins taken from vending machines in the state capitol building.[6]

Naturally, government agencies are well aware of the potential for corruption and other misconduct. Within the federal government (the model is similar, if more limited, at the state and local levels), there are several avenues for reporting misconduct by government employees and officials. The Office of Government Ethics, which is part of the executive branch, perhaps surprisingly has no "investigative or prosecutorial authority," nor does it deal with complaints.[7] Rather, it is charged with "promulgating and maintaining enforceable standards of ethical conduct" for employees of executive branch agencies, overseeing the financial disclosure system, and keeping ethics programs compliant with federal laws and regulations, in addition to public outreach, ethics training, and technical assistance to "state, local, and foreign governments and international organizations."[8]

For executive branch agencies, the primary responsibility for investigating misconduct falls to the agency's Office of the Inspector General (IG). IGs are charged primarily to "detect and prevent fraud, waste, abuse, and violations of the law and to promote economy, efficiency, and effectiveness in the operations of the Federal Government." Formally established by the Inspector General Act of 1978 (as subsequently amended) and the IG Reform Act of 2008, IG offices now exist in 73 agencies.[9] As their mission implies, IG offices tend to focus more on wasteful practices and the failure of agencies to be responsive to their clients. Criminal acts are certainly within their purview, but more serious crimes are typically investigated by the FBI.

Observers are sometimes cynical about IG investigations because these offices are part of the agency they are investigating. This leads to a legitimate wonder about "who watches the watchers." (Pity the poor IG staffs; they are typically not exactly the most popular members of their agencies while simultaneously facing questions about their effectiveness from outsiders.) Having an outside agency come in to investigate when matters are serious helps eliminate this stigma.

Federal law enforcement agencies that are part of the Department of Justice (DOJ), as well as DOJ attorneys, fall under the jurisdiction of the Office of Professional Responsibility (OPR). (The department does have its own IG office as well.) In this case, DOJ attorneys are subject to OPR when "accused of engaging in misconduct in connection with their duties to investigate, litigate, or provide legal advice."[7] Other types of alleged misconduct are instead handled by the Legal Counsel's Office in the Executive Office for U.S. Attorneys. Wardens and correctional staff of federal prisons are investigated by the Office of Internal Affairs of the Bureau of Prisons.

In the judicial branch, allegations of misconduct are reported to the office of the Clerk of the U.S. Court of Appeals for the circuit where the judge in question presides. In the legislative branch, senators fall under the responsibility of the Senate Select Committee on Ethics. Representatives are investigated by the House Committee on Ethics or the Office of Congressional Ethics.

It is one thing for a concerned (or aggrieved) citizen to complain about an unresponsive agency or suspicions of criminal acts. However, much of what happens inside government is hidden from the view of outsiders. That means revelations of misconduct often must come from those on the inside: the "whistle-blowers."

Of course, for someone to report wrongdoing by coworkers or even a supervisor and thereby put their livelihood at risk takes courage. The first effort at protecting federal workers came in 1989 with the Whistleblower Protection Act (WPA). However, the statute was (in the opinion of many experts) poorly written, making whistle-blowers ineligible for protection if they were not the first person to disclose misconduct, made their disclosure to a supervisor or coworker, revealed the consequences of a policy decision, or were still performing their job when they made the disclosure.[10] Moreover, judicial action over the years further eroded WPA protections. From 1994 until June 2012, administrative hearing outcomes at the Merit Systems Protection Board (MSPB) were 3 in favor of whistle-blowers and 224 against. Analysis of MSPB data showed that by 2010, federal whistle-blowers were nine times more likely to be fired than they were in 1992.[11]

The Congressional response was the Whistleblower Protection Enhancement Act (WPEA) of 2012. The legislation was introduced in four congressional sessions before finally passing (by unanimous votes in both chambers) in the autumn of 2012. The WPEA significantly expanded protections for whistle-blowers and simplified the process of disciplining those found to have illegally retaliated against them. It also imposes restrictions on the limitations on whistle-blowing that can be justified by national security concerns.[12]

Finally, there are some advocates who claim that systemic misconduct within the criminal justice system has resulted (and continues to result) in wrongful convictions. While honest mistakes are acknowledged, they claim that deliberate acts on the part of some law enforcement personnel and prosecutors are unacceptably common. Examples of such alleged law enforcement misconduct include coercing false confessions, deceiving jurors, influencing witnesses, withholding evidence, and soliciting unreliable evidence from confidential informants. On the prosecutorial side, allegations include withholding, mishandling, or destroying evidence; using witnesses known to be unreliable; presenting inaccurate forensic evidence; and discouraging defense witnesses from testifying.[13]

Individual fraud and the government

It was President Franklin D. Roosevelt who, as the nation wallowed in the grip of the Great Depression, created the foundations of the modern welfare state. As originally conceived, these programs were intended as a social safety net to protect the most vulnerable. (Although few realize it today, the formal name of Social Security was Old Age, Survivors, and Disability Insurance—hence the abbreviation OASDI in the deductions section of many pay stubs.) However, once "free money" is available, inevitably a few will attempt to obtain something to which they are not entitled.

The Social Security Disability Insurance (SSDI) program is one seen as particularly vulnerable. A 2012 report from the Senate Permanent Subcommittee on Investigations reviewed 300 SSDI awards and found that in over one-quarter of them, the award of benefits "failed to properly address insufficient, contradictory, or incomplete evidence." The report also cites Social Security Administration (SSA) internal review data that similarly found a 22% error rate in disability award decisions.[14]

In August 2011, 10.614 million SSDI beneficiaries received $128.9 billion in payments. Using the SSA's lower error rate of 22% indicates approximately $28.358 billion in fraudulent (or at least unjustified) benefits. Most beneficiaries remain in the program, too: In 2011, only 12.4% terminated benefits for medical improvement, return to work, or "other" causes. The vast majority reached full retirement age (51.7%) or died (36.1%).[15]

Other common forms of individual fraud include making false claims and failing to accurately disclose information in applying for benefits. Major disasters create ample opportunity for false benefit claims. The Government Accountability Office estimated in 2006 that "improper and potentially fraudulent individual assistance payments" made by relief programs for Hurricanes Katrina and Rita totaled between $600 million and $1.4 billion, a fraud rate of about 16%.[16] Given the magnitude of the relief programs for these storms, prosecutions continued for years. For example, a New Orleans man was convicted on November 8, 2011, for fraudulently obtaining almost $25,000 from the Federal Emergency Management Agency in September 2005 and sentenced to 2 years and 2 months in prison.[17]

Many federal benefit programs such as the Supplemental Nutrition Assistance Program (SNAP) and the Department of Housing and Urban Development's Section 8 housing assistance program are means-tested, meaning eligibility is based on a combination of family size and household income. Fraudulent disclosure is accomplished by concealing or falsifying income, misreporting family size, and similar methods.

SNAP was particularly subject to fraud when the benefit was issued as paper "food stamps," as retailers and others would accept them as cash (albeit at a discounted face value) or in payment for prohibited items such as alcohol, tobacco, and lottery tickets. SNAP was converted to an Electronic Benefit Transfer system in part to combat fraud. Although this measure has helped somewhat, it is still possible to defraud the system. Typically a retailer will process a sale transaction in which no merchandise actually changes hands. The retailer gives the beneficiary cash equal to a percentage of the "sale" and in turn receives reimbursement from the U.S. Department of Agriculture (USDA).

Fortunately, the electronic trail does make it easier to trace fraud as funds make their way through the banking system. The USDA reported 782,945 fraud investigations in fiscal 2010 (conducted by state agencies, since the program is administered through the states) that resulted in the disqualification of 44,483 beneficiaries and the recoupment of $287 million ($67.2 million of which was obtained fraudulently). The USDA says that the SNAP fraud rate has been reduced from 4% to 1%.[18]

Fraud by an individual against the federal government is covered by various sections of Title 18 USC, Part I, Chapter 47. For example, § 1040 addresses "Fraud in connection with major disaster or emergency benefits," and § 1014 deals with "Loan and credit applications generally; renewals and discounts; crop insurance." Penalties vary, but for the statutes cited here are a fine and/or up to 30 years in prison (§ 1040) and a fine of up to $1 million and/or up to 30 years in prison (§ 1014).[19]

Business fraud and the government

If the benefits available to individuals prompt people to attempt to defraud the government, the money potentially involved in doing business with the government has produced some truly epic schemes. In addition to the tremendous sums the government spends on supplies ranging from paper clips to fighter planes, in many cases the procurement standards are quite exacting and preclude the use of off-the-shelf items. This is particularly true when it comes to that bonanza of government spending: defense contracting.

Fraud by defense contractors became notorious during the Civil War, starting from the opening days of the conflict. The U.S. Army paid for uniforms that literally fell apart in the rain, firearms that would not fire, munitions filled with sawdust instead of gunpowder, and horses and mules that were old, lame, and on occasion blind as well.[20] Unconscionable though it might be, a shameful number of suppliers were more than willing to fulfill their contracts with goods only charitably described as "substandard."

This was the first major war for the United States as a nation, so no systems or laws were in place to detect and prevent military procurement fraud. Moreover, in some cases, members of the military were also involved, willing to enrich themselves at the expense of the war effort and those on the front lines. The first effort at enforcement was the creation of the Select Committee on Government Contracts at the behest (and under the chairmanship) of Charles Van Wyck, a congressman from New York, in July 1861. The committee forged ahead with its investigations, holding numerous hearings, interviewing hundreds of witnesses, and eventually issuing three reports totaling over 3000 pages.[21]

Its findings were a catalog of infamy. Both the Department of War and the Department of the Navy had routinely awarded bids not through a public announcement process to the lowest bidder but to cronies of the secretaries, Simon Cameron and Gideon Welles. The Navy used private agents compensated by commission to purchase ships—some of which proved to be not even seaworthy. Major Justus McKinstry, the quartermaster of the Western Department, was eventually court-martialed on 63 counts related to bribery and fraud based on the committee's findings. Some members of the government attacked the committee—some in defense of their political turf and others because they did not find the committee to be zealous enough—but public outrage (some stemming from complaints from soldiers in letters home) kept it alive.[22]

Finally, Congress took direct action. On March 2, 1863—the final day of the congressional session—the Federal Civil False Claims Act (FCFCA) was passed. It established what were for the time especially harsh financial penalties: up to $5000, plus twice the amount defrauded plus $2000 per claim. Prison time was also an option. At the time, the DOJ did not exist, nor did any significant federal law enforcement. As such, the law was written with a *qui tam* (Latin for "who as well," shorthand for "he who prosecutes for himself as well as the king") provision that enabled a private citizen—a whistle-blower—to bring suit against a person or company alleged to have committed fraud against the government. Significantly, the *qui tam* principle entitles the whistle-blower to a portion of what is recovered. This provides an incentive for those who may be aware of wrongdoing to disclose it.

The FCFCA was substantially weakened during World War II, but in 1986, the law was amended and strengthened. Since that time, it has produced over $20 billion in recovered funds and penalties, to say nothing of its probable deterrent effect.[23]

Fraud in government contracting takes several common forms. A basic one—the sort seen so often during the Civil War—is product substitution. In this case, the contractor provides a substandard product or includes substandard components. "Substandard" may simply mean foreign-made in some cases; contracts (particularly defense contracts) mandate that all components be made domestically. A similar violation is failing to comply with contract specifications. Those specifications do not only address components; they may also require specific manufacturing or testing procedures.

Improper cost allocation is a form of creative accounting. For example, the contractor may allocate portions of its overhead costs not legitimately associated with fulfilling the contract to what it charges the government. In the most egregious cases, the contractor may bill the government for work done for other clients. Cross-charging takes places when a contractor has multiple government contracts, some fixed cost, and some cost-plus. The contractor takes expenses associated with fulfillment of the fixed cost contract and charges them to the cost-plus contracts. Finally, there is another law governing government contracting: the Truth in Negotiations Act. In simple terms, a contractor that is a sole supplier of a given product cannot charge the government more than it charges other clients (assuming the specifications are the same, of course).

Such fraud is not the sole purview of defense contractors, either. In 2010, an interior designer hired to decorate the new Washington headquarters of Immigration and Customs Enforcement pled guilty to a felony charge of conspiracy to defraud the government. She was alleged to have misrepresented contractors as company employees, lied about their qualifications, and created false documents to substantiate those claims to secure a $1.3 million contract through the General Services Administration. The maximum penalty was a $250,000 fine and 5 years in prison.

A variety of statutes address business fraud against the government. When more than one person is involved, by definition a conspiracy exists. Title 18 USC § 286, for example, establishes penalties for conspiracy to defraud the government with respect to claims: a fine and/or imprisonment for up to 10 years. While the potential for illicit profits is tremendous—even for interior designers—getting caught carries a stiff price.

Cybercrime

Cybercrime might not seem to belong in the midst of a discussion about government- and business-related crimes. A decade ago, that would probably have been true. However, as cybercrime and cybercriminals have become more sophisticated, the focus of their efforts has shifted, "focusing less on theft of financial information and more on business espionage and accessing government information."[24] While individuals certainly suffer financially from cybercrime, businesses and governments are exposed to losses far more significant.

Cybercrime falls into nine major categories:

1. Viruses and worms: The first form of major cybercrime, debuting when an e-mail-borne virus infected almost 45 million computers around the world in 2000, viruses and worms are self-contained (and usually self-replicating) computer programs. While some are merely malicious, others duplicate information stored on the system and may transmit it to the software's author or another destination.
2. Spam: The most prevalent form of cybercrime, spam is unsolicited e-mail. In most cases, it advertises something for sale, although spam can be the vehicle for other forms of attack such as phishing. Despite aggressive efforts at filtering and blocking spam, it continues to increase. In 2010, spam increased worldwide 1.4% over 2009 to an overall rate of 89.1%—yes, on average 9 of every 10 e-mails is spam. In 2010, Italy suffered the highest spam rate at 94%.

3. Trojans: A specific type of virus, like its namesake the Trojan looks legitimate. While it may perform whatever function it purports to have, unknown to the user it also takes other actions. Common Trojans are keyloggers that steal user name and password information or those that open a "backdoor" to give the author access to the infected computer. Some simply destroy data.

4. Malware: Sometimes the term "malware" is used as a general name for harmful computer programs including viruses, worms, and Trojans. Used more specifically, the term refers to software that takes control of a computer (without the user's knowledge, of course) for the purpose of gaining access to a network or to create a "bot," a computer used to generate spam or spread various types of malware as part of a "botnet."

5. Scareware: Some harmful software comes disguised as something beneficial, often an antivirus program. The name "scareware" derives from the fact that the software usually warns the user of some dire event, typically a serious infection of the computer, and prompts them to download and install the program. That program is of course the harmful software. To add insult to injury, many scareware authors require the victim to pay for removal of the malware by "purchasing" or "subscribing to" the supposed antivirus software.

6. Denial of service (DoS): The DoS or sometimes distributed denial of service attack is aimed at websites or in some cases networks in an attempt to shut them down. Typically, these attacks flood the site or network with repeated requests for access, overloading and "crashing" them.

7. Phishing: The phishing attack, normally mounted by e-mail, attempts to mislead the victim by posing as a legitimate communication from an official source such as a bank or credit card company. Typically these warn of some problem and ask the recipient to confirm critical information such as passwords, account numbers, or Social Security numbers. The most effective attacks are tailored to the victim, such as originating with an organization of which the recipient is a member or a bank of which they are a customer, and are called "spear phishing."

8. Fiscal fraud: These attacks are normally aimed at government channels such as tax payment websites in an attempt to stop tax collection, or as a means of attempting to fraudulently claim government benefits.

9. Carders: Cybercriminals specializing in carding often use one or more of the tools mentioned here, such as Trojans or phishing, to collect credit card numbers. These valid account numbers can then be loaded onto blank cards and used to make purchases or obtain cash.

Some authorities add a 10th category: state cyberattacks. These are state-sponsored or state-sanctioned illicit cyberactivities intended to achieve various ends, and for that reason they blur the lines among crime, terrorism, espionage, and acts of war. This category is discussed in the section "Government-sponsored crime and terrorism."

From 2008 to 2009, the financial losses to cybercrime in the United States more than doubled from $265 million to $560 million (and this is only what was reported). The threat is not only from traditional cybercriminals; a departing employee seeking financial gain or simply revenge can use his or her knowledge to cause serious damage. In fact, a survey of businesses by global accounting and consulting firm KPMG revealed that almost two-thirds of respondents had serious concerns about three specific types of internally originated cybercrime: theft of customer or employee data by an insider or ex-employee, deliberate exploitation of weak points in business processes or systems by a knowledgeable insider or ex-employee, and theft of intellectual property or sensitive business data by an insider or ex-employee.[25]

The costs of cybercrime are far more than simply direct losses. The very real and substantial threat requires companies and governments to take extensive defensive and preventive measures such as antivirus software, firewalls, IT security procedures, and even insurance. Such measures are estimated to account for nearly half of the approximately $43 billion lost to cybercrime annually in the United Kingdom, for example. (Loss of intellectual property accounts for about $14 billion and espionage for about $11–$12 billion.)[26]

There are also indirect costs. Business operations can be interrupted by substantial attacks or disruptions. Data lost to damage or theft can set back research and development by weeks, months, or years. Stolen intellectual property can deprive a company of income or a return on its development costs. When customer or employee data are compromised, a company's reputation can suffer, and such losses often result in the need to compensate victims or pay for identity theft monitoring, to say nothing of the possibility of fines imposed by regulatory agencies.

While it might seem likely that most business-related cybercrime targets major corporations, research does not bear out that assumption. A report from Verizon recorded 621 confirmed incidents of data breach in 2012, and of those almost half targeted companies with less than 1000 employees. Almost a third—193—took place at companies with less than 100 employees. A similar report from computer security company Symantec indicated that 31% of cyberattacks in 2012 victimized companies with less than 250 employees, an increase of 18% over 2011.[27] Moreover, *The Wall Street Journal* has reported that almost 60% of small businesses will close within 6 months of a cyberattack because of the substantial financial impact.[28]

It is a simple matter of risk: Small companies rarely have the resources to implement a full-scale security solution comparable to what is within the capabilities of an Apple, Amazon, or Walmart. Small business owners also tend to assume they are "under the radar" since cybercriminals would have no reason to be interested in their company. Yet, small businesses have customer and employee information, credit card data, and bank accounts too. There is also an even more insidious reason for targeting small companies in growth industries like IT and health care: If a cybercriminal gains access to such a company, he or she can lie in wait until it is acquired by a larger corporation. The odds are good that as the acquired company's systems are integrated, the intruder will retain that access—in a sense using the small company as a Trojan horse to get him "through the gate" and past the more sophisticated security used by the parent.

The Ponemon Institute conducted a survey of senior business leaders and IT professionals in the United States, United Kingdom, Germany, Hong Kong, and Brazil in 2012. The average worldwide employee count for U.S. respondents was 9219, so the sampling is weighted toward large enterprises. (The report does caution that because it is a voluntary, web-based survey, it is subject to nonresponse, sampling-frame, and self-reporting biases.) The report was compiled from data from 2618 respondents.

Surprisingly, the surveyed businesses reported an average of 79 cyberattacks per week that produced some disruption of the business. The United States had the second-highest rate after Germany, at 82. The primary concern among U.S. executives was DoS attacks. In the opinion of the majority of respondents, the foremost motivation of cybercriminals is financial, followed by the theft of customer data. As for cost, the average reported cost of a single incident in the United States is $276,671, an amount composed of investigation, investment in IT security, and restoration of the reputation of the company and/or brand. Reported costs are between $200,000 and $300,000 in 30% of incidents and between $300,000 and $400,000 in 22%.[29]

The most dangerous threats today originate with sophisticated, highly organized cybercriminal organizations structured much like a legitimate business. The "business model" includes multilevel hierarchies, marketing, competition, and even outsourcing. Cybersecurity firm Fortinet describes the "corporate structure" of these groups.[30]

At the top are the "executives," who create the business model and establish the foundation of the operation. Rarely do they participate directly in illicit activities; instead, they recruit "affiliates," who serve as the mid-level management. In smaller organizations, the affiliates often perform the work themselves, but in larger ones the affiliates often use recruiters to locate and hire the frontline workers, what Fortinet calls the "infantry." The main job of the infantry is to infect as many computers as possible. "Mules" handle the transactions that transfer the organization's profits, keeping the amounts small enough to avoid triggering antimoney laundering measures.

Both advertisements and illicit software tools are usually placed on public, if underground, websites. Much of this illicit software is provided as open source code, some of it extensively documented, and more experienced infantry modify the software. This makes detecting and blocking such malware more difficult since it is constantly evolving. For example, a popular crimeware module called Zeus has appeared—and continues to appear—in numerous variations over the years.

Converting cyberattacks into profit takes place in several ways. At the individual computer level, a popular technique is scareware, described at the beginning of this section in the list of cybercrime categories. On average, computer users are charged between $50 and $100 to remove the "virus" they believe has infected their machine. A more recent version of scareware is ransomware. There is no subtlety or misdirection involved: The malware encrypts the user's data and holds it hostage until a ransom is paid, usually in the range of $100. Similar techniques have been used against corporate networks, but the ransoms are in the thousands or hundreds of thousands of dollars.

The most powerful tool of the cybercrime syndicate, however, is the botnet. As mentioned previously, bots are infected computers that the cybercriminal can control. Botnets can be used for a variety of purposes, often offered on a contract basis to interested parties. In the past, one of the major applications was the generation of spam, and that remains the case. However, using the power of distributed computing, botnets can accomplish frightening things. For example, passwords can be broken using various types of cracking software; Jack the Ripper is a popular version. However, these single-computer programs may take weeks to determine a password. In comparison, a botnet can crack the same password within hours. For a batch of 300 million attempts—about 20 minutes of work for a botnet—the price is about $17.

For those not familiar with the world of cybercrime, the scale might be difficult to believe. A task force was organized to uncover and take down the Mariposa botnet, which it accomplished in March 2010. That botnet included over 12 million computers, and more frighteningly over half of those belonged to Fortune 1000 companies, including over 40 banks. A Dutch cybercrime unit uncovered a botnet based on the Bredolab malware in October 2010. The man who was arrested controlled 143 servers that managed about 29 million bots. Dutch prosecutors alleged that he was generating $139,000 monthly from spam-generation contracts alone.

Combating highly organized cybercrime like this has proved extremely difficult. First, detecting and blocking the various forms of crimeware is next to impossible because the software evolves so rapidly. Cybersecurity firms spend most of their time reacting to new threats as it is rarely possible to be proactive—after all, releasing new security software into the marketplace gives cybercriminals the opportunity to study it and devise ways around it at their leisure.

Second, prosecutions (and arrests, for that matter) are very rare. Identifying and locating the individuals responsible for cybercrime usually means crossing national borders, if they can even be tracked that far. Governments have very limited resources for an enforcement effort that would require far more than is available, to say nothing of a high level of international cooperation. Also, both China and Russia are notorious for turning a blind eye to the servers that are absolutely necessary to all of this cybercrime.

Third, cybercrime has become "consumerized": The necessary tools are widely available online, and using them effectively no longer requires much in the way of technical know-how. This is hardly unprecedented. In the early days of the Internet (all the way back in the 1990s), a significant amount of damage was done not by true "hackers" but by so-called script kiddies, many of them teenagers, who downloaded and used malware written by others.

Some cybercrime is politically motivated. The loosely organized so-called hacktivist group Anonymous has been in the media frequently. The group tends to pick its targets based on its own ill-defined moral code, and those targets are not always governments: It has made high-profile attacks on Mexican drug cartels. But most politically motivated hackers go after governments or transnational organizations. Anonymous has allegedly attempted cyberattacks against the U.S. Marine Corps base at Quantico, Virginia, because U.S. Army intelligence analyst Bradley Manning, accused of stealing about 250,000 documents and passing them to WikiLeaks, was housed there pending trial. The European Union headquarters was targeted in March 2011 during preparations for an economic summit, and hackers penetrated the French Finance Ministry in December 2010 and stole documents containing confidential information regarding the upcoming G-20 Summit.[29]

As dangerous as these cybercrime and activist organizations can be, however, they are hard-pressed to rival the damage that can be done by state-sponsored cybercrime. Information technology is now yet another tool in the kit of the soldier, spy, or terrorist.

Government-sponsored crime and terrorism

Terrorism is hardly new. Many authorities date its origin to the first century AD. Jewish resistance fighters in occupied Palestine known as Zealots attacked Roman soldiers and destroyed property. (This was the group that ultimately committed suicide at Masada.)[31] However, for the most part, the Zealots confined their attacks to military targets, which by most definitions makes them resistance fighters rather than terrorists. By comparison, the Shi'ite Muslim sect Nizari Isma'ilis, popularly known as the hashashins ("hashish eaters," from which the word "assassin" derives) used indiscriminate murder, including of women and children, to spread terror.[32] The sect used these tactics against its Sunni Muslim rivals from 1090 to 1275, but also engaged in more conventional resistance against European military forces during the Crusades from 1095 to 1291.

The term "terrorism" originated during the French Revolution and the Reign of Terror under the French revolutionary Robespierre. This was when terror was used as a tactic by the state to suppress counterrevolutionary forces, crack down on profiteering and hoarding, and prevent anarchy. French leaders were unapologetic; Robespierre himself claimed that "Terror is nothing but justice, prompt, severe, and inflexible." About 12,000 people were executed during this period.[33]

Terrorism as a tool to oppose (and if possible overthrow) the state was first used in the 1870s in Czarist Russia. It had three main goals, which echo the general purposes of terrorism wherever and whenever it is practiced: to draw public attention to the opposition's grievances (the anti-Czarist forces used the term "the propaganda of the dead"), to undermine public confidence in the government and thereby destabilize it, and to prompt overly harsh reactions from the government to further arouse the populace and also attract international sympathy.[34]

Similar tactics were used by various anarchist political movements (and individuals) through the late nineteenth and early twentieth centuries, up to and shortly after World War I. In some cases, bombs were planted and detonated in public places, such as a wagon loaded with explosives (forerunner of the modern car bomb) that blew up on Wall Street across from the headquarters of J. P. Morgan & Company in 1920, but for the most part anarchists targeted government officials. From 1880 to 1920, four European heads of state, Russian Czar Alexander II, and two U.S. presidents were assassinated; an anarchist bomb killed nine police officers in November 1917 in Milwaukee; and a bomb severely damaged the home of the U.S. Attorney General in Washington, D.C. in 1919.[35] What is today called "collateral damage" to innocent bystanders was limited as much as possible, something that significantly distinguishes terrorism in this period from its modern counterpart.

It was during the Cold War that state-sponsored terrorism became widespread. Various Marxist, socialist, and "liberation" movements in Europe and throughout the Third World achieved new levels of operational, financial, intelligence, and political coordination, something generally acknowledged to have been encouraged and supported by the Soviet Union and its allies and client states. This phenomenon was at its height from the mid-1960s until the late 1980s, when Cuba, Iraq, Algeria, and Sudan provided training facilities for various groups. The most intensive terrorism centered on the Middle East because of the Arab–Israeli conflict and sponsorship of the two sides by the United States and U.S.S.R., respectively.

Following the fall of the Soviet Union and the Persian Gulf War, terrorism morphed into the tool primarily of nonstate actors that we are familiar with today. From 1993 to 2001, the United States was targeted on seven occasions: the 1993 World Trade Center attack; the 1995 bombing of a U.S. military headquarters facility in Saudi Arabia; the 1996 bombing of the Khobar Towers military barracks, also in Saudi Arabia; a 1997 attack on a tourist site in Egypt that killed 58; the 1998 U.S. embassy attacks in Kenya and Tanzania; the 2000 attack on the USS Cole in a Yemeni port; and of course 9/11. The vast majority of those killed in these attacks were not military or government personnel.

Some of these groups still enjoy state sponsorship today. The Taliban provided safe haven for training facilities for Al-Qaeda in Afghanistan, for example, and Iran provides extensive support to Hezbollah as a means to extend its influence into Lebanon and Syria and pressure Israel. (Hezbollah fighters have been assisting the Syrian regime during the 2012–2013 civil war at Iran's behest.) Although the groups they support commit numerous criminal acts, the responsible governments have a degree of insulation, if not exactly plausible deniability.

In Colombia in the 1970s and 1980s, at the height of the cocaine cartels, the government did not exactly support criminal organizations. However, it did turn a blind eye to many activities, many authorities accepted bribes, and the government enacted policies that made it easy for citizens to for all intents and purposes invest in the cartels. Mexico now faces some of the same issues with its drug cartels. While cooperation with the cartels is certainly not an official government policy, many observers have opined that the Mexican government seeks a certain degree of accommodation for two main reasons. One is the sheer power of the cartels and the difficulty Mexico has faced in combating them, often resorting to the use of military forces because local law enforcement was simply too corrupt to be reliable. The other is that the drug trade brings billions of dollars (a consensus number is $40 billion) into the Mexican economy. While the level of violence produced by inter-cartel competition is unacceptable, eradicating them entirely would not necessarily be wholly desirable even if it were practical. In addition, most of the violence—and the worst of it—occurs in the regions along the U.S.–Mexico border. Historically, Mexico has enjoyed little control of this area in any event, so the current level of lawlessness there is not a significant concern. So long as the violence does not spread into the Mexican heartland, the government will have little interest in eradicating the drug trade.[36]

While cybercrime is, as we have seen, largely the purview of international syndicates, many of the same techniques are now used by various governments. This should come as no surprise, really; the Internet is just another domain available to be militarized. As with most military power, it matters little what a particular nation wants to do: It must be prepared to deal with what other nations choose to do.

China and Russia are believed to routinely attack—sometimes successfully and sometimes not—U.S. government and corporate networks. Lockheed Martin, a major defense contract, and NASA have both been subject to espionage attacks. A European security expert summed up the difference between China and Russia thus: "The Chinese are notable for the sheer volume of what they do. The Russians are less active, but what they do is very sophisticated."[37]

One signature of government-sponsored or government-sanctioned cybercrime is the advanced persistent threat (APT), a highly sophisticated (and dangerous) form of malware. Cybercrime organizations are beginning to use APT as well, but most of these techniques originated with government professionals. In fact, the most successful APTs enter target networks not through the Internet as most crimeware does, but through a person on the inside who compromises the system. This is a classic hallmark of a foreign intelligence service. Make no mistake: The threat is very real. In 2008, the Department of Defense (DOD) suffered a breach of its secure network for classified data that is physically isolated from the public Internet. The malicious code was introduced through a flash drive, meaning a person with access to one of the network's computers was responsible. As a result, the DOD banned the use of all removable media on military computers in November 2008.[29]

Similarly, in 2009, the network for the DOD's F-35 Lightning II Joint Strike Fighter—at $300 billion the most expensive weapons program in history—was breached. It stands to reason that either a foreign government or an organization intending to sell data to a foreign government was responsible; after all, this data would not do a nonmilitary organization any good otherwise. What is particularly scary, and what points to likely involvement by an intelligence service, is that the stolen data was encrypted. As a result, investigators had no way to determine exactly what data had been stolen or even how much data.[29]

The world has seen cyberwarfare as a complement to conventional warfare already. In 2007, Estonia, one of the Baltic states and a former Soviet satellite, suffered a protracted DoS attack that the media dubbed "Web War I." The main targets were servers at government agencies, media outlets, and banks. When Russia invaded Georgia in 2008, the nation suffered similar attacks. (The presumed culprit in both cases was naturally Russia.)[29]

It is with events like this that the lines between crime, terrorism, and warfare begin to blur. Soldiers who kill at the behest of their national government (assuming that killing follows the laws of land warfare) are not guilty of murder, after all, so is a hacker who attempts to cripple a critical infrastructure in another country also at the behest of his national government guilty of cybercrime? Most authorities would say no, and at this point cybercrime transitions to information warfare. The distinction might seem merely academic or semantic, but hostile acts in cyberspace can have real consequences in the physical world: Israeli security expert Amos Guiora noted in a December 2012 interview that a hostile cyberact by one nation against another constitutes an act of war and can legitimately be answered with conventional military action.[38]

This leads us to consideration of the legal quandary that now confronts the United States: how to address terrorism. On the one hand, the U.S. government has treated terrorists as criminals. Many have been tried in federal criminal court—nearly 500 since 9/11 as of early 2013. In March 2013, for example, one of Osama bin Laden's sons-in-law, Sulaiman Abu Ghaith, was arraigned in federal court in Manhattan and subsequently cooperated with investigators.[39] Others have been tried by special military tribunals at the Guantanamo Bay, Cuba detention facility.

The use of traditional criminal prosecution against terrorists stems primarily from the fact that the body of international law on armed conflict—the so-called Geneva Conventions, as well as others—does not address terrorists. The primary focus is on uniformed military personnel, of course. Military personnel who don the uniform of opposing forces or civilian clothes to conceal their identity can legitimately be executed as spies if captured. The only major concession to irregular forces is a relatively recent addition, and it permits nonmilitary resistance fighters to be treated as soldiers under the law of war so long as they carry their weapons openly and use some sort of identifying clothing or other mark, such as all wearing an armband of a particular color.

In short, the law of war deals with the forces of a state. Even resistance forces are fighting in defense of their nation, an identifiable political entity. Terrorists who act on behalf of a nonstate actor like Al-Qaeda, however, are not fighting for a government. The law of war is therefore silent on how they should or can be treated. This is why many have been critical of the indefinite detentions at Guantanamo Bay: Under international law, the detainees are not prisoners of war who could be held until the end of the conflict, but civil law does not permit indefinite detention without arraignment and eventual trial.

There are difficulties with treating terrorists as criminals, however. A criminal cannot be deprived of life or liberty without due process, whereas in wartime an enemy soldier can be killed on sight. In other words, if a terrorist is a criminal he cannot be killed preemptively, whereas if he is a combatant he can. Yet, the nature of combat makes the notion of treating a terrorist like a criminal ridiculous in many respects. Imagine positively identifying a terrorist hideout and having to attempt to arrest its occupants rather than mounting an immediate assault or air strike.

The importance of establishing a viable legal model for combating terrorism should not be underestimated. Treating those who can be defined as combatants as criminals establishes a dangerous precedent, since by that rationale U.S. military personnel could theoretically face criminal charges from other countries for participating in normal military operations. The amorphous legal framework currently in use leaves much to be desired, especially as it has forced the United States to violate basic legal premises such as habeas corpus and given rise to controversy over "execution without benefit of trial" in the case of drone-launched missile strikes against identified terrorist leaders.

Corporate misconduct

Just as the concentration of money represented by government contracts and benefits lures criminals, the money that passes through U.S. businesses on a daily basis creates an even greater attraction. There are naturally those criminals who have an eye on siphoning off an illicit share of those funds, but they will be addressed in the section "White-collar crime." Here, we consider misconduct and criminal activity by companies.

In many cases, it is possible to identify individuals within companies who are responsible for misconduct. But bear in mind that a corporation is a legal entity, a "person" if you will, in the eyes of the law. Sometimes misconduct is so pervasive, the responsibility of so many people, or simply not possible to pin on a few select individuals that the company itself must be punished.

A recent and fairly dramatic example of this is BP. Because of the size and complexity of the case that resulted from the 2010 catastrophic failure of the company's Deepwater Horizon platform that resulted in the largest oil spill in history, this is a very educational case study. ("Complex" is perhaps a mild understatement: The 2013 criminal trial produced some "70 million" pages of evidence.)

First, the criminal charges: In November 2012, BP entered guilty pleas to 14 criminal counts, including 11 felony counts of seaman's manslaughter. (The other three charges were misdemeanor charges under the Clean Water Act and Migratory Bird Treaty Act, plus an additional felony charge of obstruction of justice.) BP agreed to a $4 billion fine to be paid over 5 years.[40]

These charges were against the company itself. In addition, the two senior supervisors present on the rig at the time of the accident were indicted on 23 counts that included involuntary manslaughter, accused of ignoring warning signs of the impending blowout. A senior BP executive, former vice president David Rainey, was also indicted for obstruction of justice, accused of concealing critical information from law enforcement and government agencies during the spill response. We can thus see how both a corporation and individuals within that corporation can be criminally charged.[41]

Next is the inevitable civil litigation. Understand that BP is not the only company accused of misconduct in this affair. Petroleum exploration and production is a highly complex process, and many specialized services are required at various stages. In the case of the Deepwater Horizon, the rig itself was owned by Transocean, and Halliburton was responsible for casing the well (in essence lining the boreshaft with cement). BP naturally has a vested interest in shifting as much blame as possible to these stakeholders, and observers estimated that its trial defense might have managed to shift up to 30% or so to them, most of it accruing to Halliburton.

The key issue of the civil litigation for BP was whether it would be found grossly negligent. A gross negligence finding would substantially increase the civil penalties, even beyond the $42 billion BP allocated before the trial. For example, its exposure under the Clean Water Act alone would be as much as $17.5 billion. It would also open the door to punitive damage awards to the various litigants, which include Louisiana, Alabama, Mississippi, and Florida, adding another layer of cost beyond actual damages. A third set of penalties related to natural resource damage remained at the time of this writing as yet unexplored. In short, a bad outcome in civil court will produce financial consequences for BP far beyond the $4 billion criminal fine.

The lead-up to the criminal charges against BP prompted much discussion of the so-called corporate death penalty in the media. At least in recent history, this "death penalty" has been nothing more than a myth. A clerk for a U.S. District Court judge in Houston compiled an analysis of 51 publicly traded companies that were convicted on criminal charges between 2001 and 2010. Of those, 36 showed no significant effect—their stock had not been delisted or downgraded to another exchange, they had not been acquired or merged or even changed names, and obviously they remained in business. Eleven of the remaining companies had undergone favorable mergers or acquisitions, and of the four business failures, none could reasonably be attributed to the convictions.[42]

In fact, BP's guilty plea was unusual. Historically the DOJ has used alternatives to criminal conviction, primarily deferred prosecution agreements. The rationale is that a serious conviction would be the equivalent of the hypothetical corporate death penalty, destroying the company and throwing thousands of people out of work and costing creditors, bondholders, and shareholders millions as a result. A DOJ spokesperson has summed up the official position favoring deferred prosecution in most cases, saying that it "achieve[s] these results without causing the loss of jobs, the loss of pensions, and other significant consequences to innocent parties who played no role in the criminal conduct, were unaware of it, or were unable to prevent it."[43] The evidence for this assumption is Arthur Andersen, one of the "Big Five" accounting firms that in 2001 had a notorious client: Enron. When the extent of Enron's fraud was revealed, it became clear that as its outside auditor Arthur Andersen should have objected to many of the company's accounting and finance practices. Moreover, it was difficult to reach any conclusion other than that the large sums of money Arthur Andersen made from consulting services for Enron constituted a substantial conflict of interest and was probably a significant reason that Enron's questionable practices were "given a pass" by the accounting firm.

The government aggressively pursued Arthur Andersen. (In the case of Enron, the company imploded on its own. Instead, its senior executives were indicted and prosecuted.) Found guilty in 2002 of obstruction of justice, the accounting firm lost its clients and quickly withered away. But in May 2005, the U.S. Supreme Court overturned that conviction, ruling that the trial judge had established an unfairly "low hurdle for the jury to reach a guilty verdict."[44] After that the DOJ embraced a more cautious strategy.

It is instructive, in fact, to compare DOJ policies from before and after this watershed moment. A June 16, 1999, policy document entitled Federal Prosecution of Corporations opens with the words, "Corporations should not be treated leniently because of their artificial nature nor should they be subject to harsher treatment. Vigorous enforcement of the criminal laws against corporate wrongdoers, where appropriate, results in great benefits for law enforcement and the public, particularly in the area of white collar crime." It continues, "prosecutors should be aware of the important public benefits that may flow from indicting a corporation in appropriate cases. For instance, corporations are likely to take immediate remedial steps when one is indicted for criminal conduct that is pervasive throughout a particular industry, and thus an indictment often provides a unique opportunity for deterrence on a massive scale." In the following paragraph it adds, "Charging a corporation, however, does not mean that individual directors, officers, employees, or shareholders should not also be charged."[45]

Compare those exhortations to the tone of current policy. While the words above are still present, the document opens with very different language: "… federal prosecutors and corporate leaders typically share common goals. For example, directors and officers owe a fiduciary duty to a corporation's shareholders, the corporation's true owners, and they owe duties of honest dealing to the investing public in connection with the corporation's regulatory filings and public statements. The faithful execution of these duties by corporate leadership serves the same values in promoting public trust and confidence that our criminal cases are designed to serve." Other sentences mention that while pursuing "the investigation and prosecution of criminal wrongdoing if it is discovered … prosecutors should be mindful of the common cause we share with responsible corporate leaders" and remind prosecutors that "corporate prosecutions can potentially harm blameless investors, employees, and others."[46]

But advocates for stronger corporate prosecution, including law clerk Gabriel Markoff who conducted the aforementioned study, say that historical evidence shows that the risk of actually putting a convicted company out of business is minimal. Markoff specifically insists that the DOJ can evaluate defendants and determine whether a conviction would actually constitute a significant risk and act accordingly. By no means is he suggesting that prosecutors ruthlessly pursue charges no matter the circumstances.[42] However, since a corporation cannot be imprisoned, the only real penalties (aside from possible damage to its reputation) are financial. Mary Ramirez, a former assistant U.S. attorney who now teaches at the Washburn University School of Law, says, "I worry and so do a lot of economists that we have created no disincentives for committing fraud or white-collar crime, in particular in the financial space."[43] After all, if the decision as to whether to follow the law or circumvent it comes down to a calculation of likely profits, the chance of getting caught, and the size of potential penalties, the law is not being well-served.

To see deferred prosecution in action, we will consider the 2010 deferred prosecution agreement with Panalpina World Transport. Panalpina, which provided transport services to the oil and gas industry, was alleged to have extensively violated the Foreign Corrupt Practices Act (FCPA), bribing foreign officials in at least seven countries (Angola, Azerbaijan, Brazil, Kazakhstan, Nigeria, Russia, and Turkmenistan) between 2002 and 2007, making "thousands of payments."[47]

The centerpiece of the agreement was a fine of $70,560,000 payable in four annual installments. The potential fine for the company's offenses, calculated based on a weighting scale that takes into account (among other things) the company's size, the degree to which it cooperated with law enforcement, and the size and frequency of its offenses, was $72,800,000–$145,600,000, so clearly Panalpina negotiated a favorable arrangement. In addition to the fine, the company was required to cooperate with any additional criminal investigations, "implement a compliance and ethics program designed to prevent and detect violations of the FCPA," review its internal controls, and report periodically to the DOJ regarding its compliance with the agreement. It also pled guilty to two charges, one of violating the FCPA and one of conspiracy to commit an offense against the United States.[48]

Panalpina is a private company, so information on its revenue is not publicly available. Moreover, the company operates numerous subsidiaries, meaning it has multiple revenue streams. But what does a global company with over 15,000 employees working in the lucrative oil and gas sector probably make? How much of an impact is less than $18 million a year for 4 years likely to have?

Although many complain about corporate behavior, few realize that companies can be criminally charged just as individuals can. But except for the grossest scandals that generate tremendous public outrage at the magnitude of Enron or Deepwater Horizon, the DOJ has tended to pursue much less dramatic legal action against corporate offenders.

White-collar crime

Although the FBI somewhat flippantly describes white-collar crime as "lying, cheating, and stealing" on its website,[49] the more academic definition comes to us from criminologist and Indiana University professor Edwin H. Sutherland, who in an address to the American Sociological Association on December 27, 1939, introduced the concept, defining it as "a crime committed by a person of respectability and high social status in the course of his occupation."[50] The automatic equation of respectability and high social status and use of the pronoun "he" does date this definition to an earlier era, but it still holds much validity.

The National White Collar Crime Center (NWC3) offers a much more detailed and much broader definition that reflects modern realities: "illegal or unethical acts that violate fiduciary responsibility or public trust for personal or organizational gain." The definition spans both organizational and individual offenders and encompasses not only traditional forms of economic crime (e.g., embezzlement, money laundering, insurance fraud), but also high-tech crimes (such as Internet fraud), as well as crimes committed both inside and outside of the occupational setting."[51] Consequently, this discussion will of necessity overlap somewhat with the prior exploration of corporate crime.

The most recent white-collar crime survey conducted by the NWC3 revealed that in the prior 12 months, 24% of households and 17% of individuals had experienced at least one of the following crimes: mortgage fraud, credit card fraud, identity theft, fraudulent (unnecessary) home or car repairs, price misrepresentation, or financial loss resulting from fraudulent information from stockbrokers, fraudulent business ventures, or Internet scams. Of these incidents, 54.7% were reported to an outside agency (such as a credit card company or consumer protection agency), but only 11.7% of the time did that reporting include law enforcement.[52] As an indication of public opinion, a majority of survey respondents agreed with the proposition that white-collar crime contributed to the 2008 financial crisis and subsequent recession.

In pursuing white-collar criminals, the FBI has established 11 programs to combat the major categories it defines: money laundering, bankruptcy fraud, corporate fraud, financial institution fraud, health-care fraud, hedge fund fraud, insurance fraud, mass marketing fraud, mortgage fraud, piracy and intellectual property theft, and securities and commodities fraud.[49] To gain an understanding of the widely varied nature of white-collar crime, we will examine several common scams.

Pump-and-dump stock scams: In 2010, the FBI concluded an investigation of over 40 such schemes involving professionals who most would assume to be trustworthy—certified public accountants, attorneys, financial advisors, and stockbrokers—working in conjunction with CEOs. The pump-and-dump scam almost always involves "penny stocks," those that trade at share prices under $1. The primary reason is that these companies trade on exchanges that have very lenient (if any) listing criteria and are not subject to the extensive disclosure requirements of the Securities and Exchange Commission required of larger companies, meaning there is little hard information to contradict whatever the scammers may claim. Such low-priced stocks also enjoy the psychological perception of being a "bargain" to most victims.

The basic mechanism of the scam is quite simple. The scammers use various resources to spread positive information about the company, including press releases, Internet bulletin board and chat room postings, and even comments from "stock analysts." In some cases, the victims are not specifically targeted, but are rather anyone who picks up on the "chatter" and buys the stock. In others, such as those uncovered by this particular FBI investigation, people were specifically and personally encouraged to buy these stocks. Before starting the scam, the criminals purchase millions of shares at rock-bottom prices. They then publicize the stock. As more and more people buy, the stock price climbs. The deal looks better and better, and the number of buyers grows. Finally, before anything can shatter the illusion, the scammers sell their shares for a handsome profit, sending the stock price plummeting and leaving the victims with nearly worthless shares.[53]

Timeshare fraud: A timeshare is a partial ownership in a piece of real estate (generally some form of vacation property) that gives the owner the right to use it for certain blocks of time each year. Although this is a legitimate practice, the industry is subject to widespread fraud by illicit companies and by criminals posing as representatives of legitimate companies. Most scams focus on timeshare owners who are trying to sell. The scammers use high-pressure techniques to convince the sellers to place the property with them—sometimes claiming they have a buyer ready to make an immediate purchase—and demand upfront fees ranging from hundreds to thousands of dollars. Once the fee is paid, of course, the victim never hears from the "broker" again.[54]

Work-at-home scams: In yet another confirmation of the aphorism that "if it sounds too good to be true, it probably is," the work-at-home scam promises hundreds or thousands of dollars weekly for simple work: stuffing envelopes, medical billing, and typing are popular "jobs." There are different variations on the scheme. The victim may have to purchase a several-hundred-dollar "startup" kit with training materials, inventory, and the like, which of course is worthless. It may be a pyramid scheme in which the victim becomes a "distributor" and purchases expensive product inventories and promotional materials and makes money by recruiting "downstream" distributors, receiving a cut of their sales. The further down the "pyramid" the victim is, the less money (if any) he or she will make.

"Mystery shopping" is another popular version. While there are legitimate mystery shoppers, in this scheme the "employer" sends the victim a large check to cover expenses. The victim withdraws funds, often sending a large percentage through one or more money transfer services, only to learn that the "expense check" was counterfeit. Finally, some of these schemes do actually pay. However, the victim is laundering funds for a criminal enterprise, usually by reshipping merchandise or money, and when law enforcement catches up, the real criminals remain anonymous. To add insult to injury, given the types of personal information employers normally request, these scammers collect everything they need to commit identity theft, and the victim suffers twice.[55]

Illegal pharmacies: Many prescription drugs are not cheap, and for those without health insurance or without a prescription for certain medications (such as Viagra), cheap "offshore" pharmacies have a strong allure. Such "pharmacies" are easy to find on the Internet, and for that matter are a popular subject of spam e-mails. In most cases, the scammers do ship products to the victims. However, exactly what they are selling is highly questionable. Often the "drugs" are outright fakes with no medicinal value. At best they are expired, counterfeit, or mislabeled, and the prescriptions written by the doctors they use take no real consideration of the patient's medical condition or possible drug interactions.[56]

Home theft: Although it might seem hard to believe, there are criminals who will steal houses right out from under the legitimate owners. (Fortunately, this crime remains fairly rare.) The process is actually not all that complicated. While occupied homes are certainly targeted, vacation and rental homes tend to be somewhat easier targets. The scammers collect enough personal information about the actual owners to create sufficient documentation to pose as the owners. From there, it is a simple matter of filling out the proper paperwork and filing it with the authorities to transfer ownership. Once the scammers own it, they typically sell it to another unsuspecting victim. One version of the scheme that defrauded over 100 Los Angeles homeowners and produced $12 million in illicit profits posed as a rescue program for struggling homeowners—common enough in the wake of the 2008 mortgage scandal. The criminals claimed to be refinancing their mortgages but instead purchased the homes under fake identities, kept the mortgage loan proceeds, and never made any payments. The homeowners lost title to their homes and the mortgage lenders lost the money they loaned.[57]

The highest profile white-collar crime cases receive plenty of play in the media. The Bernard Madoff Ponzi scheme that defrauded sophisticated investors out of billions of dollars is a good example. But in the space of 1 week in July 2013, the FBI announced convictions in three white-collar crimes: a $4 million Ponzi scheme run by a Denver business owner, a father and son who operated another Ponzi scheme aimed at members of the Church of Latter Day Saints to the tune of $100 million, and a fugitive finally captured and sentenced for a $14 million loan fraud scam. Clearly white-collar crime is pervasive and costly.

Organized crime

Crime, criminals, and the law enforcement officers who fight them have long captured the public imagination and been the basis of books, movies, and television shows. Some of the most popular have focused on America's various organized crime "families."

Organized crime dates to the 1920s when the main targets of government law enforcement were men like Al Capone and Charles "Lucky" Luciano. Organized crime has its origins in the Prohibition era, when the amount of money to be made smuggling liquor to sate the demands of Americans made large, complex criminal enterprises both necessary and cost-effective. Naturally, once established, these organizations branched out into much more than smuggling. Throughout the 1920s, Capone's Chicago crime family engaged in prostitution, gambling, narcotics, robbery, "protection" rackets, and the routine bribery and murder that were just part of doing business.[58]

Charles "Lucky" Luciano ran a very similar enterprise in New York City. During the 1920s, numerous members of the Italian—predominantly Sicilian—Mafia emigrated to the United States, often illegally, following in the footsteps of those who had come beginning in the 1880s. They eventually founded La Cosa Nostra (LCN), the American Mafia, under Luciano's leadership. Even after he was deported to Italy in 1946, he continued to function as a liaison between the Sicilian and American Mafias; even today LCN continues to cooperate with the various Italian organized crime families.[59]

It was Luciano who created the hierarchical structure that put the "organized" into organized crime. Once he consolidated control by murdering his primary rival, Joseph Masseria, in 1931, he established five "families" in New York City, divided the criminal activity in the city among them, and eventually established the LCN Commission composed of seven family bosses. The Genovese and Gambino families emerged as the most powerful factions in the LCN.[60]

The U.S. government gradually became aware of the extent of Mafia activity through the 1950s, and federal law enforcement began making its first significant inroads against organized crime late in that decade. In 1963, the FBI recruited its first high-level informant from the LCN, Joseph Valachi. He provided a detailed look at the structure and operations of the Mafia.

The various families were involved in a broad array of criminal activities: drug trafficking, extortion, gambling, loan sharking, pornography, prostitution, stock manipulation, tax fraud, labor racketeering, and the infiltration of legitimate businesses, along with the associated "management" activities like murder, assault, arson, money laundering, and corruption of public officials.

Extensive investigations of the various families proceeded through the 1970s and 1980s. By the late 1980s, the government's efforts began to pay substantial dividends, leading to successful prosecutions of major Mafia figures like Anthony "Fat Tony" Salerno and four other New York bosses in 1985, John Gotti in 1992, and Vincent "the Chin" Gigante in 1997.

Although arrests and convictions of significant LCN figures have continued through the 2000s, beginning in the 1990s, new organized crime groups began to appear on the U.S. landscape. After the fall of the Soviet Union, Russian organized crime expanded rapidly and soon made the move into the United States. The FBI has also seen major groups from countries like Armenia and Albania as well as new activity from long-established criminal organizations in China and other Asian countries. The fight against organized crime will not end even if law enforcement successfully puts an end to LCN.

Summary

According to urban legend, the famous bank robber Willie Sutton once claimed that he robbed banks "because that's where the money is." (Sutton corrected that myth in his autobiography, saying the phrase apparently came from a reporter but definitely not from him.) It is for the same reason that government and business attract so much criminal attention or are the vehicles of criminal activity. Today the Internet makes theft a simple and anonymous process, and the person who would never dream of committing a mugging or an armed robbery will not hesitate to bilk unsuspecting victims out of thousands or millions of dollars.

Corporations and even governments can commit crimes, although where governments are concerned it is often the case that those who make the laws can make any act legal. The company that commits crimes can even be directly subject to criminal penalties, something demonstrated repeatedly over the years. Compared to crime committed by an individual, organized and white-collar crimes all too often merely take wrongdoing to an epic scale.

Practicum

1. There have been numerous high-profile convictions of political figures for criminal activity, particularly corruption, over the years. Why do you think we continue to see members of government engage in such acts?
2. How widespread do you think the abuses of power alleged by some advocates within law enforcement circles actually are?
3. What are the characteristics of government benefit programs that, in your opinion, make them so vulnerable to fraud?
4. Do you see any risks inherent in the *qui tam* principle in the reporting of government misconduct?
5. In your opinion, what distinguishes an act of terrorism from an act of armed resistance?
6. In your opinion, can a government engage in terrorism?
7. Do you feel the government should have the ability to shut down a corporation convicted of malfeasance? Why or why not?
8. How do you think the government should determine criminal penalties against companies?

Resources

U.S. Office of Government Ethics, http://www.oge.gov/home.aspx
Council of the Inspectors General on Integrity and Efficiency, http://www.ignet.gov/index.html
Department of Justice Office of Public Affairs, http://www.justice.gov/opa/
National White Collar Crime Center, http://www.nw3c.org/
Federal Bureau of Investigation Organized Crime Center, http://www.fbi.gov/about-us/investigate/organizedcrime

References

1. King, L. W. (1997). *Hammurabi's code of laws* (Trans.). Evansville, IN: University of Evansville. Retrieved June 20, 2013, from http://eawc.evansville.edu/anthology/hammurabi.htm
2. Acton, J. (2013). *Lord acton quote archive*. Acton Institute. Retrieved June 20, 2013, from http://www.acton.org/research/lord-acton-quote-archive
3. The Watergate Story, Part 1: The Post Investigates. (2002). Retrieved June 20, 2013, from http://www.washingtonpost .com/wp-srv/politics/special/watergate/part1.html
4. Davey, M. (2011, December 7). Blagojevich sentenced to 14 years in prison. *The New York Times.* Retrieved June 20, 2013, from http://www.nytimes.com/2011/12/08/us/blagojevich-expresses-remorse-in-courtroom-speech.html?ref=rodrblagojevich&_r=0
5. Davey, M. (2009, April 2). Blagojevich charged with 16 corruption felonies. *The New York Times.* Retrieved June 20, 2013, from http://www.nytimes.com/2009/04/03/us/03illinois .html?ref=rodrblagojevich
6. Buettner, R. (2010, July 31). Running government as a cash business. *The New York Times.* Retrieved June 20, 2013, from http://www.nytimes.com/2010/08/01/weekinreview/01buettner. html?ref=rodrblagojevich
7. U.S. Office of Government Ethics (a). (2013). *Where to Report Misconduct in ....* Retrieved June 22, 2013, from http://www.oge.gov/About/Mission-and-Responsibilities/Where-to-Report-Misconduct-in---/
8. U.S. Office of Government Ethics (b). *Mission & responsibilities.* Retrieved June 22, 2013 from http://www.oge.gov/About/Mission-and-Responsibilities/Mission---Responsibilities/
9. Council of the Inspectors General on Integrity and Efficiency. (2013). Retrieved June 22, 2013, from http://www.ignet.gov/index.html
10. Government Accountability Project (a). (2012). *Whistleblower Protection Enhancement ACT (WPEA).* Retrieved June 24, 2013 from http://www.whistleblower.org/program-areas/legislation/wpea
11. Government Accountability Project (a). (2012). *Whistleblower Protection Enhancement ACT (WPEA).* Retrieved June 24, 2013, from http://www.whistleblower.org/program-areas/legislation/wpea
12. Government Accountability Project (b). (2012). *WPEA Rights.* Retrieved June 24, 2013, from http://www.whistleblower.org/program-areas/legislation/wpea/the-protections
13. Innocence Project. (2013). *Government misconduct.* Retrieved June 24, 2013, from http://www.innocenceproject.org/understand/Government-Misconduct.php
14. U.S. Senate Permanent Subcommittee on Investigations. (2012, September 13). *Social Security disability programs: Improving the quality of benefit award decisions* (pp. 3–4). Washington, DC: U.S. Senate. June 25, 2013, Retrieved from http://www.coburn.senate.gov/public/index.cfm?a=Files.Serve&File_id=6f2d2252-50e8-4257-8c6f-0c342896d904
15. U.S. Senate Permanent Subcommittee on Investigations. (2012, September 13). *Social Security disability programs: Improving the quality of benefit award decisions* (pp. 7–8). Washington, DC: U.S. Senate. Retrieved June 25, 2013, from http://www.coburn.senate.gov/public/index.cfm?a=Files .Serve&File_id=6f2d2252-50e8-4257-8c6f-0c342896d904
16. Kutz, G. D., & Ryan, J. J. (2006, June 14). *Testimony before the Subcommittee on Investigations, Committee on Homeland Security, House of Representatives: Hurricanes Katrina and Rita disaster relief.* Washington, DC: Government Accountability Office. Retrieved June 25, 2013, from http://www.gao.gov/new.items/d06844t.pdf
17. U.S. Attorney's Office, Northern District of Georgia. (2012, February 2). *New Orleans man sentenced for FEMA fraud.* Washington, DC: Department of Justice. June 25, 2013, Retrieved from http://www.justice.gov/usao/gan/press/2012/02-02-12.html
18. Food and Nutrition Service. (2011, December). *USDA efforts to reduce waste, fraud and abuse in the Supplemental Nutrition Assistance Program* (SNAP). Washington, DC: Department of Agriculture. Retrieved June 25, 2013, from http://www.fns.usda.gov/sites/default/files/Integrity.pdf
19. Legal Information Institute. (2013). *18 USC chapter 47—Fraud and false statements.* Ithaca, NY: Cornell Law School. Retrieved June 25, 2013, from http://www.law.cornell.edu/uscode/text/18/part-I/chapter-47

20. Greenbaum, M. (2013, March 7). The civil war's war on fraud. *The New York Times*. Retrieved June 27, 2013, from http://opinionator.blogs.nytimes.com/2013/03/07/the-civil-wars-war-on-fraud/

21. Greenbaum, M. (2013, March 7). The civil war's war on fraud. *The New York Times*. Retrieved June 27, 2013, from http://opinionator.blogs.nytimes.com/2013/03/07/the-civil-wars-war-on-fraud/

22. Greenbaum, M. (2013, March 7). The civil war's war on fraud. *The New York Times*. Retrieved June 27, 2013, from http://opinionator.blogs.nytimes.com/2013/03/07/the-civil-wars-war-on-fraud/

23. Greenbaum, M. (2013, March 7). The civil war's war on fraud. *The New York Times*. Retrieved from http://opinionator.blogs.nytimes.com/2013/03/07/the-civil-wars-war-on-fraud/

24. KPMG International Cooperative. (July 2011). Cyber crime—A growing challenge for governments. *Issues Monitor, 8*, 1.

25. KPMG International Cooperative. (July 2011). Cyber crime—A growing challenge for governments. *Issues Monitor, 8*, 5.

26. KPMG International Cooperative. (July 2011). Cyber crime—A growing challenge for governments. *Issues Monitor, 8*, 6.

27. Kavilanz, P. (2013, April 23). Cybercrime's easiest prey: Small businesses. *CNNMoney*. Retrieved June 30, 2013, from http://money.cnn.com/2013/04/22/smallbusiness/small-business-cybercrime/index.html

28. Fox Business. (2013, March 22). Most small businesses don't recover June 30, 2013, from cybercrime. *The Wall Street Journal*. Retrieved June 30, 2013, from http://online.wsj.com/article/SB10001424127887324557804578376291878413744.html

29. Ponemon Institute. (2012, May). *The impact of cybercrime on business*. Retrieved June 30, 2013, from http://www.ponemon.org/local/upload/file/Impact_of_Cybercrime_on_Business_FINAL.pdf

30. Fortinet. (2013). Cybercriminals today mirror legitimate business processes. *Fortinet*. Retrieved June 30, 2013, from http://www.fortinet.com/sites/default/files/whitepapers/Cybercrime_Report.pdf

31. Criminal Justice Council. (2012, February 27). *The history of terrorism: More than 200 years of development*. Delaware Criminal Justice Council. Retrieved June 30, 2013, from http://cjc.delaware.gov/terrorism/history.shtml

32. Criminal Justice Council. (2012, February 27). *The history of terrorism: More than 200 years of development*. Delaware Criminal Justice Council. Retrieved June 30, 2013, from http://cjc.delaware.gov/terrorism/history.shtml

33. Digital History. (2012). *Terrorism in historical perspective. Digital history*. Houston, TX: University of Houston. Retrieved June 30, 2013, from http://www.digitalhistory.uh.edu/topic_display.cfm?tcid=94

34. Digital History. (2012.) *Terrorism in historical perspective. Digital history*. Houston, TX: University of Houston. Retrieved June 30, 2013, from http://www.digitalhistory.uh.edu/topic_display.cfm?tcid=94

35. Digital History. (2012.) *Terrorism in historical perspective. Digital history*. Houston, TX: University of Houston. Retrieved June 30, 2013, from http://www.digitalhistory.uh.edu/topic_display.cfm?tcid=94

36. Friedman, G. (2012, August 21). Mexico's strategy. *Stratfor*. Retrieved June 30, 2013, from http://www.stratfor.com/weekly/mexicos-strategy [via subscription only]

37. Blitz, J. (2011, November 1). Security: A huge challenge from China, Russia and organised crime. *Financial Times*. Retrieved June 30, 2013, from http://www.ft.com/intl/cms/s/0/b43488b0-fe2a-11e0-a1eb-00144feabdc0.html#axzz2YssyBvDw

38. Guiora, A. (2012, December 6). *Interview by Israel Knowledge@Wharton*. Philadelphia: Wharton School, University of Pennsylvania. Retrieved July 1, 2013, from http://kw.wharton.upenn.edu/israel/security-expert-amos-guiora-cyber-terrorism-poses-an-enormous-threat/

39. Eviatar, D. (2013, March 9). Keep terrorism trials in U.S. courts. *Reuters*. Retrieved July 1, 2013, from http://blogs.reuters.com/great-debate/2013/03/08/keep-terrorism-trials-in-u-s-courts/

40. Mufson, S. (2012, November 15). BP settles criminal charges for $4 billion in spill; supervisors indicted on manslaughter. *The Washington Post*. Retrieved July 1, 2013, from http://articles.washingtonpost.com/2012-11-15/business/35505450_1_bp-rig-supervisors-bp-settlement-deepwater-horizon

41. Mufson, S. (2012, November 15). BP settles criminal charges for $4 billion in spill; supervisors indicted on manslaughter. *The Washington Post*. Retrieved July 1, 2013, from http://articles.washingtonpost.com/2012-11-15/business/35505450_1_bp-rig-supervisors-bp-settlement-deepwater-horizon

42. (2012, August 27). The myth of the corporate death penalty. *Corporate Crime Reporter*. Retrieved July 2, 2013, from http://www.corporatecrimereporter.com/news/200/markoffthemythcorporatedeathpenalty08272012/

43. Morgenson, G. (2011, July 7). As wall St. Polices itself, prosecutors use softer approach. *The New York Times*. Retrieved July 2, 2013, from http://www.nytimes.com/2011/07/08/business/in-shift-federal-prosecutors-are-lenient-as-companies-break-the-law.html?pagewanted=all&_r=0

44. Greenhouse, L. (2005, May 31). Justices unanimously overturn conviction of Arthur Andersen. *The New York Times*. Retrieved July 2, 2013, from http://www.nytimes.com/2005/05/31/business/31wire-andersen.html?pagewanted=1

45. Office of the Deputy Attorney General. (1999, June 16). *Federal prosecution of corporations*. Washington, DC: Department of Justice. Retrieved July 2, 2013, from http://www.justice.gov/criminal/fraud/documents/reports/1999/charging-corps.PDF

46. *Title 9, Chapter 9-28.000: Principles of federal prosecution of business organizations*. Washington, DC: Department of Justice. Retrieved August 28, 2008, from http://www.justice.gov/opa/documents/corp-charging-guidelines.pdf

47. Luck, S. K. (2010, November 4). *United States of America v. Panalpina World Transport (Holding) Ltd*. Houston, TX: U.S. District Court for the Southern District of Texas, Houston Division. Retrieved July 7, 2013, from http://www.justice.gov/opa/documents/panalpina-world-transport-dpa.pdf

48. Luck, S. K. (2010, Nov. 4). *United States of America v. Panalpina World Transport (Holding) Ltd*. Houston, TX: U.S. District Court for the Southern District of Texas, Houston Division. Retrieved July 7, 2013, from http://www.justice.gov/opa/documents/panalpina-world-transport-dpa.pdf

49. Federal Bureau of Investigation. (2013). *White-collar crime*. Washington, DC: Author. Retrieved July 7, 2013, from http://www.fbi.gov/about-us/investigate/white_collar

50. Huff, R., Desilets, C., & Kane, J. (2010, December). *The 2010 national public survey on white collar crime* (p. 11). Fairmont, WV: National White Collar Crime Center. Retrieved July 7, 2013, from http://www.nw3c.org/docs/publications/2010-national-public-survey-on-white-collar-crime.pdf?sfvrsn=8

51. Huff, R., Desilets, C., & Kane, J. (2010, December). *The 2010 national public survey on white collar crime* (p. 11). Fairmont, WV: National White Collar Crime Center. Retrieved July 7, 2013, from http://www.nw3c.org/docs/publications/2010-national-public-survey-on-white-collar-crime.pdf?sfvrsn=8

52. Huff, R., Desilets, C., & Kane, J. (2010, December). *The 2010 national public survey on white collar crime* (p. 8). Fairmont, WV: National White Collar Crime Center. Retrieved July 7, 2013, from http://www.nw3c.org/docs/publications/2010-national-public-survey-on-white-collar-crime.pdf?sfvrsn=8

53. Federal Bureau of Investigation. (2010, January 29). *Investors beware: Stock fraud case offers lessons*. Washington, DC: Author. Retrieved July 8, 2013, from http://www.fbi.gov/news/stories/2010/january/fraud_012910

54. Federal Bureau of Investigation. (2012, February 17). *Trying to sell that timeshare? Beware of fraudsters*. Washington, DC: Author. Retrieved July 8, 2013, from http://www.fbi.gov/news/stories/2012/february/timeshare-fraud_021712

55. Federal Bureau of Investigation. (2009, April 17). *Work-at-home scams: Job one: Do not take the bait*. Washington, DC: Author. Retrieved July 8, 2013, from http://www.fbi.gov/news/stories/2009/april/workathome_041709

56. Federal Bureau of Investigation. (2009, March 3). *Don't put your health in the hands of crooks.* Washington, DC: Author. Retrieved July 8, 2013, from http://www.fbi.gov/news/stories/2009/march/pharmacy_030309

57. Federal Bureau of Investigation. (2008, March 25). *House stealing: The latest scam on the block.* Washington, DC: Author. Retrieved July 8, 2013, from http://www.fbi.gov/news/stories/2008/march/housestealing_032508

58. Federal Bureau of Investigation. (2005, March 28). *Solving Scarface: How the law finally caught up with Al Capone.* Washington, DC: Author. Retrieved July 10, 2013, from http://www.fbi.gov/news/stories/2005/march/capone_032805

59. Federal Bureau of Investigation. (2013). *Italian organized crime.* Washington, DC: Author. Retrieved July 10, 2013, from http://www.fbi.gov/about-us/investigate/organizedcrime/italian_mafia#italianoc_genovese

60. Federal Bureau of Investigation. (2013). *Italian organized crime.* Washington, DC: Author. Retrieved July 10, 2013, from http://www.fbi.gov/about-us/investigate/organizedcrime/italian_mafia#italianoc_genovese

chapter twelve

Drugs and the justice system

Chapter objectives

After studying this chapter, you should understand and be able to explain

- Where various illegal drugs originated and how they have been viewed, used, and abused in the United States
- The demographics of illegal drug users and the nature of drug abuse
- How drug court programs function and what research has revealed about their effectiveness
- The nature of drug trafficking within the United States
- The nature of international drug trafficking and major drug trafficking organizations, with special emphasis on the most significant Mexican cartels
- How drug trafficking organizations launder the funds generated by drug sales.
- The agencies primarily responsible for combating drug trafficking and the tactics they use
- Perceived weaknesses in current antidrug efforts

Introduction

In 1954, President Dwight Eisenhower appointed a five-member Cabinet-level committee and directed them to "stamp out narcotic addiction." Although many drugs—opiates and cocaine among them—had enjoyed a certain respectability and were widely used in the late nineteenth and early twentieth centuries, by the time of the Great Depression all of today's illegal drugs had been outlawed and lost their social acceptability. In a nation preoccupied first by economic crisis and then by a world war, drug use dropped out of the mainstream and nearly disappeared.

The end of World War II and the rejection of middle-class values by the Baby Boomer Generation brought drugs back to the forefront. The 1960s counterculture glorified drugs and many U.S. soldiers in Vietnam took advantage of easy access to heroin and marijuana. By 1973, President Richard Nixon found it necessary to establish the Drug Enforcement Administration (DEA) and became the first U.S. government official to publicly refer to the "War on Drugs" when he declared "an all-out global war on the drug menace." President Bill Clinton appointed as his "drug czar" retired Army general and Desert Storm hero Barry McCaffrey. Yet 40 years and $2.5 trillion later, despite the killing or capture of such drug kingpins as Pablo Escobar and a string of Mexican cartel leaders, the use of illegal drugs in America has actually increased. Moreover, the aggressive pursuit of the Colombian cartels drove the cocaine trade into Mexico, and now the violence created by intense competition among Mexican drug trafficking organizations threatens to spill across the border into the United States.[1]

Six major categories of drugs are scheduled by the DEA: amphetamines, powder cocaine, crack cocaine, lysergic acid diethylamide (LSD), marijuana, and opiates. In addition, prescription drugs are sold and used illegally, constituting a seventh category.

The popularity of specific drugs has waxed and waned over the years, but all remain part of the marketplace and components of a $400 billion worldwide underground industry.

History of illegal drugs in America

Of the major illegal drugs, marijuana has the longest history in the United States. The hemp plant (*Cannabis sativa*) was cultivated beginning with the Jamestown settlers early in the seventeenth century, albeit for its fibers for the manufacture of rope, sails, and even clothing. During the first half of the nineteenth century, hemp was a major plantation crop, and not only in the South—substantial cultivation took place in New York, Nebraska, and California as well as South Carolina, Kentucky, Georgia, and Mississippi.[2] In addition to the commercial product represented by hemp, the smoking of hashish (prepared from the resin of the plant and therefore stronger than the dried leaves and buds) enjoyed a certain degree of popularity in the United States and even more in France. From 1850 to 1937, marijuana saw extensive medicinal use across the country and was widely available in retail shops. Recreational use, however, was uncommon.

That changed in the wake of the Mexican Revolution in 1910, as recreational use in Mexico was far more common and Mexican immigrants to the United States brought the habit with them. The Volstead Act of 1920, which created the practical framework for Prohibition, had the unintended consequence of further increasing the popularity of marijuana by making it an alternative to alcohol. However, the economic strains created by the Great Depression led to an increase in racial tensions, and during the 1930s, marijuana became linked in the popular imagination to Mexicans and to a lesser extent African Americans.[3] Finally, the Marijuana Tax Act of 1937 outlawed the drug. The "beatnik" movement acquired the recreational use of marijuana from African-American jazz culture and brought it into mainstream middle-class society in the 1960s.

Opiates (opium and heroin) enjoyed broad popularity during the nineteenth century, especially among the upper and middle classes, and given this "respectability" were often prescribed by doctors as well as being available for retail purchase, normally in liquid form. Chinese workers who came to the United States in the mid-nineteenth century for railroad construction introduced the smoking of opium. The first widespread problem with opiate addiction arose in the early 1900s. Ironically enough the culprit was heroin, a synthetic version of morphine, which had been introduced to combat the problem of morphine addiction that had grown out of the painkiller's widespread use during the Civil War.[2] In the 1950s and 1960s, heroin entered mainstream American culture in much the same manner that marijuana did.

Cocaine followed a developmental path similar to that of opiates, initially being hailed as a useful and beneficial drug. The German army gave it to trainees to combat fatigue, and no less a personage than Sigmund Freud praised its properties extensively in writing. The U.S. Army's surgeon general endorsed its use in 1886, the same year John Pemberton introduced Coca-Cola—which did indeed contain coca extract until the early twentieth century.[2] Often combined with opium in "medicinal tonics," cocaine had captured 200,000 U.S. addicts by 1902. Cocaine was outlawed by the Harrison Narcotics Tax Act of 1914, though there were racial overtones to its banning as well: Where marijuana was linked in particular to Mexicans, cocaine-using African Americans were demonized, particularly in the South.[3] Cocaine returned to popularity in the 1970s as the members of the 1960s counterculture, now entering the workforce, adopted it as a glamorous "party drug."

Unlike the plant-derived drugs such as marijuana, opium, and cocaine, amphetamines are synthetic, and the first one was created in 1887. It was widely adopted for various medical uses beginning in the 1920s, given to military personnel during World War II to fight fatigue and enhance endurance, and prescribed afterward as an antidepressant. However, abuse of the drug had already begun in the 1930s, when an amphetamine was sold over-the-counter with the brand name Benzedrine. In the postwar years, illegal use was common among over-the-road truck drivers, athletes, and students. The drug's popularity declined during the 1970s, but in the 1990s a new version—methamphetamine—emerged. Usage has been overwhelmingly among white Americans, particularly rural and blue-collar populations, and as its popularity has increased, Mexican cartels have undertaken industrial-scale production.

LSD is another purely synthetic drug, an accidental discovery by Swiss chemist Albert Hofmann in 1943. The first use of LSD was also accidental: Hofmann absorbed a small dose through the skin of his fingertips. Given the drug's psychotropic properties, psychiatry professors at the University of Zurich began investigating LSD. As the Cold War intensified in the 1950s, the U.S. military and intelligence community assessed the potential for LSD as an interrogation drug, while the medical community pursued possible applications for treating psychosis, depression, and even epilepsy.

In the early 1960s, amateur chemists began synthesizing LSD, making the drug much more widely available. LSD was outlawed in the United States in 1966, and much of what was produced for the black market was of low quality and strength. As the counterculture movement of the late 1960s waned, the popularity of LSD declined with it until the 1990s, when rave culture revived it. Nearly all of the current supply of the drug is believed to originate in Northern California at a strength roughly 10% of what was produced in the 1960s.

Although crack is merely processed cocaine, it warrants a category of its own because of the significant differences between it and the powder form of the drug. Although cocaine was expensive, crack was cheap and powerful and used disproportionately by the poor. The racial associations with certain drugs seen in the early twentieth century emerged once again as extremely harsh penalties were assessed for crack offenses as compared to powder cocaine—a sentencing ratio of 100 to 1, in fact.[2] (The threshold for felony possession was set at 5 g for crack but 500 g for powder cocaine.) As a result, during the 1980s, the U.S. prison population began to swell. The U.S. Sentencing Commission examined crack cocaine sentencing guidelines beginning in 1994. Research revealed that about two-thirds of crack users were either white or Hispanic, yet 84.5% of those convicted for possession of crack and 88.3% of those convicted for trafficking were African Americans.[8] Nevertheless, it took until 2010 for Congress to enact the sentencing reforms first recommended by the commission in 1995.

Finally, the most significant and growing drug problem involves not illegal drugs, but rather illegal use of prescription drugs. The 2010 National Survey on Drug Use and Health (NSDUH) reported that 20,044 of 36,450 overdose deaths in 2008 resulted from prescription drugs, meaning they killed more people than all illegal drugs combined.[4] So-called "prescription mills" masquerading as pain clinics have issued millions of technically legal but not medically necessary prescriptions for such pain medications as OxyContin, Percocet, Lortab, Vicodin, and Darvocet. Of about 7 million people reporting "nonmedical" use of a prescription drug in the past month in 2010, 5.1 million had abused a painkiller, 2.6 million a sedative or tranquilizer (such as Valium, Xanax, Ambien, or Seconal), and 1.1 million a stimulant (such as Adderall or Dexedrine).[5]

Drug use and drug abuse

The major source of data on illicit drug use by Americans is the NSDUH conducted by the Substance Abuse and Mental Health Services Administration of the U.S. Department of Health and Human Services. The survey breaks illicit drug use into nine categories:

1. Marijuana (including hashish)
2. Cocaine (including crack cocaine)
3. Heroin
4. Hallucinogens (including LSD, phencyclidine (PCP), peyote, mescaline, psilocybin, and methylenedioxy-N-methylamphetimine (MDMA) or "Ecstasy")
5. Inhalants (a broad category that includes gasoline, spray paint, glue, cleaning fluids, aerosols, amyl nitrate, and nitrous oxide)
6. Prescription pain relievers
7. Prescription tranquilizers
8. Prescription stimulants (includes methamphetamine, which is derived from over-the-counter medications)
9. Prescription sedatives

The NSDUH methodology considers a "current" drug user to be one who has used an illegal drug within the past month. For reporting purposes, the four categories of prescription drugs are combined under the term "psychotherapeutics." The 2011 survey reported 22.5 million people (age 12 or older) as current drug users, or 8.7% of the population. For statistical purposes, this was essentially flat compared to 2010 (8.9%) and 2009 (8.7%), but the 2009–2011 rates were slightly higher than that of the 2002–2008 period:

- 2002: 8.3%
- 2003: 8.2%
- 2004: 7.9%
- 2005: 8.1%
- 2006: 8.3%
- 2007: 8.0%
- 2008: 8.1%

Of the 22.5 million reporting drug use, the vast majority had used marijuana: 18.1 million. The other significant category was psychotherapeutics at 6.1 million. The remaining categories were cocaine at 1.4 million, hallucinogens at 1.0 million, inhalants at 0.6 million, and heroin at 0.3 million.[6]

On an age basis, usage climbs rapidly through the adolescent years. Illicit drug usage in 2011 was 3.3% for the 12–13 age group, rising to 9.2% for the 14–15 age group and to 17.2% for 16- and 17-year-olds. Usage by age group peaked with the 18–20 segment at 23.8%, declining somewhat to 19.9% for ages 21–25 and even more sharply to 14.9% for ages 26–29. For ages 30–34 and 35–39, usage rates were 11.1% and 8.2%, respectively. After age 40, usage rates were 6.4% for ages 40–44, 6.7% for ages 45–49, and 50–54, and 6.0% for the 55–59 cohort. Among the elderly, drug use was 2.7% among 60- to 64-year-olds and 1.0% at ages 65 and above.[7]

An intriguing aspect of age as a factor in drug use appeared consistently in several different studies from 1997 to 2002 involving New York City drug users. Arrestees born between 1945 and 1954 were predominantly heroin users. The majority of those born from

1955 to 1969 used crack cocaine while avoiding heroin. Those born in 1970 and afterward demonstrated "strong norms against heroin and crack use" and preferred "blunts," marijuana incorporated into an inexpensive cigar.[8]

On a gender basis, a larger proportion of males use illicit drugs, with the female usage rate not much more than half that of males: In 2011, 6.5% of females aged 12 and older reported drug use versus 11.1% of males. Among adolescents, the gender gap was about half as much: For 12- to 17-year-olds, 6.7% of females and 9.0% of males used drugs. On a gender-related note, 5.0% of pregnant women aged 15–44 reported drug use compared to 10.8% among members of that age group who were not pregnant. Age played a significant role in use by pregnant women: For women aged 15–17 the rate was 20.9%, dropping sharply to 8.2% among those aged 18–25 and even more sharply to 2.2% among those aged 26–44.[9]

Perhaps surprisingly (at least superficially), the majority of reported users were employed: 13.1 million of 19.9 million users aged 18 or older were employed (either part time or full time). However, this is merely a function of the overall rate of employment among the population. On a percentage basis for the same age group, 17.2% of unemployed persons reported drug use compared to 9.3% of those employed full time and 3.8% employed part time. Education level also plays a role. For the same cohort (18 and older), usage rates were 5.4% for college graduates, 10.4% among those with some college, 8.9% among high school graduates, and 11.1% among those without a high school diploma or GED.[10]

Finally, a set of statistics of particular interest given both the composition of prison populations and historical associations between racist assumptions and the banning of certain drugs is usage by ethnicity. The lowest rate was among those self-identified as Asian at 3.8%. The second-lowest was 8.4% among Hispanics, followed by 8.7% among whites, 10.0% among African Americans, 11.0% among Hawaiians and other Pacific Islanders, and 13.4% among Native Americans and Alaska Natives. Interestingly, the highest rate by a slight margin was 13.5% among those of two or more races. (The report does caution that the sample sizes for the groups with the three highest rates—Hawaiians and Pacific Islanders, Native Americans and Alaska Natives, and mixed-race individuals—were relatively small and therefore statistically less reliable.)

The American Psychiatric Association does consider drug abuse to be a form of mental illness. The current *Diagnostic and Statistical Manual of Mental Disorders* (*DSM-IV*) establishes separate categories for substance abuse and dependence. The terms have been the subject of some debate in the mental health community, and in fact the clinical term "dependence" was included in the *DSM-IV* by the margin of a single vote.[11] Among medical professionals, dependence generally refers to physical dependence that results in withdrawal symptoms when the drug is discontinued, whereas addiction is psychological dependence.

The latest revision, *DSM-V*, eliminates substance abuse and dependence in favor of "addictions and related disorders." Increasingly, research is demonstrating that repeated drug use can result in structural and chemical changes in the brain. Marijuana was long considered to be nonaddictive, but it is now known that physical withdrawal is uncommon instead because tetrahydrocannabinol (THC) is stored in fat cells and clears from the body only gradually. As such, the concept of physical dependence is no longer distinct from what was once considered "psychological dependence."[12]

In addition to being a disorder in itself, many chronic drug abusers have what is known as a co-occurring disorder, meaning they have a second serious mental illness. Disorders commonly associated with drug abuse include posttraumatic stress disorder, generalized anxiety disorder, bipolar disorder, schizophrenia, obsessive-compulsive disorder, panic disorder, antisocial personality disorder, and attention deficit hyperactivity disorder. Conversely, certain psychological disorders carry an increased risk of drug abuse:[13]

- Antisocial personality disorder: 15.5%
- Manic episode: 14.5%
- Schizophrenia: 10.1%
- Panic disorder: 4.3%
- Major depressive episode: 4.1%
- Obsessive-compulsive disorder: 3.4%
- Phobias: 2.1%

The mental illness perspective on drug abuse is part of the impetus behind initiatives to replace traditional criminal prosecution and penalties with treatment programs backed by punitive measures to ensure compliance. Attempts to interdict drugs on the supply side have been expensive and only marginally successful, as the section on "Enforcement activities" will explore. The alternative, focusing efforts on reducing demand, was initially attempted through relatively stiff penalties for drug possession, minimum sentencing requirements, and "three strikes" laws. However, if we accept that the addict is in fact uncontrollably dependent, some form of treatment becomes the rational alternative.

The drug court alternative

As mentioned in Chapter 11, all 50 states now have some form of drug court; the federal system took longer to adopt the concept, and what was established was not an exact equivalent of the state model. Rather than emphasizing punitive measures, drug courts attempt first and foremost to resolve the offender's drug dependency issues. The mainstay of this effort is a drug treatment program, with enforcement accomplished through random urine drug tests and regular reporting to a parole officer. Their use, however, is restricted to nonviolent offenders with no (or at most a minor) criminal history and to personal-use possession charges, not to drug trafficking offenses. A defendant cannot request adjudication through the drug court system, but rather must be referred by the prosecutor or judge. In many cases, a guilty plea will be a prerequisite to diversion into this system. Assuming the defendant successfully completes the treatment program, there will be no further punishment, and many jurisdictions will remove the offense from the defendant's record entirely. Failure, however, means a return to the conventional criminal court system and more likely than not jail time.[14]

The first drug court was the Miami-Dade County Felony Drug Court, established in 1989. The National Institute of Justice (NIJ) reported more than 2600 drug courts nationwide as of December 31, 2011. The majority of them (1435) handle adult offenders, but there are numerous specialized types:

- Juvenile drug courts: 458
- Family drug courts: 329
- Tribal drug courts: 79
- Designated DUI courts: 192
- Campus drug courts: 5
- Reentry drug courts: 31
- Federal reentry drug courts: 46

- Veterans drug courts: 95
- Co-occurring disorder courts: 20[15]

The most significant question for any alternative sentencing program is whether it is more effective than traditional procedures. NIJ has funded studies of various drug court systems, the most comprehensive of which was a 10-year evaluation of the Multnomah County drug court in Portland, Oregon. Overall, research points to reductions in both recidivism and costs produced by these programs. A study of the Pensacola, Florida, and Kansas City, Missouri, drug courts published in 2002 reported reductions in felony rearrest rates from 40% to 12% and from 50% to 35% over the course of a 2-year follow-up.[16]

The Multnomah County study tracked 6500 offenders from 1991 to 2001. Looking even farther out—5 years or more—recidivism rates were conclusively lower, although the exact degree of improvement (which varied from 17% to 26%) was affected by changes in the assigned judges and variations in program procedures over the course of the study. Moreover, the average cost reduction for the drug court compared to traditional criminal courts was $1392 per offender. Adding in the reduction in recidivism, direct costs to the system were estimated to have decreased by $6,744 per defendant, and if victimization costs are factored in, the amount rises to $12,218.[17]

The NIJ underwrote another study, the Multisite Adult Drug Court Evaluation (MADCE), to determine what factors make a drug court program effective. The 5-year study used a sample of approximately 1800 offenders (1157 from drug courts and 627 from traditional criminal court systems) across 23 drug courts and 6 criminal court control groups drawn from 29 urban, suburban, and rural jurisdictions in Florida, Georgia, Illinois, New York, Pennsylvania, North Carolina, South Carolina, and Washington. The study addressed four primary research questions:

1. What is the impact of adult drug courts on alcohol and other drug use, criminal recidivism, employment, and other functional outcomes?
2. What community, program, and offender characteristics predict these short- and long-term outcomes?
3. How do changes in short-term outcomes—such as offender perceptions and attitudes—mediate the impact of programs on long-term outcomes?
4. Are there cost savings attributable to drug court programs?[18]

The study confirmed the findings of other research. For example, an oral swab drug test conducted 18 months after completion of sentence showed drug use among 46% of traditional offenders but 29% of drug court defendants, and 43% of traditional offenders reported some form of criminal activity in the 6 months before the survey versus 31% of drug court defendants.[19] Although far from perfection, this is nevertheless a significant improvement.

In considering what offenders are the best candidates for drug courts, the study looked at violent versus nonviolent offenders. Statutes typically bar violent offenders from these programs, but the MADCE results indicated that "participants with violence histories reduced substance abuse just as much in Drug Court as those without violence histories and reduced criminal activity even more."[20] Interestingly, the cost savings estimated by other studies were not echoed by the MADCE. The economic benefit returned to the community by the drug courts averaged $2 for every $1 of investment, but this was essentially the same as that produced by traditional criminal courts. Rossman and Zweig[21] suggest that the drug courts in the MADCE "reduced low-level criminal offenses that are typically not associated with high incarceration or victimization costs. This suggests Drug Courts will need to target more serious offenders to reap significant cost benefits for their communities."

As for maximizing the effectiveness of drug courts, the study identified four best practices: "greater leverage over their participants," meaning the defendant was advised before entering the program of the consequences of failure and that judicial status hearings were held at least twice monthly; "greater predictability of sanctions," based on a written policy for addressing infractions disseminated to all participants; "consistent point of entry," "either at preadjudication or postadjudication, but not both"; and "positive judicial attributes," specifically judges who were "respectful, fair, attentive, enthusiastic, consistent, predictable, caring, and knowledgeable."[22]

The MADCE also quantified the frequency of various aspects of drug court programs that enhanced effectiveness. In addition to the aforementioned twice-monthly minimum for judicial hearings, Rossman and Zweig[23] recommend urine drug tests at least twice weekly, clinical case management sessions at least weekly, and formal substance abuse treatment lasting at least 35 days.

The federal justice system in 2000 created what it calls the Reentry Court Initiative under the auspices of the Office of Justice Programs. The various Reentry Court Programs are not standardized across all districts, which is somewhat surprising for a federal program, and not all are strictly speaking drug courts: "reentry courts that target the general population of returning offenders have to meet a diverse set of needs extending far beyond substance abuse treatment."[24] The most significant difference is that these federal programs are an alternative to traditional supervised release, not an alternative to traditional sentencing. Broadly speaking, the intent is to assist offenders with substance abuse problems to deal with addiction to reduce the risk of recidivism. For example, one of the first federal reentry programs was established in the District of Oregon in 2005 because of a sharp rise in methamphetamine abuse that had sent "the District of Oregon's revocation rate … above the national average."[25]

Because these federal programs were established relatively recently, there has been less evaluation of their effectiveness thus far. However, the ubiquity of drug courts at the state level and the backing of various interested groups such as the Drug Policy Alliance (DPA) and the National Association of Drug Court Professionals make it highly likely that these programs will remain a fixture of drug enforcement efforts. Significant shifts in public opinion regarding drug use have also strengthened support for an emphasis on treatment over punitive measures, albeit for those who use—not sell—illegal drugs.

Domestic drug trade

The drug trade in America was once a predominantly American issue. As previously discussed, most of today's illegal drugs were legal until the early twentieth century. Although it was necessary to address overseas cultivation of opium poppies and coca bushes to some extent, for the most part, enforcement was the responsibility of domestic law enforcement agencies. In the first three decades of the twentieth century, the social acceptability of heroin, cocaine, and marijuana (at least among the middle and upper classes) sharply declined. By the outbreak of World War II, illegal drug use had become a minimal social issue.[26]

The counterculture that arose among the postwar generation that came of age in the 1960s brought illegal drugs back to the forefront. The values of the generation that had rejected drugs were dismissed by many young people, so the social stigma that accompanied drug use was not an issue for them. Because the Baby Boomer Generation was so large, its embrace of illegal drugs fueled a massive boom in the drug trade. It was this boom that gave rise to the DEA, which was established in 1973.

As the demand for drugs rose, existing criminal organizations stepped in to answer it. U.S.-organized crime syndicates evolved during the Prohibition era to smuggle and distribute liquor. Once Prohibition was repealed, eliminating their major source of revenue, these organizations shifted their emphasis to both illegal gambling and the control of legal gambling operations. In the 1960s, heroin trafficking in particular was a focus, but aggressive efforts by federal law enforcement mostly dismantled those distribution networks in the 1970s.[27]

Generally speaking, drug distribution networks may be divided into wholesale and retail levels. The retail operation has two categories of personnel: The retail seller "is the functional, if illegal, equivalent of retail clerks in stores. They collect money from someone (usually the final retail customer) purchasing a commodity."[8] The other category includes "a loose assortment of roles in which an 'actor' is responsible for either, but never for both, drugs or money. They act as 'holders,' 'transporters,' 'mules,' 'deliverers,' 'counters,' 'lookouts,' 'backups,' or 'muscle.'"[8]

Wholesale distribution similarly has two tiers. The layer that sells to retailers purchases various drugs in large quantities either by weight or by value. Their suppliers in turn are the high-level distributors who have contacts with overseas producers (or may be an extension of such an organization) and who typically deal in terms of entire shipments. Because of the complexity of financing such large transactions, dividing shipments into wholesale parcels, and transporting these parcels across the country, the highest domestic distribution level is typically some form of organized criminal enterprise.[8]

There are significant distinctions between the upper and lower levels of drug distribution. The retail levels tend to draw extensively from among the poorest members of society; Johnson notes that "almost no low-level distributors and few sellers pay for their own apartment/home or support a family," and many in fact "live at severe poverty levels." They tend to have extensive criminal histories, shift among the various aforementioned distribution roles frequently as circumstances dictate, do the most dangerous work, and typically receive payment only on completion of assigned tasks. It is also rare for anyone at this level to "advance" into wholesale operations. Almost all retail distributors partake of the product they sell, and some actually receive drugs instead of money as payment.[8]

Although law enforcement certainly prefers to interdict networks at the upper wholesale levels, the fact is that more than 80% of drug offense arrests involve retail distributors. Wholesale operators are sufficiently sophisticated and savvy that they conceal their illegal activities from friends and even family; usually only their business associates will be aware of their criminal activity. Working through low-level personnel particularly for dangerous tasks insulates these individuals from much of the risk associated with the trade.[8]

Drug sales networks are either private or public. Public networks are those typically portrayed in fiction media and match the popular perception of "drug dealing": the corner dealer selling in a park, alley, bar, housing project, or similar setting. There is typically no personal relationship between seller and buyer, although a "regular" customer may know where to locate a particular dealer. Private networks involve sales between people who know each other. Because of these personal relationships and the lack of any need to conduct a transaction in a public place, private networks are next to impossible to identify—let alone infiltrate—for law enforcement. Most working-class and middle-class drug users obtain their supply through such networks.[8]

Small distributors tend to prefer acting as freelancers (i.e., working as independent public dealers) when this is an option. However, freelancers face a number of challenges.

First, because almost all of them are users as well as distributors, they often use much or all of their supply before making any sales. Second, organized distribution enterprises tend to drive off freelancers from the more lucrative sales areas. Third, such independents are particularly vulnerable to law enforcement. Researchers found that in New York City, freelancers would sometimes band together in informal cooperatives in an attempt to overcome some of these difficulties, though each member maintained strict control of his or her drug supply and money.[8]

Finally, some dealers were found to have organized their activities as a business enterprise. They would hire "managers" on a salary basis who in turn managed "day laborers" for the various low-level distribution roles. In most cases, those laborers were compensated with drugs rather than cash, and typically they handled only the delivery half of transactions, with someone else collecting payment from the customer.[8]

It is difficult to clearly distinguish between domestic and international trafficking operations, as discussed in the section on "International drug trade." Most overseas smuggling operations have organic distribution networks within the United States, just as domestic distribution networks often have links to production sources outside the country. However, certain drugs are produced predominantly within the United States. High-quality marijuana is grown, particularly on the West Coast, although substantial quantities still enter from foreign sources. Likewise, methamphetamine was originally a domestic product; as enforcement efforts have located and destroyed more and more production laboratories, Mexican cartels have ramped up to industrial-scale methamphetamine production and begun smuggling the drug into the United States as well. Current LSD supplies come from a few producers, most thought to be located in California.[28]

Despite these instances of domestic drug production, however, the bulk of illicit drugs distributed in this country come from overseas.

International drug trade

Although marijuana was certainly cultivated in the United States—it had been a plantation crop in the nineteenth century, after all—varieties from Central and South America were particularly prized. As author Mark Bowden[29] notes in *Killing Pablo*, "Colombian dope was … plentiful and highly potent, a fact that the world's marijuana-smoking millions quickly discovered. It was soon the worldwide gold standard for pot." Colombia had long been the domain of the *contrabandistas*, crime syndicates that specialized in smuggling. For decades, the cargo had been gold and emeralds; later in the twentieth century it included hard-to-find (and heavily taxed) consumer goods. But in the 1960s, the *contrabandistas* began shipping marijuana north. By the early 1970s, cocaine (with a substantially higher value per unit of volume) had displaced marijuana as the primary cargo. In 1975, one of the first Colombian cocaine kingpins, Fabio Restrepo of Medellín, was flying cargoes of 40–60 kg cocaine into Miami one to two times yearly, and at that time 1 g would fetch a street price in excess of $40,000.[30]

Such external sources of supply fed into various domestic distribution networks. The Colombian smuggling channels often terminated with young, upper-class Colombian men who had been educated in the United States, spoke English, and moved easily in the upper- and upper-middle-class social circles that represented the primary cocaine market. These were the simple forerunners of what would later become "a vast infrastructure of multiple cells functioning in many major metropolitan areas," each of which "performs a specific function within the organization, *e.g.* transportation, local distribution, or money movement."[28]

One of the first major international drug sources to receive widespread public attention was the "French Connection" of the 1970s, popularized by an eponymous motion picture. Since the 1950s, various American mafia families had been involved in smuggling and distributing illegal drugs, though not all—some considered the drug trade immoral or dishonorable and would not participate in it; others participated but would only distribute drugs to certain minorities or ethnic groups. The French Connection was a broad label for this activity, which focused primarily on the smuggling of Turkish opium. The first shipment leg took the drug to the French port of Marseilles and then to Paris. The next leg was by air into New York City, at which point the mafia families took possession for distribution across the United States.

Southeast Asia was another major source of heroin, particularly during the Vietnam War era, with most of the drug production originating from the so-called "Golden Triangle" region at the conjunction of Thailand, Laos, and Myanmar. As of 1987, the portion of U.S. heroin originating in Southeast Asia was estimated at 18%; by 1990, it had reached 45%. In certain regions, the change was even more dramatic. For New York City, the proportions changed from 5% in 1984 to 80% by 1990.[31] In 1993, Colombian heroin began to dominate the markets along the U.S. East Coast. The gain in market share resulted from aggressive marketing of a product with substantially higher quality at a lower price as well as from exploitation of existing distribution channels already in use for the cocaine trade. Both Asian and South American heroin comes mainly by courier via air, but larger shipments (typically in the range of 50 kg) were intercepted in seaborne cargo.[28] From 2002 to 2006, South American smugglers began shifting their air travel entry point from New York to Miami.[32]

West of the Mississippi, Mexican heroin dominates the market. The long land border with Texas, New Mexico, Arizona, and California greatly simplifies transportation, although ironically despite their penchant for moving massive loads of other drugs (marijuana, cocaine, and methamphetamine) the Mexican cartels have tended to move smaller quantities of heroin in each shipment. Much like the Colombians in the eastern United States, the Mexican organizations use their existing networks to distribute heroin.

Although Afghanistan remains by far the largest producer of heroin, a fact frequently highlighted by the opium poppy eradication programs that are part of the U.S. war effort in that country, most Afghan heroin is consumed in Asia and Europe. (This is an issue of geographic proximity as well as the fact that South and Central American suppliers control the U.S. heroin market.) Ironically, it was the U.S.-led defeat of the Taliban regime that caused Afghan heroin production to skyrocket, from about 7 metric tons in 2001 to 582 metric tons in 2004. Despite the fact that output has decreased in most of the world's other production areas, the surge in Afghan heroin caused overall global output to increase nonetheless.

In urban markets, the retail distribution is usually handled by street gangs, whereas in rural areas (where in any event heroin is much less common) independent dealers control the majority of sales. The Colombian, Dominican, and Mexican criminal enterprises that handle the smuggling serve as the wholesale source to these retailers.

The concept of the international drug cartel owes its fame (or infamy), however, primarily to the Colombian cocaine cartels of the late 1970s and the 1980s. These were the Medellín and Cali cartels, named for the Colombian cities where they originated. The Medellín cartel was synonymous with Pablo Escobar, although he was not the man who founded it. That had been accomplished by Fabio Restrepo, who as previously mentioned in 1975 was making one or two cocaine shipments a year to Miami. It was never proved that Pablo Escobar killed Restrepo, nor did Escobar ever make such a claim (though in fairness he never discouraged anyone from making that assumption, either), but it was widely assumed that he was responsible. In any event, responsible or not, in 1975, Restrepo was murdered and Escobar was suddenly in charge of his smuggling operation.[29]

Pablo Escobar in particular introduced high levels of organization into his criminal enterprise. Not every kilo of cocaine heading north came from Escobar's labs, but he had such tight control of the smuggling routes that he could impose "a tax on every kilo shipped." Product from small independent producers was included with loads from the Medellín cartel for a fee of 10% of the street price. In return, Escobar provided insurance: He reimbursed the cost of any shipment confiscated or otherwise lost, albeit only at the wholesale (Colombian) cost. As less than a tenth of shipments were being intercepted, this policy never posed the least threat to his profit margins.[29]

The heyday of cocaine—all of it originating in South America—lasted from the mid-1970s until 1986. In June of that year, Len Bias, a University of Maryland basketball player who had been picked second in the NBA draft, died at a party as a result of cocaine use. The public perception of the drug shifted, particularly among those who used it. The drug lost its glamor and appeal, a process only accelerated by the epidemic of crack cocaine, which was a drug of the poor and one that was spawning violence on the streets of America.[29] (The previously discussed generational nature of drug preferences becomes clearer in this historical context: Those reaching their late teens around this time would have been influenced by the abrupt and widespread decline in the popularity of cocaine.)

Nevertheless, cocaine has not stopped flowing into the United States, and it still originates in South America. The key difference is that the aggressive enforcement efforts aimed at the Colombian cartels—Escobar himself was finally run to ground and killed by police at the end of 1993—made their traditional trans-Caribbean smuggling routes too risky. Faced with no other way to bring their product to market (which includes Europe and Africa in addition to the United States), the Colombian cartels turned to overland smuggling through Mexico. So it was that the success of the DEA and its local partners in Colombia at interdicting cocaine trafficking inadvertently spawned a decade of intense violence much closer to home: just across the border in Mexico.

Mexican drug cartels

In discussing the fractured landscape of the Mexican drug trade, it is not even truly accurate to use the term "cartel." That word implies a monopoly or near-monopoly on the production and/or distribution of some product. Although Pablo Escobar's Medellín cartel was truly a cartel—the Cali cartel rose only as Escobar's organization declined—the various Mexican organizations continue to struggle for dominance. The term frequently used in government and some law enforcement circles is DTO (for drug trafficking organization), although the DEA does use "cartel" instead.

Escobar's focus in building the Medellín cartel was on control of the smuggling routes. Similarly, the various Mexican DTOs are primarily concerned with what are called "plazas": the smuggling routes across the U.S.–Mexico border. Producing drugs is not the issue; getting them to customers is.

Understand that any overview of the DTOs is a snapshot, as the landscape is constantly changing as groups lose power struggles, senior leaders are killed or captured, groups fracture, or one DTO mounts an effort to seize territory from another. That being said, what follows addresses the broad outlines and some of the background of the major DTOs. (All information is drawn from the April 15, 2013 Congressional Research Service report entitled *Mexico's Drug Trafficking Organizations: Source and Scope of the Violence*.)[33]

Tijuana Cartel/Arellano Felix Organization (AFO): Emblematic of the chronic corruption problems within Mexican law enforcement at all levels, AFO was founded by a Sinaloa police officer, Miguel Angel Felix Gallardo. Gallardo himself was arrested in 1989 for the 1985 murder of a DEA Special Agent named Enrique "Kiki" Camarena, but his group included leaders of smaller DTOs including Amado Carrillo Fuentes, Rafael Caro Quintero, and Joaquin "El Chapo" Guzmán, as well as the seven brothers and four sisters of the Arellano Felix family. Based in Tijuana (hence its alternative name) and controlling the lucrative plazas into California, AFO shared dominance with the Juárez DTO. In October 2008, the last of the five Arellano Felix brothers participating in the drug trade was arrested. AFO split into two factions shortly thereafter, and other DTOs, seeing an opportunity, also moved in to take control of the Tijuana-San Diego plaza. One of AFO's lieutenants defected to the Sinaloa DTO but was subsequently arrested in January 2010. Violence in the Tijuana area has slackened since then, and while Mexican law enforcement might deserve credit for that, the more likely explanation is that the various DTOs reached an agreement on use of the plaza. The rumor is that the current AFO leader, Fernando Sanchez Arellano, has reached a pay-for-use arrangement with Sinaloa.

Sinaloa: This DTO was founded by one of the original members of AFO, Joaquin "El Chapo" Guzmán, who is probably the most infamous billionaire fugitive in Mexico (and number one on the country's list of top narco-traffickers). Sinaloa dominated South America-to-U.S. cocaine smuggling. Described by Jane's Information Group as "a complex organization containing a number of semi-autonomous groups" rather than "a strictly vertical and hierarchical structure," this DTO was estimated in 2010 to control 45% of the Mexican drug trade—and this was despite the collapse of an alliance with the Beltrán Leyva and Juárez DTOs in 2008. With a presence in 50 countries as far away as Southeast Asia, Sinaloa has been described as "the most powerful mafia organization in the Western Hemisphere." The DTO controlled (as of January 2012) the states of Sinaloa, Sonora, and Baja California Sur; nearly all of Baja California Norte; substantial portions of Chihuahua, Durango, Nayarit, Jalisco, Colima, and Oaxaca; and a small portion of Quintana Roo along the Mexico–Belize border.

Juárez/Vicente Carrillo Fuentes Organization: Currently under the leadership of Vicente Carrillo Fuentes, this DTO is based around the Ciudad Juárez-El Paso plaza. Since splitting with Sinaloa in 2008, Juárez (along with La Línea, its enforcement arm) has contested control of this vital route with its former ally. The battle has been carried out directly and through proxy street gangs within Ciudad Juárez itself, with Los Aztecas fighting on behalf of the Juárez DTO and Artistas Asesinos and the Mexicales fighting for Sinaloa. The prolonged combat has made Chihuahua the Mexican state with the highest murder rate. Some observers opine that Juárez is in permanent and irreversible decline and that its loss of the Ciudad Juárez plaza to Sinaloa is inevitable. La Línea suffered the loss of its leader, José Antonio Acosta "El Diego" Hernández, who was arrested in July 2011, extradited to the United States, and ultimately sentenced to four consecutive life sentences.

Gulf: Headquartered in Matamoros, across the Rio Grande from Brownsville, Texas, the Gulf DTO dates to the Prohibition era. It was one of the first to establish ties to the Cali cartel in the 1980s under the leadership of Juan García Abrego. The Gulf DTO was formidable around the turn of the century; although Abrego's successor Osiel Cárdenas Guillén was arrested in 2003, he continued to run his DTO from prison until he was finally extradited to the United States in 2007, where he is now serving a 25-year sentence. One of the Gulf DTOs major contributions to the Mexican drug trafficking landscape is Los Zetas, another DTO. Los Zetas started out as the Gulf DTO's enforcement arm and is particularly notorious because it was originally made up of

Mexican special operations soldiers who defected to the cartel. Osiel Guillén's brother Antonio Ezequiél Cárdenas "Tony Tormenta" Guillén took control of the organization after Osiel's extradition, but Antonio was killed in early November 2010 during a firefight with Mexican marines. Los Zetas took advantage of the opening and moved to seize territory including Tamaulipas, Nuevo León, and Veracruz, initiating a fight that lasted through 2011. Scrambling to retain its holdings, the Gulf cartel formed alliances with Sinaloa and La Familia Michoacána against Los Zetas, and the ensuing battles rose to the level of urban warfare, including attacks on military posts and blockades intended to keep police from intervening in cartel battles. Antonio's successor Eduardo "El Coss" Costilla was arrested in September 2012, at which point the Gulf DTO split into competing factions struggling to reunify and control the organization.

Los Zetas: Los Zetas began its move away from the Gulf DTO in 2008 when it began freelancing its enforcement services to other DTOs, primarily Juárez and Beltrán Leyva. Sometime between 2008 and 2010—there is no consensus on exactly when—Los Zetas split from the Gulf cartel entirely. It began aggressive expansion into Central America, particularly Guatemala, in an attempt to take control of cocaine smuggling routes out of South America. The DTO's rapid rise to power prompted enhanced enforcement efforts against it by both U.S. and Mexican authorities, causing the loss of several important members. Los Zetas leader Heriberto Lazcano Lazcano was killed by Mexican marines in October 2012, and the new leader Miguel Angel Treviño "Z-40" Morales may not fully control all factions within the organization.

Beltrán Leyva Organization (BLO): Another member of the Sinaloa federation, BLO is based in Sonora along the Arizona border with its primary plaza in the twin cities of Nogales, Mexico and Nogales, Arizona. In January 2008, Alfredo Beltrán Leyva, brother of BLO leader Arturo Leyva, was arrested, and Sinaloa leader "El Chapo" Guzmán was blamed, leading to the split between the two organizations. BLO does not control wide swathes of territory comparable to many other DTOs, but it does operate smuggling routes through the states of Sinaloa, Durango, Sonora, Jalisco, Michoacán, Guerrero, and Morelos. BLO was historically among the most sophisticated of the DTOs. It had well-established links with Colombian cocaine producers, controlled multiple drug transport routes, and had extensive reach into the high levels of the Mexican government. BLO lost its leader during a raid by Mexican marines; of the two remaining Beltrán brothers Carlos was arrested in January 2010, leaving Hector in control. However, he faced an internal power struggle with Gerardo "La Barbie" Alvarez-Vazquez, a Mexican-American from Laredo, Texas, until Vazquez was arrested in August 2010. Nevertheless, BLO fractured. Hector retains the leadership of the South Pacific Cartel, whereas the Independent Cartel of Acapulco is composed of those who were loyal to Vazquez.

La Familia Michoacána/Knights Templar (LFM): LFM is a study in contradictions, or at the very least irony. It dates to the 1980s, when it was founded as an antidrug vigilante group, yet today it is known for its use of extreme violence and violence for the sake of symbolism, at least partly because of the religious elements it blends into its image. The DTO's members are known for making donations of food, providing medical care, and even building schools. LFM specializes in methamphetamine but also deals in heroin, cocaine, and marijuana, although because of its "principles" it does not distribute methamphetamine in Mexico. LFM lost its leader, Nazario Moreno "El Más Loco" González, in a December 2010 firefight with Mexican "Federales," and his successor José de Jésus Méndez Vargas was arrested in June 2011. The Knights Templar, under the leadership of Servando "La Tuta" Gomez, has emerged as a successor organization. It maintains the same pseudoreligious image and has published a 22-page manifesto explaining its "ethics." It is believed that the Knights Templar has fought with remnants of the original LFM in the states of Michoacán, Mexico, Morelos, and Guerrero.

It is important to note that drug trafficking is not the sole pursuit of the Mexican DTOs. Most engage in other types of organized crimes. LFM and the Knights Templar, for example, are known for extortion, and Los Zetas is the most diversified of all the DTOs, involved in stealing petroleum from PEMEX, Mexico's state oil company, among other things. Other activities include kidnapping, assassination for hire, auto and resource theft, prostitution, software piracy, and human smuggling. For this reason, the DEA has begun to apply the term "transnational criminal organization" rather than DTO.[27]

One significant lesson of the Mexican cartels is that targeting the senior leadership of DTOs is only marginally effective. The loss of a strong leader typically has one of two results: Either a new leader takes control of the organization or competing factions within the DTO devolve into infighting. When a DTO splinters, a new DTO of equal or nearly equal strength may emerge, or rival DTOs may descend on the weakened organization in the hope of seizing whatever spoils are available. In short, destabilizing the system by eliminating leaders tends to produce elevated levels of violence.

Money laundering and the drug trade

It is no secret that the drug trade generates huge sums of money—at least for those at the wholesale level. (As noted in the section on "Domestic drug trade," frontline sellers and couriers frequently live in poverty and as often as not are paid in drugs rather than cash.) As the cocaine boom headed toward its peak, Bowden notes that "between 1976 and 1980 bank deposits in Colombia's four major cities more than doubled." During the presidency of Alfonso López Michelsen, policies were changed so that Colombia's central bank was allowed to convert unlimited quantities of dollars into Colombian pesos. The government even established "speculative investment funds" that paid stratospheric rates of return. Although they were represented as legitimate investment vehicles, it was common knowledge that the real destination of the money was the cocaine trade, meaning that anyone who could afford to invest could participate vicariously in the drug trade with the government's implicit blessing.[29]

To put a value on "huge sums of money," the Office of National Drug Control Policy estimates U.S. spending on illegal drugs at $65 billion annually.[34] The United Nations Office of Drugs and Crime estimates a worldwide total of over $400 billion. Of that, only about $1 billion is seized by law enforcement, so tremendous sums still flow through the underground global economy.[35] The DEA has focused extensive efforts on tracking and disrupting the financial infrastructure that underlies DTOs, since after demand reduction eliminating the financial incentives of drug trafficking is the most efficient method of attack. The financial channels also represent a chokepoint that is easier to target than smuggling routes or individual dealers. Investigation and prosecution are aided by the fact that the number, size, and complexity of transactions mean detailed recordkeeping is unavoidable. And while drugs flow from top to bottom in a DTO, money flows from bottom to top, meaning following the money is a path to the organization's leadership.

Former DEA agent and money laundering expert Robert Mazur, who spent many years undercover investigating the Colombian cartels' financial activities, reports that "a segment of the international banking and business community solicits business relationships with people who possess 'flight capital,' which constitutes money-seeking-secrecy from governments." He identifies several varieties of flight capital: proceeds of the illegal arms trade, white-collar crime, and tax evasion; money diverted to nations under economic sanctions; and national assets stolen by regime insiders. Drug profits, of course, top the list.

The bitter truth is that global banks play a significant role in money laundering. The headlines periodically blare revelations of another supposedly legitimate bank that has turned out to be processing illegal funds. A recent example is HSBC, fined $2 billion by the U.S. government in 2012 for money laundering. It is believed to have laundered at least $881 million for clients that included the Sinaloa cartel and Colombia's Norte del Valle cartel, and the U.S. Department of Justice described its internal controls as "knowingly and willfully lax."[36] Other institutions that have recently admitted complicity in money laundering include Bank Atlantic (2006), Union Bank of California (2007), American Express Bank International (2007), Lloyds (2009), UBS (2009), Credit Suisse (2009), Wachovia Bank (2010), Deutsche Bank (2010), ABM Amro Holding NY (2010), and Barclays Bank (2010).[35] As you can see, the list includes major multinational banks with household and (at least in the past) respected names—UBS, Deutsche Bank, Lloyds, Barclays, Credit Suisse, and Wachovia—and to put it bluntly, these are just the ones that have been caught. Although several of these banks are based in Europe, Mazur does not mince words: "the trail of the greatest portion of illicit drug sales around the globe runs through the U.S. banking system."[35]

It was the Colombian cartels that first mastered large-scale money laundering to handle the tremendous sums flowing south from U.S. markets. Although the cocaine trade is not what it once was, total money laundering in Colombia is now estimated at $8 billion annually, about 3% of gross domestic product. Cartels establish businesses not only in Colombia but across Central and South America to provide front organizations for laundering.[37]

The obscenely large profits from his cocaine trafficking meant that Pablo Escobar had to find creative ways to launder those dollars. Escobar's brother Roberto advised Pablo on financial matters and later related some of the techniques that they used. An American economist and Wall Street professional invested money in stocks and directly into various companies under false names. One of the first avenues Roberto used was real estate: Drug proceeds were used to buy property, which was then resold. High-dollar art and collectibles—goods that could easily be resold—were also common choices; Escobar bought paintings by Picasso, Botero, and Dali in addition to furniture and other antiques. He also took advantage of Colombia's substantial emerald trade (about 60% of the global market). In response to orders from legitimate overseas buyers, the cartel would ship low-quality stones that had been treated with oil; the deception would not be revealed until after payment had been made. The problem was that these laundering methods were expensive, in some cases costing half or more of the total proceeds.[38]

Today, it is the Mexican cartels that are at the forefront of money laundering, simply because they control the lion's share of drug proceeds. Much of the money generated by drug sales is returned to Mexico by what the DEA calls bulk currency smuggling. This is no minor undertaking given the quantities of cash involved: $20 million weighs about 1176 pounds, equivalent to a young elephant.[39] In fact, many of the same enforcement tactics used to detect drug smuggling into the country are just as effective at identifying cash being smuggled out of it. Some proceeds are also returned to Mexico via remittances, the money that Mexicans working in the United States send to family members still in Mexico.

The United States has taken steps to detect and if not prevent then at least complicate the processing of large sums of cash. For example, any bank deposit of $10,000 or more is automatically reported to federal authorities, and restrictions have been proposed on cash purchases of big-ticket items such as houses, cars, and boats.[40] Evading these deposit limits through a practice known as "structuring" funds into amounts just under the $10,000 threshold is itself a crime.

Even more sophisticated money laundering techniques are now favored. The prevalent method is called trade-based money laundering, which is notoriously hard to detect and even harder to prove. The process uses drug sale proceeds to purchase some form of commodity. That commodity is then exported to the DTO's home country where it is sold. Once the initial purchase has been made, the proceeds of the resale of the goods can be presented as the source of funds to purchase further products, in just the same manner as any business would operate, and laundering the "seed money" is not particularly complicated.

To make the laundering chain even harder to follow a third country is often involved, frequently as the source of the goods. Taiwan and China are popular options. In many cases, transactional documents are adulterated; U.S. customs officials have reported invoices and customs declarations that were either undervalued or overvalued. In other words, the invoice showing the purchase of the commodity (with drug proceeds) is doctored to show a higher purchase price to support a higher customs declaration, which accounts for even more value than the goods themselves would represent. As one Immigration and Customs Enforcement (ICE) officer explained to the *Los Angeles Times*,

> You generate all this paperwork on both sides of the border showing that the product you're importing has this much value on it, when in reality you paid less for it. Now you've got paper earnings of a million dollars. You didn't really earn that, but it gives you a piece of paper to take to [Mexican financial authorities] to say: "This million dollars in my bank account—it's legitimate. It came from this here, see?"[40]

One of the greatest complications of trade-based money laundering is the overall value of the trade between the United States and Mexico: about $400 billion annually. Although several 100 million dollars is substantial, when diluted within such a large volume it becomes extremely hard to identify.

One of the pioneers of this style of money laundering—at least in Mexico—is believed to have been Blanca Cazares, who is alleged to have laundered funds for the Sinaloa DTO. She imported silk from China into Los Angeles, paying for it with drug funds. The fabric was then exported to Mexico and sold in a chain of retail shops at substantial prices, thereby converting the dollars into pesos.[40]

In 2010, another such scheme was uncovered in Los Angeles. The Angel Toy Company was indicted and its top three executives arrested. Large sums of cash in small bills had been regularly delivered by couriers to the company's workshop, where workers "structured" the cash and deposited it into company accounts. Angel Toys imported toys from Asian manufacturers and exported them to Bogota to be sold in retail stores.[40]

The fight against money laundering is like any other aspect of the War on Drugs: The enemy is constantly introducing new techniques that law enforcement must identify, understand, and counter. In response, the drug traffickers shift to new tactics. U.S. agencies have begun training Mexican customs and law enforcement personnel and enhancing the level of cooperation between the two countries' customs agencies. Technology and data interchange among countries will also be vital parts of a successful counter to these new money laundering techniques.

Enforcement activities

U.S. law enforcement efforts against illegal drugs are based on the Controlled Substances Act (CSA). It divides substances into five schedules. Schedules II through V cover substances with recognized medical applications and regulate their manufacture, distribution, and use. The higher schedule numbers represent decreasing levels of danger and addiction potential. As such, Schedule I substances are those that have no medical use and may not be possessed or consumed even with a prescription. Anyone who handles Schedule II through V substances, whether as a manufacturer, distributor, retailer, prescriber, researcher, or end user (such as a hospital or clinic), must register with the DEA, which is charged with primary responsibility for enforcing the CSA.[41]

Interdicting illegal drugs at the country's borders is a tremendous challenge. About 60 million people enter the United States annually by air on over 675,000 commercial and private flights, 6 million by sea on 90,000 passenger and merchant vessels and 157,000 private vessels, and 370 million by land. The Canadian and Mexican border crossings deal with approximately 116 million vehicles. Seaborne commerce brings 9 million shipping containers and 400 million tons of cargo.[42]

Even knowing the exact scope of the challenge can be problematic. During the 1970s, U. S. estimates of cocaine smuggling from South America were inaccurate by a full order of magnitude. In 1975, the official estimate was that between 500 and 600 kg were arriving from South America annually. That was the same year that a fortuitous bust in Cali by Colombian police found more than 600 kg of cocaine in a single aircraft.[29]

Today, the lion's share of enforcement efforts is directed at the U.S.–Mexico border. A report from the U.S. International Narcotics Control Strategy indicates that 90% of cocaine reaching the U.S. market crosses that border. Half of imported marijuana enters via Arizona alone.[1] For that reason, ICE and U.S. Customs and Border Protection play a vital role in the interdiction of illegal drug shipments. However, the primary responsibility for antidrug efforts rests with the DEA. Its official mission is

> to enforce the controlled substances laws and regulations of the United States and bring to the criminal and civil justice system of the United States, or any other competent jurisdiction, those organizations and principal members of organizations, involved in the growing, manufacture, or distribution of controlled substances appearing in or destined for illicit traffic in the United States; and to recommend and support non-enforcement programs aimed at reducing the availability of illicit controlled substances on the domestic and international markets.[43]

Because the investigation of drug crimes may fall to law enforcement agencies at any level, from a local police department or sheriff's office to the Federal Bureau of Investigation, one of the DEA's most important responsibilities is the "coordination and cooperation with federal, state, and local law enforcement officials on mutual drug enforcement efforts and enhancement of such efforts through exploitation of potential interstate and international investigations beyond local or limited federal jurisdictions and resources."[43] This coordination extends overseas as well, and under the auspices of the U.S. Department of State, the DEA interfaces with foreign law enforcement agencies and transnational organizations such as Interpol and the United Nations.

There are two basic approaches to combatting drugs: the supply side and the demand side. Reducing supply means eradicating crops, arresting suppliers, interdicting smuggling routes, and confiscating drugs. Reducing demand means using education and prevention programs in combination with rehabilitation programs for drug-use offenders. The general proportion of antidrug funding has generally been 60% against supply and 40% against demand. Other related efforts have focused on building up the rule of law in major countries of origin, Mexico foremost among them. For example, in 2008 and 2009, about 70% of the U.S. Department of State's antidrug budget assigned to Mexico went to border security, including helicopters and other equipment. Beginning in 2010, funding emphasis shifted to such activities as training prison guards, supporting antigang programs aimed at at-risk youth, and professional development for prosecutors and judges.[44]

Corruption has, after all, been one of the key weaknesses in the drug fight, particularly in embattled Mexico. It was Pablo Escobar who made what came to be known as *plata o plomo*, a trademark of the drug cartel. Law enforcement and government officials had a choice: accept payoffs to ignore cartel activity (*plata*, silver) or die for refusing (*plomo*, lead).[29] The huge sums of money involved in the drug trade would by themselves buy plenty of cooperation; combined with the threat of death (for oneself and often for one's family as well) bribes were hard to refuse.

In fact, Mexico's Institutional Revolutionary Party (PRI), which ruled Mexico for 71 years straight, is blamed by some observers for the evolution of Mexican DTOs during most of the twentieth century, up to the time that cocaine smuggling routes began shifting to trans-Mexican overland routes. It is believed that the PRI accommodated a limited amount of drug activity in limited areas under what has been characterized as "a working relationship between Mexican authorities and drug lords" that lasted into the 1990s.[33]

The forms corruption takes range from simply "looking the other way" and ignoring DTO activities to active support and protection. In some of the most egregious cases, law enforcement officers (particularly in local police forces, which have been especially vulnerable to corruption) have actually carried out assassinations and other attacks. Although the Federal Police or "Federales" had a reputation of relative reliability (and were in fact expanded from 6,500 personnel to 37,000 during the 2006–2012 presidency of Felipe Calderón), that force has not been immune to problems, either. Federal Police attacked and killed three fellow officers in June 2012, and 12 were arrested and charged for the ambush of two U.S. law enforcement agents and a Mexican Navy captain in August 2012.[33] For that reason, the Mexican military has been used in some of the most troubled areas (the advantage being that military personnel are not local to the area where they are operating and so do not have contacts with the area's criminal organizations), and a review of cartel leaders killed will show that many died battling Mexican marines.

Some of the most obvious signs of the extent of corruption have been the results of arrests of state and local officials. Federal officers arrested 28 state and local officials, including 10 mayors, in May 2009, for involvement in drug trafficking. Of those 28 officials, 27 were later released when the charges against them did not hold up in court. The mayor of Cancún was arrested in 2010 and released 14 months later when his prosecution similarly failed, and yet another mayor, from Tijuana, was released only 2 weeks after being arrested in June 2011 because of procedural errors.[33]

Mexico is hardly unique in its problems with corruption. Colombia was no better, and the various Central American countries aside the current smuggling routes have the same issues. The sheer amounts of money available combined with the relative poverty typical of such countries and the violence associated with DTOs makes refusing bribery a difficult proposition for even the most well-intentioned official.

Criticisms of the "War on Drugs"

A variety of interest groups oppose the "War on Drugs" for several reasons. Some would like to see limited or even across-the-board legalization of Schedule I substances. Some have ethical objections to the motivations assumed to underlie drug statutes. Some point to the tremendous costs, including the swelling prison population, incurred in generating relatively limited results. Others are concerned about what they perceive as a degradation of civil rights in the pursuit of drug offenders.

The racial assumptions of many early drug statutes are seen by some as calling into question the justification for those laws. Opium laws in the 1870s were enacted with Chinese immigrants as their target. The first anticocaine laws were motivated by stories of how the drug caused uncontrollable violence in African Americans and were passed in the South. Mexican immigrants were the target of early-twentieth-century antimarijuana laws.[3] Although there is at least some truth in these assertions, broad statements that the standards of the CSA have nothing to do with scientific assessments of risk are not accurate. Opiates, for example, are indisputably highly addictive.

One of the major factors behind the tremendous increase in the U.S. prison population (and the cost associated with housing those inmates) has been the incarceration of nonviolent drug offenders. The number of inmates sentenced for such offenses multiplied eightfold from 50,000 in 1980 to more than 400,000 in 1997,[3] and the total correctional population rose from just less than 2 million in 1980 to peak at more than 7 million in 2007 and stood at 6,995,900 in 2011. (Note that the Bureau of Justice Statistics uses the term "correctional population" to include those on probation or parole. The total number of individuals actually incarcerated was 2,239,800 in 2011.)[45] Of 1,362,028 inmates under state jurisdiction at the end of 2010, as many as 237,000 or 17.4% were sentenced for drug offenses (of all types), down from 258,100 out of 1,209,130 or 21.4% as of December 31, 2000. For federal inmates, the proportions were much higher. At the end of 2011, a total of 94,600 were serving sentences for drug offenses out of a total population of 197,050, a rate of 48.0%. As with the state trend, the federal rate was higher in 2000: 70,500 out of 125,044 or 56.4%.[46]

The DPA raises concerns about what it calls "the militarization of domestic drug law enforcement." It cites 40,000 "paramilitary-style SWAT raids" conducted annually, at least some (the DPA claims "mostly") for nonviolent and misdemeanor offenses. Several U.S. Supreme Court decisions have enhanced search rights for law enforcement, although by no means have such decisions been across the board in favor of police actions.

Concurrent with the 2012 federal elections, voters in Washington and Colorado passed initiatives that legalized recreational marijuana use in those states. (A total of 18 states—Alaska, Arizona, California, Colorado, Connecticut, Delaware, Hawaii, Maine, Massachusetts, Michigan, Montana, Nevada, New Jersey, New Mexico, Oregon, Rhode Island, Vermont, and Washington—and the District of Columbia have already made the medical use of marijuana legal.) Oregon decriminalized the possession of small quantities (one ounce or less) of marijuana in 1973, though the drug was not legal—possession within those limits was subject to citation and a $100 fine, later raised to a maximum of $1000 in 1989.[47] The Supremacy Clause of the Constitution, which requires that if a state law contradicts federal law the state law is invalidated, technically makes these moves irrelevant, but the key issue is whether the federal government will pursue action against those states.

Although public support for legalizing marijuana has grown in recent years, there is virtually no chance that any other Schedule I substances would be legalized in the foreseeable future, which means the drug trade will continue to be a challenge facing the nation. Efforts to attack the supply side of the trade have had only marginal success. During the first decade of the twenty-first century, drug-use rates remained basically steady and overdose fatalities actually increased despite continued enforcement efforts.[3] In this era of shrinking government budgets, it is likely that the debate will focus on which measures deliver the best results for the cost.

Summary

If there is one consistent feature of the U.S. "War on Drugs," it is the resilient nature of the enemy. Success in one arena is almost always counterbalanced by frustration in another. Eradication programs might reduce drug cultivation in Peru and Bolivia only to cause production to increase in Brazil and Colombia. The crackdown on trans-Caribbean cocaine smuggling by the Colombian cartels led to a shift to land-based routes through Mexico across the southwestern U.S. border. The resultant breaking of the Colombian monopoly led to the rise of powerful and competing cartels in Mexico, with violence that occasionally spills across the border. The flow of Southeast Asian heroin has ebbed and flowed depending on enforcement efforts and competing supply sources.

If there is a lesson to be learned, it is that demand reduction will be the most effective means of combating illegal drug use. So long as there is a market for their product, criminal enterprises will find ways to bring drugs into the country. The sharply diminished illicit drug activity seen in the 1920s, 1930s, and 1940s was to a great extent the result of social attitudes that considered such activity anathema. Certainly, social mores do not eliminate all socially unacceptable acts; some are merely driven into the shadows. Moreover, attitudes shift over time, and indeed it was the rejection of the values espoused by their parents that in part drove the adoption of drugs by the Baby Boomer Generation. The point, however, is that what curbed illicit drug use was reduced demand, not enforcement activity that reduced supply. With government budgets steadily shrinking, alternatives to traditional incarceration—particularly for those guilty only of possessing personal-use quantities—will likely be considered from the standpoints of both effectiveness and cost control.

Questions in review

1. Explain the transitions in social attitudes toward what are now Schedule I substances from the late nineteenth century into the early twentieth century up to World War II and through the postwar period.
2. Why do you think the abuse of prescription drugs represents such a significant problem compared to all other categories of illicit drugs?
3. Why do you think the penalties associated with crack cocaine were so much harsher than those levied on powder cocaine?
4. Do you think drug court programs would be effective for violent offenders? Why or why not?
5. How does the nature of retail-level actors in the drug trade differ from the popular notions contained in movies, television shows, and other media?
6. Summarize how enforcement activity against the Colombian cartels resulted in the unintended consequence of empowering the Mexican DTOs and thereby bringing drug violence closer to the United States.
7. Describe two or three methods of money laundering other than those discussed in the text that might be effective. How might your methods be detected and countered by law enforcement?

8. What do you think might be the most effective means of combating corruption among government and law enforcement officials in Central and South American countries and others involved in the drug trade?
9. Why do you think the proportion of drug offenders is so much higher in the federal prison population than in the state populations?
10. Explain what factors might complicate federal enforcement of existing antidrug statutes in states that have legalized the medical and/or recreational use of marijuana.

Resources

Drug Enforcement Administration Resource Center, www.justice.gov/dea/resource-center/statistics.html
Substance Abuse and Mental Health Services Administration National Survey on Drug Use and Health, www.samhsa.gov/data/NSDUH/aspx
National Institute of Justice drug court information, http://www.nij.gov/topics/courts/drug-courts/

References

1. Suddath, C. (2009, March 25). The War on Drugs. *Time*. Retrieved April 20, 2013, from http://www.time.com/time/world/article/0,8599,1887488,00.html
2. Public Broadcasting Corporation. (2000). A social history of America's most popular illegal drugs. *Frontline: Drug wars*. Boston: WGBH-TV. Retrieved April 20, 2013, from http://www.pbs.org/wgbh/pages/frontline/shows/drugs/buyers/socialhistory.html
3. Drug Policy Alliance. (2013). *A brief history of the drug war*. New York: Drug Policy Alliance. Retrieved April 20, 2013, from http://www.drugpolicy.org/new-solutions-drug-policy/brief-history-drug-war
4. Dave, D., & Schmidt, M. S. (2012, July 16). Rise in pill abuse forces new look at U.S. Drug fight. *The New York Times*. Retrieved April 22, 2013, from http://www.nytimes.com/2012/07/17/world/americas/us-priority-on-illegal-drugs-debated-as-abuse-rises.html?pagewanted=all&_r=0
5. National Institutes of Health. (2011, October). *Commonly abused prescription drugs*. Washington, DC: U.S. Department of Health and Human Services. Retrieved April 22, 2013, from http://www.drugabuse.gov/sites/default/files/rx_drugs_placemat_508c_10052011.pdf
6. Substance Abuse and Mental Health Services Administration. (2012, September). *Results from the National Survey on Drug Use and Health: Summary of National Findings*, NSDUH Series H-44, HHS Publication No. (SMA) 12-4713. Rockville, MD: Author.
7. Substance Abuse and Mental Health Services Administration. (2012, September). *Results from the National Survey on Drug Use and Health: Summary of National Findings*, NSDUH Series H-44, HHS Publication No. (SMA) 12-4713. Rockville, MD: Author.
8. Johnson, B. D. (2003). Patterns of drug distribution: Implications and issues. *Substance Use & Misuse*, *38*(11–13), 1789–1806. Retrieved April 25, 2013, from http://www.ncbi.nlm.nih.gov/pmc/articles/PMC1975811/
9. Johnson, B. D. (2003). Patterns of drug distribution: Implications and issues. *Substance Use & Misuse*, *38*(11–13), 1789–1806. Retrieved April 25, 2013, from http://www.ncbi.nlm.nih.gov/pmc/articles/PMC1975811/
10. Johnson, B. D. (2003). Patterns of drug distribution: Implications and issues. *Substance Use & Misuse*, *38*(11–13), 1789–1806. Retrieved April 25, 2013, from http://www.ncbi.nlm.nih.gov/pmc/articles/PMC1975811/
11. Curley, B. (2010, March). DSM-V – Major changes to addictive disease classifications. *Recovery Today Online*. Retrieved April 25, 2013, from http://www.recoverytoday.net/articles/143-dsm-v-major-changes-to-addictive-disease-classifications/
12. Markel, H. (2012, June 5). The D.S.M. gets addiction right. *The New York Times*. Retrieved April 25, 2013, from http://www.nytimes.com/2012/06/06/opinion/the-dsm-gets-addiction-right.html

13. National Drug Intelligence Center. (2004, April). *Drug abuse and mental illness fast facts.* Washington, DC: U.S. Department of Justice, National Drug Intelligence Center. Retrieved from http://www.justice.gov/archive/ndic/pubs7/7343/index.htm

14. Families Against Mandatory Minimums. (2011). *Alternatives to incarceration fact sheet* (p. 2). Washington, DC: Families Against Mandatory Minimums Foundation. Retrieved from http://www.famm.org/repository/files/alternatives%20in%20a%20nutshell%207.30 .09%5B1%5Dfinal.pdf

15. National Institute of Justice. (2012, May 15). *Drug courts.* Washington, DC: U.S. Department of Justice, Office of Justice Programs. Retrieved from http://www.nij.gov/topics/courts/ drug-courts/

16. Truitt, L., Rhodes, W. M., Hoffmann, N. G., Seeherman, A. M., Jalbert, S. K., Kane, M., Finn P. (2002, March). *Evaluating treatment drug courts in Kansas City, Missouri and Pensacola, Florida: Final reports for phase I and phase II.* Abstract retrieved from https://www.ncjrs.gov/App/ Publications/abstract.aspx?ID=198477

17. Finigan, M. W., Carey, S. M., & Cox, A. (2007, April). *Impact of a mature drug court over 10 years of operation: Recidivism and costs (final report).* Abstract retrieved from https://www.ncjrs.gov/ App/Publications/abstract.aspx?ID=241017

18. National Institute of Justice. (2012, November 5). *NIJ's multisite adult drug court evaluation.* Washington, DC: U.S. Department of Justice, Office of Justice Programs. Retrieved from http:// www.nij.gov/nij/topics/courts/drug-courts/madce.htm

19. Rossman, S. B., & Zweig, J. M. (2012, May). *What have we learned from the multisite adult drug court evaluation? Implications for policy and practice* (pp. 2–3). Alexandria, VA: National Association of Drug Court Professionals. Retrieved April 26, 2013, from http://www.nadcp.org/sites/default/ files/nadcp/Multisite%20Adult%20Drug%20Court%20Evaluation%20-%20NADCP.pdf

20. Rossman, S. B., & Zweig, J. M. (2012, May). *What have we learned from the multisite adult drug court evaluation? Implications for policy and practice* (p. 3). Alexandria, VA: National Association of Drug Court Professionals. Retrieved April 26, 2013, from http://www.nadcp.org/sites/default/ files/nadcp/Multisite%20Adult%20Drug%20Court%20Evaluation%20-%20NADCP.pdf

21. Rossman, S. B., & Zweig, J. M. (2012, May). *What have we learned from the multisite adult drug court evaluation? Implications for policy and practice* (p. 3). Alexandria, VA: National Association of Drug Court Professionals. Retrieved April 26, 2013, from http://www.nadcp.org/sites/default/ files/nadcp/Multisite%20Adult%20Drug%20Court%20Evaluation%20-%20NADCP.pdf

22. Rossman, S. B., & Zweig, J. M. (2012, May). *What have we learned from the multisite adult drug court evaluation? Implications for policy and practice* (pp. 3–4). Alexandria, VA: National Association of Drug Court Professionals. Retrieved April 26, 2013, from http://www.nadcp.org/sites/default/ files/nadcp/Multisite%20Adult%20Drug%20Court%20Evaluation%20-%20NADCP.pdf

23. Rossman, S. B., & Zweig, J. M. (2012, May). *What have we learned from the multisite adult drug court evaluation? Implications for policy and practice* (p. 4). Alexandria, VA: National Association of Drug Court Professionals. Retrieved April 26, 2013, from http://www.nadcp.org/sites/default/ files/nadcp/Multisite%20Adult%20Drug%20Court%20Evaluation%20-%20NADCP.pdf

24. Lindquist, C., Hardison, J., & Lattimore, P. (2004) The reentry court initiative: Court-based strategies for managing released prisoners. *Justice Research and Policy, 6*(1), 97–118.

25. Close, D. W., Aubin, M., & Alltucker, K. (2008). *The District of Oregon Reentry Court Evaluation, Policy Recommendations, and Replication Strategies.* Portland, OR: United States District Court, District of Oregon. Retrieved April 27, 2013, from http://www.ussc.gov/Education_and_ Training/Annual_National_Training_Seminar/2009/008c_Reentry_Court_Doc.pdf

26. DEA Museum, & Visitors Center. (2013). *Illegal drugs in America: A modern history: Enforcing new drug laws, 1919–1950s.* Washington, DC: Drug Enforcement Administration. Retrieved April 27, 2013, from http://www.deamuseum.org/museum_idaendl.html

27. West, B. (2012, February 16). Meth in Mexico: A turning point in the drug war? *STRATFOR.* Retrieved April 27, 2013, from http://www.stratfor.com/weekly/meth-mexico-turning-point-drug-war

28. Almanac of Policy Issues. (2004, May). *Drug trafficking in the United States.* Retrieved April 30, 2013, from http://www.policyalmanac.org/crime/archive/drug_trafficking.shtml

29. Bowden, M. (2001). *Killing Pablo: The hunt for the world's greatest outlaw* (p. 17). New York: Atlantic Monthly Press.

30. Bowden, M. (2001). *Killing Pablo: The hunt for the world's greatest outlaw* (p. 23). New York: Atlantic Monthly Press.
31. Erlanger, S. (1990, February 11). Southeast Asia is now no. 1 source of U.S. heroin. *The New York Times*. Retrieved April 30, 2013, from http://www.nytimes.com/1990/02/11/world/south-east-asia-is-now-no-1-source-of-us-heroin.html?pagewanted=all&src=pm
32. National Drug Intelligence Center. (2006, January). *National drug threat assessment 2006*. Washington, DC: U.S. Department of Justice. Retrieved May 2, 2013, from http://www.justice.gov/archive/ndic/pubs11/18862/heroin.htm
33. Beittel, J. S. (2013, April 15). *Mexico's drug trafficking organizations: Source and scope of the violence*. Washington, DC: Congressional Research Service. Retrieved from http://www.fas.org/sgp/crs/row/R41576.pdf
34. Drug Enforcement Administration. (2013). *DEA programs: Money laundering*. Retrieved May 3, 2013, from http://www.justice.gov/dea/ops/money.shtml
35. Mazur, R. (2012, March 22). Attacking drug cartels through undercover money laundering operations. *CTC Sentinel*. West Point, NY: Combating Terrorism Center, United States Military Academy. Retrieved May 3, 2013, from http://www.ctc.usma.edu/posts/attacking-drug-cartels-through-undercover-money-laundering-operations
36. Landers, K. (2012, December 12). US fines HSBC $2 billion for money laundering. *ABC News Radio*. Retrieved May 3, 2013, from http://www.abc.net.au/am/content/2012/s3652017.htm
37. Public Intelligence. (2011, September 21). *Colombian money laundering totals $8 billion each year*. Retrieved May 3, 2013, from http://publicintelligence.net/colombian-money-laundering-totals-8-billion-each-year/
38. Escobar, R., & Fisher, D. (2009). *The accountant's story: Inside the violent world of the Medellín cartel* (Kindle ed., pp. 1019–1124). New York: Grand Central Publishing.
39. Kestenbaum, D. (2012, November 21). How the government set up a fake bank to launder drug money. *National Public Radio*. Retrieved May 4, 2013, from http://www.npr.org/blogs/money/2012/11/21/165508343/how-the-government-set-up-a-fake-bank-to-launder-drug-money
40. Wilkinson, T., & Ellingwood, K. (2011, December 19). Cartels use legitimate trade to launder money, U.S., Mexico say. *Los Angeles Times*. Retrieved May 4, 2013, from http://articles.latimes.com/2011/dec/19/world/la-fg-mexico-money-laundering-trade-20111219/2
41. Yeh, B. T. (2012, December 13). *The controlled substances act: Regulatory requirements*. Washington, DC: Congressional Research Service. Retrieved May 4, 2013, from http://www.fas.org/sgp/crs/misc/RL34635.pdf
42. Drug Enforcement Administration. (2004, May). *Drug trafficking in the United States*. Retrieved May 5, 2013, from http://www.policyalmanac.org/crime/archive/drug_trafficking.shtml
43. Drug Enforcement Administration. (2013). *DEA Mission Statement*. Retrieved May 5, 2013, from http://www.justice.gov/dea/about/mission.shtml
44. Cave, D., & Schmidt, M. S. (2012, July 16). Rise in pill abuse forces new look at U.S. drug fight. *The New York Times*. Retrieved May 5, 2013, from http://www.nytimes.com/2012/07/17/world/americas/us-priority-on-illegal-drugs-debated-as-abuse-rises.html?pagewanted=all&_r=1&
45. Glaze, L. E., & Parks, E. (2012, November). Correctional populations in the United States, 2011. Washington, DC: U.S. Department of Justice, Office of Justice Programs, Bureau of Justice Statistics.
46. Carson, E. A., & Sabol, W. J. (2012, December). *Prisoners in 2011* (p. 10). Washington, DC: U.S. Department of Justice, Office of Justice Programs, Bureau of Justice Statistics.
47. Wong, P. (2013, April 3). Oregon legislators consider bill to legalize pot. *USA Today*. Retrieved May 5, 2013, from http://www.usatoday.com/story/news/nation/2013/04/03/oregon-marijuana-legalization/2049071/

chapter thirteen

Changing nature of crime and crime causation

Introduction

This text was developed by three individuals who have studied the policing, nature of crime, and crime causation for many years. We are not going to tell you that we can predict what the crime situation will be 10 or 20 years from now. Instead, in this chapter, we discuss some of the trends that are likely to continue to influence crime patterns, trends, causes, and the labeling of some behaviors as "criminal," into the foreseeable future.

Globalization of crime

Crime is no longer an intranational problem—it is becoming increasingly international. According to the United Nations, more crimes than ever are crossing international borders:

> Globalization and growing economic interdependence have encouraged and promoted the transformation of crime beyond borders in all parts of the world. Improved communications and information technologies, increased blurring of national borders, greater mobility of people, goods and services across countries, and the emergence of a globalized economy have moved crime further away from its domestic base.[1]

Organized crime in the present day is inextricably linked to the concept of globalization. The specific crimes that fall into this trend of globalization are vast and varied, as with

- Smuggling humans across international borders, sometimes to be used in sex trafficking or other forms of human slavery
- Smuggling drugs or firearms across national borders
- The cross-national shipment of counterfeit goods, ranging from software to designer handbags to medication
- Wildlife smuggling, including the transportation of exotic or endangered species
- Online predation and exploitation committed by individuals from different nations, as with the production and distribution of child pornography
- International phishing, hacking, denial of service, and other cybercrimes that can be carried out without regard to geography

The globalization of crime has fed the need for cross-national task forces. For example, in 2010, the Federal Bureau of Investigation (FBI) engaged in its first joint venture with "Europol," the law enforcement agency of the European Union, in "Operation Atlantic," an effort to capture online predators. FBI agents worked "covertly [to] set up an electronic dragnet on a peer-to-peer network targeting pedophiles located in European Union (EU) countries" and sent their findings to Europol.[2] As of March 2012, the effort had resulted in the identification of offenders in "France, Italy, the Netherlands, Spain, and the United Kingdom."[3]

U.S. Customs and Border Protection has made a number of seizures of counterfeit goods at the nation's borders, including

- More than 10,000 pounds of cocaine, worth more than $841 million, detected on speedboats in the waters of the Western Caribbean, the Eastern Pacific, and off the coast of Columbia. The seizures necessitated assistance from the Ecuadorian Navy, Columbian Air Force, U.S. Coast Guard, and U.S. Navy.[4]
- More than 70,000 counterfeit products discovered on a shipment from China at the port of Newark, New Jersey, worth an estimated $3.9 million. The products included "razor blades, toys, sunglasses, markers, and batteries" that were in violation of intellectual property laws.[5]
- Almost 2,900 pairs of jeans falsely labeled as "Levi Strauss & Co.," worth an estimated $194,000, seized at the border in Laredo, Texas.[6]
- Cargo containers at the Port of New York/Newark that contained counterfeit watches with the labels of "Rolex, Tag Heuer, Omega, and Breitling," which would have garnered almost $62 million if sold at the manufacturer's suggested retail price.[7]

Although many cross-national crimes are economically driven, this is not true in all cases: The motivations for these crimes are likely as varied as the crimes themselves.

Evolving responses to crime

Situational crime prevention

In the 1970s, a growing skepticism emerged surrounding the potential for convicted criminals to be rehabilitated. An academic article published in 1974[8] famously concluded "nothing works"—or at least consistently and with confidence—in the treatment of offenders. This led to an emphasis on crime prevention strategies that are not wedded to the transformation of offenders, including situational crime prevention efforts that instead focus on transforming the environment to discourage criminal activity (see Chapter 3). Ronald V. Clarke points out that relative to rehabilitative strategies that aim to reduce recidivism, these strategies are focused on stopping crime before it starts. Technology has facilitated the ongoing growth of situational crime prevention tactics. Consider the following figures from a survey of retail stores regarding their loss prevention strategies:[9]

- 94.4% used burglar alarms.
- 73.3% used live, visible closed circuit television.
- 61.9% used check approval database screening systems.
- 50.8% used live, hidden closed circuit television.
- 50.8% used a digital video recording system.
- 42.4% used "acousto-magnetic, electronic security tags."
- 32.2% had silent alarms in place.
- 28% used radio frequency electronic security tags.
- 17.8% used microwave electronic security tags.

Any one of these efforts to prevent crime would have been unheard of in the times of Cesare Beccaria and Jeremy Bentham. The applicability of situational crime prevention is not limited to retail. A host of public and private organizations and agencies—schools, hospitals, transit systems, shops and malls, manufacturing businesses and phone companies, local parks and entertainment facilities, and pubs and parking lots—whose products, services, and operations spawn opportunities for a vast range of different crimes, stand to benefit from various situational crime prevention strategies.[10]

The changing nature of technology has interesting implications for theories that focus on the circumstances of the crime (rather than the criminal). For example, routine activities theory (Chapter 3) highlights that crime is most likely when a motivated offender, suitable target, and lack of a capable guardian converge in time and space. This often brings to mind a burglar stumbling on an unoccupied home, or a motivated sexual offender encountering a potential victim in an otherwise isolated area, but can this model equally be applied to emerging forms of crime? For example, the crime of phishing (Chapter 10) can entail an e-mail sent from China or the United Kingdom to a victim in California, who, hours later, unsuspectingly clicks the fraudulent link and sends his or her banking information to the offender. What implications do such crimes have for the dimensions of time and space highlighted by routine activities theory? What does this say about the changing nature of criminal opportunities more generally? Finally, what would capable guardianship look like in this situation?

Technology has changed the face of "capable guardianship." Companies now sell home security cameras that can be viewed by homeowners online and activated or deactivated through the homeowners' phones. Such crime detection devices are increasingly accessible to the general public: In July of 2013, a vacationing couple who had installed a $150 "Dropcam" to keep an eye on their dog between visits from the dog sitter received notification on their iPhone that the camera's motion detection sensor had been activated. When they opened the app for the camera, instead of seeing the dog sitter as expected, they saw a live feed of their home being burglarized. The technology enabled the homeowners to notify the police, who successfully recovered all stolen items.[11]

> **TRANSIT BUS ROBBERIES IN SAN FRANCISCO IN THE 1960s**
>
> William McDonald, in his unpublished dissertation submitted to the University of California in 1970, reported an analysis of a survey of assaults and robberies on transit bus drivers in the Bay Area of California. At the start of his study, there were concerns about these crimes. During the course of his study, the transit bus companies changed their procedures and required passengers to have correct change only and to deposit fares into a box. The bus driver did not have access to the fare box. As a result of this change, there was a significant decrease in robberies of bus drivers. Accordingly, McDonald shifted his focus to assaults on transit bus drivers.[12]
>
> **Question: Were the actions of the transit companies an early form of situational crime prevention?**
>
> Note: The transit bus drivers in Moscow, Soviet Union, in the 1980s had closed compartments that could not be entered by the passengers. The drivers had their own separate entrances to the bus. Regardless of broader crime trends and social contexts, we can likely conclude with confidence that the Soviet Union transit organizations did not have much of a problem with assaults on bus drivers!

Community policing

Policing expert Lawrence Sherman has suggested that police can reduce crime by treating suspects and citizens with respect, as the resulting increase in police legitimacy will compel individuals to comply with the law. This is consistent with a broader trend toward community policing, which holds that police and area residents should work in partnership to improve quality of life. Can any of the theories in this text account for the idea that officers may be able to reduce crime by showing greater respect to the public? If so, which theories?

SHOULD WE PUNISH THE VICTIM?

Art Buchwald for many years wrote a daily satirical column in the *Washington Post* newspaper on political events. On February 4, 1969, after a recent outbreak of robberies in the District of Columbia, Buchwald indicated that maybe we should punish a store owner every time the owner's store got robbed. He noted that many people do not take precautions against robberies until after they have been robbed. According to him, if the store owner knew that he or she would get punished if the store was robbed, the owner would take precautions to make sure this did not happen. According to Buchwald, once the would-be robbers know that store owners have taken preventive steps to prevent robberies, the robbers will be less likely to rob.[13] Although the argument was satirical, it does serve as an interesting intellectual exercise in considering problem-solving approaches to criminal behavior.

Problem-oriented policing

Researcher Lawrence Sherman has stated that simply increasing the number of officers in a police department is unlikely to reduce crime unless they are focused on specific objectives, tasks, places, times, and people. Prior research has called into question the ability of response times or random patrols to have a discernible impact on crime. By contrast, focusing efforts on "hot spots" (high-crime areas) and problem-solving strategies hold more promise.[14]

If we (the United States as a whole) have learned anything in the past five decades, it is that law enforcement needs to be more strategic in the use of police assets in preventing crime. Simply targeting a particular problem does not guarantee success, as evidenced by the "War on Drugs." President Nixon first declared this "war" on July 17, 1971, when he asked Congress for $84 million to combat what he characterized as the new "public enemy number one." More than 40 years and billions of dollars later, the United States is currently the world's largest illegal drug market place. The authors are not condoning the use of illegal drugs, but rather making the point that heavy-handed criminal justice strategies have yet to show effectiveness in curbing that use.

Instead of investing vast amounts of money in tough-on-crime crackdowns, history should teach us that it is more effective to strategically target the application of resources for maximum benefit. Similar strategies are being used in other fields: In recent years, Major League Baseball has used analytics to assist managers to make decisions regarding the placement of defensive players. With proper data analysis, it is possible to predict with some degree of accuracy where the ball will go if the batter hits a ball that is thrown in a particular way, for example, a high fastball. This prediction allows the managers to place their fielders in the positions where the ball is likely to be hit. Along the same lines, law enforcement should use all data available to them to allocate their resources and manpower to those locations and circumstances where it is most likely to have an impact.

Reductions in incarceration

For years, even as researchers have argued that too many people were being confined too long for minor offenses, the prison population continued to grow—to the point that the United States incarcerates a greater portion of its population than any other nation in the world. It was only recently that the trend started to reverse. The United States experienced its first slight decrease in incarceration in 2009,[15] after nearly 40 years of unrelenting growth. Consistent with critical criminologists' perspective that imprisonment rates are as much a reflection of state practices as of the amount of harmful behavior that actually takes place in society, it appears that this shift in the correctional population is based primarily on factors unrelated to the crime rate—namely, tightening state budgets, and the Supreme Court decision in *Brown v. Plata* (2011), which ordered a dramatic reduction in California's prison population because of unconstitutionally crowded conditions. The current reductions in prison population are not the result of state and federal officials listening to the researchers, but the recent economic downturn in the United States.

Texas provides a good example of criminal justice reforms due to economic conditions. In the 1980s and 1990s, Texas had surplus money because of the energy boom, and the state built new prisons at a record-breaking pace. In 2007, the Texas Legislative Budget Board declared that 17,000 new prison beds would be needed by the year 2012. The cost of the new beds was estimated at about $2 billion dollars. Even though the state had a multibillion-dollar budget surplus in 2007, there were signs that in the next few years the surplus would disappear. Instead of approving the new prison construction, the state legislature directed a small amount of state funds toward alternatives to incarceration. Those alternatives included drug courts, increased electronic monitoring, and better parole and probation monitoring practices. Crime rates in the state continued to drop, and in 2011, for the first time in state history, Texas closed one of its prisons because the beds were no longer needed.[16]

During the 1980s and 1990s, mandatory minimums held popularity with conservative and liberal policy makers, correctional officer unions, and the prison building industries. At the federal level, these stringent sentencing policies inflated the U.S. Bureau of Prisons budget by about $200 million a year from 1980 to 2010. In August 2013, U.S. Attorney General Eric Holder announced that the Department of Justice would no longer pursue mandatory sentences for a broad array of drug crimes—a reform that he indicated was partially driven by the need to reduce government expenses.

Changing definitions of "criminal"

In sharp contrast to the "Just Say No" campaign and harsh antidrug laws of the 1980s, recent years have seen increasing legal acceptance of medical marijuana in many states and the legalization of recreational marijuana in Washington State and Colorado. At the time of this writing, additional cities, including Portland, Maine, had voted in favor of recreational marijuana decriminalization or legalization. Initially, the federal government vowed to continue to enforce its marijuana laws even where the drug was no longer illegal under state law, but (as indicated above) the Department of Justice has since changed course, now intending to limit prosecutions to the following eight priorities:[17]

1. Preventing the distribution of marijuana to minors
2. Preventing revenue from the sale of marijuana from going to criminal enterprises, gangs, and cartels
3. Preventing the diversion of marijuana from states where it is legal under state law in some form to other states

4. Preventing state-authorized marijuana activity from being used as a cover or pretext for the trafficking of other illegal drugs or other illegal activity
5. Preventing violence and the use of firearms in the cultivation and distribution of marijuana
6. Preventing drugged driving and the exacerbation of other adverse public health consequences associated with marijuana use
7. Preventing the growth of marijuana on public lands and the attendant public safety and environmental dangers posed by marijuana production on public lands
8. Preventing marijuana possession or use on federal property

On August 29, 2013, the U.S. Department of Justice issued the following press release regarding its marijuana policies:

JUSTICE DEPARTMENT ANNOUNCES UPDATE TO MARIJUANA ENFORCEMENT POLICY[18]

Today, the U.S. Department of Justice announced an update to its federal marijuana enforcement policy in light of recent state ballot initiatives that legalize, under state law, the possession of small amounts of marijuana and provide for the regulation of marijuana production, processing, and sale.

In a new memorandum outlining the policy, the Department makes clear that marijuana remains an illegal drug under the Controlled Substances Act and that federal prosecutors will continue to aggressively enforce this statute. To this end, the Department identifies eight enforcement areas that federal prosecutors should prioritize. These are the same enforcement priorities that have traditionally driven the Department's efforts in this area.

Outside of these enforcement priorities, however, the federal government has traditionally relied on state and local authorities to address marijuana activity through enforcement of their own narcotics laws. This guidance continues that policy.

For states such as Colorado and Washington that have enacted laws to authorize the production, distribution, and possession of marijuana, the Department expects these states to establish strict regulatory schemes that protect the eight federal interests identified in the Department's guidance. These schemes must be tough in practice, not just on paper, and include strong, state-based enforcement efforts, backed by adequate funding. On the basis of assurances that those states will impose an appropriately strict regulatory system, the Department has informed the governors of both states that it is deferring its right to challenge their legalization laws at this time. But if any of the stated harms do materialize—either despite a strict regulatory scheme or because of the lack of one—federal prosecutors will act aggressively to bring individual prosecutions focused on federal enforcement priorities and the Department may challenge the regulatory scheme themselves in these states.

War on Drugs

In June 1971, President Nixon declared a "War on Drugs." He dramatically increased the size and presence of federal drug control agencies and pushed through measures such as mandatory sentencing and no-knock warrants. Nixon temporarily placed marijuana in Schedule I, the most restrictive category of drugs. Forty plus years later, the overall results of the "War on Drugs" is that the United States is presently the world's largest illegal drug market. And Mexico is currently involved in a relatively unsuccessful fight against the drug cartels that import drugs into the United States.

The term "War on Drugs" is commonly applied to a campaign of prohibition, military aid, and military intervention, with the stated aim being to define and reduce the illegal drug trade. Generally, the war includes a set of drug policies that are intended to discourage the production, distribution, and consumption of what the involved nations and the United Nations define as illegal psychoactive drugs. The term was popularized by the media shortly after a press conference in June 1971 by U.S. President Richard Nixon where he declared drug abuse "public enemy number one."

Most researchers agree that despite the billions of dollars spent to fight the war, it has been a failure. For example, on May 13, 2009, the Director of the Office of National Drug Control Policy stated that although it did not plan to significantly alter drug enforcement policy, the Obama administration would not use the term "War on Drugs," as the Director claimed it was "counterproductive."

States are rapidly changing their views of substance abuse, especially those involving the use of marijuana. It is too early to predict the new directions that will be used to fight or control illegal substances; it is clear that there will be a significant departure from past practices.

References

1. Office on Drugs and Crime, United Nations. (2002, September). *Global programme against transnational organize crime: Results of a pilot survey of forty selected organized criminal groups in sixteen countries* (p. 2). Retrieved October 3, 2013, from http://www.unodc.org/pdf/crime/publications/Pilot_survey .pdf
2. Federal Bureau of Investigation. (March 1, 2012). *Operation Atlantic: Taking international aim at child predators*. Retrieved October 3, 2013, from http://www.fbi.gov/news/stories/2012/march/predators_030112/predators_030112
3. Federal Bureau of Investigation. (March 1, 2012). *Operation Atlantic: Taking international aim at child predators*. Retrieved October 3, 2013, from http://www.fbi.gov/news/stories/2012/march/predators_030112/predators_030112
4. Customs and Border Patrol. (May 23, 2013). *CBP disrupts $840 million in narcotics: Trackers spot 4 separate cocaine smuggling attempts*. Retrieved October 3, 2013, from http://www.cbp.gov/xp/cgov/newsroom/news_releases/national/05232013_6.xml
5. Customs and Border Patrol. (August 27, 2013). *CBP seizes $3.9 million in counterfeit consumer goods*. Retrieved October 3, 2013, from http://www.cbp.gov/xp/cgov/newsroom/news_releases/national/08272013_3.xml
6. NBC Dallas-Fort Worth. (June 22, 2012). *Thousands of fake jeans seized at Laredo Border*. Retrieved October 3, 2013, from http://www.nbcdfw.com/news/local/Thousands-of-Fake-Jeans-Seized-at-Laredo-Border-160002155.html
7. Customs and Border Patrol. (November 21, 2012). *Counterfeit watches seized by CBP*. Retrieved October 3, 2013, from http://www.cbp.gov/xp/cgov/newsroom/news_releases/local/2012_news_releases/november_2012/11212012_2.xml
8. Martinson, R. (1974). What works? Questions and answers about prison reform. *The Public Interest*, 35, 22–54.
9. Hollinger, R. C., & Davis, J. L. (2003). *2002 National Retail Security Survey: Final report*. p. 22. Gainesville, FA: University of Florida. Retrieved October 8, 2013, from http://www.pitnet.com/nrss_2002.pdf
10. Clarke, R. V. (Ed.). (1997). *Situational crime prevention: Successful case studies* (2nd ed.). Albany, NY: Harrow and Heston.

11. Rapaport, D. (2013, July 18). Woman sees home burglar via phone app while on vacation. *ABC News*. Retrieved October 2, 2013, from http://abcnews.go.com/blogs/headlines/2013/07/woman-sees-home-burglar-via-phone-app-while-on-vacation/

12. McDonald, W. (1970). *The victim: A social psychological study of criminal victimization*. (Unpublished dissertation). Berkeley, CA: University of California.

13. Art Buchwald. (1969, February 4). Comments on victim interaction. *Washington Post*, p. 6.

14. Sherman, L. W. (n.d.). Policing for crime prevention. In L. W. Sherman, D. Gottfredson, D. MacKenzie, J. Eck, P. Reuter, & S. Bushway (Eds.), *Preventing crime: What works, what doesn't, what's promising. A Report to the United States Congress*. Retrieved October 14, 2013, from https://www.ncjrs.gov/works/chapter8.htm

15. Glaze, L. E. (2001). *Correctional populations in the United States, 2010 (NCJ 236319)*. Washington, DC: Bureau of Justice Statistics.

16. Reddy, V. (2013, August 24). Criminal justice reforms in Texas can set tone for U.S. *Houston Chronicle*, p. B-1.

17. List drawn verbatim from Cole, J. M. (2013, August 29). *Memorandum for all United States attorneys: Guidance regarding marijuana enforcement*. Washington, DC: U.S. Department of Justice, Office of the Deputy Attorney General. Retrieved October 12, 2013, from http://www.justice.gov/iso/opa/resources/3052013829132756857467.pdf

18. Memo drawn in its entirety from United States Department of Justice. (2013, August 29). *Justice department announces update to marijuana enforcement policy*. Washington, DC: Author. Retrieved October 14, 2013, from http://www.justice.gov/opa/pr/2013/August/13-opa-974.html

Index